Dł

Signal Processing, Image Processing and Pattern Recognition

Prentice Hall International Series in Acoustics, Speech and Signal Processing

Signal Processing,
Image Processing
and Pattern Recognition

Stephen P. Banks

Prentice Hall

New York   London   Toronto   Sydney   Tokyo   Singapore

First published 1990 by
Prentice Hall International (UK) Ltd
66 Wood Lane End, Hemel Hempstead
Hertfordshire HP2 4RG
A division of
Simon & Schuster International Group

Typeset in 10/12pt Times
by KEYTEC, Bridport, Dorset

Printed and bound in Great Britain
at the University Press, Cambridge

Library of Congress Cataloging-in-Publication Data

Banks, Stephen P.
    Signal processing : image processing and pattern recognition / Stephen Banks.
      p. cm.
    Includes bibliographical references and index.
    ISBN 0–13–812587–2 : $60.00
    1. Image processing—Digital techniques. 2. Pattern recognition systems. I. Title.
TA1632.B35 1991
621.36'7—dc20
    90-7559
    CIP

British Library Cataloguing in Publication Data

Banks, Stephen P. (Stephen Paul) *1949–*
  Signal processing.
  1. Digital signals. Processing 2. Image processing
  3. Pattern recognition
  I. Title
  621.3822

  ISBN 0–13–812587–2
  ISBN 0–13–812579–1 pbk

---

1 2 3 4 5 94 93 92 91 90

Contents

Contents

Preface

This book has developed from a number of courses at Sheffield University given to undergraduate and postgraduate students over a number of years. The intention is to provide an introduction to modern signal processing and its related fields of image processing and pattern recognition. The applications of this subject are virtually limitless and range from the fairly mundane use of digital filters in modern digital audio and video systems to the more challenging field of machine intelligence for robotics, neural computers and automatic vehicles.

The book is written in three sections so that each area (one-dimensional signal processing, image processing and pattern recognition) may be studied independently, although the main object of the book is to show the connections between these three topics. The level is fairly elementary in much of the book, but certain more advanced ideas have been included which introduce the reader to some areas of current research. Thus computer vision, syntactic pattern recognition and neural networks are discussed in some detail.

The mathematical level required of the reader is not particularly high – undergraduate analysis and probability theory should suffice, although certain sections require the more sophisticated ideas of Hilbert space and generalized orthogonal functions. It is also assumed that the reader is familiar with the Pascal programming language.

In Part I we cover rather briefly many aspects of one-dimensional signal processing (since much of this is well known and appears in many other texts). However, an extensive treatment of analog filters (essential for infinite impulse response (IIR) design) is included since this topic is often relegated to long forgotten analog systems textbooks. Other chapters include discrete systems and signals, nonrecursive filters, fast Fourier transform FFT, IIR design, quantization effects and hardware and software design.

Two-dimensional signal processing and image processing form the material of Part II. Many of the ideas of Part I are generalized to two-dimensional systems – in particular, stability is discussed in detail since it is much more difficult in this case. Images are usually formed from a large number of individual pixels which generally produce significant amounts of data, and so data compression techniques are particularly important here. This is discussed in detail along with many of the techniques for picture enhancement and restoration. Finally, parallel processing methods are introduced with specific reference to systolic arrays and transputers.

Part III is concerned with pattern recognition and can be regarded as being made up of three parts. These are the decision-theoretic approach which is dealt with in detail in Chapters 16–19, syntactic methods (Chapter 20) in which we discuss abstract languages, machines and parsing, and, finally, in Chapter 21, neural networks are covered from a systems viewpoint. Indeed, Chapter 21 can be read independently as an introduction to neural networks.

The book can be used as the basis of courses on signal processing, image processing and pattern recognition either separately or as an integrated course. It is aimed at senior undergraduate and postgraduate students, but should also be useful to professional engineers and scientists who require an introduction to this important field.

S.P.B.

One-dimensional Digital Signal Processing

1

Discrete Signals and Systems

1.1 Introduction

In this chapter we shall introduce the basic properties of discrete signals and discrete systems which operate on them to produce a processed form of the input signal. A discrete system can be thought of as an algorithm which will usually be implemented on a (special or general purpose) computer. Since we are interested mainly in the processing of data we shall use the term 'filter' interchangeably with the term 'discrete system'. This chaper will be concerned entirely with analysis of systems – the design of filters with specified response characteristics will be considered later.

1.2 Discrete signals

A discrete signal is just a sequence of (complex) numbers $\{x(n)\}$ where n is an integer in the range $-\infty < n < \infty$. Denoting by $\mathbb{C}$ the set of complex numbers and by $\mathbb{Z}$ the set of integers, it follows that a discrete signal is a function

$$x : \mathbb{Z} \to \mathbb{C}$$

Since confusion often arises in the notation for discrete signals we shall be particularly careful in our own notation. Thus, when considering a discrete signal as a whole we shall denote it by a single letter such as x or by the notation $\{x(n)\}_{n \in \mathbb{Z}} = \{ \ldots, x(-1), x(0), x(1), \ldots \}$ to emphasize the range of values of n. When we write $x(n)$ we mean the *value* of the sequence at the particular 'point' n. Hence, $x(n)$ is a complex number, whereas x is a function. This may seem overly pedantic, but we shall see shortly that it is justified.

A discrete signal may be specified *a priori*, without any reference to a continuous-time system, or it may be obtained by sampling a continuous-time signal. Sampling is usually, although not exclusively, done at fixed intervals; in this case, if $x(t)$ is a continuous-time signal and we sample at intervals of length T, then we obtain the sequence $\{x(nT)\}_{n \in \mathbb{Z}}$. The above notation is recovered if we set $T = 1$. When we wish to process a sampled signal by computer, then we must digitize each sample $x(nT)$. This is because numbers are stored in computers to a finite number of significant figures and so only a finite number of distinct levels can be distinguished. Rounding $x(nT)$ to its 'nearest' level results in a quantized signal value $x_q(nT)$. The quantized signal x_q is called a *digital* signal to distinguish it from a discrete signal. In this chapter we are interested only in discrete signals, leaving the discussion of the effects of rounding errors to a later chapter.

In continuous-time systems a number of special signals are of particular importance, namely the impulse (δ-function), the step function and the exponential and sinusoidal functions. The corresponding discrete signals are shown in Figure 1.1. It is also important to define the delay operator which we introduce in the following way. For any discrete signal x and any integer n_0 we define the signal x^{n_0} by

$$x^{n_0}(n) = x(n - n_0)$$

For example,

$$u_0^{n_0}(n) = \begin{cases} 1 \text{ if } n = n_0 \\ 0 \text{ if } n \neq n_0 \end{cases}$$

where u_0 is the unit impulse.

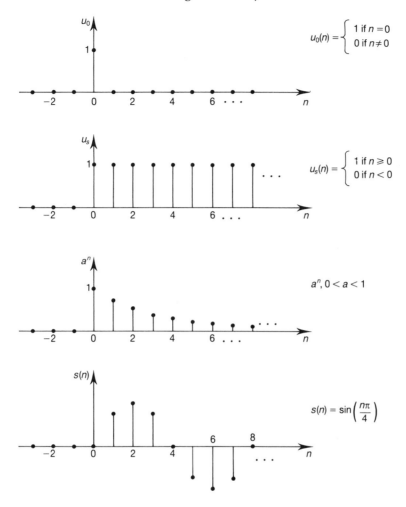

Figure 1.1 Important discrete signals.

1.3 Discrete systems

As we have stated above, a discrete system is just an algorithm which operates on an input sequence x and produces an output sequence y. Hence we may regard a (discrete) system as a function

$$\phi : \mathbb{C}^{\mathbb{Z}} \to \mathbb{C}^{\mathbb{Z}}$$

where $\mathbb{C}^{\mathbb{Z}}$ is the set of all sequences with complex values (Figure 1.2). A general

Figure 1.2   General discrete system.

discrete system of this kind will have few, if any, reasonable properties, which will simplify the analysis of the system, and so we are led to search for a class of systems which may be studied generally, but for which we may obtain useful results. Obvious properties of this kind are linearity and time-invariance, since we already know that these properties enable us to derive the whole of classical continuous-time system theory.

In order to define linearity we must define what we mean by the addition of discrete signals and by the muliplication of discrete signals by scalars, i.e. we must make $\mathbb{C}^{\mathbb{Z}}$ into a vector space (of infinite dimension). Thus if x_1, $x_2 \in \mathbb{C}^{\mathbb{Z}}$ and α, $\beta \in \mathbb{C}$, then we define the signal $\alpha x_1 + \beta x_2$ by

$$(\alpha x_1 + \beta x_2)(n) = \alpha(x_1(n)) + \beta(x_2(n))$$

i.e. we define the vector space operations pointwise.

Now let ϕ be a system. Then we say that ϕ is *linear* if

$$\phi(\alpha x_1 + \beta x_2) = \alpha\phi(x_1) + \beta\phi(x_2)$$

for any signals x_1, $x_2 \in \mathbb{C}^{\mathbb{Z}}$ and scalars α, $\beta \in \mathbb{C}$. A system ϕ is called *shift-* (or *time-*) *invariant*[1] if

$$y = \phi(x) \Rightarrow y^{n_0} = \phi(x^{n_0}) \quad \text{for all } x \in \mathbb{C}^{\mathbb{Z}}, n_0 \in \mathbb{Z}$$

i.e. if any input signal x produces some output y, then the delayed input x produces the same output, but delayed by the same interval.

We are now in a position to derive the input–output equation for a general linear, shift-invariant system. Let

$$h = \phi(u_0)$$

i.e. h is the impulse response of the system. For any input signal x, we have

$$x(n) = \sum_{m=-\infty}^{\infty} x(m)u_0(n - m) \tag{1.3.1}$$

since $u_0(k) = 0$ unless $k = 0$, and so the terms in the sum on the right-hand side are all zero apart from when $m = n$. Equation (1.3.1) is an expression for the nth term of the signal x; written in terms of whole signals it becomes

$$x = \sum_{m=-\infty}^{\infty} x(m)u_0^m \tag{1.3.2}$$

[1]In picture processing, the independent variable n is a spatial variable.

Note that on the right-hand side of (1.3.2), $x(m)$ is a scaler and u_0^m is the delayed unit impulse signal. Thus,

$$y \triangleq \phi(x) = \phi \left\{ \sum_{m=-\infty}^{\infty} x(m)u_0^m \right\}$$

$$= \sum_{m=-\infty}^{\infty} \phi(x(m)u_0^m) \quad \text{by linearity of } \phi$$

$$= \sum_{m=-\infty}^{\infty} x(m)\phi(u_0^m) \quad \text{by linearity of } \phi$$

$$= \sum_{m=-\infty}^{\infty} x(m)h^m \quad \text{by shift-invariance of } \phi$$

(Note that this is valid only for those inputs for which the summations converge absolutely and, strictly speaking, we should use a limiting argument since we have only assumed linearity with respect to finite summations.) This is again an equation of signals; converting back to pointwise values we have

$$y(n) = \sum_{m=-\infty}^{\infty} x(m)h(n-m) \tag{1.3.3}$$

Note that, as can easily be checked, we can also write (1.3.3) in the form

$$y(n) = \sum_{m=-\infty}^{\infty} x(n-m)h(m) \tag{1.3.4}$$

The right-hand side of (1.3.3) (or (1.3.4)) is called the *discrete convolution* of the signals x and h, and each of these equations expresses the fact that, for a linear, shift-invariant system, the response to any input can be found by convolving the input with the response of the system to the unit impulse. This implies that a linear, shift-invariant system is completely characterized by its impulse response.

Before proceeding we shall briefly return to the issue of the notation of sequences which we discussed above. Recall that we are denoting a sequence by x or by $\{x(n)\}$ and its value at n by $x(n)$. Thus, we have written the input – output relation for a general system as $y = \phi(x)$. This is often incorrectly written as

$$y(n) = \phi(x(n)) \tag{1.3.5}$$

Although the expression (1.3.5) is intended to be interpreted as $y = \phi(x)$, or $\{y(n)\} = \phi(\{x(n)\})$, it appears to mean the following: the output y at time n depends on (is a function of) the input only at time n. Such a system is called *memoryless* since it requires only the input at the current time (or spatial coordinate) to generate the current output. Clearly, from (1.3.3), a linear, shift-invariant system is *not* memoryless, in general.

1.4 Causality and stability

We have seen that a linear, shift-invariant system has the input – output relation (1.3.3) (or (1.3.4)). Clearly, the output at the current time n depends on the input x at future times. Such a filter could not be made to operate in real time since the computer algorithm which implements the filter would have to anticipate future values of the input. For this reason we say that a filter is *causal* (or *realizable*) if the output at any time depends only on the input up to that time. From (1.3.3) we have

$$y(n) = \ldots + x(n-1)h(1) + x(n)h(0) + x(n+1)h(-1) + \ldots$$

and it follows that a linear, shift-invariant system is causal if and only if

$$h(n) = 0 \text{ for } n < 0 \tag{1.4.1}$$

i.e. the impulse response coefficients vanish for negative times.

Another important property of systems is that of stability. We say that a signal x is *bounded* if we have

$$|x(n)| \leq M \quad \text{for all } n \in \mathbb{Z}$$

for some $M \geq 0$ independent of n, and we say that a system is *stable* if a bounded input produces a bounded output. We shall now prove the following characterization of stability.

THEOREM
A linear, shift-invariant system is stable if and only if

$$\sum_{m=-\infty}^{\infty} |h(m)| < \infty$$

Proof If $\sum_{m=-\infty}^{\infty} |h(m)| = \infty$ we shall prove that the system is unstable by finding a bounded input which produces an unbounded output. Thus, define the input

$$x(n) = \begin{cases} +1 & \text{if } h(-n) \geq 0 \\ -1 & \text{if } h(-n) < 0 \end{cases}$$

Then, by (1.3.3),

$$y(0) = \sum_{m=-\infty}^{\infty} x(m)h(-m) = \sum_{m=-\infty}^{\infty} |h(m)| = \infty$$

and so the output is not bounded.

Conversely, assume that $\sum_{m=-\infty}^{\infty} |h(m)| < \infty$ and let x be a bounded input. Then $|x(n)| \leq M$ for all n and for some $M \geq 0$. Hence,

$$|y(n)| = \left| \sum_{m=-\infty}^{\infty} x(m)h(n-m) \right| < \sum_{m=-\infty}^{\infty} |x(m)| \cdot |h(n-m)|$$

$$< M \sum_{m=-\infty}^{\infty} |h(n-m)| = M \sum_{m=-\infty}^{\infty} |h(m)| < \infty$$

and so the system is stable.

1.5 Frequency response

We have seen that a linear, shift-invariant system can be characterized by its impulse response h. From the theory of linear, continuous-time systems, we also expect that we can specify a discrete system in terms of its response to sinusoidal inputs; this is indeed the case. Let $x = \{e^{j\omega n}\}$ be a discrete complex sinusoidal input. (This is merely a convenient device for studying frequency responses – to find the response of a system to sine and cosine inputs we just take the real and imaginary parts of the output.) Then by (1.3.4) we have

$$y(n) = \sum_{m=-\infty}^{\infty} h(m) e^{-j\omega m}$$

$$= e^{j\omega n} \sum_{m=-\infty}^{\infty} h(m) e^{-j\omega m}$$

$$= H(e^{j\omega})\, x(n)$$

or, in terms of sequences,

$$y = H(e^{j\omega}) x \qquad\qquad (1.5.1)$$

where

$$H(e^{j\omega}) = \sum_{m=-\infty}^{\infty} h(m) e^{-j\omega m} \qquad\qquad (1.5.2)$$

$H(e^{j\omega})$ is called the *frequency response* of the system since, by (1.5.1), the output from a linear, shift-invariant system with a (complex) sinusoidal input is the same sequence multiplied by the complex factor $H(e^{j\omega})$. If we write

$$H(e^{j\omega}) = A(\omega) e^{j\phi(\omega)}$$

then we have

$$e^{j\omega n} H(e^{j\omega}) = A(\omega) e^{j(\omega n + \phi(\omega))}$$

and so the response $y(n)$ is given by

$$y(n) = A(\omega) \cos(\omega n + \phi(\omega)) + jA(\omega) \sin(\omega n + \phi(\omega))$$

Hence the response to a (real) sine wave of unit amplitude and zero phase shift is a sine wave with amplitude $A(\omega)$ and phase shift ϕ (by equating real and imaginary parts).

The first point to note about (1.5.2) is that, unlike the continuous-time case, where the frequency response is aperiodic, we have

$$H(e^{j\omega}) = H(e^{j(\omega+2k\pi)})$$

for any $k \in \mathbb{Z}$. Hence, the frequency response of a discrete system is periodic with period 2π. This is because if we sample the function $x(t) = \sin \omega t$ at the instants $t = n$, then we obtain the same sequence as that obtained by sampling the function $x(t) = \sin(\omega + 2\pi)t$ at the same instants. Hence a discrete system cannot distinguish between the two signals (see Figure 1.3).

It follows that we need to consider the frequency response of a discrete system only for frequencies in the interval $[0, 2\pi]$. In fact, we can even restrict our attention to the frequency interval $[0, \pi]$ because of further symmetry properties of $H(e^{j\omega})$ which we now derive.

LEMMA 1

$|H(e^{j\omega})|$ is symmetric (for $\omega \in [0, 2\pi]$) about $\omega = \pi$.

Proof Since $\{h(n)\}$ is a real sequence (for a real filter) we have, for $0 \leqslant \omega \leqslant \pi$,

$$|H(e^{j\omega})|^2 = (\Sigma h(n) \cdot \cos \omega n)^2 + (\Sigma h(n) \cdot \sin \omega n)^2$$
$$= (\Sigma h(n) \cdot \cos(2\pi - \omega)n)^2 + (\Sigma h(n) \cdot \sin(2\pi - \omega)n)^2$$
$$= |H(e^{j(2\pi-\omega)})|^2$$

LEMMA 2

arg $H(e^{j\omega})$ is antisymmetric about $\omega = \pi$

The proof of this statement is similar to that of lemma 1.

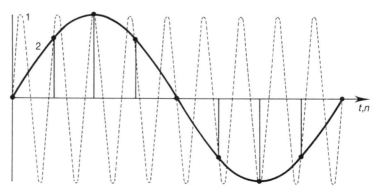

Figure 1.3 Sampling sine waves of different frequencies: $1 \sin\left(\dfrac{n\pi}{4} + 2\pi n\right)$; $2 \sin\left(\dfrac{n\pi}{4}\right)$.

Example   Consider the first-order system

$$y(n) = x(n) + Ky(n - 1) \tag{1.5.3}$$

with the initial condition $y(-1) = 0$, where $0 < |K| < 1$. Then the impulse response is given by solving this equation with input $x = u_0$.
When $n = 0$ we have

$$y(0) = u_0(0) + Ky(-1) = 1$$

and when $n > 0$ we have

$$y(n) = Ky(n - 1) \tag{1.5.4}$$

so that we can replace the original equation (1.5.3) by the homogeneous equation (1.5.4) with the initial condition $y(0) = 1$. The solution of (1.5.4) with this initial condition is clearly

$$y(n) = K^n \quad (n \geqslant 0)$$

Since $y(-1) = 0$ and $K \neq 0$, it follows from (1.5.3) that $y(n) = 0$ if $n < 0$ (for the input $x = u_0$). Hence the impulse response of the system (1.5.3) is given by

$$h(n) = \begin{cases} K^n & n \geqslant 0 \\ 0 & n < 0 \end{cases}$$

Hence,

$$H(e^{j\omega}) = \sum_{n=0}^{\infty} K^n e^{-j\omega n}$$

$$= \frac{1}{1 - Ke^{-j\omega}}$$

since $|K| < 1$ and so

$$|H(e^{j\omega})|^2 = \frac{1}{1 - 2K\cos\omega + K^2}$$

and

$$\arg H(e^{j\omega}) = \omega - \arctan\left(\frac{\sin\omega}{\cos\omega - K}\right)$$

Returning to the general theory, recall that the frequency response of a system with impulse response $\{h(n)\}$ is given by

$$H(e^{j\omega}) = \sum_{n=-\infty}^{\infty} h(n)e^{-j\omega n}$$

Similarly, we define the *frequency spectrum* of a general signal x by

$$X(e^{j\omega}) = \sum_{n=-\infty}^{\infty} x(n)e^{-j\omega n} \tag{1.5.3}$$

The right-hand side of (1.5.3) can be interpreted as the (complex) Fourier series of the periodic function $X(e^{j\omega})$. We can invert this relation by using the orthogonality of the function $e^{-j\omega n}$, i.e.

$$\int_{\pi}^{\pi} e^{-j\omega n} e^{j\omega m} d\omega = \begin{cases} 0 & \text{if } m \neq n \\ 2\pi & \text{if } m = n \end{cases}$$

Hence, multiplying both sides of (1.5.3) by $e^{j\omega m}$ and integrating between $-\pi$ and π gives

$$x(m) = \frac{1}{2\pi} \int_{-\pi}^{\pi} X(e^{j\omega}) e^{j\omega m} d\omega \quad -\infty < m < \infty \tag{1.5.4}$$

Now, if $\phi : \mathbb{C}^{\mathbb{Z}} \to \mathbb{C}^{\mathbb{Z}}$ is a linear, shift-invariant system, then operating on the input signal x, defined by (1.5.4), gives

$$y(n) = (\phi(x))(n) = \phi\left(\frac{1}{2\pi} \int_{-\pi}^{\pi} X(e^{j\omega}) e^{j\omega \cdot} d\omega\right)(n)$$

$$= \left\{\frac{1}{2\pi} \int_{-\pi}^{\pi} X(e^{j\omega}) \phi(e^{j\omega \cdot}) d\omega\right\}(n)$$

where $e^{j\omega \cdot}$ denotes the sequence $\{e^{j\omega n}\}$. (The last equality follows by linearity since the integral can be written as the limit of the sums of exponential sequences.) Hence,

$$y(n) = \frac{1}{2\pi} \int_{-\pi}^{\pi} X(e^{j\omega}) H(e^{j\omega}) e^{j\omega n} d\omega \tag{1.5.5}$$

by the definition of the frequency response H of ϕ. Writing y in terms of its frequency spectrum $Y(e^{j\omega})$ we have

$$y(n) = \frac{1}{2\pi} \int_{-\pi}^{\pi} Y(e^{j\omega}) e^{j\omega n} d\omega \tag{1.5.6}$$

and so, by the uniqueness of Fourier series, (1.5.5) and (1.5.6) imply that

$$Y(e^{j\omega}) = H(e^{j\omega}) X(e^{j\omega}) \tag{1.5.7}$$

Thus, the frequency spectrum of the output of a linear, shift-invariant system equals the product of the frequency spectrum of the input and the frequency response of the system. We shall relate this to the 'transfer function' and the Z-transformation operator to be introduced later.

1.6 The sampling theorem

Up to now we have been interested mainly in discrete signals which are defined without reference to any continuous signal, i.e. are just given as a sequence of numbers. Many discrete signals are, of course, obtained by sampling a continuous-time signal at fixed time intervals of length T. In this case a discrete signal will be written as a sequence of the form $\{x(nT)\}_{n \in \mathbb{Z}}$, and the Fourier transform pair (1.5.3) and (1.5.4) becomes

$$X(e^{j\omega T}) = \sum_{n=-\infty}^{\infty} x(nT)e^{-j\omega T} \tag{1.6.1}$$

and

$$x(nT) = \frac{T}{2\pi} \int_{-\pi/T}^{\pi/T} X(e^{j\omega T})e^{j\omega nT}d\omega \tag{1.6.2}$$

Moreover, $X(e^{j\omega T})$ is now periodic with period $2\pi/T$. We define

$$\omega_s = \frac{2\pi}{T} \tag{1.6.3}$$

and call ω_s the *sampling (or angular) frequency*, in rads/s.

Since $\{x(nT)\}$ has been derived from a continuous-time signal $x(t)$ we can also define the frequency spectrum of $x(t)$ by the Fourier transform of x:

$$X_C(j\Omega) \triangleq \int_{-\infty}^{\infty} x(t)e^{-j\Omega t}dt \tag{1.6.4}$$

We can again recover $x(t)$ by inverse Fourier transformation:

$$x(t) = \frac{1}{2\pi} \int_{-\infty}^{\infty} X_C(j\Omega)e^{j\Omega t}d\Omega \tag{1.6.5}$$

(The subscript 'C' is introduced to distinguish the continuous-time frequency spectrum from that of the discrete sampled version.) To establish a relation between $X(e^{j\omega T})$ and $X_C(j\Omega)$ note that (1.6.5) implies

$$x(nT) = \frac{1}{2\pi} \int_{-\infty}^{\infty} X_C(j\Omega)e^{j\Omega nT}d\Omega$$

$$= \frac{1}{2\pi} \sum_{m=-\infty}^{\infty} \int_{(2m-1)\pi/T}^{(2m+1)\pi/T} X_C(j\Omega)e^{j\Omega nT}d\Omega$$

If we replace Ω by $\omega + 2\pi m/T$ in the mth integral, we have

$$x(nT) = \frac{T}{2\pi} \int_{-\pi/T}^{\pi/T} \frac{1}{T} \sum_{m=-\infty}^{\infty} X_C(j[\omega + 2\pi m/T]e^{j\omega nT}d\omega$$

Comparing this with the general expression (1.6.2), the uniqueness of Fourier series implies that

$$X(e^{j\omega t}) = \frac{1}{T} \sum_{m=-\infty}^{\infty} X_C(j[\omega + 2m\pi/T]) \tag{1.6.6}$$

From the definition (1.6.3) we can expand this relation in the form

$$X(e^{j\omega T}) = \frac{1}{T}(\ldots + X_C(j[\omega - \omega_s]) + X_C(j\omega) + X_C(j[\omega + \omega_s]) + \ldots) \tag{1.6.7}$$

Hence, modulo the factor $1/T$, $X(e^{j\omega T})$ (the frequency spectrum of the sampled signal) is equal to $X_C(j\omega)$ (the frequency spectrum of the continuous-time signal), plus the 'sidebands' $X_C(j\omega + jm\omega_s)$, $m \neq 0$.

Suppose that $x(t)$ is *bandlimited* in the sense that

$$|X_C(j\omega)| = 0 \quad \text{for } |\omega| > \omega_c \tag{1.6.8}$$

Then if

$$\omega_c < \omega_s/2 \tag{1.6.9}$$

if follows from (1.6.7) that

$$X(e^{j\omega T}) = \frac{1}{T}X_C(j\omega), \; \omega \in [-\omega_s/2, \, \omega_s/2] \tag{1.6.10}$$

The relations (1.6.9) and (1.6.10) essentially embody the sampling theorem. Stated formally, we have proved the following.

The sampling theorem

If a continuous-time signal $x(t)$ is bandlimited with cutoff frequency ω_c and we sample at least twice this frequency, then the frequency spectrum of the sampled signal and that of the continuous-time signal are equal on the 'baseband' $[-\omega_s/2, \omega_s/2]$ (modulo the factor $1/T$). (See Figures 1.4, 1.5.)

Since a knowledge of $X_C(j\omega)$ implies (by inverse Fourier transformation) a knowledge of $x(t)$, it follows from the sampling theorem that if we sample fast

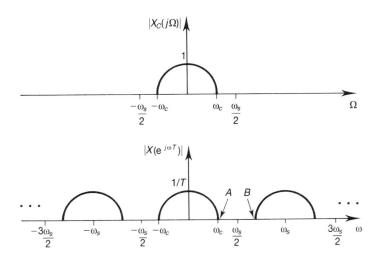

Figure 1.4   Continuous and discrete frequency responses.

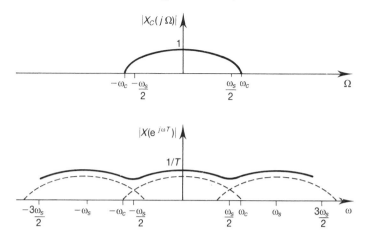

Figure 1.5 Frequency responses and aliasing.

enough, then we can (theoretically) reconstruct $x(t)$ from the discrete frequency spectrum $X(e^{j\omega T})$. This can be proved as follows. If the conditions of the sampling theorem hold, then we have from (1.6.5), (1.6.8) and (1.6.10),

$$x(t) = \frac{1}{2\pi} \int_{-\infty}^{\infty} X_C(j\Omega) e^{j\Omega T} d\Omega$$

$$= \frac{T}{2\pi} \int_{-\omega_s/2}^{\omega_s/2} X(e^{j\omega T}) e^{j\omega t} d\omega$$

$$= \frac{T}{2\pi} \int_{-\omega_s/2}^{\omega_s/2} \left(\sum_{k=-\infty}^{\infty} x(kT) e^{-j\omega kT} \right) e^{j\omega t} d\omega$$

$$= \frac{T}{2\pi} \sum_{k=-\infty}^{\infty} x(kT) \int_{-\omega_s/2}^{\omega_s/2} e^{j(t-kT)\omega} d\omega$$

$$= \sum_{k=-\infty}^{\infty} x(kT) \left(\frac{\sin\left[\omega_s(t-kT)/2\right]}{\omega_s(t-kT)/2} \right) \tag{1.6.11}$$

Using (1.6.11) we can reconstruct $x(t)$ from the samples $x(kT)$. This reconstruction amounts to passing $\{x(kT\}$ through an ideal lowpass filter.

Suppose again that conditions (1.6.8) and (1.6.9) hold for a continuous-time signal $x(t)$. Then the graphical representation of (1.6.10) is shown in Figure 1.4. Consider the effect of reducing the sampling frequency ω_s so that ω_s approaches and becomes less than $2\omega_c$. Then the upper frequency point A in Figure 1.4 will approach the point B and as $\omega_s/2$ becomes smaller than ω_c the first side-band starting at B will begin to interfere with the base-band component at A. This is shown in Figure 1.5. Interference of this kind, due to insufficiently high sampling rate, is called *aliasing* or *frequency folding*. To avoid such effects, a continuous-time signal is often preprocessed by passing it through an analog lowpass filter with cutoff $\omega_s/2$.

1.7 The Z-transform and general linear systems

The Laplace transform is a device for translating a linear time-variant differential equation into an algebraic equation. A similar device can be used for discrete systems; this is called the *Z-transform* and it transforms a linear, shift-invariant system into an algebraic equation. The Z-transform of a sequence x, denoted by $Z\{x\}$ or $X(z)$, is defined by

$$X(z) = \sum_{n=-\infty}^{\infty} x(n)z^{-n} \tag{1.7.1}$$

where z is a complex variable, and exists for all $z \in \mathbb{C}$ for which the series on the right-hand side of (1.7.1) converges absolutely. If x, x_1 and x_2 are generic discrete signals, then the following gives the basic properties of the Z-transform:

(a) LINEARITY

$$Z\{ax_1 + bx_2\} = aZ\{x_1\} + bZ\{x_2\}, \quad a, b \in \mathbb{C}$$

(b) TRANSLATION

$$Z\{x(n + m)\} = z^m Z(x), \ m \in \mathbb{Z}$$

Proof

$$Z\{x(n + m)\} = \sum_{n=-\infty}^{\infty} x(n + m)z^{-n} = z^m \sum_{n=-\infty}^{\infty} x(n + m)z^{-(n+m)}$$

$$= z^m \sum_{n=-\infty}^{\infty} x(n)z^{-n} = z^m Z\{x\}$$

(c) COMPLEX SCALE CHANGE

$$Z\{c^{-n}x(n)\} = X(cz)$$

Proof

$$Z\{c^{-n}x(n)\} = \sum_{n=-\infty}^{\infty} x(n)c^{-n}z^{-n}$$

$$= X(cz)$$

(d) COMPLEX DIFFERENTIATION

$$Z\{nx(n)\} = \frac{-z\,\mathrm{d}X(z)}{\mathrm{d}z}$$

Proof

$$Z\{nx(n)\} = \sum_{n=-\infty}^{\infty} nx(n)z^{-n} = -z \sum_{n=-\infty}^{\infty} x(n)(-n)z^{-n-1}$$

$$= -z \sum_{n=-\infty}^{\infty} x(n) \cdot \frac{d(z^{-n})}{dz}$$

$$= -z \frac{dX(z)}{dz}$$

(e) REAL CONVOLUTION

$$Z\left\{ \sum_{k=-\infty}^{\infty} x_1(k)x_2(n-k) \right\} = X_1(z)X_2(z) = Z\left\{ \sum_{k=-\infty}^{\infty} x_1(n-k)x_2(k) \right\}$$

Proof

$$Z\left\{ \sum_{k=-\infty}^{\infty} x_1(k)x_2(n-k) \right\} = \sum_{n=-\infty}^{\infty} \sum_{k=-\infty}^{\infty} x_1(k)x_2(n-k)z^{-n}$$

$$= \sum_{k=-\infty}^{\infty} x_1(k)z^{-k} \sum_{n=-\infty}^{\infty} x_2(n-k)z^{-(n-k)}$$

$$= X_1(z)X_2(z)$$

We can also define the one-sided Z-transform of a signal x by

$$Z_1\{x\} = \sum_{n=0}^{\infty} x(n)z^{-n}(\triangleq X_I(z))$$

This is the same as the two-sided Z-transform if $x(n) = 0$ for $n < 0$, and the results (a) – (e) above hold with the following modifications in cases (b) and (e):

(b') TRANSLATION
If $m > 0$ then

$$Z_1\{x(n-m)\} = z^{-m}\left\{ \sum_{k=-m}^{-1} x(k)z^{-k} + X_I(z) \right\} \qquad (1.7.2)$$

Proof

$$Z_1\{x(n-m)\} = \sum_{n=0}^{\infty} x(n-m)z^{-n} = z^{-m}\sum_{n=0}^{\infty} x(n-m)z^{-(n-m)}$$

$$= z^{-m}\left\{ \sum_{k=-m}^{\infty} x(k)z^{-k} \right\}$$

$$= z^{-m}\left\{ \sum_{k=-m}^{-1} x(k)z^{-k} + X_I(z) \right\}$$

In particular, if $x(k) = 0$ for $k < 0$ then $Z_1\{x(n-m)\} = z^{-m}X(z)$.

(c') REAL CONVOLUTION

$$Z_I\left\{ \sum_{k=0}^{n} x_1(k)x_2(n-k) \right\} = Z_I\left\{ \sum_{k=0}^{n} x_1(n-k)x_2(k) \right\} = X_{1I}(z)X_{2I}(z)$$

In the sequel we shall not preserve the notational distinction between the one- and two-sided Z-transforms and denote either by Z without the subscript I. Since we shall be concerned almost entirely with signals which are zero for $n < 0$, this should not cause any confusion.

Two important signals are the unit impulse u_0 and the general geometric series $x_c = \{c^n\}$. These have the respective Z-transforms

$$U_0(z) = 1 \tag{1.7.4}$$

and

$$X_C(z) = \frac{1}{1 - cz^{-1}} \tag{1.7.5}$$

The latter is important because any rational function with distinct poles can be written as a sum of terms of the form $1/(1 - cz^{-1})$ by partial fraction expansion. Hence, inverting a Z-transform of this type is particularly easy.

In general, we can derive an inverse Z-transform expression for any function $X(z)$. In fact, since

$$X(z) = \sum_{n=-\infty}^{\infty} x(n)z^{-n}$$

we have

$$x(n) = \frac{1}{2\pi j} \oint_{\Gamma} X(z)z^{n-1}\mathrm{d}z \tag{1.7.6}$$

by Cauchy's theorem, where Γ is a counterclockwise contour enclosing the sigularities of X (assuming the integral exists). If X is a rational function and

$$X(z)z^{n-1} = \frac{R(z)}{\Pi_{i=1}^{k}(z - p_i)^{m_i}}$$

then, by (1.7.6) and the residue theorem,

$$x(n) = \sum_{i=1}^{k} \operatorname*{res}_{z=p_i}\{X(z)z^{n-1}\}$$

$$= \sum_{i=1}^{k} \frac{1}{(m_i - 1)!} \lim_{z \to p_i} \frac{\mathrm{d}^{m_i-1}}{\mathrm{d}z^{m_i-1}}[(z - p_i)^{m_i}X(z)z^{n-1}] \tag{1.7.7}$$

Finally, we note that there is a dual of the real convolution which relates the Z-transform of a product of signals to the *complex convolution* of their individual Z-transforms. In fact,

$$Z\{x_1 x_2\} = \frac{1}{2\pi j} \oint_{\Gamma_1} X_1(v) X_2(z/v) v^{-1} \mathrm{d}v$$

$$= \frac{1}{2\pi j} \oint_{\Gamma_2} X_1(z/v) X_2(v) v^{-1} \mathrm{d}v \qquad (1.7.8)$$

where Γ_1 is a contour in the common region of convergence of $X_1(v)$ and $X_2(z/v)$, and similarly for Γ_2.

Proof of (1.7.8)

$$Z\{x_1 x_2\} = \sum_{n=-\infty}^{\infty} [x_1(n) x_2(n)] z^{-n}$$

$$= \sum_{n=-\infty}^{\infty} x_1(n) \left\{ \frac{1}{2\pi j} \oint_{\Gamma_2} X_2(v) v^{n-1} \mathrm{d}v \right\} z^{-n}$$

$$= \frac{1}{2\pi j} \oint_{\Gamma_2} \left\{ \sum_{n=-\infty}^{\infty} x_1(n) (z/v)^{-n} \right\} X_2(v) v^{-1} \mathrm{d}v$$

$$= \frac{1}{2\pi j} \oint_{\Gamma_2} X_1(z/v) X_2(v) v^{-1} \mathrm{d}v$$

Returning now to linear systems theory, recall from (1.3.3) that any linear, shift-invariant system is characterized by its impulse response $h(n)$ so that for any input $x(n)$ the output $y(n)$ is given by

$$y(n) = \sum_{k=-\infty}^{\infty} x(k) h(n-k) \qquad (1.7.9)$$

Hence, by the real convolution theorem, we have

$$Y(z) = H(z) X(z) \qquad (1.7.10)$$

Thus, the Z-transform of the impulse response equals the quotient of the Z-transforms of the output and input and we call $H(z)$ the *transfer function* of the system. We have seen that (1.7.9) holds for any linear, shift-invariant system. In the remainder of this book we shall restrict our attention mainly to a special subclass of such systems. These are systems with rational transfer functions of the form

$$H(z) = \frac{\sum_{i=0}^{m} a_i z^{-i}}{1 + \sum_{i=1}^{n} b_i z^{-i}} \qquad (1.7.11)$$

for some constants $a_0, \ldots, a_m, b_1, \ldots, b_n$. Using (1.7.2) we see that, by taking inverse Z-transforms, y and x are related by the difference equation

$$y(n) = \sum_{i=0}^{m} a_i x(n-i) - \sum_{i=1}^{n} b_i y(n-i), \quad y(-n) = \ldots = y(-1) = 0 \qquad (1.7.12)$$

The initial conditions in (1.7.12) are necessary for causality. If at least one of the bs in this equation is non-zero, we say that (1.7.12) represents a *recursive filter* and, conversely, if all the bs are zero it is called a *nonrecursive* filter. (In the latter case, $y(n)$ can be determined without evaluating $y(k)$ for earlier values of $k < n$.)

Alternatively, we can write (1.7.11) in the form

$$H(z) = \frac{z^{n-m}\sum_{i=0}^{m}d_i z^{m-i}}{z^n + \sum_{i=1}^{n}b_i z^{n-i}} = K \cdot \frac{\prod_{i=1}^{n}(z - z_i)}{\prod_{i=1}^{n}(z - p_i)} \tag{1.7.13}$$

where z_i and p_i are the zeros and poles of $H(z)$ respectively. As in the case of continuous-time systems, the pole locations have important implications for stability. In fact, we have

THEOREM

The system (with transfer function) (1.7.13) is stable (in the bounded-input–bounded-output sense) if and only if the poles p_i are inside the unit circle, i.e. $|p_i| < 1$ for $1 \leqslant i \leqslant n$.

Proof First note that the Z-transform of the sequence

$$x = \{k(k - 1)(k - 2) \ldots (k - m + 1)a^k)\} \tag{1.7.14}$$

is given by

$$X(z) = \frac{m(az^{-1})^m}{(1 - az^{-1})^{m+1}}$$

If the transfer function $H(z)$ has l poles with respective multiplicities m_i, $1 \leqslant i \leqslant l$, then we can write

$$H(z) = \sum_{i=1}^{l} \sum_{j=2}^{m_i} \frac{A_{ij}(j - 1)(p_i z^{-1})^{j-1}}{(1 - p_i z^{-1})^j} + \sum_{i=1}^{l} \frac{B_i}{(1 - p_i z^{-1})}$$

for some (complex) constants A_{ij}, B_i, by partial fraction expansion. (Here $A_{ij} = 0$ if $m_i = 1$.) Hence, $\{h(n)\}$ is a sum of sequences of the form (1.7.14). The theorem follows easily apart from the case when $H(z)$ has a nonrepeated pole on the unit circle. Then the impulse response contains a term of the form

$$Z^{-1}\left\{\frac{A}{1 - pz^{-1}}\right\} = Ap^k$$

where $|p| = 1$ and so we can choose the bounded input $x = \{p^k\}$ which will give an unbounded output.

Bibliographical notes

There are many texts on discrete signals and systems; see, for example, Antoniou (1979); Rabiner and Gold (1975). The theory of difference equations is presented in Levy and Lessman (1959), and the theory of discrete systems and the Z-transform as applied in control theory is given in Banks (1986).

Exercises

1 Show that $u_s = \Sigma_{k=0}^{\infty} u_0^k$, where u_s and u_0 are the unit step and unit impulse sequences, respectively. (In particular, show that the infinite sum makes sense.)

2 Explain in detail the steps involved in proving the convolution theorem (1.3.3) (or (1.3.4)), paying particular attention to the existence of the infinite sum.

3 Show that a memoryless system $\phi : \mathbb{C}^{\mathbb{Z}} \to \mathbb{C}^{\mathbb{Z}}$ can be uniquely defined by a complex-valued function $f : \mathbb{C} \to \mathbb{C}$.

4 Which of the systems given in terms of their impulse responses below are stable?

(a) $h(n) = \dfrac{1}{2^n} \quad n \geqslant 0$;

(b) $h(n) = \dfrac{1}{n^2} \quad n > 0$;

(c) $h(n) = \dfrac{1}{n} \quad n > 0$ (all other values of $h(n) = 0$).

5 Prove lemma 2.

6 Discuss the frequency response behaviour of the second-order system

$$y(k) = x(k) + b_1 y(k - 1) + b_2 y(k - 2)$$

with

$$y(-1) = y(-2) = 0$$

in the spirit of the first-order example in Section 1.5.

7 Let F be a set of functions of time (defined on the interval $(-\infty, \infty)$) which are Fourier transformable and are bandlimited by ω_c, and let S_T be the sampling operator from F to $\mathbb{C}^{\mathbb{Z}}$ which associates with $f(t)$ the sequence $\{f(nT)\}$. Explain why it is possible to obtain $f(t)$ from the samples $\{f(nT)\}$ exactly if $\pi/T \geqslant \omega_c$, even though information is lost between the samples, by showing that S_T is one-to-one if and only if $T \leqslant \pi/\omega_c$. (Hint: consider $\sin(\omega_c t) \in F$.)

8 Find the Z-transforms of the sequences

(a) $\{\cos n\pi\}$;

(b) $\{\sin n\pi\}$;

For what ranges of z are they valid?
9 Solve exercise 6 by Z-transformation.
10 For which values of b_1, b_2 is the system in exercise 6 stable?

References

Antoniou, A. (1979), *Digital Filters: Analysis and design*, NY: McGraw-Hill.
Banks, S. P. (1986), *Control Systems Engineering*, Hemel Hempstead: Prentice Hall.
Levy, H. and F. Lessman (1959), *Finite Difference Equations*, London: Pitman.
Rabiner, L. R. and B. Gold (1975), *Theory and Application of Digital Signal Processing*, Englewood Cliffs, NJ: Prentice Hall.

2

Design of
Nonrecursive Filters

2.1 Introduction

Basically, the problem of the design of digital filters can be approached from two ways. The first is a direct method in which we specify the frequency response of the filter and by inverse Fourier transformation, we determine from this the impulse response coefficients. This leads to nonrecursive (or finite-impulse response) filters, and we shall present this method in this chapter. The second method consists of applying transformations from the s-plane to the z-plane to existing analog filters; this method will be discussed later. Note that there are many more techniques for designing FIR filters, some of which will be mentioned in Chapter 10.

2.2 Filter specifications

Digital filters are usually specified in the frequency domain in terms of the frequency ranges which they are to leave unaffected and those which are to be removed from any input signal. The four main types are shown in Figure 2.1. It should be remembered that the frequency response of a discrete system is periodic with period ω_s and so we need only consider the response on the interval $[-\omega_s/2, \omega_s/2]$.

In Figure 2.1 we have only shown the amplitude response of the desired filter; nothing has been said about the phase response. Of course, we would like zero phase shift over the entire frequency range, but we shall see that this is impossible, so that we must accept something less than this ideal. Suppose it is possible to achieve a linear phase shift $\phi = -\omega\lambda$ for some constant λ. Then if we split an input signal into a sum of sinusoids of the form $\sin(\omega nT)$, each such sinusoid produces the response

$$|H(e^{j\omega T})| \sin[\omega(nT - \lambda)]$$

Hence each sinusoidal component of the input signal is delayed by the same 'time' λ, and so if the amplitude response is that of a lowpass filter, for example, the output signal is an undistorted version of the part of the input signal with frequency components in the range $[-\omega_c, \omega_c]$, i.e. the filter is nondispersive.

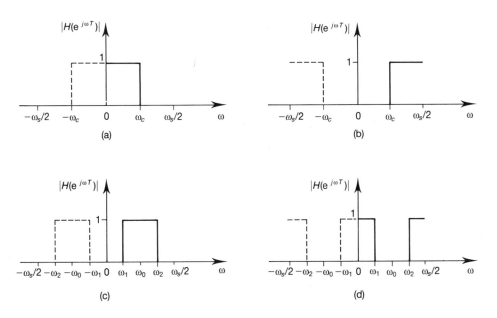

Figure 2.1   Digital filter specifications: (a) lowpass; (b) highpass; (c) bandpass; (d) bandstop.

We now show that it is possible to achieve a linear phase response in a nonrecursive filter

$$H(z) = \sum_{i=0}^{m} a_i z^{-i} \tag{2.2.1}$$

By definition of the Z-transform of the impulse response $\{h(n)\}$ of the filter we also have

$$H(z) = \sum_{i=0}^{\infty} h(i) z^{-i} \tag{2.2.2}$$

Hence, from (2.2.1) and (2.2.2) we have

$$\left. \begin{array}{ll} h(i) = a_i & 0 \leq i \leq m \\ h(i) = 0 & i > m \end{array} \right\} \tag{2.2.3}$$

and so the coefficients a_i in the difference equation defining the filter are just the impulse response coefficients.

Let m be even, say $m = 2N$, and write

$$H(e^{j\omega T}) = \sum_{k=0}^{2N} h(k) e^{-jk\omega T}$$

$$= e^{-jN\omega T}\{h(0)e^{jN\omega T} + h(1)e^{j(N-1)\omega T} + \ldots + h(N)$$

$$+ \ldots + h(2N)e^{-jN\omega T}\}$$

Then if we impose the conditions

$$\left. \begin{array}{l} h(0) = h(2N) \\ h(1) = h(2N - 1) \\ \quad\vdots \\ h(N + 1) = h(N - 1) \end{array} \right\} \tag{2.2.4}$$

then we obtain

$$H(e^{j\omega T}) = e^{-jN\omega T}\left\{h(N) + 2\sum_{i=0}^{N-1} h(i)\cos\left[(N - i)\omega T\right]\right\} \tag{2.2.5}$$

Since the expression in brackets is real the phase response of the filter is $-N\omega T$, which is a linear function of ω. Note that we can also make the coefficients $h(i)$ antisymmetric about N.

2.3 FIR design

The complete design specification of an ideal lowpass filter is shown in Figure 2.2. The amplitude and phase responses are included on the same graph.

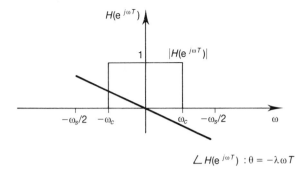

Figure 2.2 Ideal lowpass filter response.

Since we have

$$H(e^{j\omega T}) = \begin{cases} e^{-j\lambda\omega T} & |\omega| \leq \omega_c \\ 0 & \text{otherwise} \end{cases}$$

it follows from (1.5.4) that

$$h(n) = \frac{1}{\omega_s} \int_{-\omega_s/2}^{\omega_s/2} H(e^{j\omega T})e^{jn\omega T}d\omega$$

$$= \frac{1}{\omega_s} \int_{-\omega_c}^{\omega_c} e^{j(n-\lambda)\omega T}d\omega$$

$$= \frac{\omega_c T}{\pi} \cdot \frac{\sin\left[(n-\lambda)\omega_c T\right]}{(n-\lambda)\omega_c T} \qquad n = 0, \pm 1, \pm 2, \ldots$$

$$(2.3.1)$$

Suppose we try to obtain a filter with zero phase shift in the interval $[-\omega_s/2, \omega_s/2]$, then $\lambda = 0$ and if, for example, $\omega_c = \omega_s/8$, then from (2.3.1) we have

$$h(n) = \frac{1}{4} \cdot \frac{\sin n\pi/4}{n\pi/4}$$

$$= \frac{1}{4} \cdot \text{sinc}\,(n\pi/4)$$

$$(2.3.2)$$

where

$$\text{sinc}\,(x) = \frac{\sin x}{x}$$

The impulse response sequence (2.3.2) is shown in Figure 2.3. The filter with this impulse response is an ideal lowpass filter with zero phase shift. However, two points should be immediately noted. First, the filter is noncausal since $h(n) \neq 0$ for some $n < 0$ and so cannot be implemented in real time. Second, it

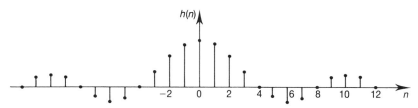

Figure 2.3 The impulse response of an ideal (zero phase shift) lowpass filter.

is not a finite impulse response filter since $h(n) \neq 0$ for infinitely many n. This means that the filter response would take an infinite time to compute (even assuming we had an infinite word-length computer). It follows that we can never achieve the ideal lowpass filter and so we must accept a compromise.

If we truncate the impulse response so that $h(n) = 0$ for $|n| > 10$, and introduce a delay of $\lambda = 10$ in (2.3.1), then we obtain the approximate impulse response $h_a(n)$ shown in Figure 2.4. By (2.2.5) we see that the frequency response of $\{h_a(n)\}$ is given by

$$H_a(e^{j\omega T}) = e^{-j10\omega T}\left\{h_a(10) + 2\sum_{i=0}^{9} h_a(i)\cos\left[(10 - i)\omega T\right]\right\} \qquad (2.3.3)$$

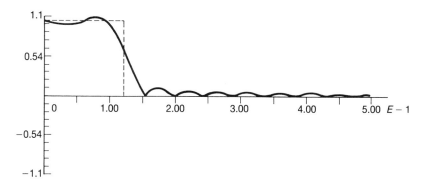

Figure 2.4 The impulse response of an approximating filter.

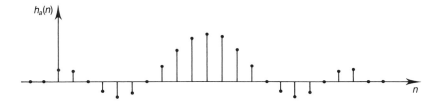

Figure 2.5 Ideal and approximate frequency responses.

This frequency response is shown in Figure 2.5 and can be compared with the ideal form in Figure 2.2. (The phase response is, of course, linear.)

2.4 Filter transformations

We can use the same method as that used in Section 2.3 to design other types of filter, e.g. highpass, bandpass, bandstop, etc. However, there is a simple method of obtaining a filter of one of these types directly from a lowpass filter. For example, if $h(n)_{LP}$ are the impulse response coefficients of a lowpass filter with cutoff $(\omega_c)_{LP}$ and sampling frequency ω_s, then

$$h(n)_{HP} = (-1)^n h(n)_{LP}$$

are the impulse response coefficients of a highpass filter with cutoff frequency

$$(\omega_c)_{HP} = (\omega_s/2) - (\omega_c)_{LP}$$

To prove this note that

$$h(n)_{HP} = \frac{1}{\omega_s} \int_{(\omega_c)_{HP}}^{\omega_s/2} e^{jn\omega T} d\omega + \int_{-\omega_s/2}^{-(\omega_c)_{HP}} e^{jn\omega T} d\omega$$

$$= \frac{1}{\omega_s} \int_{(\omega_c)_{HP}-\omega_s/2}^{0} e^{jn(\omega'+\omega_s/2)T} d\omega' + \int_{0}^{\omega_s/2-(\omega_c)_{HP}} e^{jn(\omega'-\omega_s/2)T} d\omega'$$

$$= \frac{1}{\omega_s} (\cos n\pi) \left(\int_{-(\omega_c)_{LP}}^{(\omega_c)_{LP}} e^{jn\omega' T} d\omega' \right)$$

$$= (-1)^n h(n)_{LP}$$

Hence, to design a highpass filter with cutoff $(\omega_c)_{HP}$, we design a lowpass filter with cutoff $\omega_s/2 - (\omega_c)_{HP}$ and multiply the resulting impulse response coefficients by $(-1)^n$.

The relations between lowpass and bandpass and bandstop filters are given by

(i) $h(n)_{BP} = (2 \cos n\omega_0 T) h(n)_{LP}$

$\omega_0 = $ centre frequency

$(\omega_1) = \omega_0 - (\omega_c)_{LP}$

$(\omega_2) = \omega_0 - (\omega_c)_{LP}$

(ii) $h(0)_{BS} = 1 - h(0)_{BP}, \; h(n)_{BS} = - h(n)_{BP}, \; n = +1, +2, \ldots.$

2.5 Windows

In Section 2.3 we obtained a realizable FIR filter by truncating the exact impulse response (2.2.7) and introducing a delay. Truncating an impulse response $h = \{h(n)\}$ outside the interval $|n| \leqslant N$ is equivalent to multiplying h by the sequence w_R defined by

$$w_R(n) = \begin{cases} 1 & \text{if } |n| \leqslant N \\ 0 & \text{if } |n| > N \end{cases}$$

Thus, $h_a(n)$ in (2.2.8) is given by

$$h_a(n) = h(n)w_R(n)$$

w_R is called the *rectangular window*. More generally, if $\{w(n)\}$ is any sequence we write

$$h_w(n) = h(n)w(n)$$

Using the results of Chapter 1, we see that

$$H_w(z) = \frac{1}{2\pi j} \oint_\Gamma H(v)W(z/v)v^{-1}\mathrm{d}v$$

where Γ is a contour in the common region of convergence of $H(v)$ and $W(z/v)$. Putting $v = \mathrm{e}^{j\Omega T}$, $z = \mathrm{e}^{j\omega T}$, we have

$$H_w(\mathrm{e}^{j\omega T}) = \frac{T}{2\pi} \int_0^{2\pi/T} H(\mathrm{e}^{j\Omega T})W(\mathrm{e}^{j(\omega-\Omega)T})\mathrm{d}\Omega \tag{2.5.1}$$

Consider the rectangular window, for example. We have

$$\begin{aligned}
W_R(\mathrm{e}^{j\omega T}) &= \sum_{n=-N}^{N} \mathrm{e}^{-j\omega nT} \\
&= \frac{\mathrm{e}^{j\omega NT} - \mathrm{e}^{-j\omega(2N+1)T}}{1 - \mathrm{e}^{-j\omega T}} \\
&= \frac{\sin\left(\omega(2N+1)T/2\right)}{\sin\left(\omega T/2\right)}
\end{aligned}$$

Thus the frequency spectrum of the rectangular window has large sidelobes of alternating sign. This leads to the Gibb's phenomenon when the impulse response of an ideal lowpass filter is truncated, because H_w is the convolution of the ideal frequency response H and the window W, as shown by (2.5.1). In order to overcome this problem we must therefore determine window functions whose spectrum has a large central lobe and small sidelobes. Such a function is given by the window

$$w_H(nT) = \begin{cases} \alpha + (1 - \alpha)\cos\left(\pi n/N\right) & |n| \leqslant N \\ 0 & |n| > N \end{cases}$$

For $\alpha = 0.5$ this is called the *von Hann window* and for $\alpha = 0.54$ it is called the *Hamming window*. The spectrum is given by

$$W_H(e^{j\omega T}) = \alpha \frac{\sin(\omega(2N+1)T/2)}{\sin(\omega T/2)} + \frac{1-\alpha}{2}$$
$$\times \frac{\sin[\omega(2N+1)T/2 - (2N+1)\pi/2N]}{\sin[\omega T/2 - \pi/2N]} + \frac{1-\alpha}{2}$$
$$\times \frac{\sin[\omega(2N+1)T/2 + (2N+1)\pi/2N]}{\sin[\omega T/2 + \pi/2N]} \qquad (2.5.2)$$

The first term is zero when $\omega = m\omega_s/(2N+1)$ and the second and third terms are zero when

$$\omega = \left(m + \frac{2N+1}{2N}\right)\cdot\frac{\omega_s}{(2N+1)}, \quad \omega = \left(m - \frac{2N+1}{2N}\right)\cdot\frac{\omega_s}{(2N+1)}$$

respectively, for $m = +1, +2, \ldots$. Hence, the main lobe of the frequency spectrum has width $4\omega_s/(2N+1)$ (since the three terms have a common zero at $\omega = 2\omega_s/(2N+1)$ if N is large).

The *Blackman window*, defined by

$$w_B(nT) = \begin{cases} 0.42 + 0.5\cos(n\pi/N) + 0.08\cos(2n\pi/N) & |n| \le N \\ 0 & |n| > N \end{cases}$$

has reduced ripple compared with the last two windows, but a wider main lobe width (giving a filter with a less steep transition region).

Achieving a desired trade-off between ripple-ratio and primary lobe width is particularly easy with the *Kaiser window*:

$$w_K(nT) = \begin{cases} I_0(\beta)/I_0(\alpha) & |n| \le N \\ 0 & |n| > N \end{cases}$$

where α is a parameter and

$$\beta = \alpha\{1 - (n/N)^2\}^{1/2}$$

Here, $I_0(x)$ is the zeroth-order Bessel function of the first kind, defined by the series

$$I_0(x) = 1 + \sum_{k=1}^{\infty}\left\{\frac{1}{k!}(x/2)^k\right\}^2$$

The spectrum of w_K is given by

$$W_K(e^{j\omega T}) = w_K(0) + 2\sum_{n=1}^{N} w_K(nT)\cos\omega nT \qquad (2.5.3)$$

The discrete sequence $\{w_K(nT)\}$ is the sampled form of the continuous-time function

$$w_K(t) = \begin{cases} I_0(\beta)/I_0(\alpha) & |t| \le \tau \\ 0 & |t| > \tau \end{cases}$$

where

$$\beta = \alpha\{1 - (t/\tau)^2\}^{1/2} \qquad \tau = NT$$

The spectrum of $w_K(t)$ is given by

$$W_K(j\omega) = \frac{2}{I_0(\alpha)} \cdot \frac{\sin[\tau(\omega^2 - \omega_a^2)^{1/2}]}{(\omega^2 - \omega_a^2)^{1/2}}$$

where

$$\omega_a = \alpha/\tau$$

If

$$W_K(j\omega) \approx 0 \text{ or } |\omega| \ge \omega_s/2$$

then, by the sampling theorem,

$$W_K(e^{j\omega T}) \approx \frac{1}{T} \cdot W_K(j\omega) \qquad 0 \le |\omega| < \omega_s/2$$

and so

$$W_K(e^{j\omega T}) \approx \frac{2N}{\alpha I_0(\alpha)} \cdot \frac{\sin[\alpha\{(\omega/\omega_a)^2 - 1\}^{1/2}]}{\{(\omega/\omega_a)^2 - 1\}^{1/2}}$$

Selecting α appropriately changes the ripple ratio and the main lobe as conflicting factors, and a reasonable value of α can be chosen for the particular filter being designed. In Figure 2.6 various windows are compared with the rectangular window of Fig. 2.5.

2.6 Other methods

In the final section of this chapter we shall mention briefly two other approaches to the design of FIR filters. In the first method, instead of trying to match a design frequency response over the whole interval $[0, \omega_s/2]$ we sample the required frequency response at regular intervals, say at the points $i\omega_s/2N$, $0 \le i \le N$. Then we obtain the impulse response coefficients from the inverse discrete Fourier transform (see Chapter 3). Such filters are called *frequency sampling filters*. The method can be improved by using the windowing technique, but this time in the frequency domain, to 'soften' the effect of the sharp cutoff in the ideal frequency response. (Sampling in the frequency domain leads to aliasing in the time domain for the same reason as before; we just interchange 'frequency' and 'time', which are, in a sense, dual variables.) Thus, sampling in the frequency domain implies periodicity in the time domain.

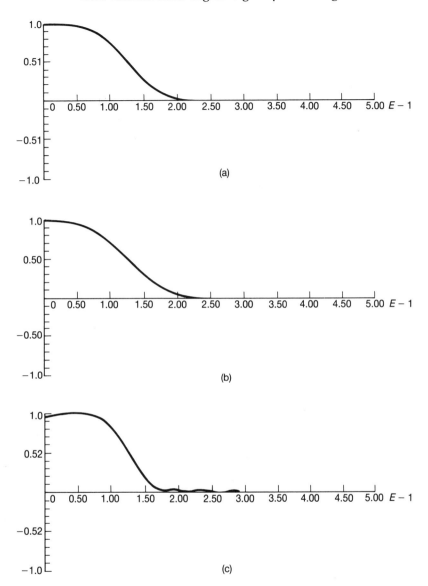

Figure 2.6   The filter of Figure 2.5 with non-rectangular windows: (a) von Hann window; (b) Blackman window; (c) Kaiser window $\beta = 4$.

The second method uses optimization theory to select the impulse response coefficients in such a way as to minimize some measure of the average error between the ideal and the practical frequency responses. If our filter is given by

$$H(z; a) = \sum_{i=0}^{N} a(i)z^{-i} + \sum_{i=1}^{N} a(N - i)z^{-(i+N)}$$

(symmetric about $i = N$ for linear phase shift), then we typically minimize the functional

$$J = \left\{ \int_{0}^{\omega_s/2} |H(e^{j\omega T}; a) - H_d(e^{j\omega T})|^p \, d\omega \right\}^{1/p} \qquad (2.6.1)$$

with respect to $a(0), \ldots, a(N)$, where H_d is the desired frequency response. If $p = 2$, then it is easy to see that the optimal solution is the same as that given in Section 2.3. If $p \neq 2$, then the equations

$$\frac{\partial J}{\partial a(i)} = 0$$

are nonlinear in $a(i)$ and so we must resort to numerical techniques of optimization.

Bibliographical notes

The derivation and application of the Kaiser window and, in particular, the choice of the parameter α is discussed in detail in Kaiser (1974). A variety of optimization techniques for choosing FIR coefficients, including the application of linear programming, can be found in Chottera and Jullien (1982), Crochiere and Rabiner (1975) and Rabiner and Herrmann (1973). The use of Tchebychev approximations for the design of linear phase FIR filters is presented in Cortelazzo and Lightner (1984). In the host windowing technique, described in Abed and Cain (1984), a filter is obtained by multiplying a 'host window', which is common to a wide class of filters, by a simple trigonometric window. It is particularly useful for designing filters with variable frequency characteristics. Finally, we note that linear phase FIR filters can be used for decimation, interpolation and narrow-band filtering (Crochiere and Rabiner (1975) and Saramaki (1984)).

Exercises

1 Show that a linear phase FIR filter may be obtained by taking the coefficients $h(i)$ antisymmetric about $h(N)$. (Compare with (2.2.4).) What is the phase response of such a filter?

2 Design a linear phase lowpass digital FIR filter with sampling frequency

1 kHz, cutoff frequency 300 Hz and delay 0.02 s. Draw a sketch of the impulse response.

3 Using the results of exercise 2, design a highpass filter with $\omega_s = 1$ kHz, delay 0.02 s. and cutoff frequency 200 Hz. Again, draw a sketch of the impulse response.

4 Prove (2.5.2) and (2.5.3).

5 If $p = 2$ in (2.6.1), show that the minimum of J when H_d is an ideal lowpass filter is attained by the values

$$a(i) = \frac{\omega_c T}{\pi} \, \text{sinc} \, \{(n - \lambda)\omega_c T\}$$

6 Show that if H_d is as in exercise 5 and, again, $p = 2$, then the minimum of the cost functional

$$J = \int_0^{\omega_s/2} W(\omega)(H(e^{j\omega T}; a) - H_d(e^{j\omega T}))^2 d\omega$$

where $W(\omega)$ is some weighting function, is attained by a vector $a = (a(0), \ldots, a(N))$ which satisfies a linear equation

$$\mathbf{Ca} = \mathbf{b}$$

and determine the matrix $\mathbf{C}$ and the vector $\mathbf{b}$.

References

Abed, A. H. M. and G. D. Cain (1984), 'The host windowing technique for FIR digital filter design', *IEEE Trans. Acoust., Speech, Signal Process.*, ASSP-**32**, 683–94.

Chottera, A. T. and G. A. Jullien (1982), 'A linear programming approach to recursive digital filter design with linear phase', *IEEE Trans. Circuits Sys.*, CAS-**29**, 139–49.

Cortelazzo, G. and M. R. Lightner (1984), 'Simultaneous design in both magnitude and group-delay of IIR and FIR filters based on multiple criterion optimization', *IEEE Trans. Acoust., Speech, Signal Process.*, ASSP-**32**, 949–67.

Crochiere, R. E. and L. R. Rabiner (1975), 'Optimum FIR digital filter implementations for decimation, interpolation and narrow-band filtering', *IEEE Trans. Acoust., Speech, Signal Process.*, ASSP-**23**, 444–56.

Kaiser, J. F. (1974), 'Nonrecursive digital filter design using the I_0-sinh window function', *Proc. 1974 IEEE Int. Symp. Circuit Theory*, pp. 20–3.

Rabiner, L. R. and O. Herrmann (1973), 'On the design of optimum FIR low-pass filters with even impulse response duration', *IEEE Trans. Audio Electroacoust.*, AU-**21**, 329–36.

Saramaki, T. (1984), 'A class of linear-phase FIR filters for decimation, interpolation and narrow-band filtering', *IEEE Trans. Acoust., Speech, Signal Process.*, ASSP-**32**, 1023–36.

3

The Discrete and Fast Fourier Transforms

3.1 Introduction

We have seen the need to compute the transform $F(e^{j\omega T})$ of a sequence $\{f(nT), n \geq 0\}$ given by

$$F(e^{j\omega T}) = \sum_{n=0}^{\infty} f(nT)e^{-j\omega nT}$$

since this represents the frequency spectrum of such a discrete signal. In the case where f is the impulse response of a finite impulse response filter, only a finite number (say N) of the terms $f(nT)$ in the sequence are nonzero, and so we have

$$F(e^{j\omega T}) = \sum_{n=0}^{N-1} f(nT)e^{-j\omega nT} \tag{3.1.1}$$

For numerical computation, we shall only evaluate (3.1.1) for a discrete set of values ω. Since $F(e^{j\omega T})$ is periodic with period $\omega_s = 2\pi/T$, it is reasonable to divide the interval $[0, \omega_s]$ into N equal parts. Then we have

$$F(k\Omega) = \sum_{n=0}^{N-1} f(nT)e^{-j\Omega Tnk} \qquad 0 \leqslant k \leqslant N - 1 \qquad (3.1.2)$$

where

$$F(k\Omega) \triangleq F(e^{jk\omega_s T/N})$$

Thus, given a sequence $f = \{f(nT), 0 \leqslant n \leqslant N - 1\}$, the sequence $F = \{F(k\Omega), 0 \leqslant k \leqslant N - 1\}$, with $\Omega = 2\pi/NT$, associated with f by (3.1.2), is called the *discrete Fourier transform* (DFT) of f.

Recalling that the Z-transform of f is given by

$$Z(f) = \sum_{n=0}^{N-1} f(nT)z^{-n}$$

we see from (3.1.2) that the discrete Fourier transform of a finite sequence is just the Z-transform of the sequence evaluated at the N points $e^{j\Omega Tk}$, $0 \leqslant k \leqslant N - 1$. These are N equally spaced points on the unit circle.

3.2 Inversion of the DFT

As with any Fourier transformation we expect the DFT given by (3.1.2) to have an inverse. To prove that this is indeed the case we multiply (3.1.2) by $e^{j\Omega Tmk}$ and sum over k:

$$\sum_{k=0}^{N-1} F(k\Omega)e^{j\Omega Tmk} = \sum_{n=0}^{N-1} f(nT) \sum_{k=0}^{N-1} e^{j\Omega Tk(m-n)} \qquad (3.2.1)$$

Consider the sum

$$S_{m,n} = \sum_{k=0}^{N-1} e^{j\Omega Tk(m-n)} = \sum_{k=0}^{N-1} (e^{j\Omega T(m-n)})^k$$

If $m \equiv n \bmod N$, then $e^{j\Omega T(m-n)} = e^{2\pi jr} = 1$ (for some r). In general,

$$S_{m,n} = \frac{1 - e^{j\Omega T(m-n)N}}{1 - e^{j\Omega T(m-n)}}$$

if $m \equiv n \bmod N$, then $e^{j\Omega T(m-n)} \neq 1$, while $e^{j\Omega T(m-n)N} = 1$. Hence, in this case, $S_{m,n} = 0$. It follows that $S_{m,n} = \delta_{m,n}N$, $0 \leqslant m, n \leqslant N - 1$ and so, by (3.2.1), we have

$$f(mT) = \frac{1}{N} \sum_{k=0}^{N-1} F(k\Omega)e^{j\Omega Tmk} \qquad (3.2.2)$$

Hence, (3.2.1) and (3.2.2) form a DFT pair.

3.3 Circular convolution

Since the convolution of two sequences is fundamental in linear discrete systems theory, it is natural to consider the corresponding concept for finite length sequences $f(nT)$, $0 \leqslant n \leqslant N - 1$. Definite the *circular convolution* of the sequences $\{x(nT)\}$, $\{y(nT)\}$, $0 \leqslant n \leqslant N - 1$ by

$$w(mT) = \sum_{n=0}^{N-1} x(nT)y([(m - n) \bmod N]T) \tag{3.3.1}$$

$$= \sum_{n=0}^{N-1} x([(m - n) \bmod N]T)y(nT) \tag{3.3.2}$$

The discrete Fourier transform of w is given by

$$W(k\Omega) = \sum_{m=0}^{N-1}\sum_{n=0}^{N-1} x([(m - n) \bmod N]T)y(nT)e^{-j\Omega Tmk}$$

$$= \sum_{n=0}^{N-1} y(nT) \sum_{m=0}^{N-1} x([(m - n) \bmod N]T)e^{-j\Omega T(m-n)k}e^{-j\Omega Tnk}$$

$$= \sum_{n=0}^{N-1} y(nT) \sum_{m=0}^{N-1} x([(m - n) \bmod N]T)e^{-j\Omega T[(m-n) \bmod N]k}e^{-j\Omega Tnk}$$

$$= X(k\Omega)Y(k\Omega)$$

and so the DFT of a circular convolution of two sequences is the product of the DFTs of the individual sequences. This is important in fast convolution algorithms, as we shall see later.

3.4 Fast Fourier transform

Evaluation of the DFT of a sequence directly, via (3.1.2), involves the order of N^2 complex multiplications and additions, which for large N requires considerable computer time. It is therefore important to find quicker methods for evaluating the right-hand side of (3.1.2). The fast Fourier transform (FFT) algorithms provide such methods, and although they require N to be composite (i.e. not a prime) number (usually a power of 2), we can usually arrange for this to be the case.

First note that (3.1.2) can be written in the form

$$F(k\Omega) = \sum_{n=0}^{N-1} f(nT)W_N^{nk}$$

where $W_N = e^{-j(2\pi/N)}$. If N is even, then we can split the sequence f into even and odd terms by defining

$$g(mT) = f(2mT)$$

$$h(mT) = f((2m + 1)T)$$

for $0 \leqslant m \leqslant N/2 - 1$. Now,

$$F(k\Omega) = \sum_{m=0}^{N/2-1} f(2mT)W_N^{2mk} + \sum_{m=0}^{N/2-1} f((2m + 1)T)W_N^{(2m+1)k}$$

$$= \sum_{m=0}^{N/2-1} g(mT)W_{N/2}^{mk} + W_N^k \sum_{m=0}^{N/2-1} h(mT)W_{N/2}^{mk}$$

$$= G(k\Omega) + W_N^k \cdot H(k\Omega) \qquad 0 \leqslant k \leqslant N - 1 \qquad (3.4.1)$$

where G and H are the DFTs of g and h, respectively, and we have used the fact that $W_N^2 = W_{N/2}$. Since $G(k\Omega)$ and $H(k\Omega)$ have period $N/2$, we can write (3.4.1) in the form

$$F(k\Omega) = G(k\Omega) + W^k H(k\Omega) \qquad 0 \leqslant k \leqslant N/2 - 1$$

$$F(k\Omega) = G((k - N/2)\Omega) + W^k H((k - N/2)\Omega) \qquad N/2 \leqslant k \leqslant N - 1$$

where we have dropped the subscript N on W_N.

Hence, we can implement the DFT of the sequence $\{f_0, f_1, \ldots, f_7\}$, for example, where $f_k = f(kT)$, as shown in Figure 3.1.

Applying the same argument to the two 4-input DFTs in Figure 3.1 we can reduce the computation of $\{F_0, \ldots, F_7\}$ to the evaluation of the signal-flow graph in Figure 3.2. Since the number of nodes in the general DFT signal-flow graph is equal to Nn where $N = 2^n$, it follows that the number of operations involved is proportional to $N\log_2 N$ rather than N^2 in the direct evaluation of

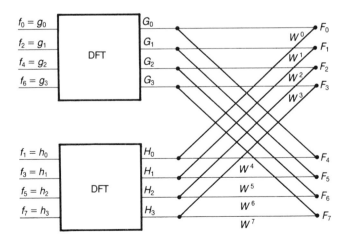

Figure 3.1 The discrete Fourier transform.

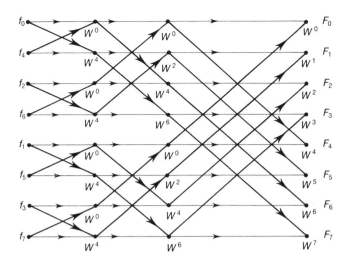

Figure 3.2 The DFT fully expanded.

the DFT. If $N = 1024$, then the *fast Fourier transform* requires only 1 per cent of the time required for direct calculation of the DFT.

The fast Fourier transform which has just been introduced is referred to as the FFT by *decimation in time*, since we divide the sequence $\{f_0, \ldots, f_{N-1}\}$ into even and odd order terms. Since the sequences $\{f_0, \ldots, f_{N-1}\}$ and $\{F_0, \ldots, F_{N-1}\}$ are dual, in an obvious sense, we can do exactly the same with the transformed sequence $\{F_0, \ldots, F_{N-1}\}$ to obtain the FFT by *decimation in frequency*. By (3.2.2) we have

$$
\begin{aligned}
f(mT) &= \frac{1}{N} \sum_{k=0}^{N-1} F(k\Omega) e^{j\Omega Tmk} \\
&= \frac{1}{N} \sum_{k=0}^{N/2-1} F(2k\Omega) W^{-2mk} + \frac{1}{N} \sum_{k=0}^{N/2-1} F((2k+1)\Omega) W^{-(2k+1)m} \\
&= \frac{1}{N} \sum_{k=0}^{N/2-1} G(k\Omega) W_{N/2}^{-mk} + W^{-m} \frac{1}{N} \sum_{k=0}^{N/2-1} H(k\Omega) W_{N/2}^{-km}
\end{aligned}
$$

where

$$
\begin{aligned}
G(k\Omega) &= F(2k\Omega) \\
H(k\Omega) &= F((2k+1)\Omega)
\end{aligned}
\qquad 0 \leqslant m \leqslant N - 1
$$

Hence,

$$
f(mT) = \tfrac{1}{2} g(mT) + \tfrac{1}{2} W^{-m} h(mT) \qquad 0 \leqslant m \leqslant N - 1
$$

where g and h are the inverse DFTs of G and H, respectively. Thus, since g and h are periodic with period $N/2$, we have

$$f(mT) = \tfrac{1}{2}g(mT) + \tfrac{1}{2}W^{-m}h(mT) \qquad 0 \leqslant m \leqslant N/2 - 1$$

$$f((m + N/2)T) = \tfrac{1}{2}g(mT) + \tfrac{1}{2}W^{-m}W^{-N/2}h(mT) \qquad 0 \leqslant m \leqslant N/2 - 1$$

However, $W^{-N/2} = -1$ and so

$$
\begin{aligned}
g(mT) &= f(mT) + f((m + N/2)T) \\
h(mT) &= W^m(f(mT) - f((m + N/2)T))
\end{aligned}
\qquad 0 \leqslant m \leqslant N/2 - 1
$$

It follows that

$$F_{2k} = F(2k\Omega) = \sum_{m=0}^{N/2-1} (f_m + f_{m+N/2})(W^2)^{mk}$$

$$F_{2k+1} = \sum_{m=0}^{N/2-1} ((f_m - f_{m+N/2})W^m)(W^2)^{mk}$$

We can draw a signal-flow graph of this algorithm for $N = 8$ as in Figure 3.3, and in fully reduced form in Figure 3.4.

3.5 Application to high-speed convolution

We have seen that the DFT of a circular convolution of sequences x, y is equal to the product of the DFTs of x and y. Computation time for the circular convolution is proportional to N^2, where the constant of proportionality k is the

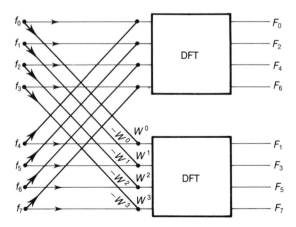

Figure 3.3   The FFT by decimation in frequency.

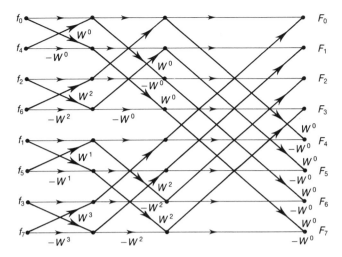

Figure 3.4 Fully reduced form of Figure 3.3.

time required to multiply two numbers and add the result to a partial sum. However, the FFT requires a computation time proportional to $N \log_2 N$ if N is a power of 2, as seen above. Hence, if we evaluate the circular convolution of two signals x, y of length N by determining the product of the FFTs of x and y and then the inverse FFT of this product, the time required is of the order of $3kN \log_2 N + \mu N$ where μ is the time required to calculate a product. For large N, the latter method is therefore faster than the direct computation of the convolution.

Of course, in most situations, we require the ordinary linear convolution of two signals rather than their circular convolution. However, if the two signals are zero outside some finite region, then their linear convolution is also zero outside some (larger) region (say for integers n such that $n \notin [0, N]$). Then by repeating the two signals periodically in the intervals $[iN, (i + 1)N]$, for all integers i, then it can be seen that the circular convolution of the periodic signals is the same as the linear convolution of the original signals in the interval $[0, N]$.

Bibliographical notes

The FFT was presented in Cooley and Tuckey (1966), although it was known much earlier (see the discussion in Brigham (1974)). The main types of algorithms are described in detail in Nussbaumer (1981). A recent technique for evaluating long period DFTs in terms of shorter ones is discussed in Kolba and Parks (1977) and Winograd (1978). Real W transformations are given in Wang (1984) together with a software implementation. A recursive cyclotomic factorization approach, suitable for microprogramming implementation, can be found in Martens (1984).

Exercises

1 Evaluate the DFT of the sequence 1, 1/2, 1/4, 1/8, 1/16, 1/32, 1/64, 1/128 by using the diagram in Figure 3.2.
2 Show in detail how Figure 3.4 is obtained from Figure 3.3.
3 Repeat exercise 1 using decimation in frequency (Figure 3.4).
4 Suppose that the discrete signals $x = \{x(nT)\}$, $y = \{y(nT)\}$ satisfy

$$x(nT) = 0 \qquad \text{if } n < 0 \text{ or } n > N$$

$$y(nT) = 0 \qquad \text{if } n < 0 \text{ or } n > M$$

Show that the linear convolution of x and y can be computed from the circular convolution of x and y extended periodically outside the range $[0, K]$ for some K. Find the minimum value of K.
5 Estimate the time required to evaluate the linear convolution by the method of exercise 4.

References

Brigham, E. Oran (1974), *The Fast Fourier Transform,* Englewood Cliffs, NJ: Prentice Hall.

Cooley, J. W. and J. W. Tuckey (1966), 'An algorithm for the machine calculation of complex Fourier series', *Math. Comput.,* **19**, 197–201.

Kolba, D. P. and T. W. Parks (1977), 'A prime factor FFT algorithm using high speed convolution', *IEEE Trans. Acoust., Speech, Signal Process.,* ASSP-**25**, 281–94.

Martens, J.-B. (1984), 'Recursive cyclotomic factorization – a new algorithm for calculating the discrete Fourier transform', *IEEE Trans. Acoust., Speech, Signal Process.,* ASSP-**32**, 750–61.

Nussbaumer, H. J. (1981), *Fast Fourier Transform and Convolution Algorithms,* Berlin: Springer-Verlag.

Wang, Z. (1984), 'Fast algorithms for the discrete W transform and for the discrete Fourier transform', *IEEE Trans. Acoust., Speech, Signal Process.,* ASSP-**32**, 803–16.

Winograd, S. (1978), 'On computing the DFT', *Math. Comput.,* **32**, 175–99.

4

Analog Filter Design

4.1 Introduction

The design of nonrecursive filters has been presented in Chapter 2, and it was seen that the parameters a_i in the filter are obtained directly by Fourier transforming the frequency response specified in each particular situation. Although recursive filters can also be designed directly by determining the coefficients a_i, b_i, using (for example) some optimization approach, such filters are usually obtained from known analog designs by using a transformation $s \rightarrow z$ from the s-plane to the z-plane. These transformations will be studied in the next chapter; in the present chapter we discuss four types of analog design, namely: Butterworth, Tchebychev, elliptic and Bessel filters.

4.2 Basic properties of analog filters

An analog filter is defined by a rational function of the form

$$G(s) = \frac{N(s)}{D(s)} = \frac{\Pi_{i=1}^{m}(s - z_i)}{\Pi_{i=1}^{n}(s - p_i)}$$

where the complex numbers z_i, p_i are respectively, the *zeros* and *poles* of G. We define the *loss function* (or *attenuation*) of G (in dB) by

$$A(\omega) = 20 \log_{10} \frac{1}{|G(j\omega)|}$$

Defining

$$L(\omega^2) = \frac{1}{G(j\omega)G(-j\omega)} = \frac{1}{|G(j\omega)|^2} \tag{4.2.1}$$

we have

$$A(\omega) = 10 \log_{10} L(\omega^2)$$

(It is easy to see that $L(\omega^2)$ is a function of ω^2 rather than ω.) It follows from (4.2.1) that

$$L(-s^2) = \frac{D(s) \cdot D(-s)}{N(s) \cdot N(-s)} \tag{4.2.2}$$

We can recover $G(s)$ from $L(-s^2)$ by selecting the left half-plane poles and zeros in the expression (4.2.2). This will guarantee realizability and the minimum phase property of the filter.

4.3 The Butterworth filter

The Butterworth lowpass filter of order n is obtained by imposing the condition that the polynomial

$$L(\omega^2) = B_0 + B_1\omega^2 + \ldots + B_n\omega^{2n}$$

is maximally flat at $\omega = 0$, i.e.

$$L(0) = 1$$

$$\frac{d^k L(\omega^2)}{d(\omega^2)^k}\bigg|_{\omega^2 = 0} = 0 \qquad 1 \leqslant k \leqslant n - 1$$

It follows that

$$L(\omega^2) = 1 + B_n\omega^{2n}$$

and if we normalize the cutoff point (or 3 dB point, where $A(\omega) \simeq 3$) at $\omega = 1$ rads/s, then $B_n = 1$ and so

$$L(\omega^2) = 1 + \omega^{2n} \tag{4.3.1}$$

The normalized transfer function is obtained from (4.2.2):

$$L(-s^2) = 1 + (-s^2)^n = 1 + (-1)^n s^{2n}$$

(putting $\omega = s/j$ in (4.3.1)), and so

$$L(-s^2) = \prod_{k=1}^{2n} (s - s_k)$$

where

$$s_k = \begin{cases} e^{j(2k-1)\pi/2n} & \text{if } n \text{ is even} \\ e^{j(k-1)\pi/n} & \text{if } n \text{ is odd} \end{cases}$$

If $p_1, \ldots, p_n$ are the left half-plane zeros of $L(-s^2)$, then we have

$$B_N(s) = \frac{1}{\prod_{i=1}^{n}(s - p_i)} \tag{4.3.2}$$

(The subscript 'N' means 'normalized'.) For example, if $n = 2$, we have

$$s_k = \cos \frac{(2k-1)\pi}{4} + j \sin \frac{(2k-1)\pi}{4} \qquad (1 \leqslant k \leqslant 4)$$

and so

$$p_1, p_2 = \frac{-1}{\sqrt{2}} \pm j \frac{1}{\sqrt{2}}$$

Thus,

$$B_N(s) = \frac{1}{s^2 + \sqrt{2}s + 1}$$

Similarly, if $n = 3$ we have

$$B_N(s) = \frac{1}{(s + 1)(s^2 + s + 1)}$$

The general pole locations of the nth order Butterworth filter are shown in Figure 4.1.
From (4.2.1) and (4.3.1), we have

$$|B_N(j\omega)|^2 = \frac{1}{1 + \omega^{2n}} \tag{4.3.3}$$

and so the amplitude response converges to the ideal lowpass response as $n \to \infty$ (see Figure 4.2).

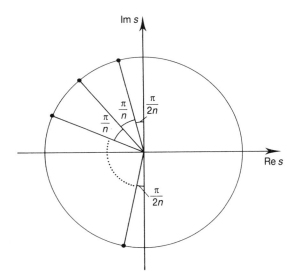

Figure 4.1   Poles of the Butterworth filter.

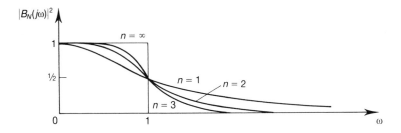

Figure 4.2   Amplitude response of the Butterworth filter.

4.4 The Tchebychev filter

In order to improve the passband characteristic of the Butterworth filter we generalize the amplitude response function (4.3.3) by replacing the polynomial ω^{2n} by a polynomial $F^2(\omega)$ so that we define

$$|T_N(j\omega)|^2 = \frac{1}{1 + F^2(\omega)} \tag{4.4.1}$$

and try to choose F so that the amplitude response is contained within some specified area in the passband, as shown in Figure 4.3(a). Therefore, it is clear that we require (as seen in Figure 4.3(b)) that

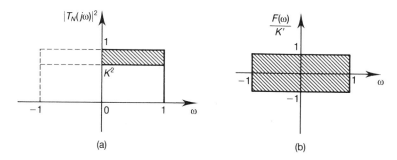

Figure 4.3 Tchebychev filter specifications: (a) ripple region; (b) transformal region.

$$|F(\omega)| \leq K' \triangleq (1/K^2 - 1)^{1/2} \quad \text{for } |\omega| \leq 1$$

(Note that no condition is placed on the amplitude response outside the cutoff region.) There is an infinite number of polynomials which satisfy this condition, and so we choose a particular set of polynomials which have extreme points with values ± 1. Such a set of functions is then given by the Tchebychev polynomials defined by

$$C_n(\omega) = \cos(n \cos^{-1}\omega) \qquad |\omega| \leq 1 \qquad (4.4.2)$$

The first six are shown in Figure 4.4.

It follows from (4.4.1) that if we choose the amplitude response

$$|T_N(j\omega)|^2 = \frac{1}{1 + \varepsilon^2 C_n^2(\omega)} \qquad (4.4.3)$$

then we can ensure that the response remains within the shaded area in Figure 4.3(a) by an appropriate choice of ε^2. The width of this area can be made arbitrarily small; however, to obtain the same rolloff outside the passband as a filter with a wider allowed ripple band, we must increase the order n of the filter.

For $\omega > 1$ we have, from (4.4.2),

$$\cos(n \cdot \cos^{-1}\omega) = \cos(jn \cdot \cosh^{-1}\omega) = \cosh(n \cdot \cosh^{-1}\omega) \qquad (4.4.4)$$

and so we can extend the definition of $C_n(\omega)$ outside the interval $[-1, 1]$ by (4.4.4). Normalized amplitude response characteristics for $n = 4$ and $n = 7$ are shown in Figure 4.5.

In order to obtain the normalized transfer funtion, note that

$$L(-s^2) = 1 + \varepsilon^2 \left[\cosh\left(n \cdot \cosh^{-1}\frac{s}{j}\right)\right]^2$$

and so if $s = \sigma + j\omega$ is a zero of $L(-s^2)$, then, if we write

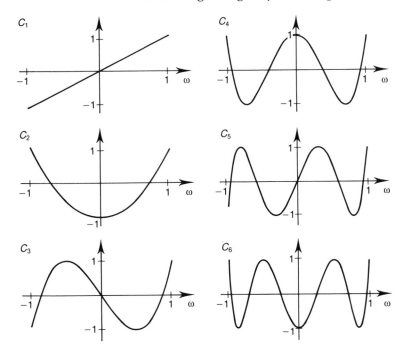

Figure 4.4   Tchebychev polynomials.

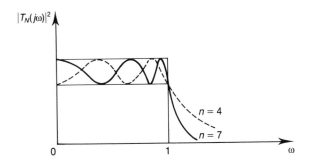

Figure 4.5   Tchebychev amplitude responses.

$$u + jv = \cosh^{-1}(-j\sigma + \omega) \qquad (4.4.5)$$

we have

$$\cosh[n(u + jv)] = \pm j/\varepsilon$$

Thus,

$$\cosh nu \cos nv = 0, \quad \sinh nu \sin nv = \pm 1/\varepsilon$$

These equations have the solutions

$$v = \frac{(2k - 1)\pi}{2n} \qquad k = 1, 2, \ldots$$

$$u = \pm \frac{1}{n} \sinh^{-1} \frac{1}{\varepsilon}$$

and so, from (4.4.4) we have

$$\left. \begin{aligned} \sigma_k &= \pm \sinh\left(\frac{1}{n} \sinh^{-1} \frac{1}{\varepsilon}\right) \sin \frac{(2k - 1)\pi}{2n} \\ &= \cosh\left(\frac{1}{n} \sinh^{-1} \frac{1}{\varepsilon}\right) \cos \frac{(2k - 1)\pi}{2n} \end{aligned} \right\} \quad k = 1, 2, \ldots, 2n$$

Moreover,

$$\frac{\sigma_k^2}{\sinh^2 u} + \frac{\omega_k^2}{\cosh^2 u} = 1$$

and so the zeros of $L(-s^2)$ are located on an ellipse (which depends on n and ε). The normalized Tchebychev filter can now be specified by choosing the left half-plane zeros of $L(-s^2)$, say $p_1, \ldots, p_n$. Thus

$$T_N(s) = \frac{T_0}{\Pi_{i=1}^n (s - p_i)}$$

To determine T_0, note that when n is odd, $C_n(0) = 0$, and when n is even $C_n(0) = 1$. Hence, by (4.4.3),

$$|T_N(0)|^2 = \begin{cases} \dfrac{1}{1 + \varepsilon^2} & \text{if } n \text{ is even} \\ 1 & \text{if } n \text{ is odd} \end{cases}$$

Hence we must choose

$$T_0 = \begin{cases} \dfrac{1}{\sqrt{(1 + \varepsilon^2)}} \Pi_{i=1}^n (-p_i) & \text{if } n \text{ is even} \\ \Pi_{i=1}^n (-p_i) & \text{if } n \text{ is odd} \end{cases}$$

4.5 The elliptic filter[1]

The main drawback with the previous filter is that we only consider the precise behaviour of the frequency response in the passband region. If we wish to

---

[1] The derivation in this section can be omitted if desired; the final expression for the filter is given by (4.5.23)–(4.5.27).

design a filter with equiripple properties in both the passband and the stopband we must allow $L(\omega^2)$ to be a rational function rather than just a polynomial. This method leads to the introduction of elliptic functions and so we first digress to present the elementary theory of such functions.

The *elliptic integral of the first kind* is defined as

$$u \equiv u(\phi, k) = \int_0^\phi \frac{d\theta}{(1 - k^2 \sin^2 \theta)} \tag{4.5.1}$$

for $0 \leqslant k < 1$. Here, ϕ is a complex variable. When ϕ is real the integral is real and satisfies the following properties:

$$u(n\pi + \phi, k) = 2nK + u(\phi, k), \; u\left(\frac{\pi}{2} + \phi, k\right) = 2K - u\left(\frac{\pi}{2} - \phi, k\right) \tag{4.5.2}$$

for $0 \leqslant \phi < \pi/2$, where K is the *complete elliptic integral of the first kind*:

$$K \overset{\triangle}{=} u\left(\frac{\pi}{2}, k\right) = \int_0^{\pi/2} \frac{d\theta}{(1 - k^2 \sin^2 \theta)} \tag{4.5.3}$$

The equations (4.5.2) follow from the periodicity (of 2π) of the integrand in (4.5.1) and the symmetry of the integrand about $\pi/2$.

Note that for a fixed k, $u(\phi, k)$ is an increasing function of ϕ (for real ϕ). Hence we may invert the function $u(., k)$, for each fixed k, and we define the inverse function of $u(., k)$ by

$$f(u(\phi, k), k) = \phi.$$

Then we define the *Jacobian elliptic functions* by

$$\left.\begin{array}{l} sn(u, k) = \sin \phi = \sin f(u, k) \\[2mm] cn(u, k) = \cos \phi \\[2mm] dn(u, k) = \sqrt{(1 - k^2 \sin^2 \phi)} \end{array}\right\} \tag{4.5.4}$$

From (4.5.2) it follows that

$$\left.\begin{array}{l} sn(u + 4mK, k) = sn(u, k) \\[2mm] cn(u + 4mK, k) = cn(u, k) \\[2mm] dn(u + 2mK, k) = dn(u, k) \end{array}\right\} \tag{4.5.5}$$

showing that sn, cn and dn are periodic with periods 4K, 4K and 2K, respectively.

Now let ϕ in (4.5.1) be a pure imaginary complex number and suppose that we perform the integral in (4.5.1) along the imaginary axis. Then if we put

$$\sin \theta = j \tan \theta', \; \sin \phi = j \tan \phi' \tag{4.5.6}$$

where θ' and ϕ' are real, we obtain

$$u \triangleq jv = \int_0^{\phi'} \frac{jd\theta'}{\sqrt{(1 - \sin^2 \theta' + k^2 \sin^2 \theta')}}$$

$$= \int_0^{\phi'} \frac{d\theta'}{\sqrt{(1 - k'^2 \sin^2 \theta')}}$$

where

$$k' = \sqrt{(1 - k^2)}$$

Thus,

$$sn(v, k') = \sin \phi'$$

$$cn(v, k') = \cos \phi'$$

$$dn(v, k') = \sqrt{(1 - k'^2 \sin^2 \phi')}$$

and so, by (4.5.6),

$$sn(jv, k) = j \tan \phi' = j \frac{\sin \phi'}{\cos \phi'} = j \frac{sn(v, k')}{cn(v, k')}$$

$$cn(jv, k) = \frac{1}{cn(v, k')} \qquad \qquad \qquad (4.5.7)$$

$$dn(jv, k) = \frac{dn(v, k')}{cn(v, k')}$$

As in the definition of K we put

$$K' = \int_0^{\pi/2} \frac{d\theta}{(1 - k'^2 \sin^2 \theta)}$$

and we then have the periodicity properties similar to (4.5.5):

$$sn(jv + j2nK', k) = sn(jv, k)$$

$$cn(jv + j4nK', k) = cn(jv, k) \qquad \qquad (4.5.8)$$

$$dn(jv + j4nK', k) = dn(jv, k)$$

The following summation formulae are the elliptic function analogs of the corresponding trigonometric formulae:

$$sn(z_1 + z_2, k) = \frac{sn(z_1, k)cn(z_2, k)dn(z_2, k) + cn(z_1, k)sn(z_2, k)dn(z_1, k)}{D}$$

$$cn(z_1 + z_2, k) = \frac{cn(z_1, k)cn(z_2, k) - sn(z_1, k)sn(z_2, k)dn(z_1, k)dn(z_2, k)}{D}$$

and

$$dn(z_1 + z_2, k) = \frac{dn(z_1, k)dn(z_2, k) - k^2 sn(z_1, k)sn(z_2, k)cn(z_1, k)cn(z_2, k)}{D}$$

$$(4.5.9)$$

where

$$D = 1 - k^2 sn^2(z_1, k)sn^2(z_2, k)$$

Using these formulae we can prove the complex periodicity properties:

$$\left. \begin{aligned} sn(z + 4mK + j2nK', k) &= sn(z, k) \\ cn(z + 4mK + j4nK', k) &= cn(z, k) \\ dn(z + 2mK + j4nK', k) &= dn(z, k) \end{aligned} \right\} \qquad (4.5.10)$$

Hence we need to specify sn, for example, only in the 'period parallelogram' $ABCDEF$ in Figure 4.6.

Using the addition formulae it can be shown that the transformation $f:z \rightarrow w$ from the z-plane to the w-plane defined by

$$w = \sqrt{k}\, sn(z, k)$$

maps the parallelogram onto the line $\text{Re}(w)$, as shown in Figure 4.7.

We have now outlined all the properties of the elliptic functions that we need to study the elliptic filters. A typical (odd order) attenuation characteristic

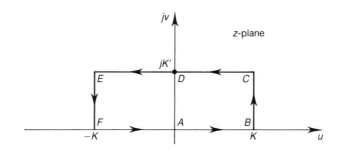

Figure 4.6   Period parallelogram.

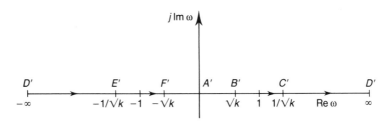

Figure 4.7   Frequency axis for elliptic functions.

is shown in Figure 4.8 (where the transition region is expanded in scale for clarity). Here, we require $\omega_a = 1/\omega_p$, $\omega_c = \sqrt{\omega_a \omega_p} = 1$ and we define the constants k, k_1 by

$$k = \omega_p^2$$

$$k_1 = \left(\frac{10^{0.1A_p} - 1}{10^{0.1A_a} - 1} \right)^{1/2} \tag{4.5.11}$$

Then we determine a rational function $F(\omega)$ such that

$$A(\omega) = 10 \log_{10} L(\omega^2)$$

where

$$L(\omega^2) = 1 + \varepsilon^2 F^2(\omega), \quad \varepsilon^2 = 10^{0.1A_p} - 1$$

From Figure 4.8 it is clear that F and L must have the properties

(i) $F(\omega) = 0$ when $\omega = 0, \pm\Omega_1, \ldots, \pm\Omega_r$

(ii) $F(\omega) = \infty$ when $\omega = \infty, \pm\Omega_{r+1}, \ldots, \pm\Omega_n$

(iii) $F^2(\omega) = 1$ when $\omega = \pm\hat{\Omega}_1, \ldots, \pm\hat{\Omega}_r, \pm\sqrt{k}$

(iv) $F^2(\omega) = \dfrac{1}{k_1^2}$ when $\omega = \pm\hat{\Omega}_{r+1}, \ldots, \pm\hat{\Omega}_n, \pm 1/\sqrt{k}$

(v) $\dfrac{\mathrm{d}L(\omega^2)}{\mathrm{d}\omega} = 0$ when $\omega = \pm\hat{\Omega}_1, \ldots, \pm\hat{\Omega}_n$

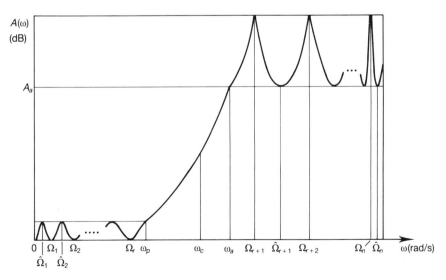

Figure 4.8 Elliptic filter characteristic with (odd) order $n + 1$, $r = n/2$.

In the following, C_1, C_2, ... will denote generic constants. From (i) and (ii) we have

$$F(\omega) = C_1 \frac{\omega(\omega^2 - \Omega_1^2) \dots (\omega^2 - \Omega_r^2)}{(\omega^2 - \Omega_{r+1}^2) \dots (\omega^2 - \Omega_n^2)} \tag{4.5.12}$$

and by (ii), (iii) and (v)

$$1 - F(\omega^2) = C_2 \frac{(\omega^2 - \hat{\Omega}_1^2)^2 \dots (\omega^2 - \hat{\Omega}_r^2)^2 (\omega^2 - k)}{(\omega^2 - \Omega_{r+1}^2)^2 \dots (\omega^2 - \Omega_n^2)^2} \tag{4.5.13}$$

Similarly by (ii), (iv) and (v)

$$1 - k_1^2 F^2(\omega) = C_3 \frac{(\omega^2 - \hat{\Omega}_{r+1}^2)^2 \dots (\omega^2 - \hat{\Omega}_n^2)^2 (\omega^2 - 1/k)}{(\omega^2 - \Omega_{r+1}^2)^2 \dots (\omega^2 - \Omega_n^2)^2} \tag{4.5.14}$$

By (v) we have

$$\frac{dF(\omega)}{d\omega} = C_4 \frac{(\omega^2 - \hat{\Omega}_1^2)^2 \dots (\omega^2 - \hat{\Omega}_n^2)^2}{(\omega^2 - \Omega_{r+1}^2)^2 \dots (\omega^2 - \Omega_n^2)^2} \tag{4.5.15}$$

From (4.5.13)–(4.5.15) we obtain

$$\left(\frac{dF(\omega)}{d\omega}\right)^2 = C_5 \frac{(1 - F^2(\omega))(1 - k_1^2 F^2(\omega))}{(1 - \omega^2/k)(1 - k\omega^2)}$$

Thus,

$$\int_0^F \frac{dx}{\sqrt{\{(1 - x^2)(1 - k_1^2 x^2)\}}} = \sqrt{C_5} \int_0^\omega \frac{dy}{\sqrt{\{(1 - y^2/k)(1 - ky^2)\}}} + C_6$$

and so

$$\int_0^F \frac{dx}{\sqrt{\{(1 - x^2)(1 - k_1^2 x^2)\}}} = C_7 \int_0^{\omega/\sqrt{k}} \frac{dy'}{\sqrt{\{(1 - y'^2)(1 - k^2 y'^2)\}}} + C_6$$

Making the transformations

$$x = \sin\theta_1, \quad F = \sin\phi_1, \quad y = \sin\theta, \quad \omega/\sqrt{k} = \sin\phi$$

we have

$$\int_0^{\phi_1} \frac{d\theta_1}{\sqrt{(1 - k_1^2 \sin^2\theta_1)}} = C_7 \int_0^\phi \frac{d\theta}{\sqrt{(1 - k^2 \sin^2\theta)}} + C_6$$

Hence,

$$\frac{\omega}{\sqrt{k}} = \sin\phi = sn(z, k) \tag{4.5.16}$$

$$F = \sin\phi_1 = sn(C_7 z + C_6, k_1) \tag{4.5.17}$$

where

$$z = \int_0^\phi \frac{d\theta}{\sqrt{(1 - k^2 \sin^2\theta)}}$$

If $z = u$ (real) for $0 \leqslant u \leqslant K$, then we have

$$\omega = \sqrt{k}\ sn(u, k)$$
$$F = sn(C_7 u + C_6, k_1)$$

As in Figures 4.7 and 4.8, ω maps the interval $[0, K]$ in the z-plane onto the interval $[0, \sqrt{k}]$ and so F must have $r + 1$ zeros in the latter interval (including $\omega = 0$) in order to satisfy (i) above. Since $F = sn(C_6, k_1)$ when $u = 0$ we have $C_6 = 0$, and since F is periodic in u with period $4K_1/C_7$ we must have

$$C_7 = (n + 1)K_1/K$$

since $n + 1$ quarter-periods of F must equal one quarter-period of ω. Thus,

$$F = sn\left(\frac{(n + 1)K_1 u}{K}, k_1\right)$$

Since F has z-plane zeros at

$$u = \frac{2Ki}{n + 1} \text{ for } i = 0, 1, \ldots, r$$

it follows that $F(\omega)$ has ω-plane zeros at

$$\Omega_i = \sqrt{k}\ sn\left(\frac{2}{n + 1}\ Ki, k\right) \qquad i = 0, 1, \ldots, r \qquad (4.5.18)$$

For $z = u + jK'$, $(0 \leqslant u \leqslant K)$, equations (4.5.16, 4.5.17) become

$$\omega = \frac{1}{\sqrt{k}\ sn(u, k)} \qquad (4.5.19)$$

$$F = sn\left(\frac{(n + 1)K_1(u + jK')}{K}, k_1\right) \qquad (4.5.20)$$

where (4.5.19) follows from the summation formula for sn. If $\omega = \infty$ then $u = 0$ and $F = \infty$ (by (ii)); hence

$$F = sn\left(\frac{j(n + 1)K_1 K'}{K}, k_1\right) = \infty$$

and so, from (4.5.7),

$$\frac{j\ sn((n + 1)K_1 K'/K, k_1')}{cn((n + 1)K_1 K'/K, k_1')} = \infty \qquad (k_1' = \sqrt{1 - k_1^2})$$

Hence

$$cn\left(\frac{(n + 1)K_1 K'}{K}, k_1'\right) = 0$$

and so

$$\frac{(n + 1)K'}{K} = \frac{K_1'}{K_1} \qquad (4.5.21)$$

which gives a constraint on A_p and A_a. Thus, (4.5.20) becomes

$$F = sn\left(\frac{(n+1)K_1 u}{K} + jK_1', k_1\right)$$

$$= \frac{1}{k_1 sn(5K_1 u/K, k_1)}$$

so that $F = \infty$ when

$$u = \frac{2K_i}{n+1} \qquad i = 0, 1, \ldots, r$$

and so $F(\omega)$ has poles at

$$\Omega_{n+1-i} = \frac{1}{\sqrt{k}\, sn(2Ki/(n+1), k)} \qquad i = 1, \ldots, r \qquad (4.5.22)$$

by (4.5.19). Note that, from (4.5.18) and (4.5.22), the poles of $F(\omega)$ are the reciprocals of the zeros, i.e.

$$\Omega_{n+1-i} = 1/\Omega_i \qquad i = 1, \ldots, r$$

From (4.5.12) we therefore obtain

$$F(\omega) = C_1' \frac{\omega(\omega^2 - \Omega_1^2) \ldots (\omega^2 - \Omega_r^2)}{(1 - \omega^2\Omega_1^2) \ldots (1 - \omega^2\Omega_r^2)}$$

To determine C_1' note that when $\omega = 1$ we have $z = K + jK'/2$ (from Figure 4.6) and $F(1) = C_1'$ and so putting $z = K + jv$ $(0 \leq v \leq k')$ in (4.5.16 and 4.5.17) we have

$$\omega = \frac{\sqrt{k}}{dn(v, k')}, \qquad F = sn\left[\frac{(n+1)K_1(K + jv)}{K}, k_1\right], \qquad \text{with } v = K'/2$$

Hence,

$$C_1' = sn\left(K_1 + \frac{jK_1'}{2}, k_1\right)$$

by (4.5.21). Thus,

$$C_1' = \frac{1}{dn(K_1'/2, k_1')} = \frac{1}{\sqrt{k_1}}$$

We now have the complete expression for $F(\omega)$:

$$F(\omega) = \frac{(-1)^r \omega}{\sqrt{k_1}} \prod_{i=1}^{r} \left(\frac{\omega^2 - \Omega_i^2}{1 - \omega^2\Omega_i^2}\right) \qquad (r = (n-1)/2)$$

and

$$\Omega_i = \sqrt{k}\, sn\left(\frac{2Ki}{n}, k\right) \qquad 1 \leq i \leq r$$

To find the poles and zeros of $L(-s^2)$ note that

$$L(z) = 1 + \varepsilon^2 sn^2\left(\frac{(n + 1)K_1 z}{K}, k_1\right)$$

where the relation

$$\frac{(n + 1)K'}{K} = \frac{K_1'}{K_1}$$

must hold.

Thus,

$$L(z) = \left[1 + j\varepsilon sn\left(\frac{(n + 1)K_1 z}{K}, k_1\right)\right]\left[1 - j\varepsilon sn\left(\frac{(n + 1)K_1 z}{K}, k_1\right)\right]$$

Since sn is an odd function of z, if z_1 is a root of the left-hand factor, then $-z_1$ is a root of the right-hand factor, and so the zeros of $L(z)$ are given by solving the equation

$$sn\left(\frac{(n + 1)K_1 z}{K}, k_1\right) = j/\varepsilon$$

We can obtain approximate solutions to this equation since k_1 is usually very small. Thus, if $k_1 \cong 0$, we have

$$sn\left(\frac{(n + 1)K_1 z}{K}, 0\right) = \sin \frac{(n + 1)K_1 z}{K} = j/\varepsilon$$

where $K_1 = \pi/2$ and so

$$\frac{-j(n + 1)\pi z}{2K} = \sinh^{-1}(1/\varepsilon) = \ln\left(\frac{1}{\varepsilon} + \sqrt{\frac{1}{\varepsilon^2} + 1}\right)$$

and so we obtain one zero of $L(z)$ at $z_0 = jv_0$ where

$$v_0 = \frac{K}{(n + 1)\pi} \ln\left(\frac{10^{0.05A_p} + 1}{10^{0.05A_p} - 1}\right)$$

from the definition of ε.

Since $sn((n + 1)K_1 z/K, k_1)$ has real period $4K/(n + 1)$, the points

$$z_i = z_0 + \frac{4K_i}{n + 1} \qquad i = 0, 1, 2, \ldots$$

are also zeros of $L(z)$. From (4.5.16) we have

$$\frac{\omega}{\sqrt{k}} = sn(z, k)$$

and so $L(\omega^2)$ has a zero at $\sqrt{k}\, sn(jv_0, k)$ whence $L(-s^2)$ has a zero at $s = \sigma_0 = j\sqrt{k}\, sn(jv_0, k)$. Similarly, $L(-s^2)$ has n distinct complex zeros at

$$j\sqrt{k}\, sn\left(jv_0 + \frac{4K_i}{n + 1}, k\right) \qquad 1 \leqslant i \leqslant n$$

i.e. at the points

$$\sigma_i \pm j\omega_i = j\sqrt{k}\,(-1)^i sn\!\left(jv_0 \pm \frac{2K_i}{n+1},\, k\right) \qquad 1 \le i \le r = n/2$$

Using the addition formula it follows that

$$\sigma_i \pm j\omega_i = \frac{(-1)^i\sigma_0 V_i \pm j\Omega_i W}{1 + \sigma_0^2 \Omega_i^2} \qquad 1 \le i \le r$$

where

$$W = \sqrt{(1 + k\sigma_0^2)\!\left(1 + \frac{\sigma_0^2}{k}\right)}$$

$$V_i = \sqrt{(1 - k\Omega_i^2)\!\left(1 - \frac{\Omega_i^2}{k}\right)}$$

$$\Omega_i = \sqrt{k}\, sn\!\left(\frac{2K_i}{n+1},\, k\right)$$

Since the poles of $L(-s^2)$ occur at the points $s = \pm j/\Omega_i$ we have a complete description of the filter.

In the case of an even-order filter with order n, similar reasoning shows that

$$F = sn\!\left(\frac{nK_1 z}{K} + K_1,\, k_1\right)$$

where

$$\frac{nK'}{K} = \frac{K_1'}{K_1}$$

Then

$$F(\omega) = \frac{(-1)^r}{k_1} \prod_{i=1}^{r} \frac{\omega^2 - \Omega_i^2}{1 - \omega^2 \Omega_i^2}$$

where $r = n/2$, and

$$\Omega_i = \sqrt{k}\, sn\!\left(\frac{(2i-1)K}{n},\, k\right) \qquad 1 \le i \le r$$

The zeros of $L(-s^2)$ are at

$$s_i = \sigma_i + j\omega_i = \frac{\sigma_0 V_i \pm j(-1)^i \Omega_i W}{1 + \sigma_0^2 \Omega_i^2}$$

We can now write the normalized transfer function in the form

$$E_N(s) = \frac{E_0}{D_0(s)} \prod_{i=1}^{r} \frac{s^2 + A_i}{s^2 + B_i s + C_i} \tag{4.5.23}$$

where

$$r = \begin{cases} (\text{order}-1)/2 & \text{if order is odd} \\ \text{order}/2 & \text{if order is even} \end{cases}$$

and

$$D_0(s) = \begin{cases} s + \sigma_0 & \text{if order is odd} \\ 1 & \text{if order is even} \end{cases}$$

The coefficients A_i, B_i, C_i are given by

$$A_i = 1/\Omega_i^2 \tag{4.5.24}$$

$$B_i = \frac{2\sigma_0 V_i}{1 + \sigma_0^2 \Omega_i^2} \tag{4.5.25}$$

$$C_i = \frac{(\sigma_0 V_i)^2 + (\Omega_i W)^2}{(1 + \sigma_0^2 \Omega_i^2)^2} \tag{4.5.26}$$

and the scaling constant E_0 is defined as

$$E_0 = \begin{cases} \sigma_0 \prod_{i=1}^{r} \dfrac{C_i}{A_i} & \text{for odd order} \\[3ex] 10^{-0.05 A_p} \prod_{i=1}^{r} \dfrac{C_i}{A_i} & \text{for even order} \end{cases} \tag{4.5.27}$$

Let us finally examine the constraint (4.5.20) in more detail. If k, A_p and A_a are specified, then the order of the filter must satisfy

$$n \geqslant \frac{K K_1'}{K' K_1}$$

where

$$K = \int_0^{\pi/2} \frac{\mathrm{d}\theta}{\sqrt{(n - \omega_p^4 \sin \theta)}}, \quad K' = \int_0^{\pi/2} \frac{\mathrm{d}\theta}{\sqrt{(1 - (1 - \omega_p^4) \sin \theta)}}$$

$$K_1 = \int_0^{\pi/2} \frac{\mathrm{d}\theta}{\sqrt{(1 - ((10^{0.1 A_p} - 1)/(10^{0.1 A_a} - 1)) \sin \theta)}}$$

$$K_1' = \int_0^{\pi/2} \frac{\mathrm{d}\theta}{\sqrt{(1 - (1 - (10^{0.1 A_p} - 1)/(10^{0.1 A_a} - 1)) \sin \theta)}}$$

4.6 The Bessel filter

The preceding filters have been designed entirely to approximate a desired amplitude response characteristic. Nothing has been said about the phase response, which should ideally be linear. The elliptic filter, in particular, has a delay characteristic which varies with frequency. To overcome this difficulty we consider the transfer function

$$H(s) = \frac{B_0}{\sum_{i=0}^{n} B_i s^i} = \frac{B_0}{s^n B(1/s)} \tag{4.6.1}$$

where

$$B_i = \frac{(2n - i)!}{2^{n-i} i!(n - i)!}$$

$B(s)$ is called the *Bessel polynomial* and it can be shown that $S^n B(1/s)$ has only left half-plane zeros. It can also be seen that

$$B\left(\frac{1}{j\omega}\right) = \frac{1}{j^n} \sqrt{\frac{\pi\omega}{2}} \, [(-1)^n J_{-\gamma}(\omega) - jJ_\gamma(\omega)]e^{j\omega} \tag{4.6.2}$$

where $\gamma = n + \frac{1}{2}$ and

$$J_\gamma(\omega) = \omega^\gamma \sum_{i=1}^{\infty} \frac{(-1)^i \omega^{2i}}{2^{2i+\gamma} i! \Gamma(\gamma + i + 1)} \tag{4.6.3}$$

From (4.6.1) and (4.6.2) we have

$$|H(j\omega)|^2 = \frac{2B_0^2}{\pi\omega^{2n+1}[J_{-\gamma}^2(\omega) + J_\gamma^2(\omega)]} \tag{4.6.4}$$

and

$$\theta(\omega) = -\omega + \tan^{-1} \frac{(-1)^n J_\gamma(\omega)}{J_{-\gamma}(\omega)}$$

Hence the group delay is given by

$$\tau = \frac{-d\theta}{d\omega} = 1 - (-1)^n \frac{(J_{-\gamma} J_\gamma' - J_\gamma J_{-\gamma}')}{J_{-\gamma}^2(\omega) + J_\gamma^2(\omega)} \tag{4.6.5}$$

From (4.6.3) and (4.6.4) we have

$$|H(j\omega)|^2 = 1 - \frac{\omega^2}{2n - 1} + \frac{2(n - 1)\omega^4}{(2n - 1)^2(2n - 3)} + \cdots$$

and from (4.6.3) and (4.6.5),

$$\tau = 1 - \frac{\omega^{2n}}{B_0^2} \, |H(j\omega)|^2$$

Thus, $|H(j\omega)| \to 1$ as $\omega \to 0$, $|H(j\omega)| \to 0$ as $\omega \to \infty$, and so (4.6.1) represents a lowpass filter. Also,

$$\tau \to 1 \text{ as } \omega \to 0 \text{ and } \frac{d^i \tau}{d\omega^i} (0) = 0 \quad 1 \leq i \leq n - 1$$

Hence the group delay is maximally flat to order $n - 1$ at $\omega = 0$ and so we can achieve a reasonably constant delay over the bandwidth. It should be realized, however, that the amplitude characteristics of the Bessel filter are very poor compared with, for example, the elliptic filter, and so the appropriate choice of filter depends very much on the application. (Note that by replacing s by Δs in (4.6.1) we can change the delay from 1 to Δ.)

4.7 Transformations

Up to now we have considered only normalized lowpass filters. In fact, other filter types can be generated by making the transformations illustrated in Table 4.1 in the filters developed above. In the case of the lowpass to lowpass transformation we have

$$j\bar{\omega} = j\omega/\lambda$$

and so the cutoff frequency is multiplied by $1/\lambda$. Similarly, for the lowpass to bandpass transformation, if ω_p and ω_a are the passband and stopband edges, then

$$j\omega = \frac{j}{b}\left(\bar{\omega} - \frac{\omega_0^2}{\bar{\omega}}\right)$$

so that

$$j\bar{\omega} = j\left\{\frac{\omega B}{2} \pm \sqrt{\omega_0^2 + \left(\frac{\omega B}{2}\right)^2}\right\}$$

Hence,

$$\bar{\omega} = \begin{cases} \omega_0 & \text{if } \omega = 0 \\ \pm\bar{\omega}_{p1}, \pm\bar{\omega}_{p2} & \text{if } \omega = \pm\omega_p \\ \pm\bar{\omega}_{a1}, \pm\bar{\omega}_{a2} & \text{if } \omega = \pm\omega_a \end{cases}$$

Table 4.1 Filter transformations

Type	Transformation (λ, ω_0, B constants)
Lowpass to lowpass	$\bar{s} = s/\lambda$
Lowpass to highpass	$\bar{s} = \lambda/s$
Lowpass to bandpass	$\dfrac{1}{B}\left(\bar{s} + \dfrac{\omega_0^2}{\bar{s}}\right) = s$
Lowpass to bandstop	$\dfrac{B\bar{s}}{\bar{s}^2 + \omega_0^2} = s$

where

$$\bar{\omega}_{x1}, \bar{\omega}_{x2} = \frac{\pm \omega_x B}{2} + \sqrt{\omega_0^2 + \left(\frac{\omega_x B}{2}\right)^2} \qquad x = p \text{ or } a$$

Bibliographical notes

The design of analog filters is now classical and more extensive treatments can be found in Grossman (1957) and Guillemin (1957). Elliptic functions and their relationships are discussed in detail in Whittaker and Watson (1965). In addition to the techniques described in this chapter – essentially consisting of the spectral factorization of a frequency domain rational function, optimization methods have also been developed. For example, in Durrani and Chapman (1980, 1984) all-pole filters are derived by using prolate spheroidal sequences. One can, of course, select the parameters in a rational function of frequency by minimizing some measure of the error between such a function and the ideal, as in FIR design.

Exercises

1 Show that $L(\omega^2) = 1/|G(j\omega)|^2$, *is a function of* ω^2.

2 Prove that we may write the nth order Butterworth filter in the form

$$B_N(s) = \frac{s_1 s_2 \ldots s_n}{\Pi_{i=1}^n (s + s_i)}$$

where $-s_i = p_i$ is the ith pole.

3 Draw a sketch of the positions of the poles of a Tchebychev filter on an ellipse.

4 Prove the equations in (4.5.2).

5 Prove the addition formula for sn (given in (4.5.9)) by following the steps below:

(a) Prove that $(d/du)sn\,u = cn\,u \cdot dn\,u$.

(b) Let $s_1 = sn\,u$, $s_2 = sn\,v$ and suppose for the moment that $v = \alpha - u$ where α is a constant. Show that

$$\left(\frac{ds_1}{du}\right)^2 = (1 - s_1^2)(1 - k^2 s^s)$$

$$\left(\frac{ds_2}{du}\right)^2 = (1 - s_2^2)(1 - k^2 s_2^2)$$

(use the fact that $(dv/du)^2 = 1$).

(c) If u is such that $cn\,u \cdot dn\,u$ and $cn\,v \cdot dn\,v$ do not vanish, show that

$$\frac{d^2 s_1}{du^2} = -(1 + k^2)s_1 + 2k^2 s_1^3, \quad \frac{d^2 s_2}{du^2} = -(1 + k^2)s_2 + 2k^2 s_2^3$$

(d) Hence show that

$$\frac{(d^2 s_1/du^2)s_2 - (d^2 s_2/du^2)s_1}{(ds_1/du)^2 s_2 - (ds_2/du)^2 s_1^2} = \frac{2k^2 s_1 s_2(s_1^2 - s_2^2)}{(s_2^2 - s_1^2)(1 - k^2 s_1^2 s_2^2)}$$

and so

$$\left(\frac{ds_1}{du}s_2 - \frac{ds_2}{du}s_1\right)^{-1}\frac{d}{du}\left(\frac{ds_1}{du}s_2 - \frac{ds_2}{du}s_1\right) = (1 - k^2 s_1^2 s_2^2)^{-1}\frac{d}{du}(1 - k^2 s_1^2 s_2^2)$$

(e) Integrate the last equation to give

$$\frac{(ds_1/du)s_2 - (ds_2/du)s_1}{1 - k^2 s_1^2 s_2^2} = \text{const}$$

(This is an integral of the equation $du + dv = 0$, as is $u + v = \alpha$.)

(f) Show that the first integral of $du + dv = 0$ in (e) is a function of $u + v$, say $f(u + v)$.

(g) Set $v = 0$ to show that $f = sn$.

6 Prove (4.6.2).

7 Design a lowpass Butterworth filter of order 2 with a cutoff frequency 200 rad/s.

8 Using the filter of exercise 7, design a bandstop Butterworth filter of order 4 with passband and stopband edges given, respectively, by

$$\omega_p = 10 \text{ rad/s}, \quad \omega_a = 400 \text{ rad/s}$$

References

Durrani, T. S. and R. Chapman (1980), 'IIR digital filter design using constrained optimization techniques', *IEE Electron. Lett.*, **16**, 843–5.

Durrani, T. S. and R. Chapman (1984), 'Optimal all-pole filter design based on discrete prolate spheroidal sequences', *IEEE Trans. Acoust., Speech, Signal Process.*, ASSP-**32**, 716–21.

Grossman, A. J. (1957), 'Synthesis of Tchebycheff parameter symmetrical filters', *Proc. IRE*, **45**, 454–73.

Guillemin, E. A. (1957), *Synthesis of Passive Networks*, NY: Wiley.

Whittaker, E. T. and G. N. Watson (1965), *A Course of Modern Analysis*, Cambridge: CUP.

5

Design of Recursive Filters

5.1 Introduction

In Chapter 2 we described various methods for the design of nonrecursive digital filters. All the methods evaluate directly the coefficients of the filter from a frequency domain specification. Analog filter designs have been in existence for many years now and a variety of these have been presented in Chapter 4. It seems reasonable, therefore, to use these analog designs in order to develop discrete filters. The technique consists of finding an appropriate transformation from the s- to the z-plane and substituting for s in the analog transfer function. One major drawback with this method, compared with nonrecursive design, is that we cannot obtain a linear phase characteristic, so that there is bound to be some distortion of the input signal.

5.2 The impulse-invariant method

In the impulse-invariant method we choose an analog filter and determine the corresponding digital filter which has impulse response coefficients equal to the values of the impulse response of the analog filter at the sampling times. This introduces aliasing into the filter and so it is usually applied only to all-pole filters (i.e. Butterworth, Bessel or Tchebychev types) which are lowpass or bandpass. For any such filter we may write its transfer function in the form (assuming simple poles)

$$G_A(s) = \sum_{i=1}^{n} \frac{A_i}{s - p_i} \tag{5.2.1}$$

Hence,

$$g_A(t) \triangleq \mathcal{L}^{-1} G_A(s) = \sum_{i=1}^{n} A_i e^{p_i t}$$

Sampling g_A, we have

$$g_A(kT) = \sum_{i=1}^{n} A_i e^{p_i kT}$$

and so the corresponding digital filter $H_D(z)$ is given by

$$H_D(z) = Z\{g_A(kT)\} = \sum_{i=1}^{n} \frac{A_i z}{z - e^{Tp_i}} \tag{5.2.2}$$

Note that a pole p_i of the analog filter gives rise to a pole e^{Tp_i} of the digital filter and so a realizable analog filter leads to a realizable digital filter. Since G_A is bandlimited (to a reasonable approximation) then $H_D(e^{j\omega t})$ approximates $G_A(j\omega)$ in the interval $[-\pi/T, \pi/T]$ and so the amplitude and phase responses of the analog filter are preserved under this transformation.

5.3 Modified impulse-invariant method

Suppose now that an analogue filter is given in the form

$$G_A(s) = \frac{KN(s)}{D(s)} = K \frac{\Pi_{i=1}^{m}(s - z_i)}{\Pi_{j=1}^{n}(s - p_j)} \tag{5.3.1}$$

where we have $m = n$. Then we cannot generally write this in the form (5.2.1) and so we proceed as follows. First write

$$G_A(s) = K G_{A1}(s)/G_{A2}(s)$$

where

$$G_{A1}(s) = 1/D(s), \ G_{A2}(s) = 1/N(s)$$

Then G_{A1} and G_{A2} can be written in the form (5.2.1) and we have

$$G_{A1}(s) = \sum_{j=1}^{n} \frac{A_j}{s - p_j}, \ G_{A2}(s) = \sum_{i=1}^{m} \frac{B_i}{s - z_i}$$

Applying the transformation in (5.2.2) we have

$$H_{D1}(z) \overset{\triangle}{=} \sum_{j=1}^{n} \frac{A_j z}{z - e^{Tp_j}}, \ H_{D2}(z) \overset{\triangle}{=} \sum_{i=1}^{m} \frac{B_i z}{z - e^{Tz_i}} \qquad (5.3.2)$$

The overall transfer function of the approximating digital filter is then

$$H_D(z) = H_{D1}(z)/H_{D2}(z) \qquad (5.3.3)$$

A problem remains, however; some of the poles of (5.3.3) may be unstable, because of the zeros of H_{D2}. This can be remedied easily, since, if p_i is a real pole, then

$$|e^{j\omega T} - p_i| = |p_i|\left|e^{-j\omega T} - \frac{1}{p_i}\right| = |p_i|\left|\left(e^{j\omega T} - \frac{1}{p_i}\right)^*\right|$$

$$= |p_i|\left|e^{j\omega T} - \frac{1}{p_i}\right|$$

and if (p_i, p_i^*) is a pair of conjugate poles, then

$$|(e^{j\omega T} - p_i)(e^{j\omega T} - p_i^*)| = |p_i|^2\left|\left(e^{j\omega T} - \frac{1}{p_i}\right)\left(e^{j\omega T} - \frac{1}{p_i^*}\right)\right|$$

Thus, an unstable pole can be replaced by its reciprocal with respect to the unit circle, without changing the loss characteristic. (Any poles on the unit circle should be decreased, slightly, in magnitude.) This method gives reasonable results for lowpass and bandpass elliptic filters. Phase response is not controlled by this method and if a good phase response is required a careful choice of analog filter must be made.

5.4 Matched Z-transformation technique

If $G_A(s)$ is an analog filter given by (5.3.1), then as an alternative to the definition (5.3.3) of the digital approximation, we can write

$$H_D(z) = (z + 1)^I K \frac{\prod_{i=1}^{m}(z - e^{z_i T})}{\prod_{j=1}^{n}(z - e^{p_i T})}$$

where I is the order of the zero of $G_A(s)$ at $s = \infty$. This method works well for highpass and bandstop filters; however, the passband ripple in Tchebychev and elliptic filters may be distorted.

5.5 *The bilinear transformation*

The main drawback with the design methods described above is that, because we are sampling the impulse response of the analog filter, aliasing is bound to occur. This can be seen more clearly by noting that the zeros and poles map according to the transformation

$$s \rightarrow z = e^{sT} \qquad (5.5.1)$$

This is a conformal transformation between the s- and the z-planes. However, it is not one-to-one since, for example, if $s = j\omega$ is imaginary, then

$$z = e^{j\omega T}$$

which is periodic in ω with period $2\pi/T$. Hence the points $s = j\omega + jn2\pi/T$ all map to the point $e^{j\omega T}$. In fact, it is easy to see that the transformation (5.5.1) maps each of the strips

$$s = \zeta + j\omega, \qquad \zeta \leqslant 0, \qquad (2n - 1)\pi/T < \omega \leqslant (2n + 1)\pi/T, \, n \in \mathbb{Z}$$

in a one-to-one way onto the closed unit disk $|z| \leqslant 1$ in the z-plane (Figure 5.1). (The corresponding strip with $\zeta > 0$ is mapped in a one-to-one way onto the exterior of the unit disk.) It can be seen that the imaginary axis in the s-plane 'wraps' around $|z| = 1$ an infinite number of times under the transformation (5.5.1). It is this repeated covering of the unit circle in the z-plane by the $j\omega$-axis of the s-plane which accounts for the aliasing in the discrete approximation to a given analog filter.

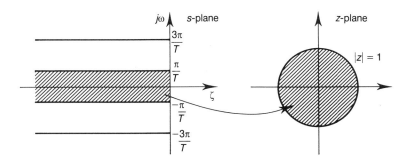

Figure 5.1 The transformation $z = e^{sT}$.

We therefore conclude that the aliasing effects in the previous design methods are due to the many-to-one nature of the transformation (5.5.1). It would seem reasonable, therefore, to find a transformation which is one-to-one and maps the $j\omega$-axis (in the s-plane) to the unit circle $|z| = 1$ in the z-plane. Such a transformation is given by

$$s = \frac{2}{T} \frac{1 - z^{-1}}{1 + z^{-1}} \qquad (5.5.2)$$

This is called the *bilinear transformation*; the factor $2/T$ is merely for convenience. It is clearly one-to-one and onto since the inverse transformation is given by

$$z = \frac{2/T + s}{2/T - s} \qquad (5.5.3)$$

If $s = j\omega$ then

$$|z| = |2/T + j\omega|/|2/T - j\omega| = 1 \qquad \text{for all } \omega$$

Hence the imaginary axis $s = j\omega$ maps to the unit circle in the z-plane. Moreover, by (5.5.2), when $z = 0$, we have $s = -2/T$ and so the left-half of the s-plane is mapped into the unit disk in the z-plane. The bilinear transformation can therefore be used to remove aliasing; note, however, that this transformation introduces a nonlinear warping of the frequency axis. This can be seen from (5.5.2) by replacing s by $j\omega$ and z by $e^{j\Omega T}$. Then we have

$$\omega = \frac{2}{T} \tan \frac{\Omega T}{2} \qquad (5.5.4)$$

Hence, if we require a digital filter which has characteristic frequencies $\Omega_1, \ldots, \Omega_k$ (i.e. passband edge, stopband edge, etc.), then we must use an analog filter with corresponding frequencies

$$\omega_i = \frac{2}{T} \tan \frac{\Omega_i T}{2} \qquad 1 \leq i \leq k \qquad (5.5.5)$$

This is known as *prewarping* the analog filter. The bilinear transform method therefore consists of the following procedure:

1. Define characteristic digital frequencies $\Omega_1, \ldots, \Omega_k$.
2. Prewarp these according to (5.5.5) to obtain analog frequencies $\omega_1, \ldots, \omega_k$.
3. Select a suitable analog filter with the frequencies $\omega_1, \ldots, \omega_k$.
4. Replace s in the analog filter by $s = (2/T)(1 - z^{-1})/(1 + z^{-1})$.

As an example, consider the following design problem:

Design a digital lowpass filter with sampling rate of 10 kHz, flat to 3 dB in the passband of 0 to 1 kHz and at least 10 dB down for frequencies above 2 kHz.

Solution We must first prewarp the frequencies 1 kHz, 2 kHz by using (5.5.5). Thus,

$$\omega_i = \frac{2}{T} \tan \left(\frac{\Omega_i T}{2} \right) \qquad i = 1, 2$$

where $\Omega_i = i \cdot 2\pi \cdot 10^3$ rad/s. Thus,

$$\omega_1 = \frac{2}{T} \times 0.325, \; \omega_2 = \frac{2}{T} \times 0.726 \qquad (5.5.6)$$

($T = 10^{-4}$, but we have left the factor $2/T$ in these expressions since it will cancel later.)

A Butterworth filter is flat to 3 dB in the passband, so we can choose the analog frequency response to be

$$|G(j\omega)|^2 = \frac{1}{1 + (\omega/\omega_c)^{2n}}$$

Note that $\omega_c = 3$ dB cutoff point $= \omega_1 = 2/T \times 0.325$. The sharpness of the cutoff specified by ω_2 will determine the order n of the filter. Thus, for $20 \log_{10} |G|$ to be ≤ 10 dB at 2 kHz we must have

$$20 \log_{10} (G(j\omega_2)) = -10 \log_{10} (1 + (\omega_2/\omega_1)^{2n})$$
$$= -10$$

and so

$$1 + (\omega_2/\omega_1)^{2n} = 10$$

Substituting the values for ω_1, ω_2 from (5.5.6) we have

$$n \cong 1.367$$

Since the order must be an integer we must choose $n = 2$ (at least). The second-order Butterworth filter is given by

$$G(s) = \frac{s_1 \cdot s_2}{(s - s_1)(s - s_2)}$$

where

$$s_1(s_2) = \omega_c(-0.707 + (-)j0.707)$$

Hence

$$G(s) = \frac{0.1056(2/T)^2}{s^2 + 0.46(2/T)s + 0.1056(2/T)^2}$$

All that remains is to replace s by $(2/T)(1 - z^{-1})/(1 + z^{-1})$. Thus, the required digital filter is

$$H = \frac{0.1056}{((1 - z^{-1})/(1 + z^{-1}))^2 + 0.46((1 - z^{-1})/(1 + z^{-1})) + 0.1056}$$

5.6 Digital filter transformations

Just as one can specify transformations between different types of analog filters (as in Section 4.7), it is possible to transform recursive digital filters from one type to another. This involves defining a map between two z-domains, say z and z' which maps the unit circle onto the unit circle (not necessarily in a one-to-one way). Such a transformation is given, as we have seen, by the bilinear transformation. A generalization of this is given by

$$z = f(z') = e^{j\zeta\pi} \prod_{i=1}^{m} \frac{z' - \bar{a}_i}{1 - a_i z'}$$

where ζ and m are integers and a_i are complex numbers. Consider first a lowpass to lowpass transformation. In this case we require only to stretch or compress the frequency axis and so a bilinear transformation of the form

$$z = e^{j\zeta\pi} \frac{z' - \bar{a}}{1 - az'}$$

should be adequate. The relevant frequencies are shown in Figure 5.2. Since $z = \pm 1$ and $z' = \pm 1$ we have

$$1 = e^{j\zeta\pi}\left(\frac{1 - \bar{a}}{1 - a}\right), \; 1 = e^{j\zeta\pi}\left(\frac{1 + \bar{a}}{1 + a}\right)$$

and so a is real and $\zeta = 0$. Thus,

$$z = \frac{z' - a}{1 - az'} \qquad (a \text{ real})$$

and since $z = e^{j\Omega_p T}$ when $z' = e^{j\omega_p T}$, we have

$$e^{j\Omega_p T} = \frac{e^{j\omega_p T} - a}{1 - ae^{j\omega_p T}}$$

which gives

$$a = \frac{\sin\left[(\Omega_p - \omega_p)T/2\right]}{\sin\left[(\Omega_p - \omega_p)T/2\right]}$$

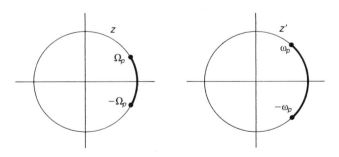

Figure 5.2 Lowpass–lowpass transformation frequencies.

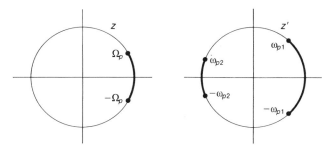

Figure 5.3 Lowpass–bandstop transformation frequencies.

Next consider a lowpass to bandstop transformation. The appropriate mapping of the z-plane and z'-plane unit circles is shown in Figure 5.3.

Since we must map the region between $-\Omega_p$ and Ω_p on the unit z-plane circle onto two regions between $-\omega_{p1}$, ω_{p1} and $-\omega_{p2}$, ω_{p2} on the z'-plane circle we require a biquadratic transformation given by

$$z = e^{j\zeta\pi} \frac{z'^2 + \alpha z' + \beta}{1 + \alpha z' + \beta z'^2}$$

It is easy to see that $e^{j\zeta\pi} = 1$ and

$$z = \frac{z'^2 - (2az'/(1 + k)) + ((1 - k)/(1 + k))}{1 - (2az'/(1 + k)) + ((1 - kz')/(1 + k))^2}$$

where

$$a = \frac{\cos\left[(\omega_{p2} + \omega_{p1})T/2\right]}{\cos\left[(\omega_{p2} - \omega_{p1})T/2\right]}$$

$$k = \tan\frac{\Omega_p T}{2} \tan\frac{(\omega_{p2} - \omega_{p1})T}{2}$$

A complete list of transformations is given in Table 5.1.

Bibliographical notes

Many other techniques exist for the design of IIR filters; for example the use of L^P optimization is considered in Deczky (1972) and Maria and Fahmy (1974), linear programming design in Chottera and Jullien (1982) and Rabiner *et al.* (1974) and multiple criterion optimization for the simultaneous design of IIR and (nonlinear phase) FIR filters is discussed in Cortelazzo and Lightner (1984). The transformations given in Table 5.1 are due to Constantinides (1970).

Table 5.1 Digital filter transformations

Type	Transformation	a, k
Lowpass to lowpass	$z = \dfrac{z' - a}{1 - az'}$	$a = \dfrac{\sin\left[(\Omega_p - \omega_p)T/2\right]}{\sin\left[(\Omega_p + \omega_p)T/2\right]}$
Lowpass to highpass	$z = -\dfrac{z' - a}{1 - az'}$	$a = \dfrac{\cos\left[(\Omega_p - \omega_p)T/2\right]}{\cos\left[(\Omega_p + \omega_p)T/2\right]}$
Lowpass to bandpass	$z = \dfrac{z'^2 - \dfrac{2akz'}{k+1} + \dfrac{k-1}{k+1}}{1 - \dfrac{2akz'}{k+1} + \dfrac{k-1}{k+1}z'^2}$	$a = \dfrac{\cos\left[(\omega_{p2} + \omega_{p1})T/2\right]}{\cos\left[(\omega_{p2} - \omega_{p1})T/2\right]}$ $k = \tan\dfrac{\Omega_p T}{2}\cos\dfrac{(\omega_{p2} - \omega_{p1})T}{2}$
Lowpass to bandstop	$z = \dfrac{z'^2 - \dfrac{2akz'}{1+k} + \dfrac{1-k}{1+k}}{1 - \dfrac{2akz'}{1+k} + \dfrac{1-k}{1+k}z'^2}$	$a = \dfrac{\cos\left[(\omega_{p2} + \omega_{p1})T/2\right]}{\cos\left[(\omega_{p2} - \omega_{p1})T/2\right]}$ $k = \tan\dfrac{\Omega_p T}{2}\tan\dfrac{(\omega_{p2} - \omega_{p1})T}{2}$

Exercises

1 Using the second-order normalized Butterworth filter, design a second-order digital filter based on the impulse invariant method. Plot the frequency responses for the analog filter and the digital filter for a variety of sampling intervals T. Comment on the results.

2 For an nth-order Butterworth filter, show that the product of the poles is $\omega_c^n(-1)^n$ and hence show that one can write the general filter in the form

$$B(s) = \frac{s_1 s_2 \cdots s_n}{\Pi_{i=1}^n (s + s_i)}$$

where $s_i = -p_i$, $1 \leqslant i \leqslant n$, and p_i are the poles.

3 Discuss the significance of the term $(z + 1)^l$ in the matched z-transformation technique (Section 5.4).

4 Design a digital filter, using the bilinear transformation method, with a sampling rate of 15 kHz, flat to 1 dB in the range 0–200 Hz and at least 12 dB down for frequencies greater than 2.5 kHz.

5 Change the filter in exercise 4 to a highpass filter by using the transformations in Table 5.1.

References

Chottera, A. T. and G. A. Jullien (1982), 'A linear programming approach to recursive digital filter design with linear phase', *IEEE Trans. Circuits Sys.,* CAS-**29**, 139–49.

Constantinides, A. G. (1970), 'Spectral transformations for digital filters', *Proc. IEEE,* **117**, 1585–90.

Cortelazzo, G. and M. R. Lightner (1984), 'Simultaneous design in both magnitude and group-delay of IIR and FIR filters based on multiple criterion optimization', *IEEE Trans. Acoust., Speech, Signal Process.,* ASSP-**32**, 949–67.

Deczky, A. G. (1972), 'Synthesis of recursive digital filters using the minimum p-error criterion', *IEEE Trans. Audio Electroacoust.,* AU-**20**, 257–63.

Maria, G. A. and M. M. Fahmy (1974), 'An L^p technique for two-dimensional digital recursive filters', *IEEE Trans. Acoust., Speech, Signal Process.,* ASSP-**22**, 15–21.

Rabiner, L. R., N. Y. Graham and H. D. Helms, (1974), 'Linear programming design of IIR digital filters with arbitrary magnitude function', *IEEE Trans. Acoust., Speech, Signal Process.,* ASSP-**22**, 117–23.

6

Quantization Effects in Filters

6.1 Introduction

In the preceding chapters it has been assumed implicitly that all the numbers involved in the implementation of a digital filter (i.e. the numbers representing the inputs, coefficients, etc.) are stored exactly, and that the results of multiplications, summations, etc., are also known exactly. In practice, of course, the filter is an algorithm implemented in computer software (or hardware, in some special purpose systems). In any case, all the values involved must be quantized in order that they can be stored in finite-length registers. This leads to quantizing errors in the filter and we shall study these effects in this chapter.

For a given filter there are basically three types of quantization errors which can occur. These are:

(a) coefficient-quantization errors;

(b) product-quantization errors;
(c) input-quantization errors;

Errors in the representation of the filter coefficients will alter the position of the poles and zeros and hence the frequency response of the filter. Product-quantization errors arise because the multiplication of two binary numbers each with n bits generates a binary number with $2n$ bits. It is therefore necessary to truncate the least significant n bits. Finally, input-quantization errors are due to the quantizing of the sampled values of the input signal, which is generally analog. Hence these errors are introduced by analog-to-digital converters.

Quantization is a nonlinear operation and so it is possible for nonlinear oscillations to occur in the output of a filter, giving rise to spurious signals – this is called the 'deadband effect'. The prediction of these limit cycles is discussed later.

6.2 Number representations

Binary numbers are stored in a computer in two basic ways – as fixed point or as floating point representations. In fixed point form, a number is stored in a register in such a way that the effective binary point is between the first and second bits of the register (the first bit being reserved for the sign of the number). This means that any binary number B in this representation satisfies $|B| < 1$. The representation of signed numbers can be chosen to be one of (at least) three forms:

(a) Signed magnitude. In this form the binary number $B = \pm 0b_{-1}b_{-2} \ldots b_{-m}$ is stored as $0b_{-1}b_{-2} \ldots b_{-m}$ (in a register of length $m + 1$) in the positive case and $1b_{-1}b_{-2} \ldots b_{-m}$ when $B < 0$. Thus the magnitude is stored in the same way and the sign is stored in the first bit as either a 0 (for $B \geqslant 0$) or a 1 (for $B < 0$).

(b) One's complement. The one's complement representation B_1 of a binary number B is given by

$$B_1 = \begin{cases} B & \text{if } B \geqslant 0 \\ 2 - 2^{-m} - |B| & \text{if } B < 0 \end{cases}$$

Thus, B_1 is obtained from B, when $B < 0$, by complementing each bit of B. Hence for example, if $m = 3$ and $B = -0.0110$, then $B_1 = 1.1001$.

(c) Two's complement. This is defined by

$$B_2 = \begin{cases} B & \text{if } B \geqslant 0 \\ \\ 2 - |B| & \text{if } B < 0 \end{cases}$$

Clearly, $B_2 = B_1 + 2^{-m}$ if $B < 0$.

The main advantage of the one's and two's complement representations is that algebraic addition (of positive and negative binary numbers) can be achieved by ordinary addition of the appropriate complemented forms[1]. Moreover, if N is given as an algebraic sum

$$N = \sum_{i=1}^{L} B_i$$

of binary numbers B_i and N has at most m bits in its binary representation, then we can evaluate N by summing the one's or two's complement forms of the B_is, even if overflow occurs in the partial sums. For example, consider the sum

$$N = \frac{11}{16} + \frac{7}{16} - \frac{3}{16}$$

Then we have

11/16	1's comp.	0.1011	2's comp.	0.1011
+ 7/16		0.0111		0.0111
18/16		1.0010		1.0010
− 3/16		1.1100		1.1101
15/16		0.1110 1		0.1111
		end around carry		ignore

Note that, in both the one's complement and two's complement cases, the first partial sum for 18/16 is incorrect.

6.3 Quantization

If we use fixed point arithmetic, then the smallest number (in absolute value) which can be represented is 2^{-m} where m is the number of bits (excluding the sign bit) in the representation. Any number whose binary representations contain bits corresponding to the bit positions 2^{-i} for $i > m$ must be quantized. We can do this in one of two ways – by truncation or rounding. Truncation consists of simply ignoring all bits in positions 2^{-i} for $i > m$. Rounding is defined as the process of changing a number to the nearest machine representable form, with an arbitrary (but fixed) definition for numbers lying exactly half-way between two machine representable forms.

[1]One's complement addition requires 'end around carry'.

Writing $Q[x]$ for the quantized form of a number x and defining $e[x]$ by

$$e[x] = x - Q[x]$$

it is easy to see that, for truncation, we have

(i) $0 \leqslant e[x] \leqslant 2^{-m}$ for one's and two's complement numbers;
(ii) $-2^{-m} < e[x] < 2^{-m}$ for signed-magnitude numbers;

and for rounding,

$$-2^{-m-1} \leqslant e[x] < 2^{-m-1} \text{ for all systems.}$$

These relationships are shown in Figure 6.1.

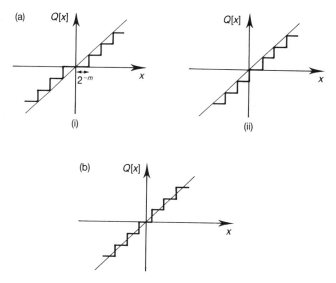

Figure 6.1   Quantization characteristics: (a) Truncation–(i) signed magnitude, (ii) one's and two's complement; (b) Rounding, all systems.

6.4 Coefficient quantization

Let $H(z)$ be a digital filter with amplitude response $A(\omega)$ which approximates an ideal amplitude response $A_I(\omega)$. If the coefficients of $H(z)$ are quantized, we obtain a response function $A_Q(\omega)$. Suppose the passband and stopband tolerances are ε_p, ε_α, respectively; then we have the frequency domain characteristics similar to those in Figure 6.2.

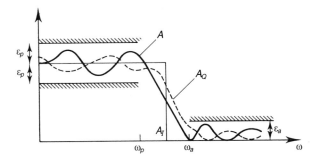

Figure 6.2 Band tolerances in coefficient quantization.

If $\Delta A = A(\omega) - A_Q(\omega)$, then the maximum value which $|\Delta A|$ can attain in order that the specification is satisfied when the coefficients are quantized is given by

$$\Delta A_{max}(\omega) = \begin{cases} \varepsilon_p - |A(\omega) - A_I(\omega)| & \text{for } \omega \le \omega_p \\ \varepsilon_a - |A(\omega) - A_I(\omega)| & \text{for } \omega \ge \omega_a \end{cases}$$

The optimum word length can thus be computed for a given filter.

The computation involved in determining the optimum word length in this way is considerable and so we usually resort to statistical techniques. Thus, suppose that $H(z)$ depends on m coefficients $c_1, \ldots, c_m$ and let Δc_i denote the error between the actual and truncated coefficient. If we assume that each Δc_i $(1 \le i \le m)$ is a random variable which is uniformly distributed, then the probability density function is

$$p(\Delta c_i) = \begin{cases} 1/q & \text{for } -q/2 \le \Delta c_i \le q/2 \\ 0 & \text{otherwise} \end{cases}$$

Thus,

$$E(\Delta c_i) = 0$$

$$\sigma^2_{\Delta c_i} = q^2/12$$

Define the *sensitivity* of $A(\omega)$ with respect to c_i by

$$S_{c_i} = \frac{\partial A(\omega)}{\partial c_i}$$

Then,

$$\Delta A = \sum_{i=1}^{m} \Delta c_i \cdot S_{c_i}$$

and

$$E(\Delta A) = 0$$

Assuming that the coefficient errors for different coefficients are statistically independent, we have

$$\sigma^2_{\Delta A} = \sum_{i=1}^{m} \sigma^2_{\Delta c_i} \cdot S^2_{c_i} = \frac{q^2}{12} S \qquad \left(S = \sum S^2_{c_i} \right)$$

If we assume that ΔA is Gaussian, then

$$p(\Delta A) = \frac{1}{\sigma_{\Delta A} \sqrt{2\pi}} \, e^{-\Delta A^2/2\sigma^2_{\Delta A}} \qquad -\infty < \Delta A < \infty$$

Thus, the probability that $\Delta A \varepsilon [-\Delta A_1, \Delta A_1]$ is

$$y = \frac{2}{\sigma_{\Delta A} \sqrt{2\pi}} \int_0^{\Delta A_1} e^{-\Delta A^2/2\sigma^2_{\Delta A}} \mathrm{d}(\Delta A)$$

$$= \frac{2}{\sqrt{2\pi}} \int_0^{x_1} e^{-x^2/2} \mathrm{d}x$$

where $x = \Delta A / \sigma_{\Delta A}$. Selecting a confidence factor y will then specify x_1 and hence $\Delta A_1 = x_1 \sigma_{\Delta A}$, and we must have

$$\Delta A_1 \leqslant \Delta A_{max}(\omega)$$

as seen above. Hence we must have

$$q \leqslant \frac{\sqrt{12} \Delta A_{max}(\omega)}{x_1 S}$$

If the word length is $m + 1$ then, since $q = 2^{-m}$ we must have

$$m + 1 \geqslant 1 + \log_2 \left(\frac{x_1 S}{\sqrt{12} \Delta A_{max}(\omega)} \right)$$

This relation specifies the minimum word length in a statistical sense.

6.5 Product quantization

In order to discuss product quantization we must first introduce the notions of discrete autocorrelation and power spectral density. If $H(z)$ is a filter with impulse response $\{h(n)\}$ and $x(n)$ and $y(n)$ are the input and output, respectively, then

$$y(i) = \sum_{k=-\infty}^{\infty} h(k) x(i - k)$$

and so

$$E(y(i)y(j)) = E\left\{ \sum_{p=-\infty}^{\infty} \sum_{q=-\infty}^{\infty} h(p)h(q)x(i-p)x(j-q) \right\}$$

Putting $j = i + k$, $q = p + n$ we have

$$r_y(k) \triangleq E(y(i)y(i+k))$$

$$= \sum_{n=-\infty}^{\infty} \sum_{p=-\infty}^{\infty} h(p)h(p+n)E(x(i-p)x(i-p+k-n))$$

Thus, if $S_y(z) = Z\{r_y(k)\}$, we have

$$S_y(z) = H(z)H(z^{-1})S_x(z)$$

$r_y(k)$ is called the autocorrelation sequence of y and $S_y(z)$ is called the *power spectral density* of y.

Now, if the input $x(n)$ is multiplied by the coefficient c_i we have

$$Q[c_i x(n)] = c_i x(n) + e_i(n)$$

where $e_i(n)$ is the quantization noise. Assuming this occurs because of rounding we have

$$p(e_i(n)) = \begin{cases} 1/q & -q/2 \leqslant e_i(n) \leqslant q/2 \\ 0 & \text{otherwise} \end{cases}$$

Hence,

$$E(e_i(n)) = 0$$

$$E(e_i^2(n)) = q^2/12$$

$$r_{e_i}(k) = E(e_i(n)e_i(n+k)) = \begin{cases} q^2/12 & \text{if } k = 0 \\ 0 & \text{otherwise} \end{cases}$$

if we assume that $e_i(n)$, $e_i(n+k)$ are independent for $k \neq 0$. Thus,

$$S_{e_i}(z) = q^2/12$$

and so e_i is a white noise process. We can also see that under this independence assumption, we have

$$r_{e_i+e_j}(k) = r_{e_i}(k) + r_{e_j}(k)$$

and

$$S_{e_i+e_j}(z) = S_{e_i}(z) + S_{e_j}(z)$$

and so the power spectral density due to different product quantization signals is the sum of the individual power spectral densities. Hence, if we consider the second-order system shown in Figure 6.3 (with multiplication errors as shown), we have

$$S_y(z) = (q^2/6)H(z)H(z^{-1}) + q^2/4$$

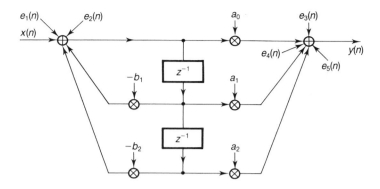

Figure 6.3   Typical second-order system.

6.6 Signal scaling

The internal signals in the fixed point implementation of a filter must not exceed the range of values which can be represented in registers of the given word length. Otherwise, overflow will occur in the registers and the signals will be distorted. Moreover, it is important that the internal signals should not have amplitudes which are too low, since the quantization steps will then be comparable with the signal sizes, giving poor signal-to-noise ratio. Thus, the input signal should be scaled (or *conditioned*) so that optimal filter performance is achieved.

Suppose that a filter is implemented in fixed point arithmetic using one's or two's complement binary representations. Each linear filter is implemented by a sequence of multiplications and summations, in which the inputs to a multiplier are either coefficients of the filter or outputs of summation operators. We wish to find a scaling factor λ such that if the input to a particular (section of the) filter is multiplied by λ, then the input to each multiplier and the output from each summation in that section of the filter is bounded by some number M if the filter input is bounded by M. (Recall that one's and two's complement arithmetic give the correct answer for a sum which is in the range of the given fixed point representation, even if overflow does occur in the partial sums.)

Consider the filter section shown in Figure 6.4. Suppose that the transfer function from the input l to the multiplier input m is $H(z)$. Then

$$v(n) = \sum_{k=0}^{\infty} \lambda h(k) x(n - k)$$

and so

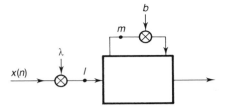

Figure 6.4 Typical filter section with scaling.

$$|v(n)| \leq \sum_{k=0}^{\infty} |\lambda h(k)|.|x(n - k)| \leq M \sum_{k=0}^{\infty} |\lambda h(k)|$$

if $|x(n)| \leq M$ for all n. Thus,

$$|v(n)| \leq M$$

if

$$\lambda \leq \frac{1}{\sum_{k=0}^{\infty} |h(k)|}$$

The best value of λ is therefore given by $1/\sum_{k=0}^{\infty} |h(k)|$. In general, if a given filter section has N multipliers with corresponding transfer functions h_i, $1 \leq i \leq N$, then we must choose

$$\lambda = \min_{1 \leq i \leq N} \left(\frac{1}{\sum_{k=0}^{\infty} |h_i(k)|} \right)$$

For a filter consisting of M sections, as shown in Figure 6.5 we must choose the λs according to

$$\lambda_i = \frac{1}{\lambda_1 \ldots \lambda_{i-1} \max_{1 \leq j \leq l_i} (\Sigma |h_{l_1}^1 * h_{l_2}^2 * \ldots * h_j^i|)} \qquad 1 \leq i \leq M$$

where h_j^i, $1 \leq j \leq l_i$ are the appropriate transfer functions for the ith section and, in particular, $h_{l_i}^i$ is the transfer function of section i.

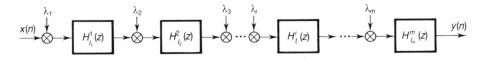

Figure 6.5 A general cascade filter.

6.7 The deadband effect

The assumption of statistically independent quantization noise between different samples made above is no longer valid for small signals, such as silent periods in speech processing. The theory developed previously does not then hold and indeed the system may lock into a stable limit cycle. To see how this can occur, consider the first-order filter

$$H(z) = \frac{Kz}{z - b}$$

i.e.

$$y(n) = Kx(n) + by(n - 1)$$

The impulse response of this filter is

$$h(n) = Kb^n$$

If $K = 10$ and $b = 0.9$, then we obtain the values $10 \times (0.9)^n$ which tend to zero as $n \to \infty$. Suppose now that we implement the filter using rounding (to the nearest integer), so that

$$Q(|x|) = \text{Int}\,(|x| + 0.5) \tag{6.7.1}$$

Then we obtain the sequence

$$y(0) = h(0) = 10$$
$$y(1) = h(1) = 9$$
$$y(2) = h(2) = \text{Int}\,(8.1 + 0.5) = 8$$
$$y(3) = h(3) = \text{Int}\,(7.2 + 0.5) = 7$$
$$y(4) = h(4) = \text{Int}\,(6.3 + 0.5) = 6$$
$$y(5) = h(5) = \text{Int}\,(5.4 + 0.5) = 5$$
$$y(6) = h(6) = \text{Int}\,(4.5 + 0.5) = 5$$
$$y(7) = h(7) = \text{Int}\,(4.5 + 0.5) = 5$$

so that, eventually, $y(n)$ tends to the constant value 5. Hence quantization has made the filter effectively unstable. In the unstable condition we have

$$Q(|y(n - 1)|) = |y(n - 1)|$$

and so, by (6.7.1),

$$\text{Int}\,\{|b|\cdot|y(n - 1)| + 0.5\} = |y(n - 1)|$$

so that we must have

$$0 \leqslant -(1 - |b|)|y(n - 1)| + 0.5 < 1$$

Thus, instability will occur when

$$|y(n - 1)| \leqslant \frac{0.5}{1 - |b|} \triangleq k$$

The interval $[-k, k]$ is called the *deadband* and the limit cycles will have amplitude $\leqslant k$ and frequency 0 or $\omega_s/2$.

In the case of a second-order filter

$$H(z) = \frac{z^2}{z^2 + b_1 z + b_2}$$

we have

$$h(n) = \frac{r^n}{\sin \theta} \sin [(n + 1)\theta]$$

where

$$r = \sqrt{b_2}, \cos \theta = \frac{-b_1}{2\sqrt{b_2}}$$

If $a_2 = 1$, then the impulse response has frequency

$$\omega = \frac{1}{T} \cos^{-1} \left(\frac{-b_1}{2}\right)$$

and so we obtain a limit cycle with this frequency if

$$Q\{|b_2 y(n - 2)|\} = |y(n - 2)|$$

and, as before, the condition for instability is

$$|y(n - 2)| \leqslant \frac{0.5}{1 - |b_2|} = k$$

To obtain general limit cycle bounds, consider the system

$$y(n) = \sum_{i=0}^{N} a_i x(n - i) - \sum_{i=1}^{N} b_i y(n - i)$$

$$= - \sum_{i=1}^{N} b_i y(n - i)$$

for zero input. If each multiplier has noise quantization error $e_i(n)$, then we have

$$y(n) = e(n) - \sum_{i=1}^{N} b_i y(n - i)$$

where

$$e(n) = \sum_{i=1}^{N} e_i(n) \tag{6.7.2}$$

We can write this in the form

$$Y(z) = H_1(z)E(z)$$

or

$$y(n) = \sum_{k=-\infty}^{n} h_1(n - k)e(k)$$

Now, assuming a limit cycle of period MT occurs, we must have

$$e(n) = e(n + M)$$

since the system is linear. Hence,

$$y(n) = \sum_{i=0}^{\infty} \sum_{k=n-(i+1)M+1}^{n-iM} h_1(n - k)e(k)$$

and putting $k = n - iM - p$, we have

$$y(n) = \sum_{i=0}^{\infty} \sum_{p=0}^{M-1} h_1(p + iM)e(n - iM - p)$$

$$= \sum_{p=0}^{M-1} e(n - p) \sum_{i=0}^{\infty} h_1(p + iM)$$

by the periodicity of e. From (6.7.2) we have

$$|e(n - p)| \leqslant Nq/2$$

and so

$$|y(n)| \leqslant \frac{Nq}{2} \sum_{p=0}^{M-1} \left| \sum_{i=0}^{\infty} h_i(p + iM) \right|$$

$$\leqslant \frac{Nq}{2} \sum_{k=0}^{\infty} |h_1(k)|$$

giving a bound on the limit cycle amplitude.

Bibliographical notes

The statistical approach to coefficient quantization is developed in Avenhaus (1972) and Crochiere (1975), and the use of coefficient sensitivity is given in Jackson (1976). The analysis of roundoff noise can be found in Jackson (1970a, b), and limit cycles and the deadband effect have been studied extensively; see, for example, Chang (1976), Ebert *et al.* (1969), Jackson (1969), Parker and Hess (1971), Sandberg and Kaiser (1972) and the references cited therein. For an algorithm for minimizing roundoff noise in cascade realizations, see Chan and Rabiner (1973).

Exercises

1 Evaluate the two's complement of the numbers
  (a) .101101 ($m = 6$)
  (b) .11101001 ($m = 8$)
  (c) 11011001 ($m = 8$).
  (Note: there is no binary point in (c).)
2 Given a filter

$$H(z) = \frac{a_2 z^2 + a_1 z + a_0}{z^2 + b_1 z + b_0}$$

where

$$a_0 = 0.365\,79, \qquad b_0 = 1$$
$$a_1 = 0.496\,89, \qquad b_1 = 0.083\,067$$
$$a_2 = 0.365\,79, \qquad b_2 = 0.463\,48$$

plot its amplitude response and the amplitude response of its implementation using binary two's complement representations of the coefficients with word length equal to 4.
3 Estimate a bound on a quantization noise limit cycle for the system

$$y(n) - 6y(n-1) + 11y(n-2) - 6y(n-3) = x(n)$$

References

Avenhaus, E. (1972), 'On the design of digital filters with coefficients of limited word length', *IEEE Trans. Audio Electroacoust.*, AU-**20**, 206–12.

Chan, D. S. K. and L. R. Rabiner (1973), 'An algorithm for minimizing roundoff noise in cascade realizations of finite impulse response digital filters', *Bell System Techn, J.*, **52**, 347–85.

Chang, T. L. (1976), 'A note on upper bounds on limit cycles in digital filters', *IEEE Trans. Acoust., Speech, Signal Process.*, ASSP-**24**, 99–100.

Crochiere, R. E. (1975), 'A new statistical approach to the coefficient word length problem for digital filters', *IEEE Trans. Circuits Sys.*, CAS-**22**, 190–6.

Ebert, P. M., J. E. Mazo and M. G. Taylor (1969), 'Overflow oscillations in digital filters', *Bell System Techn. J.*, **48**, 2999–3020.

Jackson, L. B. (1969), 'An analysis of limit cycles due to multiplication rounding in recursive digital filters', *Proc. 7th Annu. Allerton Conf. Circuit Sys. Theory*, 69–78.

Jackson, L. B. (1970a), 'On the interaction of roundoff noise and dynamic range in digital filters', *Bell System Techn. J.*, **49**, 159–84.

Jackson, L. B. (1970b), 'Roundoff noise analysis for fixed-point digital filters realized in cascade or parallel form', *IEEE Trans. Audio Electroacoust.*, AU-**18**, 107–22.

Jackson, L. B. (1976), 'Roundoff noise bounds derived from coefficient sensitivities for digital filters', *IEEE Trans. Circuits Sys.,* CAS-**23**, 481–5.

Parker, S. R. and S. F. Hess (1971), 'Limit cycle oscillations in digital filters', *IEEE Trans. Circuit Theory,* CT-**18**, 687–97.

Sandberg, I. W. and J. F. Kaiser (1972), 'A bound on limit cycles in fixed-point implementations of digital filters', *IEEE Trans. Audio Electroacoust.,* AU-**20**, 110–14.

7

Hardware and Software Implementation

7.1 Introduction

The theoretical aspects of one-dimensional filter design have been presented in the preceding six chapters. It is now important to consider various methods of implementation of these designs. Basically, two methods are available — special purpose hardware designed for each filter structure or a general purpose computer system with special purpose software. Hardware design depends on a knowledge of logic systems design and this will be discussed first, assuming only a familiarity with combinational logic. A variety of standard hardware configurations will then be developed. Software design can be accomplished via high- or low-level languages and this will be treated in the second part of this chapter.

7.2 Basic hardware blocks

Two fundamental building blocks of digital circuits are decoders and multi-plexers. A *decoder* is a device which had n inputs and 2^n outputs such that if b_i ($0 \leqslant i \leqslant n - 1$) is the n-bit binary representation of the integer i, and we input b_i to the device, then the output is

$$y = (0 \, 0 \, \ldots \, 0 \, 1 \, 0 \, \ldots \, 0)$$

where the '1' is in the ith place. An example with $n = 2$ is shown in Figure 7.1. It can be seen that we can write

$$y_i = \begin{cases} 1 & \text{if } i = \displaystyle\sum_{k=0}^{n-1} 2^k x_k \\ 0 & \text{otherwise} \end{cases} \qquad (7.2.1)$$

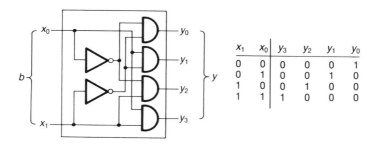

x_1	x_0	y_3	y_2	y_1	y_0
0	0	0	0	0	1
0	1	0	0	1	0
1	0	0	1	0	0
1	1	1	0	0	0

Figure 7.1 A two-input decoder.

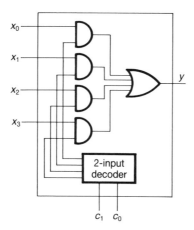

Figure 7.2 A four-input multi-plexer.

A *multiplexer* is a logic circuit which connects the output to one of 2^n inputs by appropriate choice of one out of n input selection values. Figure 7.2 shows a four-bit multiplexer with inputs x_0, x_1, x_2, x_3 selected by the control lines c_0, c_1. Many logic circuits are implemented using ROM's (read only memories). A ROM is essentially a linear collection of 'words' (binary numbers of some fixed length), each of which has an 'address' which is specified by the input. When a valid address is placed on the input lines the word which is stored in the ROM at that address is placed on the output lines. A ROM with n inputs can contain 2^n distinct words. The structure of a ROM circuit is shown in Figure 7.3.

The encoder can be implemented with diodes or transistors; a typical encoder with four eight-bit words is shown in Figure 7.4; and the words stored in the encoder are given by the truth table opposite.

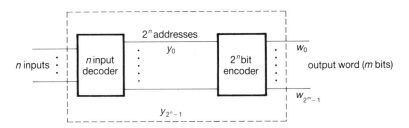

Figure 7.3   Basic ROM structure.

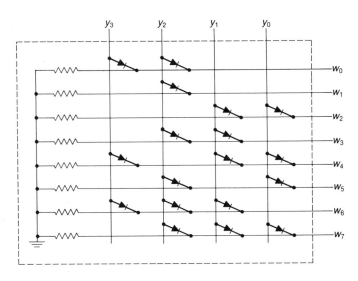

Figure 7.4   Four-input, eight-bit word encoder.

y_3	y_2	y_1	y_0	w_7	w_6	w_5	w_4	w_3	w_2	w_1	w_0
0	0	0	1	1	0	1	1	0	1	0	0
0	0	1	0	1	1	0	1	1	1	0	0
0	1	0	0	1	1	1	0	1	0	1	1
1	0	0	0	0	1	0	1	0	0	0	1

The preceding logic circuits can be used to generate many kinds of combinational logic circuits, as we shall see below. However, for sequential circuits (which are 'iterated in time' rather than 'iterated in space' as are combinational circuits) we require a device which changes state when a clock pulse is applied. Such a device is a *flip–flop* which has various configurations. We shall be interested in two types; the *JK flip–flop* and the *D (or delay) flip–flop*. The JK flip–flop is shown in Figure 7.5, together with its truth table. Here Q_n refers to the current output and Q_{n+1} represents the output after a clock pulse, for the different JK inputs. The delay flip–flop is shown in Figure 7.6(a) and merely passes on the input at the current time to the output after a clock pulse (i.e. $y_{n+1} = d_n$, independently of y_n). It can be constructed with a JK flip–flop and an inverter, as shown in the diagram.

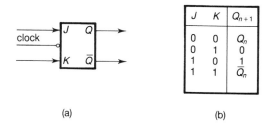

J	K	Q_{n+1}
0	0	Q_n
0	1	0
1	0	1
1	1	$\overline{Q}_n$

(a) (b)

Figure 7.5 The JK flip–flop: (a) JK flip–flop; (b) truth table.

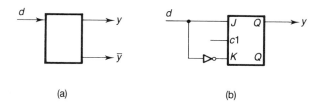

(a) (b)

Figure 7.6 The delay flip–flop: (a) D flip–flop; (b) JK implementation.

7.3 Parallel arithmetic circuits

The most basic arithmetic circuit is the half-adder which adds two binary bits and produces a sum and a carry (Figure 7.7). A full adder has three binary inputs: two summands and a carry from a lower-order summation. The outputs are again sum and carry bits, as shown in Figure 7.8.

An n-bit binary adder can then be implemented using a half-adder and $n - 1$ full adders, as shown in Figure 7.9.

Now consider the multiplication of two 4-bit binary numbers $x_3x_2x_1x_0$,

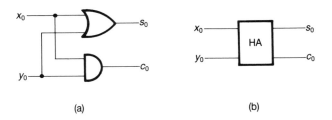

(a)   (b)

Figure 7.7   The half-adder: (a) basic circuit; (b) symbol.

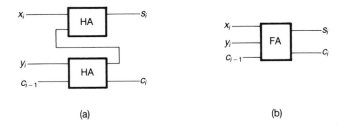

(a)   (b)

Figure 7.8   The full adder: (a) basic circuit; (b) symbol.

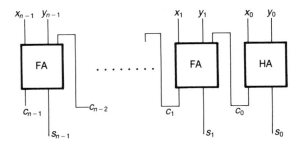

Figure 7.9 n-bit binary adder.

$y_3y_2y_1y_0$. The implementation of such a multiplication can be represented in the usual 'long-hand' form:

$$x_3x_2x_1x_0$$

$$y_3y_2y_1y_0$$

$$\alpha_3\alpha_2\alpha_1\alpha_0$$

$$\beta_3\beta_2\beta_1\beta_0$$

$$\gamma_3\gamma_2\gamma_1\gamma_0$$

$$\delta_3\delta_2\delta_1\delta_0$$

$$p_7p_6p_5p_4p_3p_2p_1p_0$$

where

$$\alpha_i = y_0x_i, \quad \beta_i = y_1x_i, \quad \gamma_i = y_2x_i, \quad \delta_i = y_3x_i$$

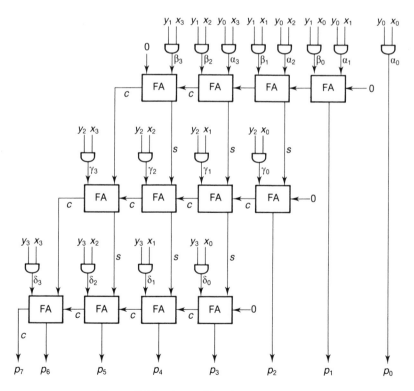

Figure 7.10 A combinational multiplier.

We can perform this operation in parallel using sixteen AND gates and an array of twelve full adders, as shown in Figure 7.10. (Note that multiplication can also be implemented by using ROMS.)

7.4 Sequential circuits

A sequential circuit is a collection of flip–flops and combinational logic gates connected as in Figure 7.11. If the clock inputs to all the flip–flops are connected to a common clock source, the sequential circuit is called *synchronous*, while if certain flip–flops have their clock inputs derived from the Q-outputs of other flip–flops it is said to be *asynchronous*. We shall consider synchronous circuits exclusively.

Many sequential circuits make use of a *shift register*, which is just a set of D-type flip–flops connected in a linear array, as shown in Figure 7.12(a). Strictly speaking, this is a *serial-in-serial-out* shift register. With an obvious symbolism, Figures 7.12(c)—(e) show other types of registers. The states of the flip–flops before and after a clock pulse are shown in Figure 7.12(b). Combinational circuits which have the same block of gates repeated several times can be implemented sequentially using a smaller number of such blocks. For example, the multiplier circuit of Figure 7.10 can be implemented using only four full adders by storing the intermediate results in shift registers (see Figure 7.13). (Actually, we could implement this circuit with a single full adder.) Similarly, the *n*-bit combinational binary adder in Figure 7.9 can be implemented sequentially using a single full adder, as shown in Figure 7.14. The circuit contains three *n*-bit shift registers and one 1-bit shift register. The 1-bit register

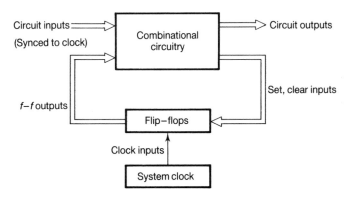

Figure 7.11   A general synchronous sequential system.

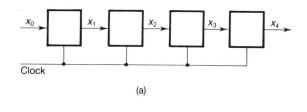

(a)

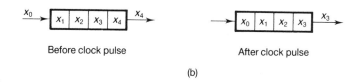

Before clock pulse   After clock pulse

(b)

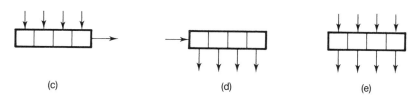

(c)   (d)   (e)

Figure 7.12 Four-bit shift registers: (a) serial in–serial out; (b) operation of (a); (c) parallel in–serial out; (d) serial in–parallel out; (e) parallel in–parallel out.

is initially reset so that the first carry bit is zero. To perform sequential subtraction we can add the two's complement of the second number to the first. The two's complement of a number is equal to the one's complement plus one, and so if we complement each bit of $y_{n-1}y_{n-2} \ldots y_0$ and set the 1-bit register to ensure that the first carry bit is one, then we obtain the sequential subtractor shown in Figure 7.15.

7.5 Filter implementation

Consider, now, the second-order filter section

$$H_2(z) = \frac{1 + a_1 z^{-1} + a_2 z^{-2}}{1 + b_1 z^{-1} + b_2 z^{-2}} \tag{7.5.1}$$

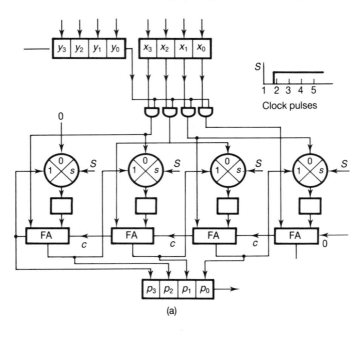

(a)

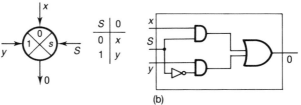

(b)

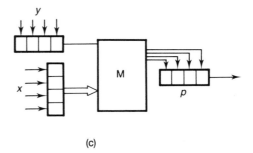

(c)

Figure 7.13   A sequential multiplier: (a) implementation;
(b) simple switch; (c) schematic diagram.

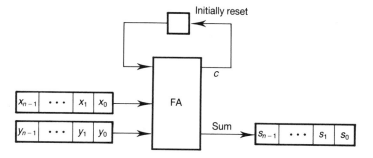

Figure 7.14 Sequential adder.

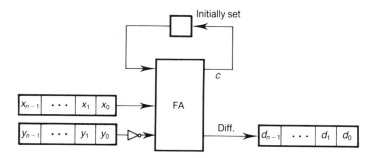

Figure 7.15 Sequential subtractor.

This can be implemented as shown in Figure 7.16 where the summation and multiplication operators use the circuitry described in the last section. (Care must be taken with the numerical robustness, however.) We have assumed n-bit numbers and we must use the $2n$-bit shift registers since multiplication introduces a delay of n clock cycles. Note that a first-order filter

$$Ha_1(z) = \frac{1 + a_1 z^{-1}}{1 + b_1 z^{-1}}$$

can be constructed in a similar way.

A general filter

$$H_n(z) = \frac{1 + a_1 z^{-1} + \ldots + a_n z^{-n}}{1 + b_1 z^{-1} + \ldots + b_n z^{-n}}$$

can be written in the form

$$H_n(z) = \frac{\Pi_{i=1}^{n_1}(z^2 + c_i z + d_i)\Pi_{i=1}^{n_2}(z + g_i)}{\Pi_{i=1}^{m_1}(z^2 + e_i z + f_i)\Pi_{i=1}^{m_2}(z + h_i)}$$

$$\triangleq H_1(z) \ldots H_k(z)$$

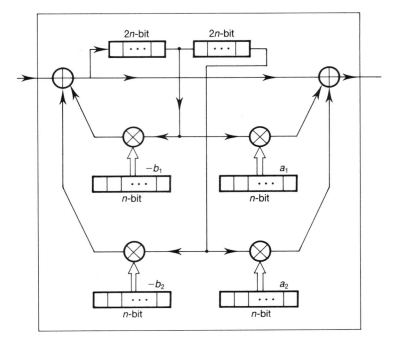

Figure 7.16   Second-order filter section.

or in the form

$$H_n(z) = \sum_{i=1}^{m_1} \frac{z(\alpha_i z + \beta_i)}{z^2 + \gamma_i z + \delta_i} + \sum_{i=1}^{m_2} \frac{z \varepsilon_i}{z + \zeta_i}$$

$$\triangleq H_1(z) + \ldots + H_l(z)$$

(by partial fraction expansion). Hence such a filter can be implemented as a cascade or parallel combination of first- and second-order filter sections.

7.6 Software design

Above, we have considered special purpose hardware for the implementation of filters. The main drawback with using such hardware is that each filter requires its own specific components, and a filter designed for one particular application cannot be used for another. The alternative approach is to use general purpose digital hardware (i.e. a computer) and implement the filter algorithm in the form of software. This has the advantage of flexibility – software designed for one application can easily be adapted to another, but has the disadvantage of being slower than special purpose hardware.

When writing software for a general purpose computer, one can choose from a wide variety of languages – FORTRAN, Pascal, MODULA-2 (high-level languages) or assembler, machine code (low-level languages). Assembly programming generates more condensed code and therefore runs faster but is difficult to write and debug. With modern high-level languages, writing good, robust code is quite easy (!?) but will not be as fast as optimally written machine code. The basic arithmetic operations can also be implemented in hardware or software – in the former case by using a microprocessor chip with hardware floating point on the chip or using a coprocessor. In the following discussion we shall choose Pascal for the software language in which to write the filter algorithms because it is now widely available and is highly structured, making software design particularly simple.

Consider first, therefore, the direct convolution implementation of an FIR filter, i.e.

$$y(n) = \sum_{i=0}^{m} a_i x(n - i) \tag{7.6.1}$$

A simple Pascal procedure which will evaluate $y(n)$ given the inputs $x(n)$, $x(n - 1), \ldots, x(n - m)$ can be written in the following way. Assuming $m + 1$ vectors $a = (a_0, \ldots, a_m)$ and $x = (x(n), x(n - 1), \ldots, x(n - m))$ have been defined by the statements

```
type
      vect = array[0 . . 20] of real;
var
      x,a:vect;
```

(where we have to specify m – here we have taken $m = 20$), then the required procedure is

```
procedure find_next_y(a,x:vect ;var y:real;m:integer);
var
      i:integer;
begin
      y:=0;
      for i:=0 to m do
          y:=y+a[i]*x[i];
end;
```

The number m can be passed as a parameter to the procedure; it must be less than or equal to 20. To apply the program to a case where $m > 20$ we must redefine the type definition of **vect** at the start of the program. (We have had to do this since dynamic arrays are not allowed in Pascal.) The current input vector x is assumed to be available. This may be updated in 'real time' by an interrupt system which reads in the current input signal from some external device, or it may be obtained as a slice of a given input sequence which has been obtained 'off-line'. To obtain k output samples $y(n), \ldots, y(n + k)$, this method requires $k(m + 1)$ additions and multiplications.

Another approach to the evaluation of (7.6.1) is to use the discrete Fourier transform. First we determine the minimum power of 2 greater than $2m + 1$, say $k \geqslant 2m - 1$ and $k = 2^l$ for some l. Then we extend the sequences $x = \{x(0), \ldots, x(m)\}$, $a = \{a_0, \ldots, a_m\}$ by adding $k - m - 2$ zeros to each one, i.e.

$$x = \{x(0), \ldots, x(m), 0, 0, \ldots, 0\}$$

$$a = \{a_0, \ldots, a_m, 0, 0, \ldots, 0\}$$

Next we evaluate the FFTs $X(i)$, $A(i)$ of these sequences, define $Y(i) = x(i)A(i)$ and invert the sequence $\{Y(0), \ldots, Y(k - 1)\}$, again by the FFT.

Given a real sequence $f = \{f_0, f_1, \ldots, f_{n-1}\}$ where $n = 2^m$, we can write a Pascal procedure to evaluate $F = \{F_0, \ldots, F_{n-1}\}$ 'in place', as shown in Figure 3.2. (Since Pascal does not allow dynamic arrays we must fix n, say $n = 16$. The program is easily modified to handle different values of n.)

```
Type
    complex=record
                realpart:real;
                imagpart:real;
            end;
    coeffs=array[0..15] of complex;
Var
    f,ord_f,weights:coeffs;
    offset,count1,count2,count3,jmp,wt_off,wt_jump:integer;
    tmp1,tmp2,tmp3,tmp4,wt1,wt2:complex;
Const
    ord_digits:array[0..15] of byte=(0,8,4,12,2,10,6,14,1,9,5,13,3,11,7,15);
Procedure complex_add(c1,c2:complex;var c3:complex);
begin
    c3.realpart:=c1.realpart+c2.realpart;
    c3.imagpart:=cl.imagpart+c2.imagpart;
end;
Procedure complex_mult(c1,c2:complex;var c3:complex);
begin
    c3.realpart:=cl.realpart*c2.realpart-cl.imagpart*c2.imagpart;
    c3.imagpart:=cl.realpart*c2.imagpart+cl.imagpart*c2.realpart;
end;
Procedure order_coeffs(f:coeffs;var ord_f:coeffs);
var
```

```
        i:integer;
begin
        for i:=0 to 15 do ord_f[i]:=f[ord_digits[i]];
end;
Procedure evaluate_weights(var weights:coeffs);
var
        i:integer;
begin
        for i:0 to 15 do
        begin
            weights[i].realpart:=cos(2*pi*i/16);
            weights[i].imagpart:=-sin(2*pi*i/16);
        end;
end;
begin
        offset:=1;
        evaluate_weights(weights);
        order_coeffs(f,ord_f);
        for count1:=1 to 4 do
        begin
            jump:=0;
            wt_off:=round(8/offset);
            for count2:=1 to wt_off do
            begin
                wt_jump:=0;
                for count3:=1 to offset do
                begin
                    wt1:=weights[wt_jump];
                    wt2:=weights[wt_jump+8];
                    complex_mult(ord_f[jump+offset],wt1,tmp1);
                    complex_mult(ord_f[jump+offset],wt2,tmp2);
                    complex_add(tmp1,ord_f[jump],tmp3);
                    complex_add(tmp2,ord_f[jump],tmp4);
                    ord_f[jump]:=tmp3;
                    ord_f[jump+offset]:=tmp4;
                    wt_jump:=wt_jump+wt_off;
                end;
                jump:=jump+2*count1;
            end;
            offset:=offset*2;
        end;
end;
```

In this program we have defined as a constant array the sequence of arguments necessary for ordering the input sequence f. These are the numbers 0,8,4,12,2,10,6,14,1,9,5,13,3,11,7,15 and can be obtained from the numbers $0, \ldots, 15$ by bit reversal. (For example, $2 = 0010$ becomes $0100 = 4$ under bit reversal.) In general, one could write a subroutine to perform bit reversal. Note also that once the length of the input sequence has been chosen (16 in this case) the evaluation of the weights W^i can be performed off-line and stored, speeding up the program.

Bibliographical notes

An introduction to basic logic circuits can be found in Hill and Peterson (1974) and Nagle *et al.* (1975). Comparisons between different hardware designs for digital filters are discussed in Peled and Liu (1974), and nonprogrammable digital filters as replacements for analog filters are considered in Tewksbury (1973).

Exercises

1 Design a 3-to-8 decoder.
2 Design a full adder from first principles (without using a half-adder).
3 Construct a system similar to that of Figure 7.16 which implements

$$H_1(z) = \frac{1 + a_1 z^{-1}}{1 + b_1 z^{-1}}$$

4 Write a procedure in Pascal to perform bit reversal on an n-bit number.

References

Hill, F. J. and G. R. Peterson (1974), *Introduction to Switching Theory and Logic Design*, NY: Wiley.

Nagle, H. T., Jr, B. D. Carroll and J. D. Irwin (1975), *An Introduction to Computer Logic*, Englewood-Cliffs, NJ: Prentice Hall.

Peled, A. and B. Liu (1974), 'A new hardware realization of digital filter', *IEEE Trans. Acoust., Speech, Signal Process.*, ASSP-**22**, 456–62.

Tewksbury, S. K. (1973), 'Special purpose hardware implementation of digital filters', *Proc. IEEE Int. Symp. Circuits Sys.*, 418–21.

Two-dimensional Signal Processing

8

Two-dimensional Discrete Systems

8.1 Introduction

The material of this chapter will be concerned with the two-dimensional counterparts of the ideas of Chapter 1. Thus we shall consider signals and systems which depend on two integer variables n_1, n_2 and derive the fundamental properties of linear systems which correspond to those of one-dimensional systems. Since the stability of two-dimensional systems is much more involved than that of one-dimensional systems we shall leave the discussion of this topic until Chapter 9.

8.2 Two-dimensional signals

A one-dimensional signal, as discussed in Chapter 1, is a sequence $\{x(n)\}$ $(n \in \mathbb{Z})$ of complex numbers (which may be obtained by sampling an analog signal – e.g. a voice waveform, seismic signal, etc.). In the same way, if we sample a two-dimensional picture x (photograph, radio map, etc.) in two directions we obtain a two-dimensional array $\{x(n_1, n_2)\}$, n_1, $n_2 \in \mathbb{Z}$. Of course, as in the one-dimensional case, we can consider abstract arrays which have not been obtained by sampling a 'real' analog picture. Thus, a *two-dimensional signal* is just a function $x : \mathbb{Z} \times \mathbb{Z} \to \mathbb{C}$.[1]

We may mention two special signals: (i) the *unit impulse* u_0 in two dimensions is defined by

$$u_0(n_1, n_2) = \begin{cases} 1 & \text{if } n_1 = n_2 = 0 \\ 0 & \text{otherwise} \end{cases}$$

and (ii) the *discrete complex sinusoid* (with frequencies ω_1, ω_2 and sampling rates T_1, T_2) is defined by

$$f(n_1, n_2) = e^{jn_1\omega_1 T_1} e^{jn_2\omega_2 T_2}$$

Again, as in the one-dimensional case, these special signals are important in the convolution and frequency response properties of linear two-dimensional systems.

8.3 Discrete systems

A two-dimensional discrete system is a function (or algorithm)

$$\phi : \mathbb{Z} \times \mathbb{Z} \to \mathbb{Z} \times \mathbb{Z}$$

i.e. to each input array $x = \{x(n_1, n_2)\}$, ϕ associates an output array $y = \{y(n_1, n_2)\}$ such that

$$y(n_1, n_2) = (\phi(x))(n_1, n_2)$$

for each n_1, $n_2 \in Z$. As in the one-dimensional case this is written in terms of arrays as

$$y = \phi(x)$$

Define the *delayed signal* $x^{(k_1, k_2)}$ by

$$x^{(k_1, k_2)}(n_1, n_2) = x(n_1 - k_1, n_2 - k_2)$$

[1]$\mathbb{Z} \times \mathbb{Z}$ is the Cartesian product of $\mathbb{Z}$ with itself – see Appendix 1.

Then the system ϕ is *shift-invariant* if

$$y = \phi(x) \Rightarrow y^{(k_1, k_2)} = \phi(x^{(k_1, k_2)})$$

for all $k_1, k_2 \in Z$. As in the one-dimensional case, we say that ϕ is *linear* if

$$\phi(\alpha x_1 + \beta x_2) = \alpha \phi(x_1) + \beta \phi(x_2)$$

for any arrays x_1, x_2.

If ϕ is a linear, shift-invariant system we define its *impulse response h* by

$$h = \phi(u_0)$$

Following the reasoning in Chapter 1, it is easy to prove that, for any input array x, the output array y is given by

$$y(n_1, n_2) = \sum_{k_1=-\infty}^{\infty} \sum_{k_2=-\infty}^{\infty} x(k_1, k_2) h(n_1 - k_1, n_2 - k_2)$$

$$= \sum_{k_1=-\infty}^{\infty} \sum_{k_2=-\infty}^{\infty} x(n_1 - k_1, n_2 - k_2) h(k_1, k_2) \qquad (8.3.1)$$

8.4 Frequency response

A discrete sinusoidal input to a system is defined by

$$x(n_1, n_2) = e^{jn_1\omega_1} e^{jn_2\omega_2}$$

and by (8.3.1) the output from a linear, shift-invariant system with such an input is given by

$$y(n_1, n_2) = \sum_{k_1=-\infty}^{\infty} \sum_{k_2=-\infty}^{\infty} h(k_1, k_2) e^{j(n_1-k_1)\omega_1} e^{j(n_2-k_2)\omega_2}$$

i.e.

$$y = x H(e^{j\omega_1}, e^{j\omega_2}) \qquad (8.4.1)$$

where

$$H(e^{j\omega_1}, e^{j\omega_2}) = \sum_{k_1=-\infty}^{\infty} \sum_{k_2=-\infty}^{\infty} h(k_1, k_2) e^{-jk_1\omega_1} e^{-jk_2\omega_2} \qquad (8.4.2)$$

Note that if h is separable in the sense that

$$h(n_1, n_2) = h_1(n_1) h_2(n_2)$$

then it follows from (8.4.2) that

$$H(e^{j\omega_1}, e^{j\omega_2}) = H_1(e^{j\omega_1}) H_2(e^{j\omega_2})$$

i.e. H is the product of the frequency responses of the one-dimensional systems $\{h_1\}$, $\{h_2\}$.

As in the one-dimensional case, H has a number of periodicity and symmetry properties. H is periodic in ω_1 and ω_2 with period 2π; thus,

$$H(e^{j(\omega_1+2k_1\pi)}, e^{j(\omega_2+2k_2\pi)}) = H(e^{j\omega_1}, e^{j\omega_2}) \tag{8.4.3}$$

Hence H is determined by its values in the square

$$S = \{(\omega_1, \omega_2) \in \mathbb{R}^2 : -\pi \leqslant \omega_1 \leqslant \pi, -\pi \leqslant \omega_2 \leqslant \pi\}$$

Secondly, if $h(n_1, n_2)$ is real for each $n_1, n_2 \in \mathbb{Z}$, then

$$H(e^{j\omega_1}, e^{j\omega_2}) = H^*(e^{-j\omega_1}, e^{-j\omega_2})$$

and H is determined by its values in the set

$$S_+ = \{(\omega_1, \omega_2) \in \mathbb{R}^2 : (\omega_1, \omega_2) \in S, \omega_1 \geqslant 0, \omega_2 \geqslant 0\}$$

8.5 The sampling theorem and signal reconstruction

As in the one-dimensional case, a two-dimensional analog signal $x(t_1, t_2)$ may be bandlimited in the sense that

$$|X_e(j\Omega_1, j\Omega_2)| = 0 \text{ if } |\Omega_1| > \omega_{c1} \text{ or } |\Omega_2| > \omega_{c2}$$

for some cutoff frequencies ω_{c1}, ω_{c2}, where X_e is the joint Fourier transform of x given by

$$X_e(j\Omega_1, j\Omega_2) = \int_{-\infty}^{\infty} \int_{-\infty}^{\infty} x(t_1, t_2)e^{-j\Omega_1 t_1}e^{-j\Omega_2 t_2}dt_1 dt_2$$

Then we have the two-dimensional sampling theorem:

If the function $x(t_1, t_2)$ is bandlimited by ω_{c1} and ω_{c2}, then x is uniquely determined by its sampled values $x(n_1 T_1, n_2 T_2)$ $(-\infty < n_1, n_2 < \infty)$ for sampling times T_1, T_2, provided that

$$T_1 \leqslant \pi/\omega_{c1}, \quad T_2 \leqslant \pi/\omega_{c2} \tag{8.5.1}$$

This follows from the relation

$$X(e^{j\omega_1 T_1}, e^{j\omega_2 T_2}) = \frac{1}{T_1}\frac{1}{T_2}\sum_{n_1=-\infty}^{\infty}\sum_{n_2=-\infty}^{\infty} X_e(j\omega_1 - jn_1\omega_{s1}, j\omega_2 - jn_2\omega_{s2}) \tag{8.5.2}$$

which is proved in the same way as the corresponding one-dimensional result. Here

$$\omega_{s1} = \frac{2\pi}{T_1}, \quad \omega_{s2} = \frac{2\pi}{T_2}$$

The reconstruction of $x(t_1, t_2)$ from its samples $x(n_1T_1, n_2T_2)$ can be achieved in the following way:

$$x(t_1, t_2) = \frac{1}{4\pi^2} \int_{-\infty}^{\infty} \int_{-\infty}^{\infty} X_e(j\Omega_1, j\Omega_2) e^{j\Omega_1 t_1} e^{j\Omega_2 t_2} d\Omega_1 d\Omega_2$$

$$= \frac{T^2}{4\pi^2} \int_{-\omega_{s1}/2}^{\omega_{s1}/2} \int_{-\omega_{s2}/2}^{\omega_{s2}/2} X(e^{j\omega_1 t_1}, e^{j\omega_2 t_2}) e^{j\omega_1 t_1} e^{j\omega_2 t_2} d\omega_1 d\omega_2$$

(by (8.5.1) and (8.5.2))

$$= \frac{T^2}{4\pi^2} \int_{-\omega_{s1}/2}^{\omega_{s1}/2} \int_{-\omega_{s2}/2}^{\omega_{s2}/2} \left(\sum_{k_1=-\infty}^{\infty} \sum_{k_2=-\infty}^{\infty} x(k_1T_1, k_2T_2) e^{-j\omega_1 k_1 T_1} e^{-j\omega_2 k_2 T_2} \right) \cdot e^{j\omega_1 t_1} e^{j\omega_2 t_2} d\omega_1 d\omega_2$$

$$= \frac{T^2}{4\pi^2} \sum_{k_1=-\infty}^{\infty} \sum_{k_2=-\infty}^{\infty} x(k_1T_1, k_2T_2) \int_{-\omega_{s1}/2}^{\omega_{s1}/2} \int_{-\omega_{s2}/2}^{\omega_{s2}/2} e^{j(t_1-k_1T_1)\omega_1} e^{j(t_2-k_2T_2)\omega_2} d\omega_1 d\omega_2$$

$$= \sum_{k_1=-\infty}^{\infty} \sum_{k_2=-\infty}^{\infty} x(k_1T_1, k_2T_2) \operatorname{sinc}(\omega_{s1}(t_1 - k_1T_1)/2) \operatorname{sinc}(\omega_{s2}(t_2 - k_2T_2)/2)$$

This is seen to be a simple extension of the one-dimensional argument.

8.6 The Z-transform and general linear systems

The definition of the two-dimensional (two-sided) Z-transform is a simple generalization of the one-dimensional case. In fact, if $\{x(n_1, n_2)\}$ is a two-dimensional signal, we define

$$X(z_1, z_2) = Z(x) = \sum_{n_1=-\infty}^{\infty} \sum_{n_2=-\infty}^{\infty} x(n_1, n_2) z_1^{-n_1} z_2^{-n_2}$$

for all complex variables z_1, z_2 for which the right-hand side is absolutely convergent.

Elementary properties of the Z-transform can be proved in a similar way to the one-dimensional case (cf. Section 1.7). Therefore we shall simply give these properties without proof:

(a) LINEARITY

$$Z(ax_1 + bx_2) = aZ(x_1) + bZ(x_2) \qquad a, b \in \mathbb{C}$$

(b) TRANSLATION

$$Z(x(n_1 + m_1, n_2 + m_2)) = z_1^{m_1} z_2^{m_2} Z(x)$$

(c) COMPLEX SCALE CHANGE

$$Z(c_1^{-n_1}c_2^{-n_2}x(n_1, n_2)) = X(c_1z_1, c_2z_2)$$

(d) COMPLEX DIFFERENTIATION

$$Z(n_1n_2x(n_1, n_2)) = z_1z_2\frac{d^2X(z_1, z_2)}{dz_1dz_2}$$

(e) REAL CONVOLUTION

$$Z(x_1*x_2) = X_1(z_1, z_2)X_2(z_1, z_2)$$

(f) INVERSE TRANSFORMATION

$$x(n_1, n_2) = \left(\frac{1}{2\pi j}\right)^2 \oint_{\Gamma_1} \oint_{\Gamma_2} X(z_1, z_2)z_1^{n_1-1}z_2^{n_2-1}dz_1dz_2$$

(g) PRODUCT

$$(xy)(n_1, n_2) = \left(\frac{1}{2\pi j}\right)^2 \oint_{\Gamma_1} \oint_{\Gamma_2} X\left(\frac{z_1}{v_1}, \frac{z_2}{v_2}\right)Y(v_1, v_2)v_1^{-1}v_2^{-1}dv_1dv_2$$

(Γ_1, Γ_2 are closed contours containing $z_1 = 0$, $z_2 = 0$ respectively.)

As in the one-dimensional case a two-dimensional linear, shift-invariant system (with rational transfer function) can be written in the form of a two-dimensional difference equation:

$$\sum_{n_1=P_1}^{M_1-1} \sum_{n_2=P_2}^{M_2-1} a_{n_1n_2}x(k_1 - n_1, k_2 - n_2) = \sum_{n_1=Q_1}^{N_1-1} \sum_{n_2=Q_2}^{N_2-1} b_{n_1n_2}y(k_1 - n_1, k_2 - n_2) \quad (8.6.1)$$

where x is the input signal, y is the output signal and $a_{n_1n_2}$, $b_{n_1n_2}$ are the system coefficients.

Taking the two-sided Z-transform of equation (8.6.1) gives the transfer function

$$H(z_1, z_2) = \frac{\sum_{n_1=P_1}^{M_1-1}\sum_{n_2=P_2}^{M_2-1} a_{n_1n_2}z_1^{-n_1}z_2^{-n_2}}{\sum_{n_1=Q_1}^{N_1-1}\sum_{n_2=Q_2}^{N_2-1} b_{n_1n_2}z_1^{-n_1}z_2^{-n_2}} \quad (8.6.2)$$

If we set $b_{00} = 1$ and $b_{n_1n_2} = 0$ if $n_1 \neq 0$ or $n_2 \neq 0$, then (8.6.1) becomes

$$y(k_1, k_2) = \sum_{n_1=P_1}^{M_1-1} \sum_{n_2=P_2}^{M_2-1} a_{n_1n_2}x(k_1 - n_1, k_2 - n_2) \quad (8.6.3)$$

and we have a nonrecursive system which defines an FIR filter, just as in the one-dimensional case. The transfer function of this system is

$$H(z_1, z_2) = \sum_{n_1=P_1}^{M_1-1} \sum_{n_2=P_2}^{M_2-1} a_{n_1n_2}z_1^{-n_1}z_2^{-n_2}$$

8.7 *Causality*

In one-dimensional filtering theory we have defined causality of a system in terms of the dependence of its output on the input at future times. Since in two-dimensional systems we are thinking mainly about 'pictures', past and future have no meaning. However, extending the one-dimensional definition in an obvious way we say that the system (8.6.1) is *causal* or a *first-quadrant filter* if

$$b_{n_1 n_2} = 0 \qquad n_1 < 0 \text{ or } n_2 < 0$$

$$a_{n_1 n_2} = 0 \qquad n_1 < 0 \text{ or } n_2 < 0$$

(i.e. a and b are nonzero only in the positive quadrant $\{(n_1, n_2) : n_1 \geqslant 0, n_2 \geqslant 0\}$). The signals x and y should satisfy the initial conditions

$$x(n_1, n_2) = 0 \qquad n_1 < 0 \text{ or } n_2 < 0$$

$$y(n_1, n_2) = 0 \qquad n_1 < 0 \text{ or } n_2 < 0$$

In this case, equation (8.6.1) can be written in the form

$y(k_1, k_2)$

$$= \sum_{n_1=0}^{M_1-1} \sum_{n_2=0}^{M_2-1} a_{n_1 n_2} x(k_1 - n_1, k_2 - n_2) - \sum_{n_1=0}^{N_1-1} \sum_{\substack{n_2=0 \\ n_1+n_2 \neq 0}}^{N_2-1} b_{n_1 n_2} y(k_1 - n_1, k_2 - n_2)$$

where we have set $b_{00} = 1$. If a and b are nonzero in the quadrants

(i) $n_1 \geqslant 0, n_2 \leqslant 0;$
(ii) $n_1 \leqslant 0, n_2 \leqslant 0;$
(iii) $n_1 \leqslant 0, n_2 \geqslant 0;$

then we obtain second-, third- and fourth-quadrant (or *nonrecursive*) filters respectively.

Another possible recursive filter structure can be obtained if a and b are nonzero in the regions

$$a_{n_1 n_2} = 0 \text{ if } (n_1, n_2) \notin \{(n_1, n_2) : 0 \leqslant n_1 \leqslant M_1 - 1, 0 \leqslant n_2 \leqslant M_2 - 1\}$$

$$b_{n_1 n_2} = 0 \text{ if } (n_1, n_2) \notin \{(n_1, n_2) : 1 \leqslant n_1 \leqslant N_1 - 1, -(N_2 - 1) \leqslant n_2 \leqslant N_2 - 1,$$

$$\text{or } n_1 = 0, 0 \leqslant n_2 \leqslant N_2 - 1\}$$

Then (again setting $b_{00} = 1$) the system (8.6.1) can be written as the *half-plane* filter

$$y(k_1, k_2) = \sum_{n_1=0}^{M_1-1} \sum_{n_2=0}^{M_2-1} a_{n_1 n_2} x(k_1 - n_1, k_2 - n_2)$$

$$- \sum_{n_1=1}^{N_1-1} \sum_{n_2=-(N_2-1)}^{N_2-1} b_{n_1 n_2} y(k_1 - n_1, k_2 - n_2) - \sum_{n_2=1}^{N_2-1} b_{0 n_2} y(k_1, k_2 - n_2)$$

$$(8.7.1)$$

y can be calculated recursively by column-wise processing.

Bibliographical notes

Most of the material of this chapter is a straightforward extension of the corresponding one-dimensional ideas. Further information on the structure of two-dimensional systems can be found in Mersereau and Duggeon (1975), Pistor (1974) and Shanks *et al.* (1972).

Exercises

1 Derive the two-dimensional convolution (8.3.1) in detail.
2 Prove directly the symmetry properties of the frequency response function $H(e^{j\omega_1}, e^{j\omega_2})$ stated in Section 8.4.
3 How fast must one sample the two-dimensional signal

$$x(t_1, t_2) = \sin(\omega_1 t_1) \sin(\omega_2 t_2)$$

to avoid aliasing?
4 Prove the properties of the Z-transform stated in Section 8.6.
5 Discuss the recursive implementation of the half-plane filter (8.7.1).

References

Mersereau, R. M. and D. E. Duggeon (1975), 'Two-dimensional digital filtering', *Proc. IEEE*, **63**(4), 610–23.
Pistor, P. (1974), 'Stability criterion for recursive filters', *IBM J. Res. Dev.*, **18** (1), 59–71.
Shanks, J. L., S. Treitel and J. H. Justice (1972), 'Stability and synthesis of two-dimensional recursive filters', *IEEE Trans. Audio Electroacoust.*, AU-**20**(2), 115–28.

9

Stability of Two-Dimensional Systems

9.1 Introduction
9.2 Basic Stability Theory
9.3 Stability Conditions via the Cepstrum
9.4 The Planar Least Squares Inverse and Stabilization
Bibliographical Notes
Exercises
References

9.1 Introduction

In this chapter we shall study the important property of stability of two-dimensional filters, which is, of course, a basic requirement of a practical realizable filter. Unlike the one-dimensional case, however, where stability is related to the poles of the filter in a simple way, we shall see that the stability of two-dimensional systems is a much more delicate idea. This is mainly due to the fact that the zeros of a two-dimensional polynomial are not isolated points in a complex plane, but form one-dimensional (in the complex sense) subvarieties of two-dimensional complex space. The separation of the irreducible components of such a polynomial is not a simple matter and so the numerical determination of the zeros of the polynomial is very involved. Nevertheless, we shall see a number of stability theorems which, to some extent, will alleviate this problem.

In Section 9.2 the Shanks and Huang stability theorems will be proved, generalizing the one-dimensional stability theory. The connection between the complex cepstrum and stability will be investigated in Section 9.3 and, finally, in

Section 9.4 we shall discuss the planar least squares inverse approximation to a filter and its application to stabilization of an unstable filter.

The mathematical background for this chapter consists of some simple two-dimensional complex variable theory, the basic ideas of which are given in Appendix 1.

9.2 Basic stability theory

We start with the two-dimensional version of the result in Chapter 1 which states that a filter is stable if and only if the impulse response sequence is absolutely summable. The proof is similar to the one-dimensional case and so we shall merely state the result as follows:

THEOREM 1
In order that a discrete two-dimensional filter with impulse response $h(n_1, n_2)$ be stable it is necessary and sufficient that

$$\sum_{n_1=-\infty}^{\infty} \sum_{n_2=-\infty}^{\infty} |h(n_1, n_2)| < \infty$$

The next theorem links Theorem 1 with the positions of the poles and zeros of the denominator of the transfer function $H(z_1, z_2)$ and can be stated in the following form:

THEOREM 2
A causal recursive filter with Z-transform

$$H(z_1, z_2) = P(z_1^{-1}, z_2^{-1})/Q(z_1^{-1}, z_2^{-1})$$

for which $Q(z_1^{-1}, z_2^{-1}) \neq 0$ if $P(z_1^{-1}, z_2^{-1}) = 0$ when $|z_1| = 1$, $|z_2| = 1$, is stable if and only if there are no zeros of Q in the region

$$D = \{(z_1, z_2): |z_1| \geq 1, |z_2| \geq 1\}$$

i.e.

$$Q(z_1^{-1}, z_2^{-1}) \neq 0 \qquad \text{for } (z_1, z_2) \in D$$

Proof Writing

$$H(z_1, z_2) = \sum_{n_1=0}^{\infty} \sum_{n_2=0}^{\infty} h(n_1, n_2)z_1^{-n_1}z_2^{-n_2}$$

we must show that

$$\sum_{n_1=0}^{\infty} \sum_{n_2=0}^{\infty} |h(n_1, n_2)| < \infty$$

if and only if $H(z_1, z_2)$ is analytic in D, by Theorem 1. To prove the 'if' part, note that if H is analytic in D, then there exists $\varepsilon > 0$ such that H is also analytic in

$$D_\varepsilon = \{(z_1, z_2) : |z_1| > 1 - \varepsilon, |z_2| > 1 - \varepsilon\}$$

(since D is closed) and so the series

$$\sum_{n_1=0}^{\infty} \sum_{n_2=0}^{\infty} h(n_1, n_2) z_1^{-n_1} z_2^{-n_2}$$

is absolutely convergent on D_ε from which the desired conclusion follows by taking $z_1 = z_2 = 1$.

For the 'only if' part we have

$$\sum_{n_1=0}^{\infty} \sum_{n_2=0}^{\infty} |h(n_1, n_2)| < \infty$$

by assumption, and so $\sum_{n_1=0}^{\infty} \sum_{n_2=0}^{\infty} h(n_1, n_2) z_1^{-n_1} z_2^{-n_2}$ is absolutely convergent on D; i.e. H is analytic on D.

The condition that $P(z_1^{-1}, z_2^{-1}) = 0 \Rightarrow Q(z_1^{-1}, z_2^{-1}) \neq 0$ for $|z_1| = 1$, $|z_2| = 1$ is described by saying that H has no *nonessential singularities of the second kind* on the set $T = \{(z_1, z_2) : |z_1| = |z_2| = 1\}$. If $P(z_1^{-1}, z_2^{-1}) = Q(z_1^{-1}, z_2^{-1}) = 0$ at some point $(z_1, z_2) \in T$, then the necessity of Theorem 2 does not hold. In fact, it can be shown that the system

$$H_1(z_1, z_2) = \frac{(1 - z_1^{-1})^8 (1 - z_2^{-1})^8}{2 - z_1^{-1} - z_2^{-1}} \tag{9.2.1}$$

is stable, while the system

$$H_2(z_1, z_2) = \frac{(1 - z_1^{-1})(1 - z_2^{-1})}{2 - z_1^{-1} - z_2^{-1}} \tag{9.2.2}$$

is unstable.

The main drawback with the application of Theorem 2 is that, as we have seen above, the separation of the zeros of a two-dimensional polynomial is not generally soluble in a closed form and requires an infinite amount of computation since we could fix z_2, say $z_2 = \bar{z}_2$, and find the roots of the one-dimensional polynomial $Q(z_1^{-1}, \bar{z}_2^{-1})$. This must be done for each $\bar{z}_2 \in \mathbb{C}$. Consider first the polynomials $Q(z_1^{-1}, \bar{z}_2^{-1})$ where $|\bar{z}_2| = 1$, and let $z_1^1, \ldots, z_1^n$ be the roots of $Q(z_1^{-1}, \bar{z}_2^{-1})$.[1] Then $z_1^1, \ldots, z_1^n$ trace out (generally intersecting) closed paths in the z_1-plane as $\bar{z}_2$ is varied around the unit circle. We can repeat this procedure for a number of other values of $\bar{z}_2$ with $|\bar{z}_2| > 1$ and we will thus map the exterior of the unit circle in the z_2-plane into a topological disk in the z_1-plane (shown as a shaded region in Figures 9.1 and 9.2 – in the latter case the region is not connected). For stability, this region should not intersect the exterior of the unit circle in the z_1-plane.

[1] Note that n is constant on each contour except, possibly, from a finite number of points.

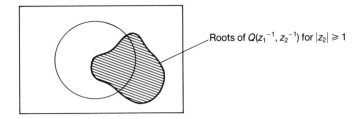

Figure 9.1   Zero map for an unstable filter.

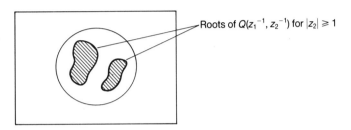

Figure 9.2   Zero map for a stable filter.

In fact, it turns out that we need not consider the roots of $Q(z_1^{-1}, z_2^{-1})$ for all $|z_2| \geq 1$, but only for $|z_2| = 1$. The result can be stated as

THEOREM 3
A causal filter satisfying the conditions of Theorem 2 is stable if and only if

(a) the map of $\partial D_2 = \{z_2 : |z_2| = 1\}$ in the z_1-plane as specified above lies outside $D_1 = \{z_1 : |z_1| \geq 1\}$;
(b) no point of $D_2 = \{z_2 : |z_2| \geq 1\}$ maps to $z_1 = \infty$.

This theorem can be proved by a simple application of the maximum modulus theorem of complex analysis. (Note that the result is true with z_1 replacing z_2 by symmetry.)

As an example, consider the filter

$$H(z_1, z_2) = \frac{1}{1 + az_1^{-1} + bz_2^{-1} + cz_1^{-1}z_2^{-1}}$$

Then

$$Q(z_1^{-1}, z_2^{-1}) = 1 + az_1^{-1} + bz_2^{-1} + cz_1^{-1}z_2^{-1}$$

and so

$$Q = 0 \text{ when } z_2^{-1} = -\frac{1 + az_1^{-1}}{b + cz_1^{-1}}$$

This is a bilinear transformation which maps circles into circles and so the image of ∂D_1 is a circle in the z_2 plane. It follows that condition (a) of Theorem 3 holds if

$$\left| \frac{1-a}{b-c} \right| > 1 \text{ and } \left| \frac{1+a}{b+c} \right| > 1$$

Condition (b) holds if $|a| < 1$.

9.3 Stability conditions via the cepstrum

In the case of one-dimensional filter design we have seen that a continuous-time recursive filter is often specified by its squared amplitude response $|G(j\omega)|^2$. From this we require to find the filter $G(s)$ in the Laplace domain which has the desired frequency response. Determining $G(s)$ from $|G(j\omega)|^2$ is usually achieved by using Wiener–Levy spectral factorization. This consists of finding the poles of $H(s) = |G(j\omega)|^2|_{j\omega=s}$ (generally $2n$ in number) and then assigning the left half-plane poles to $G(s)$. The resulting filter $G(s)$ is stable (realizable) and has the desired amplitude response.

A similar method can be used for one-dimensional discrete recursive filters. However, when we consider two-dimensional filters, this method cannot be applied because there is no fundamental theorem of algebra for two-dimensional polynomials and so we cannot separate the 'poles' of the system. In the two-dimensional case we must therefore seek another way of separating an unstable filter into causal and noncausal parts. This is provided by the cepstrum, which we will define and will then study some of its properties.

Let $b(n_1, n_2)$ be a two-dimensional signal and define its frequency spectrum as usual by

$$B(u_1, u_2) = \sum_{n_1=-\infty}^{\infty} \sum_{n_2=-\infty}^{\infty} b(n_1, n_2) e^{-j2\pi u_1 n_1} e^{-j2\pi u_2 n_2}$$
$$= B(z_1, z_2)|_{z_1=e^{j2\pi u_1}, z_2=e^{j2\pi u_2}} \tag{9.3.1}$$

The *cepstrum* $\hat{b}$ of b is defined by

$$\hat{b} = Z^{-1} \ln Z\{b\} \tag{9.3.2}$$

whenever the right-hand side exists. Thus,

$$\hat{b} = Z^{-1} \ln (B(z_1, z_2))$$

or

$$\hat{B}(z_1, z_2) = \ln (B(z_1, z_2)) \tag{9.3.3}$$

where

$$\hat{B} = Z\{\hat{b}\}$$

We shall write $\hat{b} = \mathcal{K}(b)$.

Recall that the inverse Z-transform is given by

$$\hat{b}(n_1, n_2) = \left(\frac{1}{2\pi j}\right)^2 \oint_{\Gamma_1} \oint_{\Gamma_2} \ln B(z_1, z_2) z_1^{n_1-1} z_2^{n_2-1} dz_1 dz_2$$

where we may take Γ_i to be the unit circle in the z_i-plane ($i = 1, 2$). Thus,

$$\hat{b}(n_1, n_2) = \int_0^1 \int_0^1 (\ln B(u_1, u_2)) e^{2\pi j n_1 u_1} e^{2\pi j n_2 u_2} du_1 du_2$$

Hence, $\hat{b}$ is the (two-dimensional) Fourier series of $\ln B(e^{j\theta_1}, e^{j\theta_2})$ and $B(e^{j\theta_1}, e^{j\theta_2})$ is the inverse Fourier transform of b. We can therefore write

$$\hat{b} = \mathcal{K}(b) = \mathcal{F} \ln \mathcal{F}^{-1}$$

where $\mathcal{F}$ is the operation of taking the Fourier series. Also, we have

$$b = \mathcal{K}^{-1}(\hat{b}) = \mathcal{F}^{-1} \exp \mathcal{F}$$

The basic theorem of Wiener–Levy for the one-dimensional case provides conditions under which $\mathcal{K}(b)$ exists. Before proving the two-dimensional version of this result, we first give the following definition.

DEFINITION
A two-dimensional sequence $\{x(n_1, n_2)\}$ is said to be l^1 (or *absolutely summable*) if

$$\sum_{n_1=-\infty}^{\infty} \sum_{n_2=-\infty}^{\infty} |x(n_1, n_2)| < \infty$$

The theorem can now be stated in the form:

THEOREM
If $b \in l^1$ and its transform $B(u_1, u_2)$, given by (9.3.1), is continuous and positive, then $\hat{b} = \mathcal{K}(b)$ exists and $\hat{b} \in l^1$.

Proof   We must show that if $B(u_1, u_2) > 0$ has an absolutely convergent Fourier series $b(n_1, n_2)$, then $\ln B(u_1, u_2)$ also has an absolutely convergent Fourier series. We have

$$B(u_1, u_2) = \sum_{n_1=-\infty}^{\infty} \sum_{n_2=-\infty}^{\infty} b(n_1, n_2) \exp\{-2\pi j(n_1 u_1 + n_2 u_2)\}$$

By assumption,

$$\|b\| \triangleq \sum_{n_1, n_2} |b(n_1, n_2)| < \infty$$

Since $\|b\| > 0$ we can expand $\ln(x)$ in a Taylor series about $x = \|b\|$; i.e.

$$\ln(x) = \sum_{k=0}^{\infty} \alpha_k (x - \|b\|)^k \qquad 0 < x \leqslant 2\|b\|$$

for some numbers α_k. Since $B(u_1, u_2) > 0$ we have

$$\ln(B(u_1, u_2)) = \sum_{k=0}^{\infty} \alpha_k(B(u_1, u_2) - \|b\|)^k$$

$$\leqslant \sum_{k=0}^{\infty} |\alpha_k| \|b\|^k < \infty$$

independently of u_1, u_2. The result now follows.

Having obtained conditions on b for the existence of $\mathcal{K}(b)$ we can now apply the cepstrum to the problem of spectral factorization. The method consists, basically, of writing b in the form

$$\hat{b} = \hat{b}_1 + \hat{b}_2 + \hat{b}_3 + \hat{b}_4 \qquad (9.3.4)$$

where $\hat{b}_i$ is a one-quadrant function, i.e.

$$\hat{b}_i(n_1, n_2) \neq 0 \text{ only on } Q_i$$

where

$$Q_1 = \{(n_1, n_2) : n_1 \geqslant 0, n_2 \geqslant 0\}$$
$$Q_2 = \{(n_1, n_2) : n_1 \geqslant 0, n_2 \leqslant 0\}$$
$$Q_3 = \{(n_1, n_2) : n_1 \leqslant 0, n_2 \leqslant 0\}$$
$$Q_4 = \{(n_1, n_2) : n_1 \leqslant 0, n_2 \geqslant 0\}$$

(see Figure 9.3). If we can show that each $b_i = \mathcal{K}^{-1}(\hat{b}_i)$ is recursively computable and stable then we will have

$$b = \mathcal{K}^{-1}(\hat{b}_1 + \hat{b}_2 + \hat{b}_3 + \hat{b}_4)$$
$$= \mathcal{K}^{-1}(\hat{b}_1) * \mathcal{K}^{-1}(\hat{b}_2) * \mathcal{K}^{-1}(\hat{b}_3) * \mathcal{K}^{-1}(\hat{b}_4)$$
$$= b_1 * b_2 * b_3 * b_4 \qquad (9.3.5)$$

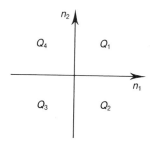

Figure 9.3   The   four-quadrant   in (n_1, n_2)-space.

since $\mathcal{K}^{-1}$ maps sums to convolutions. This is easily seen as follows:

$$\mathcal{K}^{-1}(\hat{c} + \hat{d}) = Z^{-1} \exp Z(\hat{c} + \hat{d})$$
$$= Z^{-1} \exp(\hat{C} + \hat{D})$$
$$= Z^{-1} \exp(\log \hat{C} + \log \hat{D})$$
$$= Z^{-1}(CD)$$
$$= c * d.$$

The expression (9.3.5) is then the desired factorization of b. We can always write $\hat{b}$ in the form (9.3.4), although the expression is not unique. Moreover, if $\hat{b}$ is in l^1 then it is easy to choose this representation of $\hat{b}$ so that each $\hat{b}_i$ is stable, $1 \leqslant i \leqslant 4$. It is therefore only necessary to prove the following theorem.

THEOREM
1. If we write any $\hat{b} \in l^1$ in the form (9.3.4) where each $\hat{b}_i$ is in l^1 and is nonzero in Q_i, then $b_i = \mathcal{K}^{-1}(\hat{b}_i)$ is also nonzero only in the sector Q_i.

2. If $\hat{b}_i \in l^1$ and $\hat{b}_i$ is nonzero in Q_i, then $b_i = \mathcal{K}^{-1}(\hat{b}_i)$ is recursively computable and the system $1/B_i(z_1, z_2)$ is stable.

Proof
1. Since $\hat{b}_i \in l^1$ for each i, $b_i = \mathcal{K}^{-1}(\hat{b}_i)$ exists. It is easy to check that if the two-dimensional sequences $c(n_1, n_2)$ and $d(n_1, n_2)$ are nonzero only in Q_i, then so is their convolution $(c * d)(n_1, n_2)$. To prove that $b_i = \mathcal{K}^{-1}(\hat{b}_i)$ is nonzero only in Q_i we write

$$B_i = \exp(\hat{B}_i)$$

(by (9.3.3))

$$= \sum_{k=0}^{\infty} (\hat{B}_i)^k / k!$$

and so

$$b_i = \sum_{k=0}^{\infty} (\hat{b}_i * \ldots * \hat{b}_i)/k! \tag{9.3.6}$$

where the term in parentheses represents a k-term convolution of $\hat{b}_i$. (We can evaluate the Fourier transform of B_i term by term since the series of exp converges absolutely.) By the above remark each term in the series (9.3.6) is nonzero only in Q_i and so the first part of the theorem is proved.

2. Since each b_i is nonzero only in Q_i by part (a), the system represented by b_i is recursively computable. To prove stability of the system $1/B_i(z_1, z_2)$ note that $\hat{b}_i \in l^1$ so that $\hat{B}_i$ is analytic in a region which includes the set

$$T^2 \triangleq \{(z_1, z_2): |z_1| = 1, |z_2| = 1\}$$

Hence $B_i = \exp \hat{B}_i$ has no zeros in this region and so $b_i = \mathcal{K}^{-1}(\hat{b}_i)$ is in l^1. The result now follows.

Note that we can apply this result to the filter

$$H(z_1, z_2) = \frac{A(z_1, z_2)}{B(z_1, z_2)}$$

by writing $B = B_1 B_2 B_3 B_4$. Then H can be written in the form

$$H(z_1, z_2) = (((A(z_1, z_2)/B_1(z_1, z_2))/B_2(z_1, z_2))/B_3(z_1, z_2))/B_4(z_1, z_2)$$

which can be implemented in a recursively computable and stable manner. One drawback with this method is that the sequences $\{b_i(n_1, n_2)\}$ may have infinitely many nonzero terms. It is not difficult to prove, however, that one may truncate these sequences and obtain an arbitrarily good approximation to H.

In order to derive a simple stability test we require the extension of the above definition of the cepstrum to complex functions. This will be done first in the one-dimensional case and then we shall indicate the necessary changes for two-dimensional systems. The basic problem which arises in attempting to define the complex logarithm is that the resulting function is multivalued. One way around this is to take the principal value of this function as the required logarithm. However, this function does not have the usual sum property of logarithms:

$$\log(z_1 z_2) \neq \log(z_1) + \log(z_2)$$

in general if principal values are taken. The ambiguity in the general complex logarithm comes from an arbitrary integer multiple of $2\pi j$ added to the logarithm. If $P(\omega)$ is a complex-valued function of a real variable ω, we can overcome this difficulty by defining $\log P(\omega)$ via an integral. Thus we may write

$$\log P(\omega) = \int_{\omega_0}^{\omega} \frac{1}{P(\omega)} \frac{\mathrm{d}P(\omega)}{\mathrm{d}\omega} \, \mathrm{d}\omega$$

for some fixed ω_0, provided P is differentiable and the integral exists. This specifies $\log P(\omega)$ uniquely (for a given ω_0) as a continuous function of ω. This now allows us to define the (one-dimensional) cepstrum of a signal $x(n)$ by

$$\hat{x}(n) = \frac{1}{2\pi j} \oint \log[X(z)] z^{n-1} \mathrm{d}z$$

$$= \frac{1}{2\pi} \int_{-\pi}^{\pi} \log[X(e^{j\omega})] e^{j\omega n} \mathrm{d}\omega$$

provided the Fourier transform $X(e^{j\omega})$ of $x(n)$ is nonzero and $\neq \infty$ for all ω.

The generalization of the complex cepstrum to two-dimensional systems can be defined in the following way. First consider an array $b = \{b(n_1, n_2)\}$ which is nonzero only for finitely many values of (n_1, n_2). The Fourier transform of b (from (9.3.1)) can be written

$$B(\mu_1, \mu_2) = \sum_{n_1=k_1}^{l_1} \sum_{n_2=k_2}^{l_2} b(n_1, n_2)e^{-j\mu_1 n_1}e^{-j\mu_2 n_2}$$

where k_1, k_2, l_1, l_2 define the *support* of b (i.e. the region where b is nonzero), and we have put $\mu_i = 2\pi u_i$, $i = 1, 2$. Put $z = e^{j\mu_2}$. We shall assume that $B(\mu_1, \mu_2) \neq 0$ for all μ_1, μ_2. Then

$$B_{\mu_1}(z_2) \triangleq \sum_{n_2}\left(\sum_{n_1} b(n_1, n_2)e^{-j\mu_1 n_1}\right)z_2^{-n_2}$$

B_{μ_1} has poles inside the unit circle only at $z_2 = 0$ (for each μ_1) and so we can define the 'phase' function of b by

$$\phi(\mu_1, \mu_2) = \mathrm{Im}\left\{\oint \frac{B'_{\mu_1}(z_2)}{B_{\mu_1}(z_2)}\, dz_2\right\} + \phi(\mu_1, 0)$$

where the phase $\phi(\mu_1, 0)$ can be defined as in the one-dimensional case from $B(\mu_1, 0)$. The contour of integration is the unit circle from $z_2 = 1$ to $z_2 = e^{j\mu_2}$. It is easily checked that ϕ is odd and continuous, so that

$$\phi(\mu_1, \mu_2) = -\phi(-\mu_1, -\mu_2)$$

By the residue theorem (see Appendix 1) we have, for $\mu_2 = 2\pi$,

$$\phi(\mu_1, 2\pi) = 2\pi k_1 + \phi(\mu_1, 0)$$

where $k_1 =$ (number of zeros $-$ number of poles) of $B_{\mu_1}(z_2)$ counted with multiplicity inside the unit circle. Clearly, k_1 is independent of μ_1 since $B(\mu_1, \mu_2) \neq 0$ and the roots of B_{μ_1} are continuous in μ_1. Thus,

$$\phi(\mu_1, \mu_2 + 2\pi) = \phi(\mu_1, \mu_2) + 2\pi k_1$$

Similarly,

$$\phi(\mu_1 + 2\pi, \mu_2) = \phi(\mu_1, \mu_2) + 2\pi k_2$$

for some k_2, independent of μ_2. Hence,

$$\bar{\phi}(\mu_1, \mu_2) \triangleq \phi(\mu_1, \mu_2) - k_1\mu_2 - k_2\mu_1$$

is continuous, odd and periodic. Subtracting the linear phase factor $k_1\mu_2 - k_2\mu_1$ is equivalent to translating the array b.

   The phase $\bar{\phi}$ of a finite extent array b as defined above can be extended to any array which has a ratio of polynomials for its Fourier transform by defining its phase as the difference between the phase of the numerator and that of the denominator. The resulting phase function is again continuous, odd and periodic. Thus, if $h(n_1, n_2)$ has a rational Fourier transform, then we can define its phase ϕ as before. The function $\bar{\phi}$ is then the phase of the bisequence

$$g(n_1, n_2) \triangleq h(n_1 - k_1, n_2 - k_2)$$

and so we can define the *cepstrum* of g by

$$Z^{-1}(\hat{G}(\mu_1, \mu_2)) = Z^{-1}(\ln|H(\mu_1, \mu_2)| + j\bar{\phi}(\mu_1, \mu_2))$$

We can now state a simple stability test:

THEOREM

A recursive half-plane filter $H(z_1, z_2)$ is stable if and only if its cepstrum $\hat{h}(n_1, n_2)$ has support in $\mathcal{H}$, where

$$\mathcal{H} = \{(n_1, n_2) : n_1 \geq 0, n_2 \geq 0\} \cup \{(n_1, n_2) : n_1 < 0, n_2 > 0\}$$

Proof This follows from the fact that the essential singularities of H and $\hat{H}$ are the same, so that these functions have the same regions of analyticity. Thus the coefficients in the respective power series expansions

$$H(z_1, z_2) = \sum \sum h(n_1, n_2) z_1^{-n_1} z_2^{-n_2}$$

$$\hat{H}(z_1, z_2) = \sum \sum \hat{h}(n_1, n_2) z_1^{-n_1} z_2^{-n_2}$$

must be nonzero only at the same values of (n_1, n_2). Thus

$$\text{support } h(n_1, n_2) \in \mathcal{H} \Leftrightarrow \text{support } \hat{h}(n_1, n_2) \in \mathcal{H}$$

The cepstrum $\hat{h}$ of h can be determined by using the discrete Fourier transform (DFT) rather than the z-transform, as in Figure 9.4. However, because of aliasing, this leads to an approximation $\hat{h}_a$ of $\hat{h}$. They are related by

$$\hat{h}_a(n_1, n_2) - \hat{h}(n_1, n_2) = \sum_{\substack{i=-\infty \\ i,j \neq (0,0)}}^{\infty} \sum_{j=-\infty}^{\infty} \hat{h}(n_1 + iP_1, n_2 + jP_2)$$

for a DFT of size $P_1 \times P_2$. Since the cepstrum usually decays rapidly, this gives a good approximation to $\hat{h}$.

Figure 9.4 Evaluating an approximation $\hat{h}_a$ to $\hat{h}$.

9.4 The planar least squares inverse and stabilization

In this section we shall describe a method for the stabilization of an unstable filter in which the stabilized filter is the best stable approximation to the given filter in an integral sense. The method is well known for one-dimensional filters and so we shall briefly describe this case first. Thus, let

$$H(z) = \frac{1}{b(z^{-1})}$$

by a one-dimensional recursive filter where $b(z^{-1})$ is a finite-order polynomial in z^{-1}. For any fixed $k > 0$ we wish to find a polynomial $a(z^{-1})$ of order k such that $a(z^{-1})$ has zeros inside the unit circle and $a(z^{-1}) \cong 1/b(z^{-1})$ in some sense. The obvious thing to do is to make $a(e^{-j\omega})b(e^{-j\omega})$ as close to 1 as possible in the mean square sense, i.e. to choose the coefficients of a so that the integral

$$E_1 = \frac{1}{2\pi} \int_{-\pi}^{\pi} |1 - a(e^{-j\omega})b(e^{-j\omega})|^2 d\omega \qquad (9.4.1)$$

is minimized. It can be shown that if a is chosen in this way it has zeros inside the unit circle. To obtain a stable approximation to H we repeat this procedure with a polynomial c such that the integral

$$E_2 = \frac{1}{2\pi} \int_{-\pi}^{\pi} |1 - c(e^{-j\omega})a(e^{-j\omega})|^2 d\omega \qquad (9.4.1)$$

is minimized by appropriate choice of the coefficients of c, where c is of some fixed-order k' (which may equal k). Since c also has zeros inside the unit circle, $H' = 1/c(z^{-1})$ is a stable filter. Moreover, since

$$a(z^{-1}) \cong 1/b(z^{-1}), \quad c(z^{-1}) \cong 1/a(z^{-1})$$

it follows that

$$1/c(z^{-1}) \cong 1/b(z^{-1})$$

and we have succeeded in obtaining a stable approximation to H.

For a two-dimensional filter $H(z_1, z_2) = 1/b(z_1^{-1}, z_2^{-1})$ we can generalize (9.4.1) to the integral objective function

$$E = \frac{1}{4\pi^2} \int_{-\pi}^{\pi} \int_{-\pi}^{\pi} |1 - a(e^{-j\omega_1}, e^{-j\omega_2})b(e^{-j\omega_1}, e^{-j\omega_2})|^2 d\omega_1 d\omega_2$$

where a and b are given by

$$a(z_1^{-1}, z_2^{-1}) = \sum_{n_1=0}^{N_1} \sum_{n_2=0}^{N_2} a_{n_1 n_2} z_1^{-n_1} z_2^{-n_2}$$

$$b(z_1^{-1}, z_2^{-1}) = \sum_{n_1=0}^{M_1} \sum_{n_2=0}^{M_2} b_{n_1 n_2} z_1^{-n_1} z_2^{-n_2}$$

Then, as before, we choose the coefficients $a_{n_1 n_2}$ to minimize E; the resulting polynomial a is called the *planar least square inverse* of b, and is denoted by b_I. It turns out, however, that a does not in general satisfy the conditions for stability imposed on Q in Theorem 2, so that a may have zeros in the region D.

Hence if we generalize the one-dimensional idea and try to approximate $1/b$ by $1/(b_I)_I$ the latter is not necessarily stable. However, in many cases $1/(b_I)_I$ does prove to be stable and so we have at least a tentative method of stabilization for an unstable filter. We form the double planar least square inverse of b and check to see if it is stable. A great many filters have been designed successfully by this method, but one should always be aware that the resulting filter may be unstable and so we would have to repeat the procedure with different values of N_1 and N_2. Of course, in the unlikely event that all such filters turn out to be unstable we must apply another technique.

Bibliographical notes

The basic stability results of Section 9.2 can be found in Huang (1972) and Shanks *et al.* (1972). The requirement of no nonessential singularities in Theorem 2 and the two examples given after its proof are considered in detail in Goodman (1977). Another stability test is described in Anderson and Jury by using the Schur–Cohn test. The theory of spectral factorization and the cepstrum and its application to stabilization of unstable filters is adapted from Dudgeon (1975), Ekstrom and Twogood 1977, Ekstrom and Woods (1976) and Pistor (1974). The conjecture that the planar least square inverse of an unstable polynomial is stable is due to Shanks *et al.* (1972) and the derivation of a counterexample is given in Ekstrom and Woods (1976).

Exercises

1 Prove Theorem 1 in detail.
2 Write a Pascal program to plot the diagrams corresponding to Figure 9.1 (or 9.2) for the polynomials

$$Q_1(z_1^{-1}, z_2^{-1}) = 1 - 1.5z_1^{-1} + 0.6z_1^{-2} - 1.2z_2^{-1} + 1.8z_1^{-1}z_2^{-1} - 0.72z_1^{-2}z_2^{-1}$$
$$+ 0.5z_2^{-2} - 0.75z_1^{-1}z_2^{-2} + 0.25z_1^{-2}z_2^{-2}$$

$$Q_2(z_1^{-1}, z_2^{-1}) = 1 - 1.2z_2^{-1} + 0.5z_2^{-2} - 1.5z_1^{-1} + 1.8z_1^{-1}z_2^{-1} - 0.75z_1^{-1}z_2^{-2}$$
$$+ 0.6z_1^{-2} - 0.72z_1^{-2}z_2^{-1} + 0.29z_1^{-2}z_2^{-2}$$

What conclusions can you draw about the stability of the filters $1/Q_1$, $1/Q_2$?
3 Show that the filter (9.2.1) is stable and the filter (9.7.2) is unstable.
4 Derive equations for the coefficients of b_1 in terms of those of b.

References

Anderson, B. D. O. and E. I. Jury (1973), 'Stability test for two-dimensional filters', *IEEE Trans. Audio Electroacoust.*, AU-21 (4), 366–72.

Dudgeon, D. E. (1975), 'The existence of cepstrum for two-dimensional rational polynomials', *IEEE Trans. Acoust., Speech, Signal Process.*, ASSP-23 (2), 242–3.

Ekstrom, M. P. and R. E. Twogood (1977), 'A stability test for 2-D recursive digital filters using the complex cepstrum', *IEEE Int. Conf. on Acoust., Speech and Signal Process, Rec.*, 535–8.

Ekstrom, M. P. and J. W. Woods (1976), 'Two-dimensional spectral factorization with applications in recursive digital filtering', *IEEE Trans. Acoust., Speech, Signal Process.*, ASSP-24 (2), 115–28.

Genin, Y. V. and Y. G. Kamp (1977), 'Two-dimensional stability and orthogonal polynomials on the hypercircle', *Proc. IEEE*, 65, 873–81.

Goodman, D. (1977), 'Some stability properties of two-dimensional linear shift-invariant digital filters', *IEEE Trans. Circuits Sys.*, CAS-24(4), 201–8.

Huang, T. S. (1972), 'Stability of two-dimensional recursive filters', *IEEE Trans. Audio Electroacoust.*, AU-20 (2), 158–63.

Pistor, P. (1974), 'Stability criterion for recursive filters', *IBM J. Res. Dev.* 18(1), 59–71.

Shanks, J. L., S. Treitel and J. H. Justice (1972), 'Stability and synthesis of two-dimensional recursive filters', *IEEE Trans. Audio Electroacoust.*, AU-20 (2), 115–28.

10

Design of Two-dimensional Filters

10.1 Introduction

In this chapter we shall extend the methods of Chapters 2 and 5 to obtain two-dimensional FIR and IIR filters. In the case of FIR filters the design methods fall into three basic categories. The straightforward generalization of the one-dimensional technique of inverse Fourier transformation of the frequency response followed by windowing and the method of frequency sampling will be considered in the next section. Following that the method of transforming a one-dimensional filter into a two-dimensional filter using the McClellan transform will be described in detail. Finally, we shall give a brief description of optimization techniques.

When we come to design two-dimensional IIR filters we are faced immediately with the stability problem. Many design techniques lead to unstable filters and so it is important to check the stability of an IIR filter and use the stabilization techniques described earlier if the resulting filter proves to be unstable. In the second part of this chapter we shall mention a few of the methods for designing IIR filters which have proved useful in practice. These methods include spectral transformations from known (one- or two-dimensional) designs, optimal design methods and the use of approximate separable filters which are easily shown to be stable.

10.2 Two-dimensional windows

In Section 2.3 we discussed the design of FIR filters by determining the Fourier coefficients of the desired frequency response. This method can be generalized directly; if $H(e^{j\omega_1 T_1}, e^{j\omega_2 T_2})$ is the frequency response of a desired filter then we have

$$h(n_1, n_2) = \frac{1}{\omega_{s1} \cdot \omega_{s2}} \int_{-\omega_{s1}/2}^{\omega_{s1}/2} \int_{-\omega_{s2}/2}^{\omega_{s2}/2} H(e^{j\omega_1 T_1}, e^{j\omega_2 T_2}) e^{jn_1\omega_1 T_1 + jn_2\omega_2 T_2} d\omega_1 d\omega_2$$

In particular, if

$$H(e^{j\omega_1 T_1}, e^{j\omega_2 T_2}) = \begin{cases} 1 & |\omega_1| \leq \omega_{c1}, |\omega_2| \leq \omega_{c2} \\ 0 & \text{otherwise} \end{cases}$$

then we have

$$h(n_1, n_2) = \left(\frac{\omega_{c1} T_1}{\pi}\right)\left(\frac{\omega_{c2} T_2}{\pi}\right) \text{sinc}\,[n_1\omega_{c1} T_1]\, \text{sinc}\,[n_2\omega_{c2} T_2] \qquad (10.2.1)$$

Note that h is symmetric about $n_1 = 0$ and $n_2 = 0$, giving rise, as in the one-dimensional case, to a zero phase filter. Here, we have

$$H(z_1, z_2) = H(z_1)H(z_2)$$

where $H(z_1)$ is the one-dimensional ideal lowpass filter transfer function, i.e. H is separable. We can write

$$H(z) = F(z) + F(z^{-1})$$

where $F(z)$ is the causal part of H. Thus,

$$H(z_1, z_2) = (F(z_1) + F(z_1^{-1}))(F(z_2) + F(z_2^{-1}))$$
$$= F(z_1)F(z_2) + F(z_1^{-1})F(z_2) + F(z_1)F(z_2^{-1}) + F(z_1^{-1})F(z_2^{-1})$$

It is possible to form zero phase filters from nonseparable two-dimensional transfer functions in the following ways:

(i) $H_1(z_1, z_2) = F(z_1, z_2) \cdot F(z_1^{-1}, z_2^{-1})$

(ii) $H_2(z_1, z_2) = F(z_1, z_2) + F(z_1^{-1}, z_2^{-1})$

(iii) $H_3(z_1, z_2) = F(z_1, z_2) \cdot F(z_1^{-1}, z_2) \cdot F(z_1, z_2^{-1}) \cdot F(z_1^{-1}, z_2^{-1})$

(iv) $H_4(z_1, z_2) = F(z_1, z_2) + F(z_1^{-1}, z_2) + F(z_1, z_2^{-1}) + F(z_1^{-1}, z_2^{-1})$

The above filter H is a special case of (iv).

Of course, the impulse response sequence h of an ideal lowpass filter given by (10.2.1) does not define an FIR filter and so we must truncate the sequence just as in the one-dimensional case. (We can also shift h in both directions to obtain a single-quadrant function with linear phase response.) The operation of truncation corresponds to a rectangular window

$$w(n_1, n_2) = \begin{cases} 1 & |n_1| \leq N, |n_2| \leq N \\ 0 & \text{otherwise} \end{cases}$$

However, if we wish to use more general windows such as the Kaiser or Hamming windows developed for one-dimensional systems, then it is better to use circularly symmetric filters and then use a window of the form

$$w_2(n_1, n_2) = \begin{cases} w(\sqrt{n_1^2 + n_2^2}) & \text{if } \sqrt{n_1^2 + n_2^2} \leq N \\ 0 & \text{otherwise} \end{cases}$$

where w is any one-dimensional window extended to be defined for all real arguments. If the spectrum of w_2 has a narrow band relative to that of the filter H, then it can be shown that such a window produces a good approximation to an ideal filter.

A typical circularly symmetric filter is specified by

$$H(e^{j\omega_1}, e^{j\omega_2}) = \begin{cases} 1 & \text{if } \sqrt{\omega_1^2 + \omega_2^2} \leq \omega_c \\ 0 & \text{if } \sqrt{\omega_1^2 + \omega_2^2} > \omega_c \end{cases}$$

Then

$$h(n_1, n_2) = \left(\frac{1}{2\pi}\right)\left(\frac{1}{2\pi}\right)\int_{-\pi}^{\pi}\int_{-\pi}^{\pi} H(e^{j\omega_1}e^{j\omega_2})e^{j\omega_1 n_1}e^{j\omega_2 n_2}d\omega_1 d\omega_2$$

$$= \left(\frac{\omega_c}{\omega_s}\right)\frac{J_1(2\pi(\omega_c/\omega_s)\sqrt{n_1^2 + n_2^2})}{\sqrt{n_1^2 + n_2^2}}$$

where J_1 is the first-order Bessel function given by the series

$$J_1(z) = (\tfrac{1}{2}z)\sum_{k=0}^{\infty} \frac{(-\tfrac{1}{4}z^2)^k}{k!\,\Gamma(k+1)}$$

10.3 Frequency sampling filters

Rather than finding the inverse Fourier transform of the frequency response of a desired filter we can sample the frequency response and use the discrete Fourier transform to find the impulse response coefficients. This method is called the *frequency sampling* technique. To derive the basic relations involved in this method, recall that

$$H(e^{j\omega_1}, e^{j\omega_2}) = \sum_{n_1=0}^{N_1-1} \sum_{n_2=0}^{N_2-1} h(n_1, n_2) \exp[-j(\omega_1 n_1 + \omega_2 n_2)] \qquad (10.3.1)$$

where we have normalized the sampling times to 1 for convenience. If we evaluate this relation at the points

$$\omega_{k_1} = k_1\left(\frac{2\pi}{N_1}\right) \quad 0 \le k_1 \le N_1 - 1$$

$$\omega_{k_2} = k_2\left(\frac{2\pi}{N_2}\right) \quad 0 \le k_2 \le N_2 - 1$$

then we have

$$H(k_1, k_2) \triangleq H(e^{j\omega_{k_1}}, e^{j\omega_{k_2}})$$

$$= \sum_{n_1=0}^{N_1-1} \sum_{n_2=0}^{N_2-1} h(n_1, n_2) \exp\left[-j2\pi\left(\frac{k_1 n_1}{N_1} + \frac{k_2 n_2}{N_2}\right)\right]$$

The inverse DFT follows by extending the one-dimensional expression for the DFT to two dimensions in an obvious way (cf. Chapter 3). Thus,

$$h(n_1, n_2) = \frac{1}{N_1 \cdot N_2} \sum_{k_1=0}^{N_1-1} \sum_{k_2=0}^{N_2-1} H(k_1, k_2) \exp\left[j2\pi\left(\frac{k_1 n_1}{N_1} + \frac{k_2 n_2}{N_2}\right)\right] \qquad (10.3.2)$$

By (10.3.2) and (10.3.1) we have

$$H(e^{j\omega_1}, e^{j\omega_2}) = \sum_{n_1=0}^{N_1-1} \sum_{n_2=0}^{N_2-1} \left\{ \frac{1}{N_1 \cdot N_2} \sum_{k_1=0}^{N_1-1} \sum_{k_2=0}^{N_2-1} H(k_1, k_2) \exp\left[j2\pi\left(\frac{k_1 n_1}{N_1} + \frac{k_2 n_2}{N_2}\right)\right] \right\}$$

$$\cdot \exp[-j(\omega_1 n_1 + \omega_2 n_2)]$$

$$= \sum_{k_1=0}^{N_1-1} \sum_{k_2=0}^{N_2-1} H(k_1, k_2) \cdot \left\{ \frac{1}{N_1 \cdot N_2} \cdot \sum_{n_1=0}^{N_1-1} \sum_{n_2=0}^{N_2-1} \exp\left[j2\pi\left(\frac{k_1 n_1}{N_1} + \frac{k_2 n_2}{N_2}\right)\right] \right\}$$

$$\cdot \exp[-j(\omega_1 n_1 + \omega_2 n_2)]$$

$$= \sum_{k_1=0}^{N_1-1} \sum_{k_2=0}^{N_2-1} H(k_1, k_2) \cdot A(k_1, k_2, \omega_1, \omega_2) \qquad (10.3.3)$$

where

$$A(k_1, k_2, \omega_1, \omega_2) = \frac{1}{N_1 \cdot N_2} \prod_{i=1}^{2} \left\{ \frac{1 - \exp(-jN_i\omega_i)}{1 - \exp[j((2\pi k_i/N_i) - \omega_i)]} \right\}$$

The expression (10.3.3) is the fundamental expression which allows us to reconstruct the frequency response $H(e^{j\omega_1}, e^{j\omega_2})$ from the samples by means of the interpolation functions $A(k_1, k_2, \omega_1, \omega_2)$. Just as in the case of one-dimensional filters, a two-dimensional system with the symmetry property

$$h(n_1, n_2) = h(N_1 - 1 - n_1, n_2) = h(n_1, N_2 - 1 - n_2)$$

has linear phase shift, in which case we have

$$H(e^{j\omega_1}, e^{j\omega_2}) = e^{-j\omega_1(N_1-1)/2} e^{-j\omega_2(N_2-1)/2} \cdot \sum_{n_1=0}^{N_1/2-1} \sum_{n_2=0}^{N_2/2-1} h(n_1, n_2) \prod_{i=1}^{2} \cos\left[\left(\frac{N_i - 1}{2} \right) - n_i \right]$$

$$(10.3.4)$$

Similarly, for such a filter it can be seen that

$$H(k_1, k_2) = |H(k_1, k_2)| e^{j\theta(k_1, k_2)}$$

where the amplitude and phase functions satisfy the relations

$$|H(k_1, k_2)| = |H(k_1, N_2 - k_2)| = |H(N_1 - k_1, k_2)|$$
$$\theta(k_1, k_2) = \theta(k_1) + \theta(k_2)$$

where

$$\theta(k_i) = \begin{cases} \dfrac{-2\pi}{N_i} k_i \left(\dfrac{N_i - 1}{2} \right) & k_i = 0, 1, \ldots, NU_i \\ \dfrac{2\pi}{N_i} (N_i - k_i) \left(\dfrac{N_i - 1}{2} \right) & k_i = NU_i + 1, \ldots, N_i - 1 \end{cases}$$

and

$$NU_i = \begin{cases} N_i/2 & N_i \text{ even} \\ (N_i - 1)/2 & N_i \text{ odd} \end{cases}$$

(for $i = 1, 2$). If N_1 or N_2 is even we must also have

$$\theta(k_1, N_2/2) = \theta(N_1/2, k_2) = 0$$
$$H(k_1, N_2/2) = H(N_1/2, k_2)$$

Thus from (10.3.3) we have

$$H(e^{j\omega_1}, e^{j\omega_2}) = \exp\left\{-j\left[\omega_1\left(\frac{N_1-1}{2}\right) + \omega_2\left(\frac{N_2-1}{2}\right)\right]\right\}$$

$$\cdot\frac{1}{N_1 N_2}\left[H(0,0)\alpha(\omega_1, N_1)\alpha(\omega_2, N_2)\right.$$

$$+ \sum_{k_1=1}^{NU_1}|H(k_1,0)|\alpha(\omega_2, N_2)\beta(\omega_1, k_1, N_1)$$

$$+ \sum_{k_2=1}^{NU_2}|H(0,k_2)|\alpha(\omega_1, N_1)\beta(\omega_2, k_2, N_2)$$

$$+ \left.\sum_{k_1=1}^{NU_1}\sum_{k_2=1}^{NU_2}|H(k_1,k_2)|\beta(\omega_1, k_1, N_1)\beta(\omega_2, k_2, N_2)\right]$$

$$(10.3.5)$$

where

$$\alpha(\omega, N) = \sin(\omega N/2)/\sin(\omega/2)$$

$$\beta(\omega, k, N) = \frac{\sin[(\omega/2 - \pi k/N)N]}{\sin(\omega/2 - \pi k/N)} + \frac{\sin[(\omega/2 + \pi k/N)N]}{\sin(\omega/2 + \pi k/N)}$$

and

$$NU_i = \begin{cases} N_i/2 - 1 & N_i \text{ even} \\ (N_i - 1)/2 & N_i \text{ odd} \end{cases}$$

Suppose now that we wish to design a lowpass circularly symmetric filter with

$$H(e^{j\omega_1}, e^{j\omega_2}) = \begin{cases} 1 & (\omega_1^2 + \omega_2^2)^{1/2} \leq R_1 \\ 0 & (\omega_1^2 + \omega_2^2)^{1/2} \leq R_2 \end{cases}$$

(Figure 10.1). Then we shall apply (10.3.5) with $H(k,k)$ equal to 1 for the discrete points $(e^{j\omega_{k_1}}, e^{j\omega_{k_2}})$ of Figure 10.1(b) lying in the passband, and $H(k_1, k_2)$ equal to 0 for those values in the stopband. The values of $H(k_1, k_2)$ for $(e^{j\omega_{k_1}}, e^{j\omega_{k_2}})$ in the transition band will be optimized to minimize the error between $H(e^{j\omega_1}, e^{j\omega_2})$ given by (10.3.5) and the ideal response. Thus, substituting the appropriate values for $H(k_1, k_2)$ into (10.3.5) gives

$$H(e^{j\omega_1}, e^{j\omega_2}) = H_I(\omega_1, \omega_2) + \sum_{i=1}^{L}c_i H_i(\omega_1, \omega_2) \qquad (10.3.6)$$

where H_I is the contribution to H from terms with $|H(k_1, k_2)| = 1$, L is the number of points $(e^{j\omega_{k_1}}, e^{j\omega_{k_2}})$ in the transition band, c_i is the ith value of $|H(k_1, k_2)|$ at such a point and H_i is the interpolating function associated with c_i. The resulting frequency response $H(e^{j\omega_1}, e^{j\omega_2})$, in (10.3.6) must satisfy the inequalities

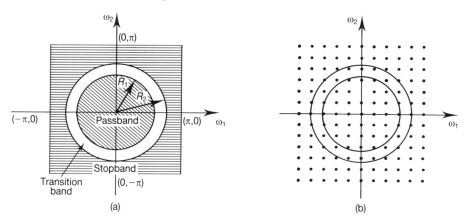

Figure 10.1 Frequency space for a cicularly symmetric filter: (a) bands; (b) sample points.

$$1 - \alpha\delta \leq H(e^{j\omega_1}, e^{j\omega_2}) \leq 1 + \alpha\delta \quad \text{in the passband}$$

$$-\delta \leq H(e^{j\omega_1}, e^{j\omega_2}) \leq \delta \qquad \text{in the stopband}$$

where we wish to minimize δ. (α is a fixed positive number which can be chosen as desired to weight the passband error or the stopband error more heavily.) Thus, we obtain the linear programming problem:

$$\text{minimize } f(c_1, \ldots, c_L, \delta) = \delta$$

subject to

$$\sum_{i=1}^{L} c_i H_i(\omega_{1l}, \omega_{2l}) - \alpha\delta \leq 1 - H_I(\omega_{1l}, \omega_{2l})$$

$$-\sum_{i=1}^{L} c_i H_i(\omega_{1l}, \omega_{2l}) - \alpha\delta \leq -1 + H_I(\omega_{1l}, \omega_{2l})$$
$$\qquad\qquad\qquad 1 \leq l \leq W_1$$

$$\sum_{i=1}^{L} c_i H_i(\omega_{1l}, \omega_{2l}) - \delta \leq -H_I(\omega_{1l}, \omega_{2l})$$

$$-\sum_{i=1}^{L} c_i H_i(\omega_{1l}, \omega_{2l}) - \delta \leq -H_I(\omega_{1l}, \omega_{2l})$$
$$\qquad\qquad\qquad W_1 + 1 \leq l \leq W_2$$

where we choose a large number of points $(\omega_{1l}, \omega_{2l})$ such that

$$(\omega_{1l}, \omega_{2l}) \text{ is in the passband for } 1 \leq l \leq W_1$$

$$(\omega_{1l}, \omega_{2l}) \text{ is in the stopband for } W_1 + 1 \leq l \leq W_2$$

This problem can be solved by using standard linear programming computer algorithms.

10.4 The McClellan Transform

As we have seen above, the amount of computation required in designing a two-dimensional filter is of the order of the square of that required to design a one-dimensional filter, if the direct methods such as those above are used. It would thus be very useful if we could derive a transformation from a one-dimensional to a two-dimensional filter, thus considerably reducing the computation and also simplifying the design. Such a transformation does indeed exist and we shall now discuss its derivation. Consider first a one-dimensional FIR filter response given by

$$H(e^{j\omega}) = \sum_{k=0}^{N-1} h(k)e^{-jk\omega}$$

We have seen in Chapter 2 that if $N = 2n + 1$ is odd and h is symmetric, so that $h(k) = h(N - 1 - k)$, $k = 0, 1, \ldots, n$, then

$$H(e^{j\omega}) = e^{-jn\omega} \sum_{k=0}^{n} b(k) \cos \omega k$$

where

$$b(0) = h(n)$$
$$b(k) = 2h(n - k) \qquad k = 1, \ldots, n$$

Thus,

$$|H(e^{j\omega})| = \left| \sum_{k=0}^{n} b(k) \cos \omega k \right|$$

Now let

$$x = \cos \omega$$

Then

$$\cos \omega k = \cos k(\arccos x) = C_k(\omega)$$

where $C_k(\omega)$ is the kth Tchebychev polynomial (cf. Chapter 4). Thus,

$$|H(e^{j\omega})| = \left| \sum_{k=0}^{n} b(k) C_k(\omega) \right|$$

$$= \left| \sum_{k=0}^{n} \hat{b}(k) x^k \right|$$

for some coefficients $\hat{b}(k)$, since C_k is a kth-order polynomial. Hence,

$$|H(e^{j\omega})| = \left| \sum_{k=0}^{n} \hat{b}(k)(\cos \omega)^k \right| \qquad (10.4.1)$$

We can now transform the filter into a two-dimensional one by substituting

$$\cos\omega = A\cos\omega_1 + B\cos\omega_2 + C\cos\omega_1\cos\omega_2 + D \qquad (10.4.2)$$

for some constants A, B, C, D. Then (10.4.1) becomes

$$F(\omega_1, \omega_2) \triangleq |H(e^{j\omega})|\Big|_{\cos\omega = A\cos\omega_1 + B\cos\omega_2 + C\cos\omega_1\cos\omega_2 + D}$$

$$= \left| \sum_{k_1=0}^{n} \sum_{k_2=0}^{n} \hat{a}(k_1, k_2)(\cos\omega_1)^{k_1} (\cos\omega_2)^{k_2} \right|$$

for some coefficients $\hat{a}(k_1, k_2)$. Reversing the argument which led to (10.4.1) we can write $F(\omega_1, \omega_2)$ in the form

$$F(\omega_1, \omega_2) = \left| \sum_{k_1=0}^{n} \sum_{k_2=0}^{n} a(k_1, k_2) \cos(\omega_1 k_1) \cos(\omega_2 k_2) \right| \qquad (10.4.3)$$

for some new coefficients $a(k_1, k_2)$.

Consider a general two-dimensional filter

$$H(e^{j\omega_1}, e^{j\omega_2}) = \sum_{k_1=0}^{N_1-1} \sum_{k_2=0}^{N_2-1} h(k_1, k_2) \exp(-j\omega_1 k_1 - j\omega_2 k_2)$$

If N_1 and N_2 are odd and we have the symmetry conditions

$$h(N_1 - k_1 - 1, k_2) = h(k_1, k_2) \quad k_1 = 0, 1, \ldots, n_1 \triangleq \tfrac{1}{2}(N_1 - 1)$$

$$h(k_1, N_2 - k_2 - 1) = h(k_1, k_2) \quad k_2 = 0, 1, \ldots, n_2 \triangleq \tfrac{1}{2}(N_2 - 1)$$

then we have

$$H(e^{j\omega_1}, e^{j\omega_2}) = \exp(-j\omega_1 n_1 - j\omega_2 n_2) \sum_{k_1=0}^{n_1} \sum_{k_2=0}^{n_2} a(k_1, k_2) \cos(\omega_1 k_1) \cos(\omega_2 k_2)$$

where

$$a(0, 0) = h(n_1, n_2)$$

$$a(0, k_2) = 2h(n_1, n_2 - k_2) \quad k_2 = 1, \ldots, n_2$$

$$a(k_1, 0) = 2h(n_1 - k_1, n_2) \quad k_1 = 1, \ldots, n_1$$

$$a(k_1, k_2) = 4h(n_1 - k_1, n_2 - k_2) \quad k_1 = 1, \ldots, n_1; k_2 = 1, \ldots, n_2$$

Thus, $|H(e^{j\omega_1}, e^{j\omega_2})|$ is of the form (10.4.3) with $n_1 = n_2 = n$, and so the transform (10.4.2) will map a one-dimensional linear phase filter on to a two-dimensional FIR filter.

To determine the types of frequency transformations which (10.4.2) produces, for different values of A, B, C, D, write the equation in the form

$$\omega_2 = \arccos\left\{ \frac{\cos\omega - D - A\cos\omega_1}{B + C\cos\omega_1} \right\} \qquad (10.4.4)$$

For each fixed ω this equation defines a curve in (ω_1, ω_2)-space along which the transformed frequency response is constant and equal to the one-dimensional response at ω. Putting $u = \cos \omega_1$, $v = \cos \omega_2$ and $x = \cos \omega$ in (10.4.4) we obtain

$$v = \frac{x - D - Au}{B + Cu} \qquad (10.4.5)$$

so that as x varies between -1 and 1, the resulting relationship between v and u defines a family of curves in the region $[-1, 1]x[-1, 1]$ of u–v space. Note that, for fixed x,

$$\frac{dv}{du} = (-AB + CD - Cx)(B + Cu)^{-2}$$

so that the sign of dv/du is constant for $u \in [-1, 1]$. Hence for each fixed x, the curve defined by (10.4.5) is either monotonically increasing or decreasing. It follows that the same is true for ω_2 as a function of ω_1 for fixed ω, from (10.4.4). In the case where dv/du is negative we can obtain contours appropriate for a circularly symmetric filter. For example, if

$$A = -B = 0.5, \ C = D = 0$$

then we obtain the contours shown in Figure 10.2

We note, finally, that the transformation (10.4.2) can be generalized to the relation

$$\cos \omega = \sum_{k_1=0}^{m_1} \sum_{k_2=0}^{m_2} A_{k_1 k_2} \cos k_1 \omega_1 \cos k_2 \omega_2 \qquad (10.4.5)$$

giving considerably more freedom in the choice of the contour lines.

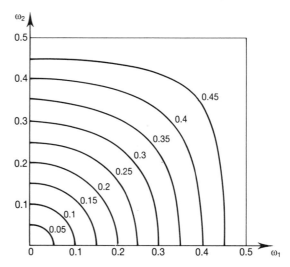

Figure 10.2 Contour lines for a circularly symmetric filter.

10.5 Optimization methods

Rather than attempting to design an FIR filter directly by inverse Fourier transformation of the desired frequency response, we can also try to find the filter coefficients which give the 'best' approximation to an ideal response. By 'best' we usually mean that the error between the real and ideal responses is minimized in some average or integral sense. Thus we define the 'cost' functional

$$E_p = \left(\frac{1}{\omega_{s1} \cdot \omega_{s2}} \int_0^{\omega_{s1}} \int_0^{\omega_{s2}} |I(e^{j\omega_1}, e^{j\omega_2}) - H(e^{j\omega_1}, e^{j\omega_2})|^p d\omega_1 d\omega_2 \right)^{1/p} \quad (10.5.1)$$

where I is the ideal frequency response and H is the actual response given by

$$H(e^{j\omega_1}, e^{j\omega_2}) = \sum_{k_1=n_1}^{n_1} \sum_{k_2=n_2}^{n_2} a_{k_1 k_2} e^{-jk_1\omega_1} e^{-jk_2\omega_2}$$

where we assume the usual symmetry conditions so that H has zero phase, i.e. H is real. If we define the error e by

$$e(\omega_1, \omega_2) = I(e^{j\omega_1}, e^{j\omega_2}) - H(e^{j\omega_1}, e^{j\omega_2})$$

then (10.5.1) can be written

$$E_p = ||e||_{L^p}$$

where $||x||_{L^p}$ (for any function x) is defined by

$$||x||_{L^p} = \left\{ \frac{1}{\omega_{s1} \cdot \omega_{s2}} \int_0^{\omega_{s1}} \int_0^{\omega_{s2}} |x(\omega_1, \omega_2)|^p d\omega_1 d\omega_2 \right\}^{1/p}$$

and is called the L^p *norm* of x. We require to find the coefficients $a_{k_1 k_2}$ of H such that

$$E_p = ||I - H||_{L^p}$$

is minimized. Hence we must solve the equations

$$\frac{\partial E_p}{\partial a_{k_1 k_2}} = 0 \quad \text{for all } k_1, k_2 \quad (10.5.2)$$

Consider the case where $p = 2$. Then we have

$$\frac{\partial E_p}{\partial a_{k_1 k_2}} = \frac{\partial}{\partial a_{k_1 k_2}} \left\{ \frac{1}{\omega_{s1} \omega_{s2}} \int_0^{\omega_{s1}} \int_0^{\omega_{s2}} \left(I - \sum_{k_1=-n_1}^{n_1} \sum_{k_2=-n_2}^{n_2} a_{k_1 k_2} e^{-jk_1\omega_1} e^{-jk_2\omega_2} \right)^2 d\omega_1 d\omega_2 \right.$$

for an ideal lowpass filter with cutoff frequencies ω_{c1}, ω_{c2}. Hence the coefficients $a_{k_1 k_2}$ must satisfy the linear equations

$$\int_0^{\omega_{s1}} \int_0^{\omega_{s2}} \left(I - \sum_{k_1=-n_1}^{n_1} \sum_{k_2=-n_2}^{n_2} a_{k_1 k_2} e^{-jk_1\omega_1} e^{-jk_2\omega_2} \right) e^{jl_1\omega_1} e^{jl_2\omega_2} \cdot d\omega_1 d\omega_2 = 0$$

for $-n_i \leq l_i \leq n_i$ ($i = 1, 2$). However,

$$\int_0^{\omega_{s1}} \int_0^{\omega_{s2}} e^{-jk_1\omega_1} e^{-jk_2\omega_2} e^{jl_1\omega_1} e^{jl_2\omega_2} \, d\omega_1 d\omega_2 = \omega_{s1}\omega_{s2}\delta_{k_1l_1}\delta_{k_2l_2}$$

and so

$$a_{l_1l_2} = \frac{1}{\omega_{s1}\omega_{s2}} \int_0^{\omega_{c1}} \int_0^{\omega_{c2}} e^{jl_1\omega_1} e^{jl_2\omega_2} d\omega_1 d\omega_2$$

$$= \frac{\omega_{c1}\omega_{c2}}{\pi^2} \cdot \text{sinc}\,(l_1\omega_{c1})\, \text{sinc}\,(l_2\omega_{c2})$$

This is precisely the same solution as is obtained by straightforward inverse Fourier transformation (cf. (2.3.1)).

The main drawback with the use of integral cost criteria is that the error between the actual and the ideal filters is only guaranteed to be small in an average sense and not at any paticular point. In fact, there is nothing to prevent the error being arbitrarily large at isolated points. There are two ways to alleviate this problem; in the first we still use an integral cost but we introduce a weighting function into (10.5.1) so that points in regions where large errors may arise (for example, at ω_{c1}, ω_{c2}) can be more heavily weighted than other points. Thus we generalize (10.5.1) in the form

$$E_{p,w} = \left\{ \frac{1}{\omega_{s1}\omega_{s2}} \int_0^{\omega_{s1}} \int_0^{\omega_{s2}} w(\omega_1, \omega_2) |[I(e^{j\omega_1}, e^{j\omega_2}) - H(e^{j\omega_1}, e^{j\omega_2})]|^p d\omega_1 d\omega_2 \right\}^{1/p}$$

where w is some positive weighting function. Again, in the case where $p = 2$ we obtain the following linear equation for the coefficients $a_{k_1k_2}$:

$$\sum_{k_1=-n_1}^{n_1} \sum_{k_2=-n_2}^{n_2} a_{k_1k_2} \int_0^{\omega_{s1}} \int_0^{\omega_{s2}} w(\omega_1, \omega_2) e^{-j(k_1-l_1)\omega_1} e^{-j(k_2-l_2)\omega_2} d\omega_1 d\omega_2$$

$$= \int_0^{\omega_{c1}} \int_0^{\omega_{c2}} w(\omega_1, \omega_2) e^{jl_1\omega_1} e^{jl_2\omega_2} d\omega_1 d\omega_2 \qquad (10.5.3)$$

This is a set of linear equations which can be solved for a $a_{k_1k_2}$ by standard numerical techniques.

For a general finite p, $1 \leqslant p < \infty$ with $p \neq 2$ the equations for $a_{k_1k_2}$ resulting from equation (10.5.2) are no longer linear and so we have to resort to more sophisticated numerical techniques. The other method of overcoming the problem of large pointwise errors in integral cost minimization is by taking $p = \infty$. Then as $p \to \infty$ it can be seen that the L^p norm of a function converges to the supremum norm, so that (10.5.1) becomes

$$E_\infty = \sup_{0 \leqslant \omega_1 \leqslant \omega_{s1}, 0 \leqslant \omega_2 \leqslant \omega_{s2}} |I(e^{j\omega_1}, e^{j\omega_2}) - H(e^{j\omega_1}, e^{j\omega_2})|$$

or, in the case of a weighting function,

$$E_{\infty,w} = \sup_{0 \leqslant \omega_1 \leqslant \omega_{s1}, 0 \leqslant \omega_2 \leqslant \omega_{s2}} w(\omega_1, \omega_2) |I(e^{j\omega_1}, e^{j\omega_2}) - H(e^{j\omega_1}, e^{j\omega_2})|$$

$$= \| I - H \|_\infty \qquad (10.5.4)$$

(We have written $||.||_{L^\infty}$ as $||.||_\infty$ for simplicity.)

The normed error function (10.5.4) can be minimized numerically, or by the following Tchebychev approximation procedure. First note that if H is assumed to be circularly symmetric, then it can be written in the form

$$H(e^{j\omega_1}, e^{j\omega_2}) = \sum_{k=0}^{n} \sum_{l=0}^{k} b_{kl} (\cos k\omega_1 \cos l\omega_2 + \cos l\omega_1 \cos k\omega_2) \quad (10.5.5)$$

$$= \sum_{i=1}^{m} a_i f_i(x)$$

$$\stackrel{\triangle}{=} f(x)$$

where

$$x = (\omega_1, \omega_2)$$

$$f_i(x) = \cos k\omega_1 \cos l\omega_2 + \cos l\omega_1 \cos k\omega_2$$

$$a_i = b_{kl}$$

with

$$i = k(k + 1)/2 + l + 1$$

$$m = (n + 1)(n + 2)/2.$$

We shall seek the best approximation to the ideal filter

$$I(e^{j\omega_1}, e^{j\omega_2}) = \begin{cases} 1 & \text{if } \omega_1^2 + \omega_2^2 \leqslant \omega_c^2 \\ 0 & \text{if } \omega_1^2 + \omega_2^2 \geqslant \omega_\sigma^2 \end{cases}$$

where ω_c and ω_σ are the passband and stopband edges, respectively. Thus, we wish to minimize

$$||I(x) - f(x)||_\infty$$

with respect to the coefficients a_i. (We have written $I(x) = I(e^{j\omega_1}, e^{j\omega_2})$.) Since $I(x)$ and $f(x)$ are circularly symmetric we can regard the sup norm as being taken over the region.

$$X = \{(\omega_1, \omega_2) : 0 \leqslant \omega_1 \leqslant \omega_{s1}, 0 \leqslant \omega_2 \leqslant \omega_1\}$$

Since the functions $f_i(x)$, $1 \leqslant i \leqslant m$, are linearly independent on X there exist m points $x_1, \ldots, x_m \in X$ such that the matrix

$$F = \begin{bmatrix} f_1(x_1) & f_1(x_2) \ldots & f_1(x_m) \\ f_2(x_1) & f_2(x_2) & f_2(x_m) \\ \vdots & & \\ f_m(x_1) & f_m(x_2) & f_m(x_m) \end{bmatrix}$$

has rank m. Put $\phi_i = (f_1(x_i), f_2(x_i), \ldots, f_m(x_i))^T$. Now let x_{m+1} be another point in X and set $\phi_{m+1} = (f_1(x_{m+1}), \ldots, f_m(x_{m+1}))^T$. Then,

$$\phi_{m+1} = \sum_{j=1}^{m} \lambda_j \phi_j \tag{10.5.8}$$

for some set of scalars λ_j. In fact, we have

$$(\lambda_1, \ldots, \lambda_m)^T = F^{-1}\phi_{m+1}$$

Let $\mathcal{F}$ be the set of all functions f of the form $\Sigma a_i f_i(x)$; i.e.

$$\mathcal{F} = \{f = \Sigma a_i f_i(x) : a_i \in \mathbb{R}, 1 \leq i \leq m)$$

Put $\lambda_{m+1} = -1$, then from (10.5.6) we have

$$\sum_{j=1}^{m+1} \lambda_j \phi_j = 0$$

and so

$$\sum_{j=1}^{m+1} \lambda_j a_i f_i(x_j) = 0$$

for each i. Hence, adding these equations we obtain

$$\sum_{j=1}^{m+1} \lambda_j f(x_j) = 0 \tag{10.5.7}$$

for all $f \in \mathcal{F}$.

A set $R = \{x_1, \ldots, x_{m+1}\} \subseteq X$ such that F is invertible, is called a *reference set* and, if we denote by h the error

$$h(x) = w(x)[f(x) - I(x)] \tag{10.5.8}$$

then f is called a *reference function* for R if

$$\operatorname{sgn} h(x_j) = \eta \operatorname{sgn} \lambda_j \quad 1 \leq j \leq m + 1 \tag{10.5.9}$$

where $\eta = \pm 1$ (independent of j) and

$$\operatorname{sgn} x = \begin{cases} 1 & \text{if } x > 0 \\ 0 & \text{if } x = 0 \\ -1 & \text{if } x < 0 \end{cases}$$

Since $\lambda_{m+1} = -1$ it follows that

$$h(x_j)h(x_{m+1})\lambda_j \leq 0 \quad 1 \leq j \leq m \tag{10.5.10}$$

We call a reference function $f \in \mathcal{F}$ a *levelled reference function* if $|h(x_j)|$ is independent of j, $1 \leq j \leq m + 1$. Put

$$|h| = |h(x_1)| = \ldots = |h(x_{m+1})|$$

$|h|$ is then called a *reference deviation*.

Then from (10.5.7), (10.5.8) and (10.5.9) we have

$$|h| = \left| \sum_{j=1}^{m+1} \lambda_j I(x_j) \right| \Big/ \left| \sum_{j=1}^{m+1} |\lambda_j| w^{-1}(x_j) \right| \qquad (10.5.11)$$

and the coefficient vector $a = (a_1, \ldots, a_m)^T$ of f is given by

$$a^T = (I(x_1) + h(x_1)/w(x_1), \ldots, I(x_m) + h(x_m)/w(x_m))F^{-1}$$

It follows from (10.5.11) that

$$|h| = \sum_{j=1}^{m+1} |\lambda_j||h(x_j)|w^{-1}(x_j) \Big/ \sum_{j=1}^{m+1} |\lambda_j| w^{-1}(x_j) \qquad (10.5.12)$$

The Tchebychev approximation algorithm is based on the following result.

THEOREM
Let R be a reference set and let f be a reference function for R. Then if $x_k \notin R$ is an arbitrary point of X, there exists $x_l \in R$ such that if we interchange x_l and x_k we obtain a new reference set R' for which f is still a reference function. Put

$$\phi_k = \sum_{j=1}^{m} \mu_j \phi_j, \quad (\mu_1, \ldots, \mu_m)^T = F^{-1}\phi_k$$

where $\phi_i = (f_1(x_i), f_2(x_i), \ldots, f_m(x_i))^T$ as before. Then the point x_l to be interchanged with x_k is given by the rule

Case 1 If

$$h(x_j)h(x_k)\mu_j \leqslant 0 \quad 1 \leqslant j \leqslant m$$

then set $x_l = x_{m+1}$.

Case 2 If there exists x_j, $1 \leqslant j \leqslant m$ such that $h(x_j)h(x_k)\mu_j > 0$ then let l be such that

$$|\lambda_l/\mu_l| = \min |\lambda_j/\mu_j|$$

where the minimum is taken over all j for which $h(x_j)h(x_k)\mu_j > 0$. The new relation between the characteristic vectors ϕ_j is given by

Case 1

$$\phi_k = \sum_{j=1}^{m} \mu_j \phi_j$$

Case 2

$$\phi_{m+1} = \frac{\lambda_l}{\mu_l} \phi_k + \sum_{\substack{j=1 \\ \neq l}}^{m} \lambda_j' \phi_j$$

where

$$\lambda'_j = \lambda_j - \lambda_l \mu_j / \mu_l \quad 1 \leq j \neq l \leq m$$

The *replacement algorithm* consists of successive interchanges of points in the reference set as in the above theorem until the optimum solution is attained. This occurs when the reference deviation $|h|$ in (10.5.12) satisfies

$$\max_X |h(x)| = |h|$$

It can be shown that the algorithm converges unless one of the λ_js in (10.5.6) becomes zero, in which case we have a *degenerate problem*. This occurs rarely and will not be discussed here, except to say that methods similar to those involved in degenerate linear programming problems can be used.

10.6 Frequency transformations

We have seen that one-dimensional filters can be transformed from one type to another (e.g. lowpass to highpass) by simple transformations. We shall study a variety of such transformations in this chapter and show that the Constantinides transforms developed in Chapter 5 can be generalized to two-dimensional filters.

In the design of one-dimensional recursive filters we applied either the impulse invariant or bilinear transforms to existing analog filters. This leads to a simple design method for two-dimensional discrete filters. First take a one-dimensional analog filter of some desired type, say $G_1(s)$, and introduce the two-dimensional filter

$$G(s_1, s_2) = G_1(s_2)$$

G is, of course, independent of s_1, but we can transform G so that it depends on two complex variables by the use of the rotation

$$\left. \begin{array}{l} s_1 = s'_1 \cos \beta + s'_2 \sin \beta \\ s_2 = s'_2 \cos \beta - s'_1 \sin \beta \end{array} \right\} \tag{10.6.1}$$

This leads to a new filter

$$\begin{aligned} \bar{G}(s'_1, s'_2 &= G(s'_1 \cos \beta + s'_2 \sin \beta, \; s'_2 \cos \beta - s'_1 \sin \beta) \\ &= G_1(s'_2 \cos \beta - s'_1 \sin \beta) \end{aligned}$$

Finally, we can use an impulse invariant or bilinear transform to discretize $\bar{G}$. Thus, for example, if we put

$$s'_1 = \frac{2}{T} \frac{1 - z_1^{-1}}{1 + z_1^{-1}}, \quad s'_2 = \frac{2}{T_2} \frac{1 - z_2^{-1}}{1 + z_2^{-1}}$$

we obtain the discrete filter

$$H(z_1, z_2) = \bar{G}(s_1', s_2') = \bar{G}\left(\frac{2}{T_1}\frac{1 - z_1^{-1}}{1 + z_1^{-1}}, \frac{2}{T_2}\frac{1 - z_2^{-1}}{1 + z_2^{-1}}\right) \qquad (10.6.2)$$

Filters H designed by this method are not particularly good, however, and so we seek more general frequency transformations. Thus we require a map $F : \mathbb{C}^2 \to \mathbb{C}^2$ which we can write in the form

$$Z_1 = F_1(z_1, z_2)$$
$$Z_2 = F_2(z_1, z_2)$$

(with $F = (F_1, F_2)$) and which satisfies the properties:

1. F maps stable first-quadrant filters to stable first-quadrant filters.
2. F maps real rational functions to real rational functions and
3. F transforms lowpass to other types of filters (highpass, bandpass, etc.). Moreover, F should map ∂D_z in z-space into ∂D_Z in Z-space, where

$$D_z = \{(z_1, z_2) : |z_1| \leq 1, |z_2| \leq 1\}$$

and

$$\partial D_z = \{(z_1, z_2) : |z_1| = 1, |z_2| = 1\}$$

Condition 1 implies that G_1 and G_2 are real and rational, while condition 2 implies that

$$|F_1(e^{-j\omega_1}, e^{-j\omega_2})| = |F_2(e^{-j\omega_1}, e^{-j\omega_2})| = 1$$

for all $\omega_1, \omega_2 \in \mathbb{R}$. Thus F_1 and F_2 must be two-dimensional all-pass transfer functions; this means that the general forms of the functions F_1 and F_2 are given by

$$Z_i = F_i(z_1, z_2) = (\pm 1)\prod_{l=1}^{K}\left\{\frac{z_1^{N_l(i)}z_2^{M_l(i)}(\sum_{n=0}^{N_l(i)}\sum_{m=0}^{M_l(i)}a_{mn}^{(i)}z_1^{-n}z_2^{-m})}{\sum_{n=0}^{N_l(i)}\sum_{m=0}^{M_l(i)}a_{mn}^{(i)}z_1^{n}z_2^{m}}\right\}$$

with $a_{00}^{(i)} = 1$. Finally, it is easy to see that condition 1 implies that F_1 and F_2 must be stable transfer functions.

Consider first the single-variable transformations

$$Z_1 = F_1(z_1) = \frac{\pm z_1^{N}(1 + \sum_{j=1}^{N}a_j^{(1)}z_1^{-j})}{(1 + \sum_{j=1}^{N}a_j^{(1)}z_1^{j})} \qquad N = 1, 2$$

$$Z_2 = F_2(z_2) = \frac{\pm z_2^{M}(1 + \sum_{j=1}^{M}a_j^{(2)}z_2^{-j})}{(1 + \sum_{j=1}^{M}a_j^{(2)}z_2^{j})} \qquad M = 1, 2$$

These are just the one-dimensional Constantinides transformations and so we can easily predict their effect on, for example, a circularly symmetric filter. Hence, for example, the transformations

$$Z_1 = -\frac{z_1 - a_1}{1 - a_1 z_1}$$
$$Z_2 = -\frac{z_2 - a_2}{1 - a_2 z_2}$$ (10.6.2)

with

$$a_i = \cos\left[(\Omega_{pi} - \omega_{pi})/2\right]/\cos\left[(\Omega_{pi} + \omega_{pi})/2\right] \quad i = 1, 2$$

map the frequency contours in Figure 10.3(a) into those of Figure 10.3(b) and transform a circularly symmetric lowpass filter into a highpass filter of the type shown in Figure 10.4 (cf. Table 5.1).

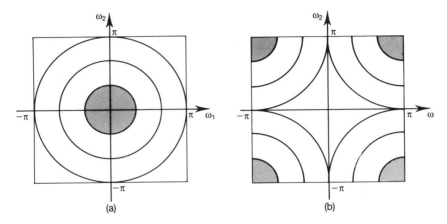

Figure 10.3 Frequency contours for the transformation: (a) z-plane; (b) Z-plane.

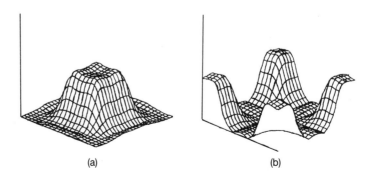

Figure 10.4 Effect of transformation (10.6.2) on a circularly symmetric lowpass filter: (a) lowpass; (b) highpass.

When we consider nonseparable transformations it is more difficult to relate the effect of the transformation on the frequency contours in terms of the parameter $a_j^{(i)}$. For example, consider the transformation

$$Z_i = \frac{\gamma_i + \beta_i z_1 + \alpha_i z_2 + z_1 z_2}{1 + \alpha_i z_1 + \beta_i z_2 + \gamma_i z_1 z_2} \quad i = 1, 2 \qquad (10.6.3)$$

We can simplify the discussion by imposing constraints on the parameters so that certain lines are mapped into some desired contours in the Z-plane. Thus, suppose we require that the ω_1 and ω_2 axes map into the line $\Omega_1 = \Omega_2$ where $Z_1 = e^{j\Omega_1}$, $Z_2 = e^{j\Omega_2}$. Then, substituting these values into (10.6.3) we have

$$\frac{\gamma_1 + \beta_1 e^{j\omega} + \alpha_1 + e^{j\omega}}{1 + \alpha_1 e^{j\omega} + \beta_1 + \gamma_1 e^{j\omega}} = \frac{\gamma_2 + \beta_2 e^{j\omega} + \alpha_2 + e^{j\omega}}{1 + \alpha_2 e^{j\omega} + \beta_2 + \gamma_2 e^{j\omega}}$$

and a similar equation with α and β interchanged. Hence we have

$$\alpha_1 = \beta_i = -\gamma_i \qquad (10.6.4)$$

If we write $(e^{j\omega_1}, e^{j\omega_2}) \rightarrow (e^{j\Omega_1}, e^{j\Omega_2})$, then we have

$$\alpha_i = \frac{e^{-j(\omega_1+\omega_2)} - e^{-j\Omega_i}}{e^{-j(\omega_1+\Omega_i)} - e^{-j(\omega_2+\Omega_i)} - e^{-j(\omega_1+\omega_2+\Omega_i)} - e^{-j\omega_2} - e^{-j\omega_1} + 1} \quad i = 1, 2 \qquad (10.6.5)$$

From Chapter 9 we know that the transformation (10.6.3) is stable if

$$|\alpha_i| < 1, \quad \left| \frac{1 + \alpha_i}{\beta_i + \gamma_i} \right| > 1, \quad \left| \frac{1 - \alpha_i}{\beta_i - \gamma_i} \right| > 1 \quad i = 1, 2$$

Hence from (10.6.4) we must have

$$-1 < |\alpha_i| < 1/3 \quad i = 1, 2 \qquad (10.6.6)$$

We can use the expression (10.6.5) to control the position of one point (Ω_1, Ω_2). If we impose the condition that $(\pi/2, \pi/2) \rightarrow (\Omega_1, \Omega_2)$, then (10.6.5) becomes

$$\alpha_i = \frac{-\tan(\Omega_i - \pi)/2}{2 + \tan(\Omega_i - \pi)/2}$$

Combining this with (10.6.6) gives a region of values of (Ω_1, Ω_2) into which $(\pi/2, \pi/2)$ can be mapped. It can now be seen that for general frequency domain transformations we can choose some of the parameters in order to achieve certain desired features of the new frequency contour maps and then choose the remaining ones to ensure stability of the resulting filter.

10.7 Optimization techniques for IIR filters

The optimization approach to the design of IIR filters is similar to that for FIR filters except that we must now ensure that the resulting filter is stable. Thus, for example, we could extend the Tchebychev minimization technique and define the error

$$E = \max_{(z_1, z_2) \in D} |I(z_1, z_2) - A(z_1, z_2)/B(z_1, z_2)| \qquad (10.7.1)$$

where $D = \{(z_1, z_2) : |z_1| \leq 1, |z_2| \leq 1\}$. Here, I is some ideal filter response and we wish to find the coefficients a_{ij}, b_{ij} in the expansions

$$A(z_1, z_2) = \sum_{i_1=0}^{m_1} \sum_{i_2=0}^{m_2} a_{i_1 i_2} z_1^{-i_1} z_2^{-i_2}$$

$$B(z_1, z_2) = \sum_{i_1=0}^{n_1} \sum_{i_2=0}^{n_2} b_{i_1 i_2} z_1^{-i_1} z_2^{-i_2}$$

which minimize E. This can be achieved by a similar method to that in Section 10.5 or by a numerical search technique, checking at each step to determine if the filter is stable.

To illustrate another optimization method we shall next discuss a technique which is similar to the L^p norm minimization approach of Section 10.5. However, we shall now discretize the frequency domain and use an 'l^p norm' to measure the error. Thus, if

$$H(z_1, z_2) = \frac{\sum_{i_1=0}^{m_1} \sum_{i_2=0}^{m_2} a_{i_1 i_2} z_1^{-i_1} z_2^{-i_2}}{1 + \sum_{\substack{j_1=0 \\ j_1+j_2 \neq 0}}^{n_1} \sum_{j_2=0}^{n_2} b_{i_1 i_2} z_1^{-j_1} z_2^{-j_2}}$$

is the transfer function of our desired filter and $I(z_1, z_2)$ is again the ideal filter characterization, then we evaluate H and I at some discrete set of points $(\omega_{1i}, \omega_{2j})$, $1 \leq i \leq M$, $1 \leq j \leq N$ and define the error

$$E = \sum_{i_1=1}^{M} \sum_{i_2=1}^{N} \{|H_{i_1 i_2}| - |I_{i_1 i_2}|\}^p$$

where

$$H_{i_1 i_2} = H(e^{j\omega_1 i_1}, e^{j\omega_2 i_2})$$

and

$$I_{i_1 i_2} = I(e^{j\omega_1 i_1}, e^{j\omega_2 i_2})$$

This can again be minimized by standard numerical techniques coupled with a stability checking algorithm.

10.8 Design of separable filters

Suppose the $|I(e^{j\omega_1}, e^{j\omega_2})|$ is an ideal or desired amplitude response and let $I_{i_1 i_2}$ denote samples of I at certain fixed points ω_{1i_1}, ω_{2i_2} for $1 \leq i_1 \leq n_1$, $1 \leq i_2 \leq n_2$, i.e.

$$I_{i_1 i_2} = |I(e^{j\omega_{1 i_1}}, e^{j\omega_{2 i_2}})|$$

To determine a separable approximation to I we consider the rank 1 matrix

$$H = \mathbf{c r}^{\mathrm{T}}$$

where

$$\mathbf{c} = (c_1, \ldots, c_{n_1})^{\mathrm{T}}, \ \mathbf{r}^{\mathrm{T}} = (r_1, \ldots, r_{n_2})$$

and then find the parameters c_i, r_j which minimize the error

$$J = \sum_{i_1=1}^{n_1} \sum_{i_2=1}^{n_2} (I_{i_1 i_2} - c_{i_1} r_{i_2})^2$$

Differentiating with respect to c_k and r_k gives the equations

$$\mathbf{c} = \frac{I \mathbf{r}}{\mathbf{r}^{\mathrm{T}} \mathbf{r}}$$

and

$$\mathbf{r} = \frac{I^{\mathrm{T}} \mathbf{c}}{\mathbf{c}^{\mathrm{T}} \mathbf{c}}$$

where I denotes the matrix $(I_{i_1 i_2})$. Hence,

$$I^{\mathrm{T}} I \mathbf{r} = (\mathbf{r}^{\mathrm{T}} \mathbf{r})(\mathbf{c}^{\mathrm{T}} \mathbf{c}) \mathbf{r} = \alpha \mathbf{r} \tag{10.8.1}$$

for some constant $\mathbf{r}$; i.e. $\mathbf{r}$ is an eigenvector of $I^{\mathrm{T}} I$. A similar argument shows that $\mathbf{c}$ is an eigenvector II^{T}.

Next we wish to find two one-dimensional filters which equal c_i and r_j, respectively, at the sample points; i.e. we require filters $C(z)$ and $R(z)$ such that

$$|C(e^{j\omega_{i_1}})| = c_{i_1} \tag{10.8.2}$$

$$|R(e^{j\omega_{i_2}})| = r_{i_2} \tag{10.8.3}$$

This can only hold if $c_{i_1} \geq 0$ and $r_{i_2} \geq 0$ for each i_1, i_2. It is not difficult to prove, however, that this must be the case for the minimum mean square error values determined above. The exact or approximate solutions of (10.8.2) and (10.8.3) for realizable filters C and R can be determined by standard one-dimensional optimization techniques. Note that if we write I in the form of its singular value decomposition (Appendix 1)

$$I = \sum_{i_1=1}^{n_2} (\lambda_i)^{1/2} \kappa_i \rho_i \tag{10.8.4}$$

where κ_i are the normalized eigencolumns of II^{T}, ρ_i are the normalized eigenrows of $I^{\mathrm{T}} I$ and λ_i are the eigenvalues of $I^{\mathrm{T}} I$, then it can be seen that in (10.8.1), we have

$$\alpha = \lambda_1, \ c = \kappa_1, \ r^{\mathrm{T}} = \rho_1$$

Bibliographical notes

Justification for the use of circularly symmetric windows is discussed in Huang (1972) and the basic theory of frequency sampling filters is taken from Hu and Rabiner (1972). Tchebychev approximation theory is derived in Cheney (1966) and its application to one-dimensional design methods can be found in Parks and McClellan (1972). Its generalization to two-dimensional nonrecursive filters is considered in Kamp and Thiran (1975). McClellan transforms were introduced in McClellan (1973) and extended to more general forms in Mersereau et al. (1976). Spectral transformations are considered in detail in Chakrabarti and Mitra (1977) and Pendergrass and Mitra (1976), while the application of Tchebychev approximation theory to IIR design can be found in Bednar (1975). The l^p design technique is covered in more detail in Maria and Fahmy (1974) and for the theory of separable filters one should consult Twogood and Mitra (1977).

Exercises

1 Find the amplitude responses of the filters $H_1, \ldots, H_4$ in (i) ... (iv) of Section 10.2 in terms of F.

2 Write a Pascal program for the design of frequency sampling filters.

3 Discuss the McClellan transformation in the case where

$$A = B = C = -D = 0.5$$

4 Write a Pascal program to solve (10.5.3) for the coefficients $a_{k_1 k_2}$, and hence design optimal two-dimensional filters by choosing a variety of different weights w.

5 Give a heuristic argument to show that

$$\|f\|_{L^p} \to \|f\|_\infty$$

as $p \to \infty$ for any $f \in L^q$, $1 \leq q \leq \infty$.

6 Implement numerically the Tchebychev replacement algorithm given in the theorem in Section 10.5.

7 Draw frequency contours, as in Figure 10.3, for the two-dimensional separable transformations corresponding to all the one-dimensional Constantinides transformations (up to order 2).

8 Prove (10.8.4) in detail.

References

Bednar, J. B. (1975), 'Spatial recursive filter design via rational Tchebychev approximation', *IEEE Trans. Circuits Sys.*, CAS-**22** (6), 572–4.

Chakrabarti, S. and S. K. Mitra (1977), 'Design of two-dimensional digital filters via spectral transformations', *Proc. IEEE*, **65**, 905–14.

Cheney, E. W. (1966), *Introduction to Approximation Theory*, NY: McGraw-Hill.

Hu, J. V. and L. R. Rabiner (1972), 'Design techniques for two-dimensional digital filters', *IEEE Trans. Audio Electroacoust.*, AU-**20** (4), 249–57.

Huang, T. S. (1972), 'Two dimensional windows', *IEEE Trans. Audio Electroacoust.*, AU-**20** (1), 88–9.

Kamp, Y. and J. P. Thiran (1975), 'Tchebychev approximation for two-dimensional non-recursive digital filters', *IEEE Trans. Circuits Sys.*, CAS-**22** (3), 208–18.

Maria, G. A. and M. M. Fahmy (1974), 'An l^p design technique for two-dimensional digital recursive filters', *IEEE Trans. Acoust., Speech, Signal Process.*, ASSP-**22** (1), 15–21.

McClellan, J. H. (1973), 'The design of two-dimensional digital filters by transformations', *Seventh Annual Princeton Conf. Inf. Sci. and Sys. Proc.*, 584 pp.

Mersereau, R. M., W. F. G. Mecklenbrauker and T. F. Quatieri Jr (1976), 'McClellan transformations for two-dimensional digital filtering: I-design', *IEEE Trans. Circuits Sys.*, CAS-**23** (7), 405–14.

Parks, T. W. and J. H. McClellan (1972), 'Tchebychev approximation for nonrecursive digital filters with linear phase', *IEEE Trans. Circuits Theory*, CT-**19** (2), 189–94.

Pendergrass, N. A. and S. K. Mitra (1976), 'Spectral transformations for two-dimensional digital filters', *IEEE Trans. Circuits Sys.*, CAS-**23** (1), 26–35.

Twogood, R. E. and S. K. Mitra (1977), 'Computer-aided design of separable two-dimensional digital filters', *IEEE Trans. Acoust., Speech, Signal Process.*, ASSP-**25** (2), 165–9.

11

Introduction to Digital Image Processing

11.1 Introduction

An *image* is a two-dimensional representation of a real physical three-dimensional scene. It can take a variety of forms from a black-and-white photograph to a moving picture on a colour television. (Similar theory to that which we shall develop in this part of the book applies to three-dimensional *holographic* images, but we shall not consider images of this type in detail.) The process of capturing the real scene in the form of an image results in a number of degrading effects, the removal of which is the basis of image processing. These degrading effects can be lack of contrast in photographs, geometric distortions in imaging systems, motion blurr or simply noise introduced by transducers or other electronic or optical devices.

There are basically two purposes for image processing: the first is to remove the effects of degradations such as those mentioned above and produce an output image for the use of human observers, while the second is to provide an output image or some enhanced version of the original scene for use in *machine vision*. In the latter case the image processing is performed as a precursor to machine pattern recognition which is discussed in detail in the last section of the book. Although the techniques of image processing for human perception and machine vision overlap, in the latter case we are interested mainly in finding and interpreting objects in a scene so that edge enhancement and thresholding operations are particularly important here.

In the case of image processing for human perception we are often influenced by the nonlinearities in the human visual response. In particular, the human eye has a logarithmic response to light intensity and so contrast enhancement techniques should take this into account. For this reason we shall continue in the next section with a study of human visual perception.

11.2 Human perception of images

For a monochrome image we can represent its spectral intensity distribution by a continuous function $I(x, y)$, or by $I(x, y, t)$ for a moving image. At any fixed value of (x, y) the number $I(x, y)$ will be proportional to the *grey level* of the image at that point. Of course, I will be bounded above by some maximum intensity I_{max} and below by zero (i.e. 'black'). Thus,

$$0 \leq I(x, y) \leq I_{max} \tag{11.2.1}$$

for each (x, y) in the image.

Colour images, on the other hand, can be represented by an intensity function $C(x, y, \lambda)$ (or $C(x, y, \lambda, t)$) which depends now on the wavelength of reflected light λ. For fixed λ, $C(x, y, \lambda)$ can be regarded as a monochrome image. Again, we can bound the function C as in (11.2.1), so that

$$0 \leq C(x, y, \lambda) \leq C_{max} \tag{11.2.2}$$

for some constant C_{max}.

The brightness response of a human observer to an image will therefore be

$$P(x, y) = \int_0^\infty C(x, y, \lambda)V(\lambda)d\lambda \tag{11.2.3}$$

where $V(\lambda)$ is the response factor of the human eye at frequency λ. More generally, if there are K sensors, each with a spectral response factor $V_i(\lambda)$, then the brightness response of the ith sensor is

$$P_i(x, y) = \int_0^\infty C(x, y, \lambda)V_i(\lambda)d\lambda \qquad 1 \leq i \leq K$$

Three types of sensor in the human eye have been identified as being associated mainly with red, green and blue light, respectively, and so we can form the three brightness response functions

$$R(x, y) = \int_0^\infty C(x, y, \lambda) V_R(\lambda) d\lambda$$

$$G(x, y) = \int_0^\infty C(x, y, \lambda) V_G(\lambda) d\lambda$$

$$B(x, y) = \int_0^\infty C(x, y, \lambda) V_B(\lambda) d\lambda$$

where V_R, V_G and V_B are the response functions for red, green and blue primaries respectively.

The perception of images by humans is dependent, of course, on the spectral energy distribution of the reflected light from the image. However, as we shall see, this is not the only influence on visual perception – indeed the way in which part of an image is perceived may depend strongly on the structure of another part of the image. Thus, what appears fairly dark grey on a white background may appear much lighter on a black background (Figure 11.1). Moreover, it is possible for two distinct spectral energy distributions to be perceived identically (so-called *metameric pairs*).

Colour perception is usually measured in terms of three parameters: brightness, hue and saturation. The *brightness* of a light source is merely the absolute intensity of the source, i.e. brightness is proportional to the electromagnetic energy radiated by the source. The *hue* of a light source is a parameter which distinguishes the colour of the source, i.e. is the source red, yellow, blue, etc.? It should be noted that perceived colours do not correspond to single wavelengths of light. Thus a monochromatic laser can produce a pure red light but not a purple one since purple can only be produced by a combination of red and blue. Most perceived colours are composed of a complex spectral energy distribution such as is shown in Figure 11.2(b). The spectral energy distribution of a helium–neon laser is shown in Figure 11.2(a).

Figure 11.1   Apparent brightness perception.

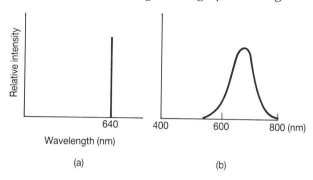

Figure 11.2 Comparison of a typical perceived red light and a pure laser light: (a) helium–neon laser; (b) typical 'red' light.

The third perceptual measure of colour is *saturation* and is the quantity which distinguishes a pure spectral light from a pastel shade of the same hue. It is merely a measure of the amount of white light added to the pure spectral colour.

Before discussing the quantitative colour measures in more detail we shall next consider human vision and outline the way in which the visual system operates. Light is focused on the retina by the lens, which can adaptively change shape according to the depth of the image. The light receptors in the retina consist of two types – rods and cones. Rods are more sensitive than cones and are responsible for *scotopic* vision at low light levels. Cones are identified with colour vision and provide *photopic* vision at high light levels. They have been found to exist in three types which are sensitive mainly to blue, red and green regions of the spectrum. Since cones are much less sensitive than rods, this accounts for our difficulty in distinguishing colours in images illuminated with low light levels, e.g. at night. It is estimated that there are of the order of 100 million receptors in the retina and only one million nerve fibres in the optic nerve, and so the receptors must be connected to the optic fibres in complex ways. The physiological basis of sight is not well understood at present and so we shall continue with some simple experimental observations on the nature of sight.

We have already mentioned the contrast effect of Figure 11.1 where the perceived nature of a grey level depends on its background. The *contrast sensitivity* of the eye is an important quantity and measures the just noticeable difference dI of an area of light of intensity $I + dI$ placed in a background of intensity I (Figure 11.3(a)). It is found that the *Weber fraction* dI/I is constant (~0.02) over much of the intensity range, but becomes highly nonlinear for low and high intensities. Moreover, the curve in Figure 11.3(a) depends on the background. In fact, if the same experiment is done with the test image in a

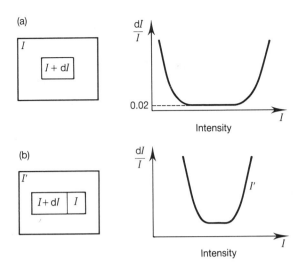

Figure 11.3 Measuring contrast sensitivity: (a) relative contrast measurement; (b) relative contrast with distinct background.

background of fixed intensity I', then the size of the constant region of dI/I is considerably reduced. Note that $d\{\log(I)\} = dI/I = $ constant; this is the reason for using log of intensities in many image processing operations.

The human eye has lower sensitivity to high and low spatial frequencies than to mid-frequencies and this leads to some interesting phenomena when observing edges between two areas of constant brightness. The *Mach band* is illustrated in Figure 11.4 where a number of strips with constant grey levels are juxtaposed. Although the strips are of constant intensity, the right side of each strip is perceived as being darker than the left. This is due to the Gibb's 'ringing' phenomenon in the human visual system.

A number of interesting colour perception properties have also been observed. First it should be noted that the hue of a perceived colour depends to a large extent on the *adaptation* of the observer. This means that when a viewer is subject to a high-intensity light of a particular hue for a period of time and then shown a scene with a variety of colours, the scene will be perceived as being shifted towards the complementary colour of the original high-intensity light. Another perceptual property of the eye is that it can be 'fooled' by high-frequency flashing lights. Thus we are familiar with the trick of spinning a disk coloured with the rainbow colours – when spinning fast enough the disk appears white. Similarly, if the *Benham disk*, shown in Figure 11.5, is spun fast enough (counterclockwise) the outer ring appears red, the middle ring appears green and the inner ring appears blue.

Figure 11.4 The Mach band effect.

Figure 11.5 The
Benham disk.

Finally, we shall note a number of visual 'illusions' in which the brain tries to interpret an image presented to it by the optic system. First we have the ability to fill in missing lines in order to interpret an image, as in Figure 11.6(a), or to fill in lines to give depth perception to a two-dimensional image – in Figure 11.6(b) we see a triangle on top of three circles and in Figure 11.6(c) we see a large triangle on top of three squares and a smaller triangle beneath the first one.

In the Zollner illusion (Figure 11.7) and the Ebbinghaus illusion (Figure 11.8) the brain incorrectly interprets the received data. In the former, the parallel lines are perceived as being skew and in the latter the central circles are perceived as being of different sizes, even though they are, in fact, the same.

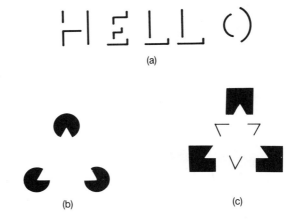

(a)

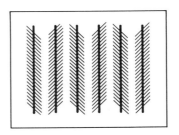

(b)   (c)

Figure 11.6 Examples of line continuation: (a) 'HELLO'; (b) apparent triangle; (c) white triangle above triangle outline.

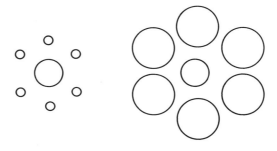

Figure 11.7 The Zöllner illusion.

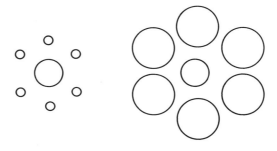

Figure 11.8 The Ebbinghaus illusion.

11.3 Colour models

We have seen that a light source is characterized by its spectral energy distribution $C(\lambda)$. The electromagnetic energy radiated by a *black body* (one which radiates the maximum possible energy at each frequency) is given by *Planck's law*:

$$C(\lambda) = \frac{a}{\lambda^5[\exp(b/\lambda T) - 1]} \qquad (11.3.1)$$

for some constants a, b, where T is the absolute temperature of the body (Figure 11.9). A real body will radiate somewhat less than this ideal value at each frequency λ, although the Sun is very close to being a black body (Figure 11.10).

In the visible spectrum (11.3.1) is often approximated by *Wien's law*

$$C(\lambda) \cong \frac{a}{\lambda^5 \exp(b/\lambda T)} \qquad (11.3.2)$$

shown in Figure 11.11.

An important quantitative measure in human visual perceptions is the *spectral sensitivity function* of the visual system, which may be obtained by averaging over a number of observers. The sensitivity function for photopic vision (cones) is called the (relative) *photopic luminosity function*, while that for scotopic vision (rods) is the (relative) *scotopic luminosity function* (Figure 11.12). It follows that the perceptual brightness of a light source with energy distribution $C(\lambda)$ is proportional to $\int_0^\infty C(\lambda)V(\lambda)d\lambda$, where $V(\lambda)$ is the relative luminosity function.

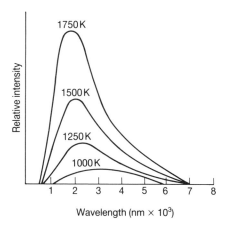

Figure 11.9   Planck's law.

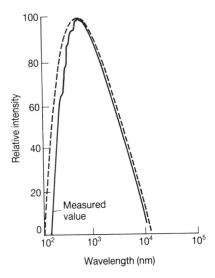

Figure 11.10   Sunlight.

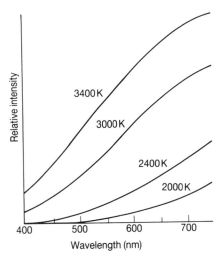

Figure 11.11   Wien's law.

In the final part of this section we shall consider the more quantitative aspects of colorimetry and their relationship with perceptual measures of colour. As we have said above, an arbitrary colour will have a spectral energy distribution which can be almost any function of frequency λ as in Figure

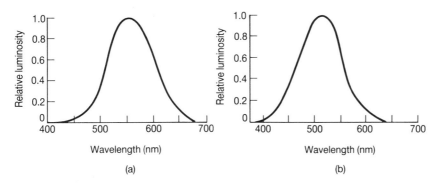

Figure 11.12 Relative luminosity functions: (a) photopic vision; (b) scotopic vision.

11.13(a). Moreover, a typical white light will not be 'true white', as in Figure 11.13(b), but will have some less than ideal characteristic. Similarly, typical primary colours used in photography, television, etc., will have distributions similar to those in Figure 11.13(c)–(e), rather than delta functions at single frequencies, as in laser light.

In subjective colour matching we try to produce the arbitrary colour $C(\lambda)$ from a linear combination of the primaries. This can be achieved either by additive or subtractive colour matching. Practically, we adjust the intensities of

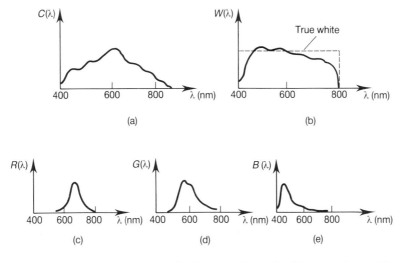

Figure 11.13 Spectral energy distributions for: (a) arbitrary colour; (b) white light; (c)–(e) standard primaries.

the primaries until the resulting superposed colour matches the given colour $C(\lambda)$, i.e.

$$C(\lambda) = I_R(C)R(\lambda) + I_G(C)G(\lambda) + I_B(C)B(\lambda) \qquad (11.3.3)$$

If we do the same with the reference white of Figure 11.13(b) we obtain

$$W(\lambda) = I_R(W)R(\lambda) + I_G(W)G(\lambda) + I_B(B)B(\lambda) \qquad (11.3.4)$$

The relative intensities

$$T_P(C) = \frac{I_P(C)}{I_P(W)} \qquad P = R, G \text{ or } B \qquad (11.3.5)$$

are called the *tristimulus values* of the colour C. It should be noted that a simple linear combination of the functions $R(\lambda)$, $G(\lambda)$ and $B(\lambda)$ cannot, in general, produce the arbitrary function $C(\lambda)$. However, because of the limited resolving power of the human eye, a good perceptual match can almost always be obtained. In subtractive colour matching a white light is passed successively through variable yellow, magenta and cyan filters and the filter dyes are changed until a match is obtained with the desired colour.

When we use three arbitrary primaries $P_i(\lambda)$ the relations (11.3.3) and (11.3.4) become

$$C(\lambda) = \sum_{i=1}^{3} I_i(C)P_i(\lambda)$$

and

$$W(\lambda) = \sum_{i=1}^{3} I_i(W)P_i(\lambda)$$

Similarly, from (11.3.5), the tristimulus values are defined by

$$T_i(C) = \frac{I_i(C)}{I_i(W)}$$

Hence we obtain

$$C(\lambda) = \sum_{i=1}^{3} T_i(C)I_i(W)P_i(\lambda) \qquad (11.3.6)$$

The tristimulus values of a colour can be regarded as rectangular coordinates in a three-dimensional colour space, as in Figure 11.14. Note, however, that for physically realizable colours we must have

$$T_i(C) \geq 0 \qquad i = 1, 2, 3$$

Some (theoretical) colours, with $T_i(C) < 0$ for some i, are not physically realizable for a given set of primaries. Note that the normalized tristimulus values

$$t_i = T_i / \sum_{j=1}^{3} T_j \qquad 1 \leq i \leq 3$$

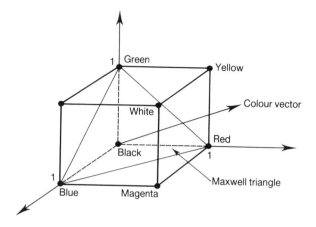

Figure 11.14   Colour space for the standard primaries.

are sometimes used, and since $t_1 + t_2 + t_3 = 1$ only two independent values, t_1 and t_2 are required. These are called *chromaticity coordinates*.

Suppose next that $s_i(\lambda)$, $1 \leq i \leq 3$ are the sensitivities of three receptors in a colour vision system, and we wish to match a colour $C(\lambda)$ by three given primaries, $P_i(\lambda)$. Then the energy from each receptor is given by

$$e_i(C) = \int C(\lambda)s_i(\lambda)\mathrm{d}\lambda \qquad 1 \leq i \leq 3$$

$$= \sum_{j=1}^{3} T_j(C)I_i(W) \int P_j(\lambda)s_i(\lambda)\mathrm{d}\lambda \qquad 1 \leq i \leq 3$$

by (11.3.6), i.e.

$$e(C) = AT(C)$$

where A is the matrix (a_{ij}) given by

$$a_{ij} = \int I_i(W)P_j(\lambda)s_i(\lambda)\mathrm{d}\lambda$$

where e, T are the obvious vectors. Thus, if A is invertible we have

$$T(C) = A^{-1}e(C) \tag{11.3.7}$$

For any colour $C(\lambda)$ we can define the tristimulus values of the narrow band signal consisting of the colour $C(\lambda)$ at a single wavelength, i.e.

$$C_\omega(\lambda) = C(\lambda)\delta(\omega - \lambda)$$

Denote these tristimulus values for a set of primaries by

$$T_{pj}(\lambda) \qquad 1 \leq j \leq 3$$

Then it is easy to show that the tristimulus values of the complete colour $C(\lambda)$ are given by

$$T_i(C) = \int C(\lambda)T_{pj}(\lambda)d\lambda$$

The tristimulus functions $T_{pj}(\lambda)$ for typical blue, green and red primaries which are necessary to match a unit energy throughout the spectrum are shown in Figure 11.15. Note that the blue and red values become negative over certain frequencies. The chromaticity diagram corresponding to Figure 11.15 is shown in Figure 11.16. From (11.3.6) we have

$$L(C) = \sum_{i=1}^{3} T_i(C) \int I_i(W)P_i(\lambda)V(\lambda)d\lambda$$

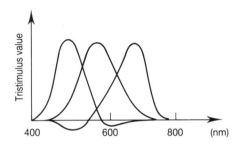

Figure 11.15 Tristimulus functions for red, green and blue primaries.

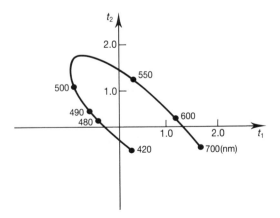

Figure 11.16 Chromaticity diagram for red, green and blue primaries.

where L is the luminance of a colour C and V is the relative luminosity function. Hence

$$L(C) = \sum_{i=1}^{3} T_i(C)L(P_i)$$

where

$$L(P) = \int I_i(W)P_i(\lambda)V(\lambda)\mathrm{d}\lambda$$

is the *luminosity coefficient* of primary i. Since

$$t_i(C) = T_i(C)/\sum_{j=1}^{3} T_j(C)$$

it follows that

$$T_i(C) = \frac{t_i(C)L(C)}{\sum_{j=1}^{3} t_j(C)L(P_j)} \tag{11.3.8}$$

Note, finally, that if we refer the colour C to two colour coordinate systems with primaries $P_i(\lambda)$ and $\widetilde{P}_i(\lambda)$, respectively, where the reference white signals are $W(\lambda)$ and $\widetilde{W}(\lambda)$, then by (11.3.7) we have

$$T(C) = A^{-1}e(C)$$

and

$$\widetilde{T}(C) = \widetilde{A}^{-1}e(C)$$

where

$$\widetilde{A} = (\widetilde{a}_{ij}) = \int I_i(\widetilde{W})\widetilde{P}_j(\lambda)s_i(\lambda)\mathrm{d}\lambda$$

Thus,

$$\widetilde{T}(C) = \widetilde{A}^{-1}AT(C)$$

and so $\widetilde{A}^{-1}A$ defines a transformation between colour coordinate systems.

11.4 Devices for picture processing

In this section we shall describe some of the main devices used in picture processing. In many systems the light from an image is focused by a lens on to a surface which is scanned in some way. There are basically two types of arrangements for this part of the system – scan-in and scan-out – as shown in Figure 11.17. In the scan-in system, light is scanned over an object (usually in the form of a laser beam) by a beam deflector, and the resulting reflected or transmitted light is focused onto a sensor. The scan-out system produces a

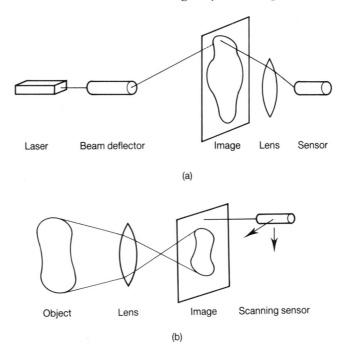

Laser   Beam deflector   Image   Lens   Sensor

(a)

Object   Lens   Image   Scanning sensor

(b)

Figure 11.17   Basic focusing systems: (a) scan-in system;
(b) scan-out system.

focused image first on some planar surface which is then scanned directly into the sensor.

A simple scanning device can be made with a galvanometer and mirror arrangement shown in Figure 11.18(a). Note, however, that for an angular movement θ of the mirror the linear distance of the image scanned is $x = d \tan \theta$ (Figure 11.18(b)). This nonlinearity (for constant θ) in horizontal distance leads to geometrical distortion, as shown in Figure 11.18(c). We shall describe methods for the correction of such distortion later.

A more common electronic scanning device is the *vidicon camera tube* shown in Figure 11.19. The image of an object is formed on a photoconductive layer through a transparent electrode. The photoconductor is an array of pixels, each consisting of a resistor and capacitor. The inner surface of this layer is scanned by an electron beam which charges the capacitors in the layer. When a pixel is not being charged by the electron beam it discharges through the resistor at a rate proportional to the incident light intensity on that pixel. When that pixel is again scanned by the electron beam the amount of discharge of the capacitor modulates the recharging current which is sensed by the external

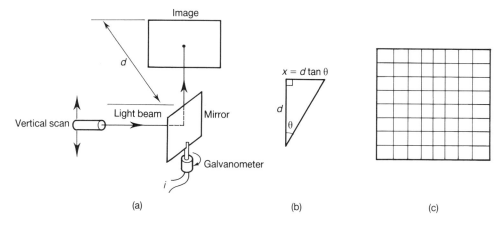

Figure 11.18 Simple mirror scanner: (a) scanning system; (b) distortion geometry; (c) distorted grid.

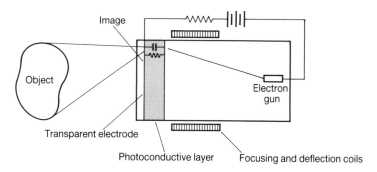

Figure 11.19 Vidicon camera tube.

circuit. The scanning rate is usually 60 frames/s (or 30 frames/s in the case of interlaced pictures).

Many modern cameras are solid state and consist of an array of photosensitive elements on an integrated chip. The operation is similar to the vidicon camera in that the video signal produced is proportional to capacitor discharge (or current flow in a transistor in the case of MOS transistors). The scanning technique is one of two types – for a MOS array, registers are used for horizontal and vertical scanning, as shown in Figure 11.20. Charge coupled devices (CCD) use an array of MOS capacitors and the charges are transferred via neighbouring elements by a series of shift pulses to a frame memory during blanking periods of the scan.

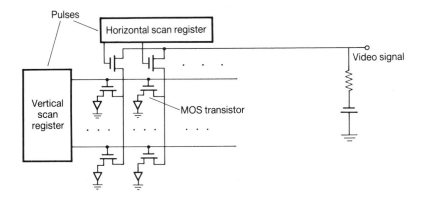

Figure 11.20 MOS camera array.

Another important means of image capture is, of course, photography. We shall describe briefly the principles of monochrome photography; the basic ideas of colour photography are similar. First consider a flat piece of some material which has light of intensity I_1 falling on one side (Figure 11.21(a)). If the transmitted light intensity is I_2 we define the *transmittance T* of the material by

$$T = \frac{I_2}{I_1} \qquad (0 \leq T \leq 1)$$

and the *optical density* by

$$D = \log \frac{I_1}{I_2} = -\log T \qquad (0 \leq D < \infty)$$

The optical density is a useful measure of transmittance since it is additive in the case of light passing through two types of material (Figure 11.21(b)). Thus, if

$$T_1 = \frac{I_2}{I_1}, \; T_2 = \frac{I_3}{I_2}, \; D_1 = \log \frac{I_1}{I_2}, \; D_2 = \log \frac{I_2}{I_3}$$

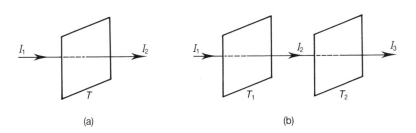

Figure 11.21 Light passing through translucent materials: (a) single sheet; (b) double sheet.

then

$$T_3 \triangleq \frac{I_3}{I_1} = T_1 T_2$$

while

$$D_3 \triangleq \log \frac{I_1}{I_3} = \log \frac{I_1}{I_2} + \log \frac{I_2}{I_3} = D_1 + D_2$$

A typical monochrome film consists of a plastic base coated with an emulsion containing silver halide grains (Figure 11.22(a)). When exposed to light, some molecules of silver halide are reduced to silver. The development process also reduces the silver halide in the emulsion but this reduction occurs much quicker in the exposed grains, at a rate proportional to the light intensity during exposure. After development, unreduced grains are washed off the base. (This process is shown in Figure 11.22(b), together with typical optical density values.) We define the *exposure* of a point on a film to be

$$E = \int_0^t I(\tau) d\tau$$

where $I(\tau)$ is the light intensity at that point at time τ and t is the time of exposure. For constant intensity I we have

$$E = tI$$

The optical density D of an exposed film is a function of E and a plot of this function (against $\log E$) is called the *Hurter–Driffield* (H–D) curve of the film (Figure 11.23). The angle γ shown on the (approximately) linear part of the curve is a measure of the contrast in the image. Note that we have the following conflicting factors for the quality of a photographic image:

1. For high resolution we require many small grains in a thin emulsion to avoid light scatter.
2. For high sensitivity at low light levels we require a thin emulsion and few grains.

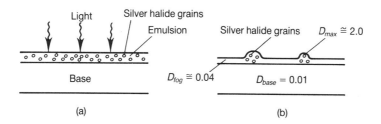

Figure 11.22   Monochrome film processing: (a) during exposure; (b) after development.

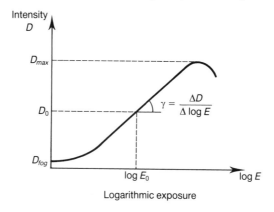

Figure 11.23 A typical Hurter–Driffield curve.

3. For high D_{max} we require a thick emulsion, usually producing 'graininess' in the image.

The resolution is usually specified in terms of the *modulation transfer function* which measures the response to sinusoidal patterns of increasing frequency. If we expose an emulsion to the spatially periodic pattern

$$\log E = \log E_0 + \sin (2\pi f x)$$

where $\log E_0$ is a point in the linear region of the H–D curve and f is the frequency, then from the H–D curve the optical density should vary according to the relation

$$D(x) = D_0 + \gamma \sin (2\pi f x)$$

However, grain size and scatter reduce the contrast and we actually obtain

$$D(x) = D_0 + \gamma M(f) \sin (2\pi f x) \qquad 0 \leqslant M(f) \leqslant 1$$

where $M(f)$ is the modulation transfer function (determined experimentally) and is shown in Figure 11.24.

Another important consideration in image processing systems is the output display. It is found that the eye can distinguish about 40–50 grey levels. However the retina has an inherent edge enhancement capacity so that if 256 successive grey levels are placed side by side the eye can distinguish the boundaries between the levels. When a white strip is placed between the grey levels the eye can no longer distinguish two neighbouring levels. In any case there is no point in having too many grey levels in comparison with the resolution of the system. For example, if the RMS noise level of the system is 1 per cent of the total range from black to white, then the display can only resolve 100 shades of grey, regardless of its intrinsic resolution.

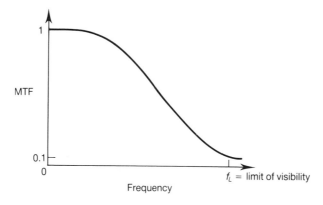

Figure 11.24 A typical modulation transfer function (MTF).

A typical image display device produces the image as an array of spots which are usually modelled by Gaussian intensities,

$$p(x, y) = e^{-(x^2+y^2)}$$

(Figure 11.25(a)). This intensity function is a maximum at the centre and is radially symmetric, so we can write

$$p(x, y) = e^{-r^2}$$
$$= e^{-(r/R)^2 \ln 2}$$
$$= e^{\ln(2^{-r^2/R^2})}$$
$$= 2^{-(r/R)^2}$$
$$\triangleq p(r)$$

Consider now the ability of a discrete set of spots to produce a flat field

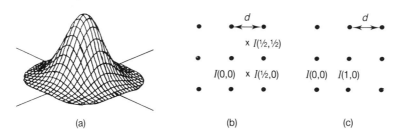

Figure 11.25 Typical display spot array: (a) spot intensity; (b) low frequency test; (c) high frequency test.

response (uniform intensity). Then each spot will have the same intensity in Figure 11.25(b) and the total intensity $I(0, 0)$ at $(0, 0)$ is given (approximately) by

$$I(0, 0) \cong 1 + 4p(d) + 4p(\sqrt{2}d)$$

Similarly, we have

$$I(\tfrac{1}{2}, 0) \cong 2p(d/2) + 4p(\sqrt{5}d/2)$$

and

$$I(\tfrac{1}{2}, \tfrac{1}{2}) \cong 4p(\sqrt{2}d/2) + 8p(\sqrt{10}d/2)$$

A plot of these three functions of d is shown in Figure 11.26 and it is seen that for the least variation in intensity we require

$$1.55R \lesssim d \lesssim 1.65R$$

A similar analysis for high-frequency response can be achieved by considering successive columns of spots with maximum and zero intensities (Figure 11.25(c)). Then

$$I(0, 0) \simeq 1 + 2p(d) + 4p(2d)$$

$$I(d, 0) \simeq 2p(d) + 4p(\sqrt{2}d)$$

If we define the *modulation factor M* by

$$M = \frac{I(0, 0) - I(1, 0)}{I(0, 0)}$$

then we obtain the graph in Figure 11.27. As is clearly seen (and, of course, is intuitively obvious) we require large d for good high-frequency response. Hence good low- and high-frequency responses are conflicting factors.

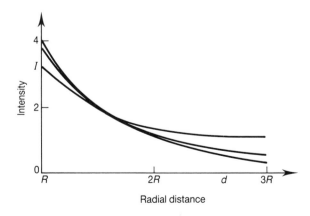

Figure 11.26   Total spot intensities at various points.

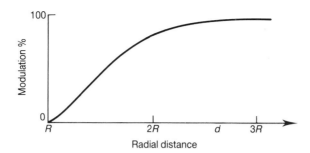

Figure 11.27 Modulation factor (in %).

We note finally in this section that a variety of techniques have been developed for obtaining range information in stereo vision. These include optical time of flight systems where an amplitude modulated laser beam is split into two parts, one of which is projected onto the object by a scanning unit and then passes to a detector, while the other goes straight to the detector. The phase difference between the two light rays is then used to compute the distance of the object. Ultrasonic ranging systems have also been employed but these are usually used only for automatic focusing of cameras, since it is difficult to produce a narrow beam of ultrasound. Triangulation is another popular method in which a light beam is projected onto the object by a rotating mirror and a photo-detector receives the reflected beam. In this method the range is given by simple triangulation (Figure 11.28). It is also possible to use a sheet of light instead of a spot – this is called the light-stripe (triangulation) method. Ranging can also be achieved by Moiré tomography, in which an interference pattern is superimposed on the object image by a pair of diffraction gratings – it has been used for many years in stress analysis.

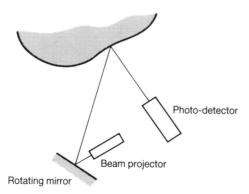

Figure 11.28 Ranging by triangulation.

11.5 Mathematical models

A typical optical imaging system is shown in Figure 11.29 and consists of a lens which focuses an object onto an image plane. We have the well-known relation

$$1/d_o + 1/d_i = 1/f$$

for the focal length f of the lens. For a lens of small aperture the spot image of a point source will be approximately the same for a spot in any position of the (x_o, y_o)-plane. Thus we may regard the spot image as the impulse response of a linear system and write

$$I(x_i, y_i) = \int_{-\infty}^{\infty} \int_{-\infty}^{\infty} \Delta(x_o - x_o', y_o - y_o')O(x_o', y_o')dx_o'dy_o'$$

where $O(x_o, y_o)$ is the object intensity function in the (x_o, y_o)-plane and $I(x_i, y_i)$ is the image intensity function in the (x_i, y_i)-plane. The impulse response Δ of the lens system is called the *point spread function* (PSF). If a point source at $(x, y, z, t) = (0, 0, 0, 0)$ emits a spherical wave, then its field amplitude at (x, y, z, t) is given by

$$u(x, y, z, t) = \frac{a}{r} \cos\left[\frac{2\pi r}{\lambda} + 2\pi\left(\frac{ct}{\lambda} + \frac{\phi(t)}{\lambda}\right)\right]$$

where λ is the mean wavelength of light, c is the speed of light and $\phi(t)$ is the phase fluctuation function. Writing $k = 2\pi/\lambda$, this may be written in the form

$$u = \mathrm{Re}\left\{\frac{a}{r}\, e^{jkr}e^{jk[ct+\phi]}\right\}$$

Coherent illumination occurs when the phase function $\phi(t)$ is independent of t (or at least all separate sources have the same functional dependence for $\phi(t)$) so that stable interference patterns between two such sources can be obtained. In cases where separate sources illuminating a scene have random phase fluctuations, stable interference is not possible.

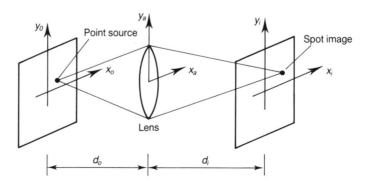

Figure 11.29 A simple lens system.

In order to obtain the PSF for a simple lens note that the converging spherical wave from a lens can be modelled as a spherical wave intercepted by an opaque screen containing a circular hole, as in Figure 11.30. The field in the pupil plane may be written in the form

$$E(x_a, y_a) = p(x_a, y_a) \frac{1}{R} e^{-jkR}$$

where p is the pupil function and $R = (x_i^2 + y_i^2 + z_i^2)^{1/2}$. Thus, by the Huygens–Fresnel principle (Appendix 1), we have the expression

$$E(x_i, y_i) = \frac{1}{j\lambda} \int \int_P p(x_a, y_a) \frac{1}{R} e^{-jkR} \frac{1}{r} e^{jkr} \cos \theta \, dx_a dy_a$$

for the field in the image plane, where λ is the (mean) wavelength of light and P is the pupil area. Now,

$$R = (x_a^2 + y_a^2 + d^2)^{1/2} \cong d[1 + \tfrac{1}{2}(x_a/d)^2 + \tfrac{1}{2}(y_a/d)^2]$$

and

$$r \cong d[1 + \tfrac{1}{2}(x_i - x_a)^2/d^2 + \tfrac{1}{2}(y_i - y_a)^2/d^2]$$

Hence,

$$E(x_i, y_i) = \frac{\lambda}{j} e^{(jk/2d)(x_i^2 + y_i^2)} \int_{-\infty}^{\infty} \int_{-\infty}^{\infty} p(\lambda dx_a', \lambda dy_a') e^{-j2\pi(x_i x_a' + y_i y_a')} dx_a' dy_a' \quad (11.5.1)$$

where $x_a' = x_a/(\lambda d)$, $y_a' = y_a/(\lambda d)$ and we have assumed small θ. Thus, the coherent PSF is proportional to the two-dimensional Fourier transform of the

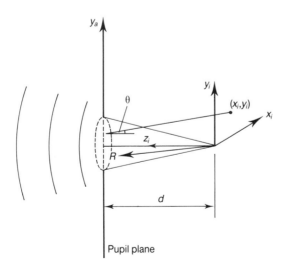

Figure 11.30   Simple lens model.

pupil function. The proportionality factor only affects the phase of the image and is usually ignored by image sensors. We can therefore write

$$i(x_i, y_i) = \int_{-\infty}^{\infty} \int_{-\infty}^{\infty} h(x_i - x_o, y_i - y_o) u(x_o, y_o) dx_o dy_o$$

for the intensity distribution of the image, where u is the projection of the object in the image plane and

$$h(x, y) = \mathcal{F}\{p(\lambda dx_a, \lambda dy_a)\}$$

Hence,

$$H(u, v) = \mathcal{F}(h)(u, v) = \mathcal{F}^2(p)(u, v) = p(-\lambda du, -\lambda dv)$$

for a symmetric pupil function.

Consider, next, the case of incoherent light. Then the observed intensity is given by

$$I(x_i, y_i) = E[u(x_i, y_i)u^*(x_i, y_i)] = E \int_{-\infty}^{\infty} \int_{-\infty}^{\infty} h(x_i - x_1, y_i - y_1)u(x_1, y_1)dx_1dy_1$$

$$\times \int_{-\infty}^{\infty} \int_{-\infty}^{\infty} h^*(x_i - x_2, y_i - y_2)u^*(x_2, y_2)dx_2dy_2$$

$$= \int_{-\infty}^{\infty} \int_{-\infty}^{\infty} \int_{-\infty}^{\infty} \int_{-\infty}^{\infty} h(x_i - x_1, y_i - y_1)h^*(x_i - x_2, y_i - y_2)$$

$$\times E(u(x_1, y_1)u^*(x_2, y_2)) \, dx_1dy_1dx_2dy_2$$

The term involving the expectation is the temporal cross-correlation of u at $(x_1, y_1)x(x_2, y_2)$. For incoherent light this is zero for distinct image point sources, while at $(x_1, y_1)x(x_1, y_1)$ it is just the image intensity at that point. Thus,

$$E(u(x_1, y_1)u^*(x_2, y_2)) = I_i(x_1, x_2)\delta(x_1 - x_2, y_1 - y_2)$$

where I_i is the image intensity. Thus, the incoherent PSF is just the power spectrum of the pupil function. The normalized Fourier transform of the incoherent PSF is the *optical transfer function* OTF given by

$$\text{OTF}(u, v) = \frac{R_p(u, v)}{R_p(0, 0)} = \frac{\int_{-\infty}^{\infty}\int_{-\infty}^{\infty} p(\lambda dx, \lambda dy)p(\lambda dx - u, \lambda dy - v) \, dxdy}{\int_{-\infty}^{\infty}\int_{-\infty}^{\infty} p^2(\lambda dx, \lambda dy) \, dxdy}$$

For a circular aperture, we have

$$h(r) = \left(\frac{2J_1[\pi(r/r_0)]}{\pi(r/r_0)}\right)^2 \qquad r_0 = \frac{\lambda d}{a}$$

The first zero is at $r_0 = 1.22\lambda d/a$ (radius of the *Airy disk*) and two point sources can just be resolved if they are separated by r_0.

We shall complete this chapter with an introduction to human vision system modelling. A basic observation in experimental vision research is that the human visual system is nonlinear (and also anisotropic, i.e. rotationally variant). A simple model of the nonlinearity is given by

$$I_{or} = \log(I_{ir}) \qquad (11.5.2)$$

where I_{ir} is the input intensity to the retina and I_{or} is the output neural signal from the retina. It is usually assumed that this nonlinearity is caused by the rods and cones. The input light to the eye passes through a lens system before meeting this nonlinearity and after the rods and cones have generated the output signal a further complex processing system is reached. Experimental observations then lead to the following model for the output signal from the visual system to the brain:

$$O = H_3(s)H_2(s)N(H_1(s)I) \qquad (11.5.3)$$

where I is the input light intensity, O is the output signal, H_1, H_2, H_3 are transfer functions of linear subsystem models and N is the point nonlinearity. As stated above, the nonlinearity may be logarithmic or it may have one of a number of other forms which have been proposed, e.g.

$$I_{or} = K_1 \log(K_2 + K_3 I_{ir}) \qquad (11.5.4)$$

or

$$I_{or} = \frac{K_1 I_{ir}}{K_2 + I_{ir}} \qquad (11.5.5)$$

or

$$I_{or} = (I_{ir})^\alpha \qquad (11.5.6)$$

for some constants K_1, K_2, K_3 and α. The linear system transfer functions H_1, H_2, H_3 are shown in the complete model of Figure 11.31.

A simple colour vision model can be derived in a similar way and such a model is shown in Figure 11.32. The signals d_{gb}, d_{yb} are related to the chrominance of the image, while d_y is a luminance value.

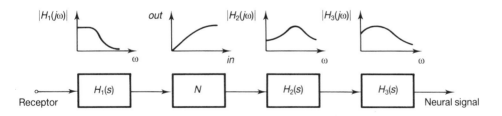

Figure 11.31   A complete monochrome vision model.

Bibliographical notes

The psychological basis of visual illusions and other aspects of visual perception are discussed in greater detail in Coren (1972), Cornsweet (1970), Land (1959),

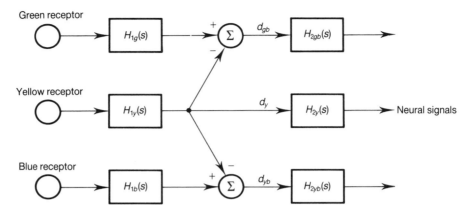

Figure 11.32   A simple colour vision model.

Luckiesh (1965) Zusne (1970), while the general nonlinear monochrome model of human vision appears in Hall and Hall (1977) and Mannos and Sakrison (1974). The colour vision model of Figure 11.32 was developed in Judd (1945) and Van der Horst *et al.* (1967). For the general theory of optics and optical system modelling, the reader should consult Shulman (1970).

Exercises

1 Make a Benham disk and check the assertions made about the apparent colours which appear when the disk is spun counterclockwise. What colours appear when the disk is spun clockwise?

2 For the scanning mirror system of Figure 11.18, derive a differential equation for the current i in the galvanometer which must be applied in order that no barrel distortion occurs.

3 Describe in detail how to obtain the range from the system in Figure 11.28.

4 Explain why constructive interference cannot occur with incoherent illumination.

5 Discuss the significance of the chrominance signals d_{gb}, d_{yb} in Figure 11.32.

References

Coren, S. (1972), 'Subjective contours and apparent depth', *Psych. Rev.*, **79**, 359–67.
Cornsweet, T. N. (1970), *Visual Perception*, NY: Academic Press.

Hall, C. F. and E. L. Hall (1977), 'A nonlinear model for the spatial characteristics of the human visual system', *IEEE Trans. Sys., Man, Cybern.*, **SMC-7** (3), 161–70.

Judd, D. B. (1945), 'Standard response functions for protanopic and deuteranopic vision', *J. Opt. Soc. Am.*, **35** (3), 199–221.

Land, E. H (1959), 'Experiments in color vision', *Scientific American*, **200** (5), 84–99.

Luckiesh, M. (1965), *Visual Illusions*, NY: Dover.

Mannos, J. L. and D. J. Sakrison (1974), 'The effects of a visual fidelity criterion on the encoding of images', *IEEE Trans. Inf. Theory*, **IT-20** (4), 525–36.

Shulman, A. R. (1970), *Optical Data Processing*, NY: Wiley.

Van der Horst, C. J. C., C. M. de Weert and M. A. Bouman (1967), 'Transfer of spatial chromaticity – contrast at threshold in the human eye', *J. Opt. Soc. Am.*, **57** (10), 1260–66.

Zusne, L. (1970), *Visual Perception of Form*, NY: Academic Press.

12

Sampling and Data Compression

12.1 Introduction

In order to perform some type of digital processing on images we must first discretize the picture in a form suitable for computer algorithms. This involves two processes as discussed for one-dimensional signals in Part 1 of the book – sampling and discretization. Although we have considered these topics in some detail in connection with one-dimensional filtering, we shall discuss them here with particular reference to images in order to be clear how they affect the digital processing algorithms. In particular, we shall consider the sampling of deterministic and stochastic images and briefly describe optimal sampling which seeks to obtain the maximum information from the image. Scalar and vector quantization will be discussed for two-dimensional images.

If we use a simple sampling technique which divides a picture into small 'pixels' and assumes a constant grey level in each pixel, then for a reasonable resolution we may have 1024×1024 pixels making up the discretized image. Thus we are usually faced with $\sim 10^6$ pixels, each with one of 256 possible grey levels. This requires 1 Mbyte of memory for each picture and so image processing is costly in both memory and time and so some form of data compression is often very useful. In this chapter we shall consider transform compression (based on Karhunen–Loève, Fourier and Hadamard transforms) and also predictive compression.

12.2 Sampling

Consider first the deterministic (monochrome) image defined by the function $F(x, y)$ which represents the light intensity or photographic density, etc., of the image. Then we can obtain ideal sampling by multiplying F by the spatial sampling 'function'

$$S(x, y) = \sum_{j_1=-\infty}^{\infty} \sum_{j_2=-\infty}^{\infty} \delta(x - j_1\Delta x, y - j_2\Delta y)$$

which consists of an infinite array of delta functions arranged in a rectangular grid with spacing $(\Delta x, \Delta y)$. Thus, we have

$$F_S(x, y) \triangleq F(x, y)S(x, y) = \sum_{j_1=-\infty}^{\infty} \sum_{j_2=-\infty}^{\infty} F(j_1\Delta x, j_2\Delta y)\delta(x - j_1\Delta x, y - j_2\Delta y)$$

Hence,

$$\mathcal{F}_S(\omega_x, \omega_y) = \frac{1}{4\pi^2} \mathcal{F}(\omega_x, \omega_y)*\zeta(\omega_x, \omega_y)$$

where we have taken the Fourier transform. Here,

$$\zeta(\omega_x, \omega_y) = \frac{4\pi^2}{\Delta x \Delta y} \sum_{j_1=-\infty}^{\infty} \sum_{j_2=-\infty}^{\infty} \delta(\omega_x - j_1\omega_{xs}, \omega_y - j_2\omega_{ys})$$

where

$$\omega_{xs} = 2\pi/\Delta x, \quad \omega_{ys} = 2\pi/\Delta y$$

are the sampling frequencies. If the image is bandlimited so that

$$\mathcal{F}(\omega_x, \omega_y) = 0 \text{ for } |\omega_x| > \omega_{xc}, |\omega_y| > \omega_{yc}$$

then we have

$$\mathcal{F}_S(\omega_x, \omega_y) = \frac{1}{\Delta x \Delta y} \int_{-\infty}^{\infty} \int_{-\infty}^{\infty} \mathcal{F}(\omega_x - u_1, \omega_y - u_2)$$

$$\sum_{j_1=-\infty}^{\infty} \sum_{j_2=-\infty}^{\infty} \delta(u_1 - j_1\omega_{xs}, u_2 - j_2\omega_{ys})\mathrm{d}u_1\mathrm{d}u_2$$

$$= \frac{1}{\Delta x \Delta y} \sum_{j_1=-\infty}^{\infty} \sum_{j_2=-\infty}^{\infty} (\omega_x - j_1\omega_{xs}, \omega_y - j_2\omega_{ys})\mathrm{d}u_1\mathrm{d}u_2$$

$$(12.2.1)$$

This again proves that sampling introduces an infinite number of 'sidebands', as we have seen in the one-dimensional case.

We can reconstruct F from the sampled version F_S as in Chapter 8. In fact, if $R(x, y)$ is a reconstruction function, then let

$$F'(x, y) = F_S(x, y)*R(x, y)$$

$$= \sum_{j_1=-\infty}^{\infty} \sum_{j_2=-\infty}^{\infty} F_S(j_1\Delta x, j_2\Delta y)R(x - j_1\Delta x, y - j_2\Delta y)$$

and so

$$\mathcal{F}'(\omega_x, \omega_y) = \frac{1}{\Delta x \Delta y} \mathcal{R}(\omega_x, \omega_y) \sum_{j_1=-\infty}^{\infty} \sum_{j_2=-\infty}^{\infty} \mathcal{F}(\omega_x - j_1\omega_{xs}, \omega_y - j_2\omega_{ys})$$

$$= \frac{1}{\Delta x \Delta y} \mathcal{R}(\omega_x, \omega_y)\mathcal{F}(\omega_x, \omega_y)$$

for $|\omega_x| \leq \omega_{xs}/2$, $|\omega_y| \leq \omega_{ys}/2$ if

$$\mathcal{F}(\omega_x, \omega_y) = 0 \text{ for } |\omega_x| > \omega_{xc}, |\omega_y| > \omega_{yc}$$

where

$$\omega_{xc} \leq \omega_{xs}/2, \omega_{yc} \leq \omega_{ys}/2$$

Hence, if

$$\mathcal{R}(\omega_x, \omega_y) = \begin{cases} 1 & |\omega_x| \leq \omega_{xR}, |\omega_y| \leq \omega_{yR} \\ 0 & \text{otherwise} \end{cases}$$

where

$$\omega_{xR} > \omega_{xc}, \omega_{yR} > \omega_{yc}$$

then

$$\mathcal{F}'(\omega_x, \omega_y) = \frac{1}{\Delta x \Delta y} \mathcal{F}(\omega_x, \omega_y)$$

and we have completely reconstructed $\mathcal{F}$ from the samples. Suitable reconstruction functions $R(x, y)$ are given by

$$R(x, y) = \frac{\omega_{xR}\omega_{yR}}{\pi^2} \text{sinc}(\omega_{xR}x) \text{sinc}(\omega_{yR}y)$$

or

$$R(x, y) = \frac{2\pi\omega_0 J_1\{\omega_0\sqrt{x^2 + y^2}\}}{\sqrt{x^2 + y^2}}$$

where $\omega_0^2 < \omega_{xc}^2 + \omega_{yc}^2$ and J_1 is the first-order Bessel function.

The above derivation assumes that $F(x, y)$ is a deterministic image. Suppose now that $F(x, y)$ is a continuous stationary random process with known mean and autocorrelation

$$R_F(\tau_x, \tau_y) \triangleq E\{F(x_1, y_1)F^*(x_2, y_2)\}$$

where

$$\tau_x = x_1 - x_2, \quad \tau_y = y_1 - y_2$$

Sampling F as before, we have

$$F_S(x, y) = F(x, y)S(x, y) = F(x, y) \sum_{j_1=-\infty}^{\infty} \sum_{j_2=-\infty}^{\infty} \delta(x - j_1\Delta x, y - j_2\Delta y)$$

and so the autocorrelation of F_S is

$$
\begin{aligned}
R_{F_S}(x_1, x_2; y_1, y_2) &= E\{F_S(x_1, y_1)F_S^*(x_2, y_2)\} \\
&= E\{F(x_1, y_1)F^*(x_2, y_2)\}S(x_1, y_1)S(x_2, y_2) \\
&= E\{F(x_1, y_1)F^*(x_2, y_2)\}S(x_1 - x_2, y_1 - y_2) \\
&= R_F(\tau_x, \tau_y)S(\tau_x, \tau_y)
\end{aligned}
$$

and so we can write

$$R_{F_S}(x_1, x_2; y_1, y_2) = R_{F_S}(\tau_x, \tau_y)$$

Taking Fourier transforms, we have

$$\mathcal{P}_{F_S}(\omega_x, \omega_y) = \frac{1}{4\pi^2} \mathcal{P}_F(\omega_x, \omega_y) * \zeta(\omega_x, \omega_y)$$

where $\mathcal{P}$ stands for 'power spectral density'. Hence, just as in (12.2.1) we have

$$\mathcal{P}_{F_S}(\omega_x, \omega_y) = \frac{1}{\Delta x \Delta y} \sum_{j_1=-\infty}^{\infty} \sum_{j_2=-\infty}^{\infty} \mathcal{P}_F(\omega_x - j_1\omega_{xs}, \omega_y - j_2\omega_{ys})$$

Again, as above, it is clear that we may obtain a reconstruction F' of F from the samples by writing

$$F'(x, y) = \sum_{j_1=-\infty}^{\infty} \sum_{j_2=-\infty}^{\infty} F(j_1\Delta x, j_2\Delta y)R(x - j_1\Delta x, y - j_2\Delta y)$$

where R is again a deterministic interpolation function. Moreover, if the Nyquist sampling conditions hold then we have

$$E\{|F(x, y) - F'(x, y)|^2\} = 0$$

i.e. the reconstructed image is 'equal' to F in the mean squared sense.

Returning to the deterministic case, we shall now consider the effects of aliasing. From (12.2.1) we have

$$\mathcal{F}_S(\omega_x, \omega_y) = \frac{1}{\Delta x \Delta y} \{\mathcal{F}(\omega_x, \omega_y) + \mathcal{F}_A(\omega_x, \omega_y)\}$$

where

$$\mathcal{F}_A(\omega_x, \omega_y) = \sum_{\substack{j_1=-\infty \\ j_1 \neq 0, j_2 \neq 0}}^{\infty} \sum_{j_2=-\infty}^{\infty} \mathcal{F}(\omega_x - j_1\omega_{xs}, \omega_y - j_2\omega_{ys})$$

is the aliasing term. Using the rectangular reconstruction filter

$$\mathcal{R}(\omega_x, \omega_y) = \begin{cases} 1 & \text{for } |\omega_x| \leqslant \omega_{xs}/2, \ |\omega_y| \leqslant \omega_{ys}/2 \\ 0 & \text{otherwise} \end{cases}$$

we obtain the reconstruction

$$F'(x, y) = F(x, y) + F_A(x, y)$$

where

$$F_A(x, y) = \frac{1}{4\pi^2} \int_{-\omega_{xs}/2}^{\omega_{xs}/2} \int_{-\omega_{ys}/2}^{\omega_{ys}/2} \mathcal{F}_A(\omega_x, \omega_y) \exp\{i[\omega_x x + \omega_y y]\} \mathrm{d}\omega_x \mathrm{d}\omega_y$$

is the aliasing artefact. The aliasing error is often reduced by passing F through a lowpass filter (for an image formed by incoherent light this can be achieved by passing the image through a lens of restricted aperture). However, the filter will degrade the image and so there is a tradeoff between aliasing error and filter degradation which must be resolved on the basis of some kind of quality measure.

Rather than use a delta function array for sampling an image we may apply a technique which will appear again in Part 3 of the book in connection with various pattern recognition algorithms. In this method we represent an image $f(x, y)$ in terms of a complete orthonormal set of functions $\phi_{mn}(x, y)$. Thus we write

$$f(x, y) = \sum_{m=0}^{\infty} \sum_{n=0}^{\infty} a_{mn} \phi_{mn}(x, y) \tag{12.2.2}$$

where the functions ϕ_{mn} satisfy the orthonormality conditions

$$\int \int_{\Omega} \phi_{mn}(x, y) \phi_{pq}^*(x, y) \mathrm{d}x \mathrm{d}y = \delta_{mp} \delta_{nq}$$

for all m, n, p, q, where Ω is some region in $\mathbb{R}^2$ and

$$\delta_{ij} = \begin{cases} 1 & \text{if } i = j \\ 0 & \text{otherwise} \end{cases} \tag{12.3.3}$$

The coefficients in (12.2.2) can be obtained in the usual way, i.e. we multiply by the function $\phi_{kl}^*(x, y)$ and integrate over Ω,

$$\int \int_{\Omega} f(x, y) \phi_{kl}(x, y) \mathrm{d}x \mathrm{d}y = \sum_{m=0}^{\infty} \sum_{n=0}^{\infty} a_{mn} \int \int_{\Omega} \phi_{mn}(x, y) \phi_{kl}^*(x, y) \mathrm{d}x \mathrm{d}y$$

$$= a_{kl} \tag{12.2.4}$$

by (12.2.3). The coefficients are the *samples* of f with respect to the o.n. basis $\{\phi_{mn}\}$. Over the rectangle $[-A/2, A/2] \times [-B/2, B/2]$ we have the familiar orthonormal functions given by the complex exponentials:

$$\phi_{mn}(x, y) = \frac{1}{\sqrt{AB}} \exp\left[j2\pi\left(\frac{mx}{A} + \frac{ny}{B}\right)\right] \qquad m, n = 0, 1, 2, \ldots$$

In this case it follows from (12.2.4) that

$$a_{kl} = \frac{1}{\sqrt{AB}} \int_{-B/2}^{B/2} \int_{-A/2}^{A/2} f(x, y) \exp\left[-j2\pi\left(\frac{kx}{A} + \frac{ly}{B}\right)\right] dx dy$$

$$= \frac{1}{\sqrt{AB}} F\left(\frac{k}{A}, \frac{l}{B}\right)$$

where F is the Fourier transform of f. The coefficients a_{kl} are called the *Fourier samples of* f. From (11.5.1) we see that the Fourier samples of a function may be obtained from an optical system by placing a transparency $f(x, y)$ in the pupil plane of the system.

Another simple orthonormal set consists of functions which are constant over small rectangular regions and zero elsewhere. This leads to *standard sampling*. Thus, define

$$\phi_{mn}(x, y) = \sqrt{\frac{MN}{AB}} \qquad \frac{mA}{M} \leq x < \frac{(m+1)A}{M}, \frac{nB}{N} \leq y < \frac{(n+1)B}{N}$$

$$= 0 \qquad \text{otherwise}$$

(for $m = 0, 1, \ldots, M-1$, $n = 0, 1, \ldots, N-1$). These functions are not complete, of course, since we cannot write any function f in the form (12.2.2) where the summation limits are finite. However, if the rectangles with sides A/M, B/N are small enough we will obtain reasonable sampling. From (12.3.4) we have

$$a_{kl} = \sqrt{MN/AB} \int_{lB/N}^{(l+1)B/N} \int_{kA/M}^{(k+1)A/M} f(x, y) dx dy$$

and so standard sampling consists of averaging f over each small rectangle.

It is possible to obtain the best set of orthonormal functions for a given set of pictures $\{f_1(x, y), \ldots, f_K(x, y)\}$. This leads to *optimal sampling* or *Karhunen–Loève sampling*. However, this theory will be considered in detail in Chapter 19 and so we shall leave further discussion of this topic until then.

12.3 Image quantization

In this section we shall consider the quantization of a sampled image – in particular, the use of vector quantization. As we have seen, an image can be sampled in a variety of ways to produce a sequence of (real) numbers representing the image. Each of these real numbers can be quantized separately (as in Part 1 of the book). However, we can often reduce the quantization error by quantizing the whole sequence considered as a vector. Thus, let $f = \{f_1, \ldots, f_N\}$ be the samples of an image regarded as an N-dimensional vector. When a scalar value f_i is quantized we choose a number of quantization levels $q_0, q_1, \ldots$ and a corresponding number of quantization values $v_0, v_1, \ldots$ such that if

$$q_l \leqslant f_i < q_{l+1}$$

then we quantize f_i to the level v_l (Figure 12.1(a)). In the case of vector quantization we divide N-dimensional sample space into disjoint regions $Q_0, Q_1, \ldots$, each containing a quantization value vector $v_0, v_1, \ldots$, as in Figure 12.1(b). The mean square quantization error is given by

$$E = \sum_{j=0}^{J-1} \int_{Q_j} \text{tr}\,[(f - v_j)(f - v_j)^{\mathrm{T}}] p(f) \mathrm{d}f$$

where J is the number of quantization regions and $p(f)$ is the probability distribution of f. To find the optimal values of v_j we must solve the equation

$$\frac{\partial E}{\partial v_j} = 0 = \int_{Q_j} (f - v_j) p(f) \mathrm{d}f$$

Thus, we obtain

$$v_j = \int_{Q_j} f p(f) \mathrm{d}f \bigg/ \int_{Q_j} p(f) \mathrm{d}f = E\{f | f \in Q_j\}$$

where E denotes expectation. This requires a knowledge of $p(f)$ and a Gaussian distribution is often assumed.

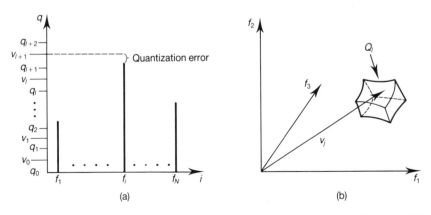

(a)   (b)

Figure 12.1 Scalar and vector quantization: (a) quantization levels; (b) quantization cell.

The optimum shape for the regions Q can also be determined. This leads to complex structures for the quantization regions, however, and so each component f_i of f is usually quantized separately over a fixed number of levels $J(i)$ ($1 \leq i \leq N$). We then choose the numbers $J(i)$ to minimize the mean square error subject to the constraint

$$J = \sum_{i=1}^{N} J(i)$$

where J is fixed. The error for the ith sample is

$$E_i = E\{f_i^2\} - \sum_{j=0}^{J(i)-1} v_{ji}^2 P\{d_{ji} \leq f_i < d_{j+1}\} \tag{12.3.1}$$

where v_{ji} is the ith component of v_j. J_i is usually taken to be a binary number, say $J_i = 2^{b_i}$. Then we minimize the mean square error over the b_i for which $B = \Sigma_{i=1}^{N} b_i$ is fixed. A variety of numerical algorithms for the selection of the b_i can be found in the literature (see Section 12.6).

12.4 Data compression by transformation

Having obtained a discrete representation of a picture, we may require to reduce to a minimum the number of bits of data we need to store or transmit the picture. In this section we shall consider the application of integral transforms to the data compression problem. It should be noted that there are strong links between the ideas developed here and those in Chapter 19 on feature selection. In fact, data compression can be regarded as a simple form of feature selection – that is, the selection of data which are most significant to the problem.

We shall first discuss Karhunen–Loève compression, in which one tries to represent a picture in terms of uncorrelated samples; the idea being that there will then be no redundant information in the data. Thus, let $f(x, y)$ be a zero mean random field (which may represent a colour image, for example) and write

$$\mathbf{f}(x, y) = \sum_{m=0}^{\infty} \sum_{n=0}^{\infty} \mathbf{a}_{mn} \phi_{mn}(x, y) \tag{12.4.1}$$

where $\{\phi_{mn}\}$ is a set of orthonormal functions. As we have seen above, we can obtain the (vector) coefficients $\mathbf{a}_{mn}$ from

$$\mathbf{a}_{mn} = \int_{-1}^{1} \int_{-1}^{1} \mathbf{f}(x, y) \phi_{mn}^*(x, y) \mathrm{d}x \mathrm{d}y \tag{12.4.2}$$

where we have normalized the images to the unit square $[-1, 1] \times [-1, 1]$ for simplicity. Suppose the data samples $\mathbf{a}_{mn}$ are uncorrelated, so that

$$E\{\mathbf{a}_{mn}\mathbf{a}_{ij}^*\} = E\{\mathbf{a}_{mn}\}E\{\mathbf{a}_{ij}^*\} \qquad m \neq i \text{ or } n \neq j$$

Then, taking the expectation of (12.4.2) we have

$$E\{\mathbf{a}_{mn}\} = \int_{-1}^{1}\int_{-1}^{1} E\{\mathbf{f}(x, y)\}\phi_{mn}^*(x, y)\mathrm{d}x\mathrm{d}y$$

$$= 0$$

for all m, n, and so $E\{\mathbf{a}_{mn}\mathbf{a}_{ij}^*\} = 0$, for $m \neq i$ or $n \neq j$. Now, by (12.4.1),

$$E\{\mathbf{f}(x, y)\mathbf{a}_{ij}^*\} = \sum_{m=0}^{\infty}\sum_{n=0}^{\infty} E\{\mathbf{a}_{mn}\mathbf{a}_{ij}^*\}\phi_{mn}(x, y)$$

$$= E\{|\mathbf{a}_{ij}|^2\}\phi_{ij}(x, y)$$

and by (12.4.2),

$$E\{\mathbf{f}(x, y)\mathbf{a}_{ij}^*\} = \int_{-1}^{1}\int_{-1}^{1} E\{\mathbf{f}(x, y)\mathbf{f}(x', y')\}\phi_{ij}(x', y')\mathrm{d}x'\mathrm{d}y'$$

$$\overset{\triangle}{=} \int_{-1}^{1}\int_{-1}^{1} R(x, y, x', y')\phi_{ij}(x', y')\mathrm{d}x'\mathrm{d}y'$$

and so, finally, we have

$$E\{|\mathbf{a}_{ij}|^2\}\phi_{ij}(x, y) = \int_{-1}^{1}\int_{-1}^{1} R(x, y, x', y')\phi_{ij}(x', y')\mathrm{d}x'\mathrm{d}y' \qquad (12.4.3)$$

Thus, in order to produce uncorrelated samples, the orthonormal functions ϕ_{ij} must satisfy the integral equation (12.4.3) (provided the random field has zero mean).

Since we are usually interested in samples images we shall consider next the discrete version of (12.4.3). Suppose, therefore, that $f(x, y)$ is sampled on an $N \times N$ sampling lattice to give the values $\mathbf{f}_{ij}$, $0 \leq i \leq N - 1$, $0 \leq j \leq N - 1$. We shall denote the matrix of values $(\mathbf{f}_{ij})$ by $\mathbf{f}$. (Using the same letter for the random field and the sampled matrix should cause no confusion.) We define the *inner product* $\langle \mathbf{g}, \mathbf{h} \rangle$ of two such matrices $\mathbf{g}$ and $\mathbf{h}$ by

$$\langle \mathbf{g}, \mathbf{h} \rangle = \sum_{m=0}^{N-1}\sum_{n=0}^{N-1} \mathbf{g}_{mn}\mathbf{h}_{mn}^*$$

Then a set of matrices $\{\phi^{(u,v)}\}$, $0 \leq u \leq N - 1$, $0 \leq v \leq N - 1$ is *orthonormal* if

$$\langle \phi^{(u,v)}, \phi^{(s,t)} \rangle = \begin{cases} 0 & \text{if } u \neq s \text{ or } v \neq t \\ 1 & \text{if } u = s \text{ and } v = t \end{cases}$$

As in (12.4.1) we can express any matrix f in terms of the o.n. set $\{\phi^{(u,v)}\}$ by

$$\mathbf{f} = \sum_{u=0}^{N-1}\sum_{v=0}^{N-1} \mathbf{a}_{uv}\phi^{(u,v)}$$

where

$$\mathbf{a}_{uv} = \langle \mathbf{f}, \phi^{(u,v)} \rangle \qquad (12.4.4)$$

(Note that **f**, **a**, etc., are matrices of vectors, so that $\mathbf{f}_{ij}$ is the (i, j)th element of **f** which is the sampled form of the vector field $\mathbf{f}(x, y)$.) It is now easy to show that the discrete version of (12.4.3) is

$$\sum_{p=0}^{N-1}\sum_{q=0}^{N-1} R(m, n, p, q)\phi_{pq}^{(u,v)} = \gamma_{uv}\phi_{mn}^{(u,v)} \tag{12.4.5}$$

where

$$R(m, m, p, q) = E\{\mathbf{f}_{mn}\mathbf{f}_{pq}\}$$

and

$$\gamma_{uv} = E\{|\mathbf{a}_{uv}|^2\}$$

Thus, (12.4.5) is a necessary condition for the samples $\mathbf{g}_{uv}$ to be uncorrelated. (It is not difficult to see that this condition is also sufficient.) Let $\mathcal{R}$ denote the operator which maps a matrix **f** into a matrix **g** where

$$\mathbf{g}_{mn} = \sum_{p=0}^{N-1}\sum_{q=0}^{N-1} R(m, n, p, q)\mathbf{f}_{pq}$$

Then (12.4.5) may be written

$$\mathcal{R}\phi^{(u,v)} = \gamma_{uv}\phi^{(u,v)}$$

Figure 12.2   Grey scale image of author's son.

and we see that the orthonormal functions $\phi^{(u,v)}$ are eigenvectors of $\mathcal{R}$ with eigenvalues γ_{uv}.

Consider now the application of these ideas to image data compression. We will determine the uncorrelated samples for the picture shown in Figure 12.2. A reasonable autocorrelation function can be shown to be

$$R(x, y, x', y') \cong \exp[-\alpha|x - x'| - \beta|y - y'|] \qquad (12.4.6)$$

If we try to solve the equation (12.4.5) directly for a 512×400 picture, then we would have to invert a $(512 \times 400)^2$ matrix, which is clearly out of the question. We shall therefore divide the picture into 32×25 subpictures, each consisting of 16×16 pixels and treat each subpicture independently. Even in this case solving (12.4.5) would require the inversion of a 256^2 matrix. Hence, instead, we shall solve (12.4.3) for the eigenvectors $\phi_{ij}(x, y)$ and their corresponding eigenvalues, on a region the size of a subpicture, and then sample the resulting functions over a 16×16 grid. Although the resulting arrays are not orthogonal, they will be approximately so and the samples obtained by using these arrays should be 'nearly' uncorrelated.

We must solve the equation

$$\lambda\phi(x, y) = \int_{-a}^{a}\int_{-b}^{b} e^{(-\alpha|x-x'|-\beta|y-y'|)}\phi(x', y')dx'dy' \qquad (12.4.7)$$

for some given values of a and b. Clearly, we may assume ϕ is separable and so we write

$$\phi(x, y) = \psi(x)\xi(y), \lambda = \mu v$$

where

$$\mu\psi(x) = \int_{-a}^{a} e^{-\alpha|x-x'|}\psi(x')dx' \qquad (12.4.8)$$

$$v\xi(y) = \int_{-b}^{b} e^{-\beta|y-y'|}\xi(y')dy' \qquad (12.4.9)$$

It is not difficult to show that the eigenvectors ψ_n and eigenvalues μ_n of (12.4.8) are given by

$$\psi_{2n}(x) = \cos\beta_n x, \; \psi_{2n-1}(x) = \sin\gamma_n x \qquad n \geqslant 1 \qquad (12.4.10)$$

where

$$\beta_n^2 = \frac{2\alpha - \alpha^2\mu_n}{\mu_n}, \qquad \frac{\alpha}{\beta_n} = \tan\beta_n a$$

$$\gamma_n^2 \frac{2\alpha - \alpha^2\mu_n}{\mu_n}, \qquad -\frac{\gamma_n}{\alpha} = \tan\gamma_n a \qquad (12.4.11)$$

Similar expressions can be written for ξ_n and v_n. This gives a set of eigenvectors and eigenvalues

$$\phi^{(m,n)}(x, y) = \xi_m(x)v_n(y), \qquad \lambda_{mn} = \mu_m v_n \qquad (12.4.12)$$

for the equation (12.4.7).

We now sample the eigenfunctions $\phi^{(m,n)}(x, y)$ over an area equal to that of a subpicture (centered at the origin) and thus obtain the matrices $\phi^{(m,n)}$ (only a finite number of which are used, i.e. N^2). If f^{ij} is the (i, j)th subpicture, then we can evaluate its coefficients in terms of these matrices according to (12.4.4), i.e.

$$\mathbf{a}_{mn}^{ij} = \langle \mathbf{f}^{ij}, \phi^{(m,n)} \rangle$$

Note that the matrices $\phi^{(m,n)}$ are not exactly orthogonal but, for fine enough sampling they will be approximately so. The subpictures can be reconstructed from the relation

$$\mathbf{f}^{ij} = \sum_{m=0}^{N-1} \sum_{n=0}^{N-1} \mathbf{a}_{mn}^{ij} \phi^{(m,n)}.$$

Data compression is achieved by choosing N to be the minimum possible so as to be compatible with some *ad hoc* measure of quality of the reconstructed picture.

In order to store the coefficients $\mathbf{a}_{mn}^{ij}$ of the subpictures we must quantize them in some way. For low values of m and n the variance of $\mathbf{a}_{mn}^{ij}$ tends to be much greater than that for large values of m and n. Hence we usually determine the variance of the coefficients from

$$\mathbf{\nabla}_{mn} \cong \frac{1}{400} \sum_{i=1}^{32} \sum_{j=1}^{25} |\mathbf{a}_{mn}^{ij}|^2$$

(assuming the pictures have zero mean), and quantize $\mathbf{a}_{mn}^{ij}/\mathbf{\nabla}_{mn}$. The reconstructed picture using 256 eigenfunctions with each coefficient quantized to sixty-four levels is shown in Figure 12.3 and with only 128 eigenfunctions and coefficients quantized to sixteen levels is shown in Figure 12.4. We can see that there is little degradation in picture quality and so a compression ratio of 3 has been achieved. (Since the first picture required $256 \times 400 \times 6$ bits of storage, while the last picture requires only $128 \times 400 \times 4$ bits.)

The main drawbacks with Karhunen–Loève compression techniques are the amount of computation required and the need for a covariance estimate such as (12.4.5). Instead of using the $\phi^{(u,v)}$ matrices determined by this method we could use other orthogonal matrix sequences. However, these will not, in general, be uncorrelated and so the resulting compression will not be optimal. Typical examples of orthogonal matrices are given by the Fourier and Hadamard transforms. In the case of the Fourier transform we obtain the matrices

$$\phi_{mn}^{(u,v)} = \frac{1}{N} \exp\left[j \frac{2\pi}{N} (mu + nv) \right] \qquad (12.4.13)$$

These matrices are clearly orthonormal. A *Hadamard matrix* is a symmetric matrix consisting of elements which are ± 1 and such that the rows (and columns) are mutually orthogonal. For example,

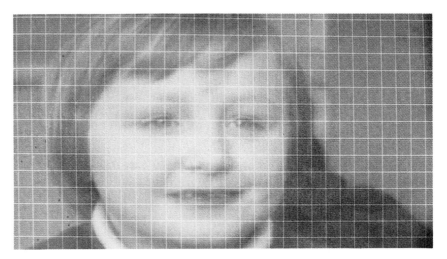

Figure 12.3   Reconstructed image from Fourier components.

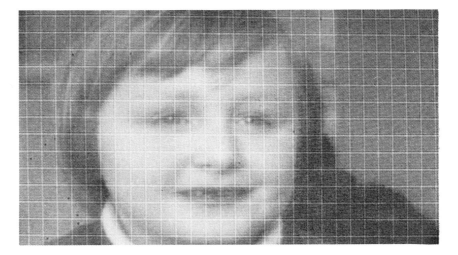

Figure 12.4   Data compressed image.

$$H_2 = \begin{bmatrix} 1 & 1 \\ 1 & -1 \end{bmatrix}$$

is a two-dimensional Hadamard matrix. It is not difficult to show that if H_J is a Hadamard matrix, then so is the matrix

$$H_{2J} = \begin{bmatrix} H_J & H_J \\ H_J & -H_J \end{bmatrix} \tag{12.4.14}$$

It is therefore easy to generate Hadamard matrices of dimensions of the power of 2. The *Hadamard transform* of a matrix f_{mn} is then defined by

$$F_{uv} = \sum_{m=0}^{N-1} \sum_{n=0}^{N-1} (H_N)_{um} f_{mn} (H_N)_{nv}$$

where N is a power of 2. This can be inverted to give

$$f_{mn} = \frac{1}{N^2} \sum_{u=0}^{N-1} \sum_{v=0}^{N-1} (H_N)_{mu} F_{uv} (H_N)_{vn} \tag{12.4.15}$$

since

$$(H_N)^{-1} = \frac{1}{N} H_N \tag{12.4.16}$$

The inverse form (12.4.15) can also be written

$$f_{mn} = \sum_{u=0}^{N-1} \sum_{v=0}^{N-1} \phi_{mn}^{(u,v)} F_{uv}$$

where

$$\phi_{mn}^{(u,v)} = (1/N)(-1)^{b(u,v,m,n)} \tag{12.4.17}$$

and

$$b(u, v, m, n) = \sum_{k=0}^{\log_2 N - 1} [b_k(u)b_k(v) + b_k(m)b_k(n)]$$

where $b_k(x)$ is the kth bit in the binary representation of x.

12.5 Predictive compression

Another approach to obtaining uncorrelated picture data is to use predictive compression. If a given picture (f_{ij}) is correlated so that

$$E\{f_{ij}f_{mn}\} \neq 0$$

for $i \neq m$ or $j \neq n$, then it should be possible to estimate f_{ij} in terms of the surrounding values f_{mn} for $m \neq i$, $n \neq j$. A simple linear estimate of f_{mn} is given by

$$\hat{f}_{mn} = a_1 f_{m-1,n} + a_2 f_{m-1,n-1} + a_3 f_{m,n-1} \tag{12.5.1}$$

where the parameters a_1, a_2, a_3 will be determined shortly. The error signal

$$e_{mn} = f_{mn} - \hat{f}_{mn}$$

should be less correlated than f_{mn}, and (e_{mn}) will then represent the compressed picture. To determine the 'best' values of a_1, a_2, a_3 in (12.5.1) we minimize the mean squared error

$$E = E\{(f_{mn} - \hat{f}_{mn})^2\}$$

If f is homogeneous (position-independent) and has zero mean, then it is easy to show that the coefficients satisfy the equations

$$a_1 R(0, 0) + a_2 R(0, 1) + a_3 R(1, 1) = R(1, 0)$$

$$a_1 R(0, 1) + a_2 R(0, 0) + a_3 R(1, 0) = R(1, 1) \qquad (12.5.2)$$

$$a_1 R(1, 1) + a_2 R(1, 0) + a_3 R(0, 0) = R(0, 1)$$

where R is the autocorrelation function defined by

$$R(m - r, n - s) = E\{\mathbf{f}_{mn} f_{rs}\}$$

If

$$R(x, y) = R(0, 0) \exp(-\alpha|x| - \beta|y|) \qquad (12.5.3)$$

then

$$a_1 = R(1, 0)/R(0, 0), \ a_2 = -R(1, 1)/R(0, 0), \ a_3 = R(0, 1)/R(0, 0)$$

$$(12.5.4)$$

and it can be shown that the variance of $(\mathbf{e}_{mn})$ is smaller than that of $(\mathbf{f}_{mn})$. Moreover, it is easy to show that

$$E\{\mathbf{e}_{mn}\mathbf{e}_{rs}\} = 0 \qquad m \neq r, n \neq s \qquad (12.5.5)$$

where R is given by (12.5.3), so that, in this case, the error signal is uncorrelated. If R does not satisfy (12.5.3), then it may be necessary to use more than the three immediate neighbours of $\mathbf{f}_{mn}$ in (12.5.1) to obtain a good estimate for $\hat{\mathbf{f}}_{mn}$.

When the error signal $\mathbf{e}_{mn}$ is quantized, it may be possible to obtain further compression by using nonlinear quantization techniques. Thus, those values which occur more frequently can be given shorter binary codes. Note, however, that at a sharp transition in a picture (at an edge, for example), $\mathbf{e}_{mn}$ is usually large. If $\mathbf{e}_{mn}$ at these points is larger than the biggest quantizer step, then the edge may be smeared, resulting in so-called 'edge busyness'.

Bibliographical notes

A detailed analysis of orthonormal functions and Hilbert space theory is given in Helmberg (1970), where the important property of completeness is discussed. The determination of optimal reconstruction points for vector quantization is considered in Curry (1970) and the shape of the quantization regions Q in Figure 12.1(b) can be found by dynamic programming, as in Bruce (1965). A number of algorithms for the minimization have been obtained; see, for example, Ready and Wintz (1972).

A justification for the autocorrelation function (12.4.5) is given in Habibi and Wintz (1971) and the use of nonuniform quantization in picture compression is discussed in Huang and Schultheiss (1963) and Wintz (1972). For further details on predictive compression, see Graham (1967), Habibi (1971), Schreiber *et al.* (1959) and Wilkins and Wintz (1970), and for a discussion of 'edge-busyness' see Arguello *et al.* (1971) and Millard and Maunsell (1971). Transform and predictive compression techniques are combined in Habibi (1974) and Habibi and Robinson (1974).

Finally, mention should be made about the *rate distortion function*, which seeks to estimate the minimum number of bits required to represent pictures (or indeed any form of information) to within some acceptable distortion. The technique seems to be difficult to apply in practice, however, and so we merely refer the reader to Berger (1971), Gallager (1968) and Shannon (1959).

Exercises

1 Show that, for scalar quantization with a large number of quantization levels, the optimum value v_i (defined in Section 12.3) is given by

$$v_i = \frac{q_{i+1} + q_i}{2}$$

i.e. half-way between the quantization levels. Find an expression for the quantization error E.

2 If the number of quantization levels is not large, show that

$$v_i = \int_{q_i}^{q_{i+1}} f p(f) \mathrm{d}f \bigg/ \int_{d_i}^{d_{i+1}} p(f) \mathrm{d}f$$

3 Show that, for any set of orthonormal functions $\{\phi_{mn}(x, y)\}$ we have

$$\sum_{i=1}^{K} \sum_{j=1}^{L} (\langle f, \phi_{ij} \rangle)^2 \leq \|f\|^2$$

for all K, L (Bessel's inequality).

4 Derive a condition for completeness of the orthonormal functions $\{\phi_{mn}\}$ from exercise 3.

5 Prove that the eigenfunctions of (12.4.7) are given by (12.4.10) and (12.4.11).

6 Prove that (12.4.4) is a Hadamard matrix.

7 Derive the equations (12.5.2).

References

Arguello, R. J., H. R. Sellner and J. A. Stuller (1971), 'The effect of channel errors in the differential pulse-code modulation transmission of sampled imagery', *IEEE Trans. Comm. Technol.*, **COM-18**, 926–33.

Berger, T. (1971), *Rate Distortion Theory: A mathematical basis for data compression*, Englewood Cliffs, NJ: Prentice Hall.

Bruce, J. D. (1965), 'Optimum quantization', *MIT research laboratory of electronics, Tech. Rep.* 429.

Curry, R. (1970), *Estimation and Control with Quantized Measurements*, Cambridge, Mass.: MIT Press.

Gallager, R. G. (1968), *Information Theory and Reliable Communication*, NY: Wiley.

Graham, D. N. (1967), 'Image transmission by two-dimensional contour coding', *Proc. IEEE*, **55**, 336–46.

Habibi, A. (1971), 'Comparison of nth order DPCM encoder with linear transformation and block quantization techniques', *IEEE Trans. Comm. Technol.*, **COM-19**, 948–56.

Habibi, A. (1974), 'Hybrid coding of pictorial data', *IEEE Trans. Comm. Technol.*, **COM-22**, 614–21.

Habibi, A. and G. S. Robinson (1974), 'A survey of digital picture coding', *Computer*, **7**, 22–34.

Habibi, A. and P. A. Wintz (1971), 'Image coding by linear transformation and block quantization', *IEEE Trans. Comm. Technol.*, **COM-19**, 50–62.

Helmberg, H. (1970), *Spectral Theory in Hilbert Spaces*, Amsterdam: North-Holland.

Huang, T. T. Y. and P. M. Schultheiss (1963), 'Block quantization of correlated Gaussian random variables', *IRE Trans. Comm. Sys.*, **CS-11**, 289–96.

Millard, J. B. and H. I. Maunsell (1971), 'Digital encoding of the video signal', *BSTJ*, **50** 459–79.

Ready, P. J. and P. A. Wintz (1972), 'Multispectral data compression through transform coding and block quantization', Purdue University, Laboratory for Applications of Remote Sensing, *Information Note 050572*.

Schreiber, W. F., C. F. Knapp and N. D. Kay (1959), 'Synthetic highs in experimental TV bandwidth reduction system', *J. Soc. Motion Picture TV Eng.*, **68**, 525–37.

Shannon, C. E. (1959), 'Coding theorems for a discrete source with a fidelity criterion', *IRE Nat. Conv. Record Pt. 4*, 142–63.

Wilkins, L. C. and P. A. Wintz (1970), 'A contour tracing algorithm for data compression for two-dimensional data', *Tech. Rep. No. TR-EE-69-3, School of Elec. Eng.*, Purdue University, W. Lafayette, Indiana.

Wintz, P. A. (1972), 'Transform picture coding', *Proc. IEEE*, **60** 809–20.

13

Picture Enhancement, Restoration and Analysis

13.1 Introduction

Modern picture processing may be divided into three main areas – enhancement, restoration and analysis. Enhancement is concerned with general improvement of the image for human observers and uses techniques such as grey scale

195

modification to increase contrast in incorrectly exposed films, edge sharpening by differentiation and noise suppression by filtering or averaging.

In most kinds of image capture systems there will be unwanted degradations introduced into the image, and it is the purpose of restoration to obtain a better representation of the object by reversing, as much as possible, the effects of the degradations. Techniques include geometric transformations, inverse filtering, Wiener and Kalman filtering, pseudoinverse operations, least squares restoration, homomorphic filtering and motion induced blurr removal.

Having obtained an acceptable image by any of these processes, one of the main applications of modern picture processing is in the field of machine vision. This requires computer software for the analysis and interpretation of images. Much of the theory of image interpretation overlaps with that of pattern recognition to be considered in the last part of the book. Thus in this chapter we shall discuss only those topics of direct relevance to image analysis, such as line extraction and representation, the Hough transform, line interpretation, realizability of line drawings, shape from shading, range processing, surface analysis and knowledge analysis as applied to images.

Of course, there is now a vast literature on the subjects we consider here and so only a small part of the results can be covered. However, many of the ideas of image processing will at least be mentioned.

13.2 Histograms and grey scale modification

Consider a monochrome image sampled and quantized to 256 grey levels (i.e. each *pixel* or picture element, where the sampled image is constant, can take one of the integer values $0, \ldots, 255$). A useful technique in image processing is to modify all pixels with the same grey level in some way. This can be achieved by first obtaining the *grey scale histogram* $H(D_i)$ of the image, which is merely a graph of the number of pixels with grey level D_i, $0 \leqslant D_i \leqslant 255$. A typical histogram is shown in Figure 13.1(a). It is customary to approximate the discrete histogram by a continuous graph, as in Figure 13.1(b), and then sums over a number of pixels become integrals; we shall use whichever formulation is more convenient. Note that, if there are N pixels in the complete image (for example, $N = 1024 \times 1024$), then

$$N = \sum_{i=0}^{255} H(D_i) \tag{13.2.1}$$

For colour images one can use either a three-dimensional histogram $H(D_R, D_B, D_G)$ ($\triangleq$ number of pixels with red level D_R, blue level D_B and green level D_G), or three one-dimensional histograms $H(D_R)$, $H(D_B)$, $H(D_G)$. The three one-dimensional functions contain less information than

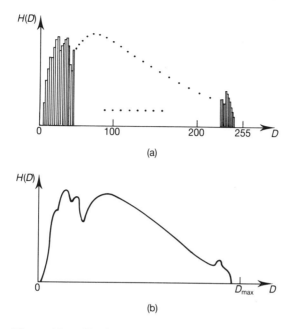

Figure 13.1 Typical histogram: (a) discrete form;
(b) continuous form.

$H(D_R, D_B, D_G)$, but are easier to use. We shall concentrate on monochromatic histograms here for simplicity.

Consider an image in which the grey levels with any given constant value D exist on closed curves and which has higher grey levels towards the centre. Then, if $A(D)$ denotes the area enclosed by the curve D = constant, we have

$$H(D) = \lim_{\Delta D \to 0} \frac{A(D) - A(D + \Delta D)}{\Delta D} = \frac{-\mathrm{d}A}{\mathrm{d}D}$$

(Note that D = constant encloses pixels with grey level $\geqslant D$.) Thus,

$$A(D) = \int_D^\infty H(D')\mathrm{d}D'$$

and so $A_I = \int_0^\infty H(D')\mathrm{d}D'$ is the area of the image. It is frequently useful to interpret the histogram as a probability density. This can be done by dividing by A_I to normalize the area of the image to 1. Thus,

$$P(D) = H(D)/A_I$$

is the pixel probability density of the image.

EXAMPLES OF HISTOGRAMS
(1) Consider the one-dimensional pulse

$$D(x) = \begin{cases} 2 - 2x & 0 \leq x \leq 1 \\ 2 + 2x & -1 \leq x \leq 0 \end{cases}$$

(Figure 13.2(a)). Then the 'area' where the image is greater than or equal to grey level D is given by $2 - D$. Thus,

$$H(D) = \frac{-\mathrm{d}A}{\mathrm{d}D} = 1$$

This histogram is shown in Figure 13.2(b).

(2) For a two-dimensional Gaussian pulse, $D(r, \theta) = \exp(-r^2)$, $0 \leq r < \infty$, $0 \leq \theta < 2\pi$ the constant D level is a circle of radius $r(D) = \sqrt{-\ln D}$ and the area enclosed by the circle is

$$A(D) = \pi(r(D))^2 = -\pi \ln D$$

Hence

$$H(d) = \pi/D \qquad \text{(Figure 13.3)}$$

The simplest type of operation we can perform on a histogram is a point transformation. Thus, if $A(x, y)$ and $B(x, y)$ are two images, then B is obtained from A to a *point transformation* if there exists a function f such that

$$B(x, y) = f(A(x, y)) \qquad (13.2.2)$$

i.e. each image pixel is transformed independently of all the others. In

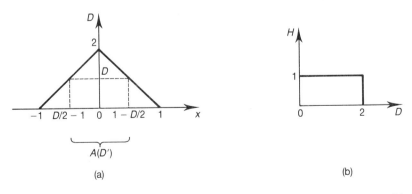

(a)   (b)

Figure 13.2 A simple one-dimensional image: (a) triangular 'image'; (b) histogram.

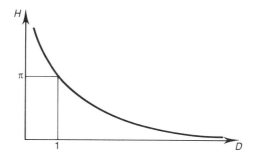

Figure 13.3　Histogram　for　a　Gaussian pulse.

particular, if f has the same value on all pixels of the A image with the same grey level, then (13.2.2) is equivalent to

$$D_B = f(D_A) \qquad (13.2.3)$$

where D_A is the grey level of any pixel in the A image and D_B is the grey level of the corresponding pixel in the B image. For example, if f is linear, we have

$$D_B = f(D_A) = aD_A + b \qquad \text{(Figure 13.4)}$$

The effect of different values of a and b is clear – if $a > 1$ then the contrast of the transformed image is increased (and is reduced if $a < 1$), $a < 0$ gives an inverted image (dark to light and vice versa) and b shifts the whole image up or down in brightness. These effects are shown in Figure 13.5; the histograms for each image are also shown.

Consider next the effect on the histogram of a general transformation $f(D)$. For simplicity we shall assume that f is monotonic. Then the output histogram can be obtained from the input histogram, as shown in Figure 13.6. The interval

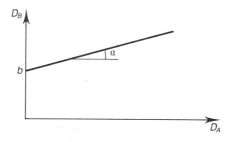

Figure 13.4　Linear point operation.

(b)

(a)

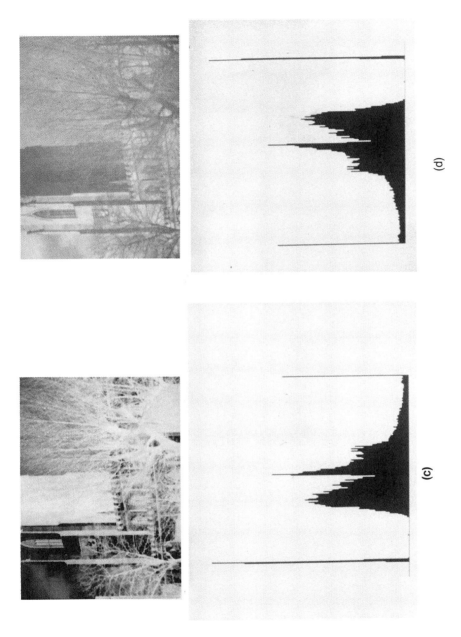

Figure 13.5 Linear grey scale modifications: (a) original image; (b) $a > 1$; (c) $a < 0$; (d) $b > 0$.

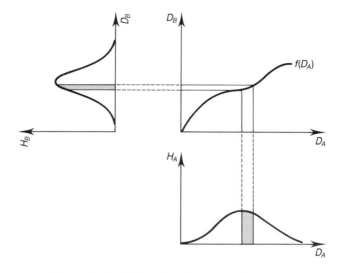

Figure 13.6 Calculating the output histogram.

$[D_A, D_A + \Delta D_A]$ is mapped by f on to the interval $[D_B, D_B + \Delta D_B]$ and so all pixels with grey levels in $[D_A, D_A + \Delta D_A]$ are mapped to pixels in $[D_B, D_B + \Delta D_B]$. It follows that

$$H_B(D_B)\Delta D_B = H_A(D_A)\Delta D_A$$

or

$$
\begin{aligned}
H_B(D_B) &= H_A(D_A)/(\mathrm{d}D_B/\mathrm{d}D_A) \\
&= H_A(D_A)/(\mathrm{d}f(D_A)/\mathrm{d}D_A) \\
&= H_A(f^{-1}(D_B))/f'(f^{-1}(D_B))
\end{aligned}
\tag{13.2.4}
$$

where

$$f' = \mathrm{d}f/\mathrm{d}D$$

For example, if $D_B = aD_A + b$, then

$$H_B(D_B) = \frac{1}{a} H_A\left(\frac{D_B - b}{a}\right)$$

and if $a > 1$ the histogram is broadened (Figure 13.7).

An important application of histogram modification is to histogram flattening, i.e. transforming an image so that each grey level appears an equal number of times. We have already observed that the normalized histogram may be regarded as a probability density. Thus, if we wish to transform an image with histogram $H_A(D_A)$ into one with a flat histogram $H_B(D_B)$, then we can write

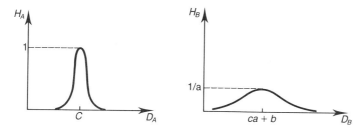

Figure 13.7   Linear histogram modification.

$$p_A(D_A) = \frac{1}{A_I} H_A(D_A), \qquad p_B(D_B) = \frac{1}{D_M}$$

where A_I is again the area of the original image and D_M is the maximum grey level. The cumulative distribution function of the original image is

$$P_A(D_A) = \int_0^{D_A} p_A(D)\mathrm{d}D = \frac{1}{A_I} \int_0^{D_A} H_A(D)\mathrm{d}D$$

Thus, if f is the desired transformation, we have, by (13.2.4),

$$\frac{\mathrm{d}f(D_A)}{\mathrm{d}D_A} = \frac{H_A(D_A)}{H_B(D_B)} = \frac{p_A(D_A)}{p_B(D_B)} = D_M p_A(D_A)$$

Hence,

$$f(D_A) = D_M P_A(D_A)$$

and so the cumulative distribution function flattens the histogram. Flattening the histogram is useful when trying to match two histograms which have been obtained from the same image by different digitizations. Thus, if we wish to match the histograms for two images A and B, then we flatten A to obtain $P_A(D_A)$ and perform the inverse of P_B to obtain $P_B^{-1}P_A(D_A)$, which is equal to H_B.

This flattening technique assumes continuous histograms, however. In the real case of digitized images with a finite number of pixels this method can be very inaccurate. A simple alternative is to change the discrete histogram into a continuous one by adding to each pixel's grey level a random number between $-\Delta D/2$ and $\Delta D/2$ (where ΔD is the separation between the discrete grey levels) so that the grey levels now range between $D_{\min} - \Delta D/2$ and $D_{\max} + \Delta D/2$, where $D_{\min}$ and $D_{\max}$ are, respectively, the minimum and maximum discrete grey levels. A function f_1 which flattens the histogram $H_1(D)$ is given by

$$f_1(D_1 - \Delta D/2) = D_1 - \Delta D/2 \qquad (13.2.5)$$

$$f_1(D_i + \Delta D/2) = [(D_M + \Delta D/2 - D_1 + \Delta D/2)/(N_1 N_2)]H_1(D_i)$$
$$+ f_1(D_i - \Delta D/2)$$

where $D_1, \ldots, D_M$ are the original discrete grey levels and the image is divided into N_1 by N_2 pixels. Between the points $D_i + \Delta D/2$, f_1 can be defined by interpolation. Now, if R is a random number uniformly distributed between 0 and 1 we can define the flattened image by

$$F_1(i, j) = \text{Trunc}[f_1(F(i, j) - \Delta D/2) + \{f_1(F(i, j) + \Delta D/2)$$
$$- f_1(F(i, j) - \Delta D/2)\}R] \tag{13.2.6}$$

where Trunc is the operation of discretizing to the nearest grey level. A similar transformation can be developed for the inverse operation to flattening a histogram, thus allowing histogram matching as before.

It can be shown that histogram equalization maximizes the zero-order brightness entropy and so, in a sense, maximizes the information in an image. However, a human's perceived brightness characteristic is not linear and so it has been argued that instead of flattening a histogram, a function should be sought which transforms a given image probability density function into one in which the perceived brightness levels are equiprobable. Thus, by (13.2.4) we have

$$p(D_B) = \frac{\mathrm{d}}{\mathrm{d}D_B} \int_0^{f^{-1}(D_B)} p(D_A)\mathrm{d}D_A \tag{13.2.6}$$

where we shall assume that $D_A \in [0, 1]$. A simple expression (similar to Weber's law) for the perceived brightness $\mathcal{B}$ is given by

$$\mathcal{B}(D_B) = \log(D_B + c) \tag{13.2.7}$$

where c is a constant. If D_B is also normalized to the interval $[0, 1]$, then we can define

$$\mathcal{B}_{\max} = \log(1 + c)$$

$$\mathcal{B}_{\min} = \log c$$

and so for $\mathcal{B}$ to be equally distributed we require

$$p(\mathcal{B}) = \frac{1}{\mathcal{B}_{\max} - \mathcal{B}_{\min}}$$

Hence, by (13.2.6), we have

$$p(D_B) = \frac{\mathrm{d}}{\mathrm{d}D_B} \int_{\mathcal{B}_{\min}}^{\mathcal{B}(D_B)} \frac{1}{\mathcal{B}_{\max} - \mathcal{B}_{\min}} \mathrm{d}\mathcal{B} = \frac{1}{(D_B + c)\log(1 + 1/c)}$$

Now, again by (13.2.6),

$$p(D_B) = \frac{1}{(D_B + c)\log(1 + 1/c)} = \frac{\mathrm{d}}{\mathrm{d}D_B} \int_0^{f^{-1}(D_B)} p(D_A)\mathrm{d}D_A$$

and so

$$D_A = F^{-1} \left\{ \frac{\log(1 + D_B/c)}{\log(1 + 1/c)} \right\}$$

where F is the cumulative distribution

$$F(D_A) = \int_0^{D_A} p(D_A) \mathrm{d} D_A$$

Finally, we have

$$D_B = f(D_A) = c\left(\exp\left[\log(1 + 1/c) \int_0^{D_A} p(D)\mathrm{d}D \right] - 1 \right) \qquad (13.2.8)$$

Transformation of a histogram by (13.2.8) is called *histogram hyperbolization*. A picture with poor dynamic range is shown in Figure 13.8(a); the same picture is shown after histogram equalization in Figure 13.8(b); and in Figure 13.8(c) after histogram hyperbolization.

Another application of histogram point operations is to the problem of photometric decalibration of nonlinear digitizer effects. We simply perform the inverse point operation on the output histogram of an image which has been obtained from a nonlinear digitizer (Figure 13.9).

Figure 13.8 (a) Original image. (b) Image after histogram equalization. (c) Image after histogram hyperbolization.

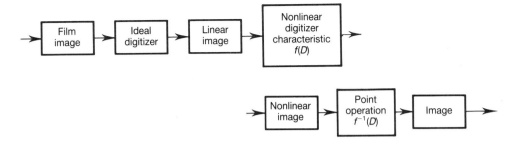

Figure 13.9 Photometric decalibration.

13.3 Noise removal and edge sharpening

Many images are contaminated with noise, usually by the image capture system. A simple method for removing additive noise when several images with identical signal components are available is by averaging the image copies. Thus, if

$$D_i(x, y) = S(x, y) + N_i(x, y) \qquad 1 \leqslant i \leqslant M$$

are M copies of an image S with additive noise N_i, and the following conditions on the expectations of the N_i hold:

$$E\{N_i(x, y)\} = 0, \; E\{N_i(x, y)N_j(x, y)\} = E\{N_i(x, y)\}E\{N_j(x, y)\} = 0 \qquad i \neq j,$$

$$E\{N_i^2(x, y)\} = \sigma^2 \text{ (independent of } i)$$

for all i, j and all x, y, then we define the image

$$\bar{D}(x, y) = \frac{1}{M} \sum_{i=1}^{M} (S + N_i)$$

If $P(x, y) = S^2(x, y)/\sigma^2$ denotes the signal/noise power ratio, then

$$\bar{P}(x, y) = \frac{S^2}{E\left\{\dfrac{1}{M} \Sigma_{i=1}^{M} N_i(x, y)\right\}^2}$$

$$= \frac{M^2 S^2}{E\{\Sigma_{i=1}^{M} N_i^2(x, y)\} + E\{\Sigma\Sigma_{i \neq j} N_i(x, y)N_j(x, y)\}}$$

$$= \frac{M^2 S^2}{\Sigma_{i=1}^{M} E\{N_i^2(x, y)\} + \Sigma\Sigma_{i \neq j} E\{N_i(x, y)\}E\{N_j(x, y)\}}$$

$$= \frac{M^2 S^2}{M \sigma^2}$$

$$= MP(x, y)$$

Hence, $\overline{SNR} = \sqrt{\overline{P(x, y)}} = \sqrt{M} \sqrt{P(x, y)} = \sqrt{M}\,SNR$, and the signal/noise ratio increases with $\sqrt{M}$.

Noise often has higher spatial frequencies than the image signal and so lowpass filtering is frequently used. It is possible to use high-order sophisticated filters such as those designed in Chapter 10. However, a simple low-order filter array will often suffice. Thus, if $f(n_1, n_2)$ is a noisy image array and $h(n_1, n_2)$ is a convolution filter, then the output filtered image $o(n_1, n_2)$ is given by

$$o(m_1, m_2) = \sum_{n_1, n_2} f(n_1, n_2) h(m_1 - n_1, m_2 - n_2)$$

Three simple lowpass filters h are given by

$$h_1 = \frac{1}{9} \begin{bmatrix} 1 & 1 & 1 \\ 1 & 1 & 1 \\ 1 & 1 & 1 \end{bmatrix}, h_2 = \frac{1}{10} \begin{bmatrix} 1 & 1 & 1 \\ 1 & 2 & 1 \\ 1 & 1 & 1 \end{bmatrix}, h_3 = \frac{1}{16} \begin{bmatrix} 1 & 2 & 1 \\ 2 & 4 & 2 \\ 1 & 2 & 1 \end{bmatrix}$$

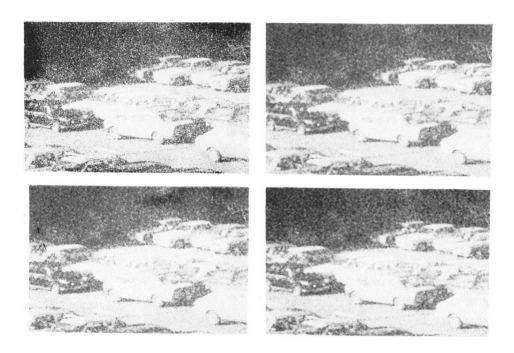

Figure 13.10   (a) Low quality image with speckle noise. (b) Image filtered with h_1. (c) Image filtered with h_2. (d) Image filtered with h_3.

(Note that we have only shown the terms $h_i(n_1, n_2)$ for $|n_1|, |n_2| \leq 1$. For $|n_1| > 1$ or $|n_2| > 1$, $h_i(n_1, n_2) = 0$, $1 \leq i \leq 3$. Also the sums of all the elements of each h_i are normalized to 1 so that the processed image is not altered with a brightness bias.) This simple type of filtering is useful for noise arising from sensors or channel transmission errors where the noise is usually discrete, uncorrelated and at isolated pixels (Figure 13.10).

Another useful application of simple 3×3 filters, this time of the highpass type, is that of edge sharpening. The quality of an image is often improved by enhancing the naturally occurring edges in order to clarify objects in the image. Simple highpass filters are given by

$$h_1 = \begin{bmatrix} 0 & -1 & 0 \\ -1 & 5 & -1 \\ 0 & -1 & 0 \end{bmatrix}, \quad h_2 = \begin{bmatrix} -1 & -1 & -1 \\ -1 & 9 & -1 \\ -1 & -1 & -1 \end{bmatrix},$$

$$h_3 = \begin{bmatrix} 1 & -2 & 1 \\ -2 & 5 & -2 \\ 1 & -2 & 1 \end{bmatrix} \tag{13.3.1}$$

The effects of these filters are shown in **Figure 13.11**.

Figure 13.11 (a) Original image. (b) Image filtered with h_1. (c) Image filtered with h_2. (d) Image filtered with h_3.

13.4 *Geometric distortion removal*

In many systems geometric distortion is inherent in the capturing process. For example, wide angle lenses are particularly prone to 'barrel' distortion; thin biological specimens used in histology may be distorted in the sectioning operation; and photographic images of planets become distorted when mapped onto a flat surface by some map projection. Let $f(x, y)$ be an image and let

$$x = a(x', y')$$

$$y = b(x', y')$$

be a spatial transformation. Then if we operate on f using this transformation we obtain the output image

$$g(x', y') = f(x, y) = f(a(x', y'), b(x', y'))$$

Note that, if f is a discrete image obtained by sampling a continuous image at regular grid points, then $(x_i, y_i) = (a(x'_1, y'_i), b(x'_i, y'_i))$, where (x'_i, y'_i) is a grid point. Hence we may have to interpolate between the known values of f at the grid points to obtain g. The simplest type of interpolation is shown in Figure 13.12 and is obtained by finding the bilinear surface which passes through four grid points. (Note that, of course, a hypersurface will not generally pass through four arbitrarily specified points.) At a general point (x, y), $f(x, y)$ is then given by

$$f(x, y) = \{f(1, 0) - f(0, 0)\}x + \{f(0, 1) - f(0, 0)\}y + \{f(1, 1) + f(0, 0)$$
$$- f(0, 1) - f(1, 0)\}xy + f(0, 0)$$

One of the most important applications of geometrical image transformations is in the correction of photographs of planets taken by spacecraft camera. The distortion arises because the planetary object which is spherical is mapped onto a flat photograph. We must also select a map projection in terms of which the final image is to be displayed. Thus, we must perform two geometrical operations: the first is the inverse of the map which projects the planetary

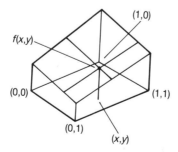

Figure 13.12   Bilinear interpolation.

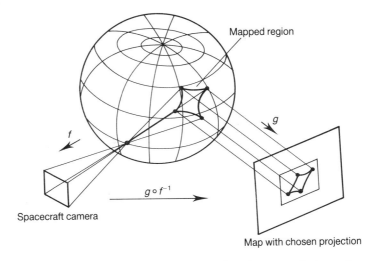

Figure 13.13 Geometrical operations for planetary photograph.

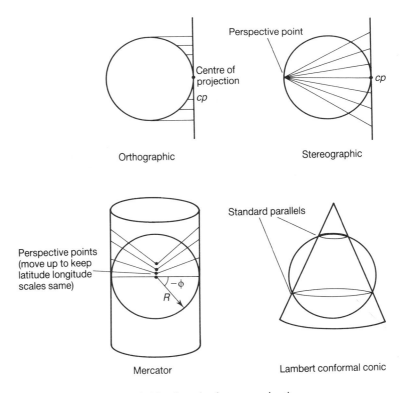

Figure 13.14 Standard map projections.

surface on to the photographic plate, and the second is the desired map projection to form the final image (Figure 13.13).

Some standard map projections are shown in Figure 13.14.

13.5 Restoration of motion degraded images

In this section we shall consider the effect of camera motion on a photographic image. Such motion causes blurring of the image which can be removed completely if we know the camera motion which caused the blurring. This is achieved by inverse filtering and will illustrate a general technique in image processing of removing any known form of (linear) degradation by applying the inverse operator of the degrading mechanism. If the image is blurred and also contains noise, then we shall use the Kalman filter in combination with the inverse filter.

To begin we need to recall some facts from systems realization theory. Thus let $H(z)$ be the transfer function of a discrete (one-dimensional) system, as considered in Part I of the book. Write H in the form

$$H(z) = c_0 + \frac{c_1}{z} + \frac{c_2}{z^2} + \ldots + \frac{c_n}{z^n} \tag{13.5.1}$$

Then we wish to find a single-input–single-output linear system of the form

$$\left. \begin{aligned} x(k+1) &= Ax(k) + bu(k) \\ y(k) &= cx(k) + du(k) \end{aligned} \right\} \tag{13.5.2}$$

where $x(k) \in \mathbb{R}^m$ (state vector), $u(k) \in \mathbb{R}$ is the input, $y(k) \in \mathbb{R}$ is the output and A, b, c are constant matrices of order $n \times n$, $n \times 1$, $1 \times n$, respectively, and $d \in \mathbb{R}$. Since the transfer function of (13.5.2) is given by

$$H(z) = \frac{Y(z)}{U(z)} = c(zI - A)^{-1}b + d \tag{13.5.3}$$

it is easy to check that the system (13.5.2) is equivalent to (13.5.1) if we choose

$$A = \begin{bmatrix} 0 & -c_2/c_0 & -c_3/c_0 & \cdots & -c_n/c_0 \\ 0 & 0 & 0 & & 0 \\ 0 & 1 & 0 & & 0 \\ 0 & 0 & 1 & & 0 \\ \vdots & & & & \\ 0 & 0 & & 1 & 0 \end{bmatrix} \tag{13.5.4}$$

$$b = (c_1 - c_0 \ 0 \ \cdots \ 0)^{\mathrm{T}}$$

$$c = (1 \ 0 \ 0 \ \cdots \ 0)$$

$$d = c_0$$

The inverse system $1/H(z)$ can be shown to be given by

$$\xi(k+1) = \hat{A}\xi(k) + \hat{b}y(k) \\ u(k) = \hat{c}\xi(k) + \hat{d}y(k) \bigg\}$$ (13.5.5)

where

$$\hat{A} = A - bd^{-1}c = \begin{bmatrix} -c_1/c_0 & -c_2/c_0 \ldots & -c_{n-1}/c_0 & -c_n/c_0 \\ 1 & 0 & 0 & 0 \\ 0 & 1 & 0 & 0 \\ \vdots & & & \\ 0 & 0 & 1 & 0 \end{bmatrix}$$ (13.5.6)

$$\hat{b} = bd^{-1} = (c_1/c_0 \; -1 \; 0 \quad \ldots \quad 0)^{\mathrm{T}}$$
$$\hat{c} = (-1/c_0 \; 0 \; 0 \; 0)$$
$$\hat{d} = 1/c_0$$

We are now ready to consider the effect of motion blur on an input image. To simplify the problem we shall assume that the motion producing the blur occurs in a straight line along the horizontal spatial coordinate. Then, we can model this blurring effect by

$$y(x_1) = \int_L h(x_1, x')u(x')\mathrm{d}x'$$

where L is the extent of the motion along x_1.

In the case of space-invariant blurring, this becomes

$$y(x_1) = \int_L h(x_1 - x')u(x')\mathrm{d}x'$$

or, in discrete form,

$$y(k) = \sum_{i=1}^{m} h(k-i)u(i)$$ (13.5.7)

where m is the extent of the blur. We can write h in the form

$$h(i) = c_0\delta_{i0} + c_1\delta_{i-1,0} + \ldots + c_m\delta_{i-m,0}$$ (13.5.8)

where

$$\delta_{ij} = \begin{cases} 1 & \text{if } i = j \\ 0 & \text{otherwise} \end{cases}$$

is the Kronecker delta.

We can now use (13.5.4) to realize the blurring system (13.5.6). Note, however, that the derivation of (13.5.4) from (13.5.3) assumes zero initial conditions. The initial values of u in our case correspond to pixels beyond the boundary of the image, i.e. the background. For zero intensity background (13.5.4) is therefore an adequate model, with $x(0) = 0$. If the background has nonzero intensity, we must include the nonzero initial condition given by

$$x_1(0) = c_1 u(-1) + c_2 u(-2) + \ldots + c_m u(-m)$$
$$x_2(0) = -c_0 u(-1)$$
$$x_3(0) = -c_0 u(-2)$$
$$\vdots$$

$$x_m(0) = -c_0 u(-m + 1)$$

Now suppose that the blur is caused by a constant velocity translation in the horizontal direction of speed v during the exposure interval $[0, T]$. Then the extent of the blur m is given by

$$m = vT$$

If $m = 10$ pixels, for example, and we take $T = 1$, then the coefficients c_i in (13.5.8) can all be taken to be $1/v$. Hence by (13.5.6) the inverse systems has dimension 10 and is of the form

$$\begin{bmatrix} \xi_1 \\ \xi_2 \\ \vdots \\ \xi_{10} \end{bmatrix}(k+1) = \begin{bmatrix} -1 & -1 & -1\ldots & & -1 \\ 1 & 0 & 0 & & 0 \\ 0 & 1 & 0 & & 0 \\ \vdots & & & & \\ 0 & 0 & 0 & 1 & 0 \end{bmatrix} \begin{bmatrix} \xi_1 \\ \xi_2 \\ \vdots \\ \xi_{10} \end{bmatrix}(k)$$

$$+ \begin{bmatrix} 1 \\ -1 \\ 0 \\ \vdots \\ 0 \end{bmatrix} y(k)$$

$$u(k) = -v\xi_1(k) + vy(k) \qquad (k = 0, 1, \ldots, N - 1)$$

where $\xi(0)$ represents the background intensity.

An example of an image with motion induced blur and its restoration by the above method is shown in Figure 13.15.

Figure 13.15 (a) Image with blur. (b) Image after filtering with inverse blur filter.

We shall next consider the removal of motion blur in the presence of additive noise. The system equation (13.5.2) is replaced by the equations

$$\left. \begin{array}{l} x(k+1) = Ax(k) + bu(k) \\ y(k) = cx(k) + du(k) + v(k) \end{array} \right\} \tag{13.5.9}$$

where v is a white noise process with

$$Ev(k) = 0$$

$$E\{v(k_1)v(k_2)\} = \sigma^2 \delta_{k_1,k_2}$$

$k, k_1, k_2 = 0, 1, \ldots, N - 1$. The variance σ^2 is assumed to be known. It is possible to derive a dynamic equation for $u(k)$ in terms of the scanning device used for obtaining the image. Thus we can write

$$\left. \begin{array}{l} r(k+1) = Er(k) + fu_1(k) \\ u(k) = gr(k) \end{array} \right\} \tag{13.5.10}$$

$k = 0, 1, \ldots, N - 1$, where $u_1(k)$ is the original image and $E\{u_1(k)\} = 0$, $E\{u_1(k_1)u^T(k_2)\} = K\delta_{k_1k_2}$. The matrices in (13.5.10) can be found by matching the response of this system to the correlation function of the scanner output. Taken together, (13.5.9) and (13.5.10) give the dynamical system

$$\left. \begin{array}{l} z(k+1) = \begin{bmatrix} A & bg \\ 0 & E \end{bmatrix} z(k) + \begin{bmatrix} 0 \\ f \end{bmatrix} u_1(k) \\[20pt] y(k) = \begin{bmatrix} c & dg \end{bmatrix} z(k) + v(k) \end{array} \right\} \tag{13.5.11}$$

where $z^T(k) = [x^T(k)\ r^T(k)]$. This is now in the form suitable for applying the standard Kalman filter, which determines an optimal estimate $\hat{z}$ of z according to the dynamics

$$
\left.
\begin{aligned}
\hat{z}(k) &= [I - F(k)\bar{c}]\bar{A}\,\hat{z}(k-1) + F(k)y(k)] \\
F(k) &= P(k)\bar{c}^{\mathrm{T}}[\bar{c}P(k)\bar{c}^{\mathrm{T}} + \sigma^2]^{-1} \\
P(k+1) &= \bar{A}[I - F(k)\bar{c}]P(k)\bar{A}^{\mathrm{T}} + \bar{B}K\bar{B}^{\mathrm{T}}
\end{aligned}
\right\} \tag{13.5.12}
$$

where

$$
\bar{A} = \begin{bmatrix} A & bg \\ 0 & E \end{bmatrix}, \quad \bar{B} = \begin{bmatrix} 0 \\ f \end{bmatrix}, \quad \bar{c} = \begin{bmatrix} c & dg \end{bmatrix}
$$

The initial conditions $P(0)$, $\hat{z}(0)$ of (13.5.12) must be determined from the given data. In cases where the value of $P(0)$ is large (i.e. the error covariance matrix is unknown), we can use an inverse filter instead. The optimal estimate of the image is given by

$$
\hat{u}(k) = [0 \; g]\hat{z}(k)
$$

13.6 Inverse filtering and Wiener deconvolution

Consider a given image $f(x, y)$ which is degraded by some spatial transfer function $h_d(x, y)$. Then if h_d is known exactly we can remove the degradation by applying the inverse filter $H_i(x, y)$ for which

$$
h_i(x, y)^*h_d(x, y) = \delta(x, y)
$$

where δ is the two-dimensional delta function (Figure 13.16a). Suppose, however, that the degraded image is corrupted by additive noise, as in Figure 13.16(b). Then we have

$$
\hat{f} = (\mathcal{F}^{-1}(H_i(\omega_x, \omega_y)[H_d(\omega_x, \omega_y)F(\omega_x, \omega_y) + N(\omega_x, \omega_y)])
$$

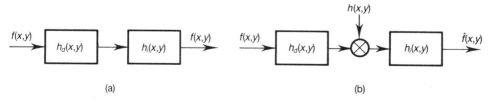

Figure 13.16 Inverse filtering: (a) two-dimensional filter and its inverse; (b) with noise injected.

where $\mathcal{F}^{-1}$ denotes inverse Fourier transformation. Since H_i is the inverse of H_d, we have

$$H_i(\omega_x, \omega_y)H_d(\omega_x, \omega_y) = 1$$

and so

$$\hat{f} = f + \mathcal{F}^{-1}(H_i(\omega_x, \omega_y)N(\omega_x, \omega_y))$$

The second term in this expression is likely to be large for high frequencies and so the detailed parts of an image will be severely degraded if nonzero noise is present when using a simple inverse filter.

We therefore consider a more sophisticated approach based on Wiener filtering. To simplify the notation we shall work in one dimension. The extension and application to two-dimensional images is immediate. Suppose, therefore, that we have a signal $s(t)$ which is contaminated with additive noise $n(t)$. Then we wish to construct a linear system $h(t)$ such that, if $x(t) = s(t) + n(t)$, then $y(t) \triangleq (h*x)(t)$ is the 'best' approximation to $s(t)$ (Figure 13.17). In order to obtain h, let $e(t) = s(t) - y(t)$ be the error and assume that $n(t)$ and $s(t)$ have known power spectral densities. The mean squared error (MSE) is given by

$$MSE = E(e^2) = \int_{-\infty}^{\infty} e^2(t)dt$$

$$= E((s - y)^2) = E(s^2 - 2sy + y^2)$$

$$= E(s^2) - 2E(sy) + E(y^2)$$

Now,

$$E(s^2) = \int_{-\infty}^{\infty} s(t)s(t)dt = R_s(0)$$

where R_s is the (known) autocorrelation of s. Similarly,

$$E(sy) = \int_{-\infty}^{\infty} h(\tau)R_{xs}(\tau)d\tau$$

$$E(y^2) = \int_{-\infty}^{\infty} \int_{-\infty}^{\infty} h(\tau)h(u)R_x(u - \tau)d\tau du$$

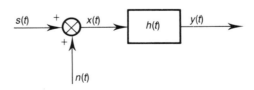

Figure 13.17 One-dimensional Wiener filtering.

since $y = h*x$. Hence,

$$MSE = R(0) - 2\int_{-\infty}^{\infty} h(\tau)R_{xs}(\tau)d\tau + \int_{-\infty}^{\infty}\int_{-\infty}^{\infty} h(\tau)h(u)R_x(u - \tau)d\tau du$$

$$\text{(13.6.1)}$$

To find the 'best' h, let $h = h_0 + g$; then

$$MSE = MSE_0 + 2\int_{-\infty}^{\infty} g(u)\left[\int_{-\infty}^{\infty} h_0(\tau)R_x(u - \tau)d\tau - R_{xs}(u)\right]du$$

$$+ \int_{-\infty}^{\infty}\int_{-\infty}^{\infty} g(u)g(\tau)R_x(u - \tau)dud\tau$$

$$\text{(13.6.2)}$$

where MSE_0 is the mean squared error calculated with h_0 instead of h. The last term in (13.6.2) can be written

$$\int_{-\infty}^{\infty} \left(\int_{-\infty}^{\infty} g(u)x(y - u)du\right)\left(\int_{-\infty}^{\infty} g(\tau)x(t - \tau)d\tau\right)dt$$

which is nonnegative. Hence, if we choose h_0 to satisfy

$$\int_{-\infty}^{\infty} h_0(\tau)R_x(u - \tau)d\tau = R_{xs}(u) \qquad \text{(13.6.3)}$$

then the second term on the right of (13.6.2) is zero and we obtain

$$MSE \geq MSE_0$$

for all g. Hence the best h_0, i.e. the one which minimizes MSE, is the solution of the integral equation (13.6.3). Since

$$R_{xy}(\tau) = (h*R_x)(\tau)$$

it follows from (13.6.3) that the Wiener filter makes the input/output cross-correlation equal to the signal/(signal + noise) cross-correlation. Moreover, again by (13.6.3), we have

$$P_{xs}(s) = H_0(s)P_x(s)$$

and so

$$H_0(s) = \frac{P_{xs}(s)}{P_x(s)} \qquad \text{(13.6.4)}$$

We can apply the Wiener filter to invert a given degradation filter in the presence of noise (Figure 13.18). This is called *Wiener deconvolution*. From Figure 13.18 we have

$$X(s) = F(s)S(s) + N(s)$$

$$Y(s) = S(s) + \frac{N(s)}{F(s)} = S(s) + K(s)$$

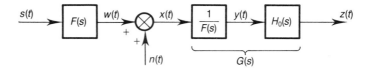

Figure 13.18   Wiener deconvolution.

where $K(s) = N(s)/F(s)$. From the general theory of Wiener filtering above, if the signal and noise are uncorrelated, we have (see exercise 5),

$$H_0(s) = \frac{P_S(s)}{P_S(s) + P_k(s)} = \frac{|S(s)|^2}{|S(s)|^2 + \left|\dfrac{N(s)}{F(s)}\right|^2}$$

and

$$G(s) = \frac{H_0(s)}{F(s)} = \frac{1}{F(s)}\left[\frac{P_S(s)}{P_S(s) + P_k(s)}\right] = \frac{F^*(s)P_S(s)}{|F(s)|^2 P_S(s) + P_n(s)}$$

Let us note, finally, that it is also possible to use pseudoinverse operations to find an approximate inverse filter. Thus, if a degraded image f_d is obtained by convolution (or a more general integral) of the original image f_i as in

$$f_d(x, y) = \int_{-\infty}^{\infty} \int_{-\infty}^{\infty} f_i(x', y')k(x, y, x', y')dx'dy'$$

then, by discretizing, we can obtain an equation of the form

$$F_d = KF_i \qquad (13.6.5)$$

where the samples in (x, y) space are arranged in the form of a vector so that (13.6.5) is a linear equation in the unknown vector F_i and K is a matrix (of some large dimension). Since K may not be invertible (or even square) we can resort to the pseudoinverse (or any other approximate inverse) to give the estimate

$$\hat{F}_i = K^\dagger F_d \qquad (13.6.6)$$

The main drawback with this method is the large size of the matrix K. However, in many cases, K is separable and can be written as a tensor product

$$K = K_1 \otimes K_2$$

in which case

$$K^\dagger = K_1^\dagger \otimes K_2^\dagger \qquad (13.6.7)$$

If significant observation noise is present, however, the generalized inverse solution is likely to be numerically unstable and so we must use a different approach, such as regression analysis. Thus, suppose that the discretized model is

$$F_d = KF_i + n \qquad (13.6.8)$$

instead of (13.6.5), where n is a noise process. Then we minimize the weighted error

$$\eta(\hat{F}_i) = (F_d - K\hat{F}_i)^{\mathrm{T}} P_n^{-1} (F_d - K\hat{F}_i)$$

where P_n is the (assumed known) covariance matrix of n. Evaluating $\partial\eta/\partial\hat{F}_i$ gives

$$-2K^{\mathrm{T}} P_n^{-1} (F_d - K\hat{F}_i) = 0$$

and if $K^{\mathrm{T}} P_n^{-1} K$ is invertible we have

$$\hat{F}_i = (K^{\mathrm{T}} P_n^{-1} K)^{-1} K^{\mathrm{T}} P_n^{-1} F_d$$

If the system (13.6.8) is underdetermined, so that K is a $p \times q$ matrix with $p < q$, then the regression solution is

$$\hat{F}_i = (P^{-1}K)^{\dagger} P^{-1} F_d + \{I - (P^{-1}K)^{\dagger} P^{-1} K\} e$$

where † is the generalized inverse, $P_n = PP^{\mathrm{T}}$ is the spectral factorization of P_n and e is an arbitrary vector. The minimum norm estimate is then

$$\hat{F}_i = (P^{-1}K)^{\dagger} P^{-1} F_d$$

and if $P = \sigma_n^2 I$ (white noise) we simply obtain (13.6.6) as in the noise free case.

13.7 Homomorphic filtering

In many practical situations signals are not combined together additively and so the normal vector space operations are not appropriate in the design of filters for such signals. It turns out, however, that in many cases the rules for combination of signals (by multiplication or convolution) can be treated as vector space operations on an appropriate vector space. Thus we introduce the notion of a homomorphic system operating between an aribtrary pair of vector spaces. A *homomorphic system N* operating between the vector spaces $(X, \bigcirc, *)$ and $(Y, \square, \dagger)$ (over the same field F) is a (memoryless) system for which

$$N(x_1 \bigcirc x_2) = N(x_1) \square N(x_2) \qquad x_1, x_2 \in X$$
$$N(c * x) = c \dagger N(x) \qquad x \in X, c \in F$$

Note that $\bigcirc$ and $\square$ are the 'addition' operations in X and Y, respectively, and $*$ and $\dagger$ represent scalar multiplication. For example, the nonlinear system N given by

$$N(x)(t) = e^{x(t)}$$

is a homomorphic system, since

$$N(x_1 + x_2)(t) = e^{x_1(t)+x_2(t)} = N(x_1)(t)N(x_2)(t) \Bigg\}$$
$$N(cx)(t) = e^{cx(t)} = (e^{x(t)})^c = (N(x))^c(t) \Bigg\}$$

$$(13.7.1)$$

For a given vector space $(X, \bigcirc, *)$ there is an invertible system α_X such that

$$\alpha_X(x_1 \bigcirc x_2) = \alpha_X(x_1) + \alpha_X(x_2) \qquad x_1, x_2 \in X$$
$$\alpha_X(c*x) = c\alpha_X(x) \qquad\qquad x \in X, c \in F$$

Thus, for any homomorphic system $N: (X, \bigcirc, *) \rightarrow (Y, \square, \dagger)$ we can write

$$N = \alpha_X \alpha_X^{-1} N \alpha_Y \alpha_Y^{-1}$$
$$= \alpha_X \tilde{N} \alpha_Y^{-1}$$

where

$$\tilde{N} = \alpha_X^{-1} N \alpha_Y$$

is a linear system.

The idea of *generalized* or *homomorphic filtering* can now be specified as follows. Suppose that a signal x and noise n are combined according to the vector space operation of the vector space $(X, \bigcirc, *)$. Then

$$\alpha_X(x \bigcirc n) = \alpha_X(x) + \alpha_X(n)$$

and we design a linear additive filter $\tilde{N}$ which removes $\alpha_X(n)$ (in some optimal way). Thus,

$$\tilde{N}(\alpha_X(x) + \alpha_X(n)) = \alpha_X(x)$$

(approximately). Finally, applying α_X^{-1} gives the signal x (Figure 13.19).

Now suppose that we consider a signal $s(k)$ which is corrupted by an unwanted convolution with a disturbance signal $d(k)$ (which may be noise, blur, etc.), so that we have a measurement of

$$y(k) = (s*d)(k)$$

Then we wish to design a homomorphic system which will provide an estimate $\hat{s}$ of s. We require the map α for which

$$\alpha(s*d) = \alpha(s) + \alpha(d) \qquad (13.7.2)$$

(We have dropped the suffix X introduced above, since the vector space is clear in this case.) The desired α is shown in Figure 13.20, where the function log is defined via an integral as in the definition of the cepstrum in order to make it

Figure 13.19   A basic homomorphic filter.

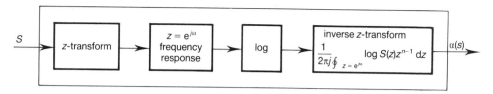

Figure 13.20 A homomorphic system for convolution.

continuous. Since (13.7.2) holds, we follow α with a liner filter L which removes $\alpha(d)$ in some optimal way and then apply α^{-1}, giving an estimate of s, i.e.

$$\hat{s} = \alpha^{-1}L\{\alpha(s*d)\}$$
$$= \alpha^{-1}L\{\alpha(s) + \alpha(d)\}$$
$$= \alpha^{-1}(\alpha(s) + \varepsilon)$$
$$= s + \alpha^{-1}(\varepsilon)$$

for some error term ε.

An example of homomorphic filtering in the case when signals are multiplied together is in photographic processing. A monochrome photographic image may be represented in the form

$$X(x, y) = I(x, y)R(x, y) > 0$$

where $X(x, y)$ is the intensity at (x, y) and $I(x, y)$, $R(x, y)$ are, respectively, the illuminance and reflectance at (x, y). To a reasonable approximation, we can regard I and R as independent. Note that I is associated with low frequencies, while R is associated with high frequencies. It is often desirable to reduce the dynamic range (i.e. the light to dark range) while enhancing the contrast. This can be achieved by filtering X to obtain

$$\hat{X}(x, y) = (I(x, y))^{\gamma_I}(R(x, y))^{\gamma_R}$$

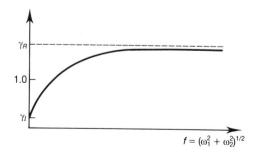

Figure 13.21 Amplitude response of L.

where $\gamma_I < 1$, $\gamma_R > 1$. To do this we introduce the homomorphic map α which is the continuous form of log to obtain

$$\alpha(X) = \log(IR) = \log(I) + \log(R) = \alpha(I) + \alpha(R)$$

and then filter $\alpha(X)$ with a linear filter L with frequency response as shown in Figure 13.21 (assuming zero phase). The complete system is shown in Figure 13.22.

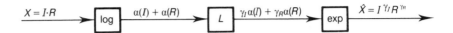

Figure 13.22   A homomorphic photographic processor.

13.8 *Image feature extraction*

In the remainder of this chapter we shall be interested in image interpretation for use in machine vision. Usually, the first operation to be performed on an image is the extraction of features corresponding to regions of the image which are regarded as separate objects. This is often begun by finding the edges and then interpreting the regions enclosed by the edges in some way.

The simplest edge-finding routines are one-dimensional and assume a knowledge of edge directions so that the processing can be carried out perpendicular to the edge. In this case we can regard the image as a one-dimensional array $f(k)$. A simple differencing operator will find well-defined edges:

$$Df(k) = f(k + l) - f(k - l)$$

where l is some positive integer. Usually l is chosen to be 1. However, for noisy images, it is better to use some form of averaging operator, such as

$$\bar{D}f(k) = \sum_{i=l_1}^{l_2} \{f(k + i) - f(k - i)\}/(l_2 - l_1 + 1)$$

where l_1 is usually 1 and $2 < l_2 < 5$.

Since the direction of edges is unlikely to be known, *a priori*, it is usually more efficient to use two-dimensional operators. Thus, if $f(m, n)$ is an image with well-defined edges, a simple 2×2 window for the edge operator is sufficient:

$$D(k_1, k_2) = [\{f(k_1, k_2) - f(k_1 + 1, k_2 + 1)\}^2$$
$$+ \{f(k_1 + 1, k_2) - f(k_1, k_2 + 1)\}^2] \qquad (13.8.1)$$

The effect of this operator is shown in Figure 13.23.

Figure 13.23 (a) Original image. (b) Image after applying a simple edge-finding algorithm.

It is also possible to use 3×3 windows based on gradient derivatives or the Laplace opertor:

$$\nabla^2 f(x, y) = \partial^2 f(x, y)/\partial x^2 + \partial^2 f(x, y)/\partial y^2$$

which can be approximated digitally by

$$D_{\mathrm{L}}(k_1, k_2) = \{f(k_1, k_2 - 1) + f(k_1 - 1, k_2) + f(k_1, k_2 + 1)$$
$$+ f(k_1 + 1, k_2) - 4f(k_1, k_2)\}/4$$

for example. These operators are often followed by thresholding in order to separate the edges from the background.

Another approach to edge finding is by the zero-crossing method. In this method lines are found by differentiating a profile and finding where the differentiated image changes sign, corresponding to a maximum (or minimum) of the original profile. The method is usually implemented by convolving the image with the Gaussian distribution

$$G(x, y) = \frac{1}{2\pi\sigma^2} \exp\left(\frac{-x^2 - y^2}{2\pi\sigma^2}\right)$$

to smooth the image, followed by the Laplacian operator. Note that $\nabla^2 G$ can be written in the rotationally invariant form

$$\nabla^2 G = \left(\frac{r^2 - 2\sigma^2}{2\pi\sigma^6}\right) \exp\left(\frac{-r^2}{2\sigma^2}\right)$$

Once a reasonable representation of the edge points in an image has been found a variety of fairly *ad hoc* edge linking and region finding algorithms can be applied. A typical region splitting method uses the minima in the histogram to divide the image into regions (Figure 13.24). There are many situations, however, when this is not particularly effective. An alternative approach is to

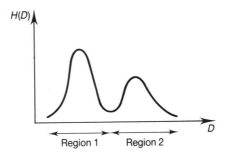

Figure 13.24   Region   splitting   by histogram.

start with small atomic regions, each consisting of pixels with similar values, and by extending each region by adding pixels or small areas with similar properties. This is usually based on thresholding and often requires some trial and error.

13.9 The Hough transform

When an image has been processed into a collection of edge points or regions it is important to be able to determine the shapes or equations of the region boundaries. In machine vision this must be done automatically and so a method by which the computer can find the presence of straight lines, circles, etc., is obviously of great importance. Such a method is provided by the *Hough transform*. To be specific, suppose we are looking for circles in an image. All such circles have equations of the form

$$(x_1 - \alpha_1)^2 + (x_2 - \alpha_2)^2 - \alpha_3^2 = 0 \qquad (13.9.1)$$

where (x_1, x_2) is a point in the image and $(\alpha_1, \alpha_2, \alpha_3)$ is a vector of parameters. Each parameter vector specifies a circle with a particular centre and radius. Given any fixed image point $(\bar{x}_1, \bar{x}_2)$ which has been determined as lying on an edge, there will be an infinity of possible circles passing through $(\bar{x}_1, \bar{x}_2)$. In fact, the parameters for all these circles satisfy

$$(\bar{x}_1 - \alpha_1)^2 + (\bar{x}_2 - \alpha_2)^2 - \alpha_3^2 = 0 \qquad (13.9.2)$$

Let $H(\bar{x}_1, \bar{x}_2)$ denote the subset of $\mathbb{R}^3$ (parameter space) consisting of all points $(\alpha_1, \alpha_2, \alpha_3)$ which satisfy (13.9.2). If $\mathcal{P}(\mathbb{R}^3)$ denotes the set of all subsets of $\mathbb{R}^3$, then the *Hough transform* is the map

$$H : \mathbb{R}^2 \to \mathcal{P}(\mathbb{R}^3)$$

given by

$$H(x_1, x_2) = \{(\alpha_1, \alpha_2, \alpha_3) \in \mathbb{R}^3 : (13.9.1) \text{ holds}\}.$$

Suppose that m given edge points $(x_1^1, x_2^1), \ldots, (x_1^m, x_2^m)$ lie on the circle

$$(x_1 - \bar{\alpha}_1)^2 + (x_2 - \bar{\alpha}_2)^2 - \bar{\alpha}_3^2 = 0 \qquad (13.9.3)$$

Then,

$$\bigcap_{i=1}^{m} H(x_1^i, x_2^i) = \{(\bar{\alpha}_1, \bar{\alpha}_2, \bar{\alpha}_3)\} \qquad (13.9.4)$$

provided the points are well spaced on the circle. (In fact, just three distinct points on a circle will do.) Equation (13.9.4) is the basis of the Hough transform method. We can interpret equation (13.9.1) by observing that, for a fixed image point (x_1, x_2) this equation defines a hypersurface in parameter (i.e. α-) space. Then we apply the Hough transform in the following way. Parameter space is discretized by dividing it into small cubes (or hypercubes in a higher dimensional space) and then each edge point (x_1, x_2) in the processed image is mapped into α-space by H. With each discrete cube in α-space we associate a number which is increased by one each time the hypersurface $H(x_1, x_2)$ passes through that cube. As more and more edge points are processed in this way the numbers associated with the cubes in α-space form a function which develops peaks at points α which correspond to circles in the image. In the example above, a peak would occur at $(\bar{\alpha}_1, \bar{\alpha}_2, \bar{\alpha}_3)$. All that remains is to identify the peaks by some kind of thresholding operation.

The same technique will work, of course, for any shape parameterized by an equation of the form

$$p(\mathbf{x}, \boldsymbol{\alpha}) = 0, \; \mathbf{x} \in \mathbb{R}^n, \; \boldsymbol{\alpha} \in \mathbb{R}^m$$

The general Hough transform $H : \mathbb{R}^n \to \mathcal{P}(\mathbb{R}^m)$ is then defined by

$$H(x) = \{\boldsymbol{\alpha} \in \mathbb{R}^m : p(\mathbf{x}, \boldsymbol{\alpha}) = 0\}$$

The main disadvantage with the above technique is that large computation times and storage requirements are involved for shapes with even a small number of parameters. However, a number of efficient algorithms have been developed which use the basic ideas of the Hough transform (see the bibliographical notes).

13.10 Interpretation of line images

In the preceding two sections we have considered methods for reducing a given image to a collection of lines. This simplifies the image considerably for computer vision but leads to the difficult problem of machine line interpretation. That is, a computer must be programmed to 'fit the lines together' into recognizable objects, some of which may be partially occluded by others. A great many attempts have been made to solve this problem with varying degrees of success. One of the most useful techniques is based on line labelling. The problem is simplified by making two assumptions:

A1. Objects are trihedral polyhedra, i.e. polyhedra in which each vertex is surrounded by exactly three sides.
A2. The objects in the image are in general position, so that a slight change in the position of the objects does not alter the junction types in the line drawing.

Since each vertex is formed by three surfaces, the vertices are all surrounded by eight octants defined by the three surfaces (Figure 13.25(a)). The possible vertex types are then as shown in Figure 13.25(b). It is clear that one, three, five or seven octants can be filled as shown. The method of labelling then proceeds as follows. Each edge or line is classified into one of three types:

L1. A convex edge. Both surfaces forming the edge are visible.
L2. A concave edge. Both surfaces forming the edge are visible.
L3. An occluding edge with one surface occluding the other.

Lines of type L1 are labelled '+', those of type L2 are labelled '−' and those of type L3 are labelled '→' or '←', such that the surface on the right side of the arrow occludes that on the left when looking along the arrow. For example, the object in Figure 13.25(b)(iii) would be labelled as in Figure 13.26, assuming it

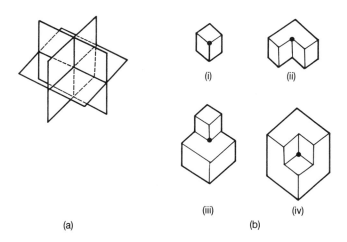

(a) (b)

Figure 13.25 The eight octants surrounding any vertex and the possible vertex types: (a) basic octants; (b) possible vertex configurations: (i) one octant, (ii) three octants, (iii) five octants, (iv) seven octants.

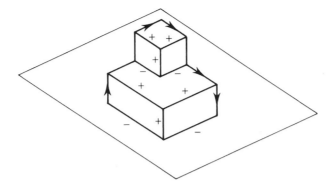

Figure 13.26   Edge labelling for a simple object.

rests on a flat surface. By examining the shapes in Figure 13.25(b) from all possible (generic) positions it can be seen that each vertex can be at the join of two or three lines which have one of only twelve possible labellings, as shown in Figure 13.27. A line joining some pair of vertices may not be completely visible – it may be partially occluded by another surface. Such a line will meet an edge line of the surface at a point which is not a vertex. These meeting points can be of four types, as in Figure 13.28. Note that the top line is shown with two arrows for convenience; in practice each line carries only one label.

Now, given any line image we can proceed to interpret objects contained in the image by trying all possible labellings for each vertex. Thus a vertex with

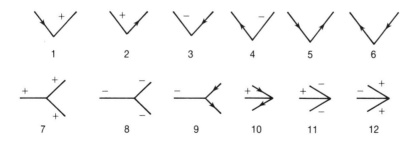

Figure 13.27   Possible labellings at any vertex.

Figure 13.28   Possible labellings for 'T' junctions.

three meeting lines can only be labelled by 7, 8, 9 or 10, 11, 12 from Figure 13.27. All inconsistencies are removed by some search technique, leaving a number of possible interpretations for the image. (Of course, a line image may have several interpretations.) This approach can be generalized to images with shadows and curved lines.

Another important consideration in two-dimensional line representations of three-dimensional scenes is that of realizability. From above we see that a line drawing which has a consistent labelling can be realized. However, the converse is not true; there are realizable line drawings which do not have consistent labellings. One method of determining the realizability of a line drawing is by mapping each surface enclosed by a set of lines into 'gradient space' and examining the possible positions of their representations in this space relative to the other surfaces in the image. A plane in space is given by a linear equation of the form

$$px + qy + z = c$$

Gradient space is the set of all points (p, q) which represent orientations of surfaces in the image.

An alternative approach to realizability is to construct polyhedra whose projections onto the image plane correspond to the given line drawing. Suppose axes are chosen so that the image plane is parallel to the (x, y)-plane, i.e. objects are projected along the z-axis. Let (x_i, y_i, z_i) be the coordinates of vertex v_i, while the equation of the plane face f_j of the object is

$$a_j x + b_j y + z + c_j = 0$$

We shall assume that no faces are parallel to the z-axis. The points (x_i, y_i) are found at the intersection of lines in the image plane and so we are left with the unknowns a_i, b_i, c_i and z_i in order to construct the objects in the scene from the image lines. If a vertex v_i lies on face f_j we have the equation

$$a_j x_i + b_j y_i + z_i + c_j = 0$$

Collecting all such equations gives a system of equations of the form

$$A\mathbf{w} = 0 \qquad\qquad\qquad (13.10.1)$$

where

$$\mathbf{w} = (z_1, \ldots, z_n, a_1, b_1, c_1, \ldots, a_m, b_m, c_m)^{\mathrm{T}}$$

The number of equations here depends on the number of visible vertices, and solution of this equation is not sufficient to solve the realizability problem. However, if we assume the image lines are labelled as above, then we obtain a set of contraints of the form

$$B\mathbf{w} < 0 \qquad\qquad\qquad (13.10.2)$$

where each element of $B\mathbf{w}$ is of the form

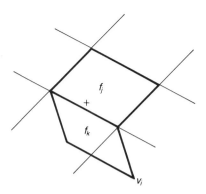

Figure 13.29 Inferring relative vertex
position.

$$a_j x_i + b_j y_i + z_i + c_j < 0$$

and represents the fact that vertex i is behind the face j. This is derived from
the labelling – thus, if vertex i is on a face f_k which intersects face f_j in a line
labelled '+', as in Figure 13.29, then vertex i can be inferred to be behind (the
infinitely extended) face f_j. The solution of (13.10.1) subject to the constraint
(13.10.2) can then be shown to solve the problem. This method can be
generalized to a so-called 'position-free' realization technique, which will deal
with small errors in the vertex positions of real images.

13.11 Shape analysis

It is possible to obtain information about the shapes of objects from monocular
images by considering the light reflected from the objects in the image. Thus,
consider a surface illuminated and observed as in Figure 13.30. At any point P
on the surface, s is the source direction, n is the normal to the surface and v is
the viewer direction. If $i(x, y, z)$ is the incident light intensity at (x, y, z) and
$\phi(\mathbf{n}, \mathbf{s}, \mathbf{v})$ is the reflectance, then the light intensity of the image at (x, y) is
given by

$$I(x, y) = ki(x, y, z)\phi(\mathbf{n}, \mathbf{s}, \mathbf{v})$$

for some constant k (depending on the camera). For a distant light source,
$i(x, y, z)$ and s are constant, so that

$$I(x, y) = ki\phi(\mathbf{n}, \mathbf{s}, \mathbf{v})$$

For a perfectly diffuse surface, reflection is uniform and reflectance is proportional to the cosine of the incidence angle α:

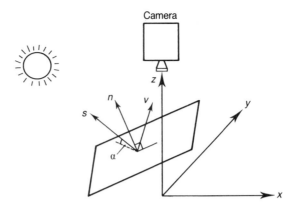

Figure 13.30 Reflectance geometry.

$$\phi(\mathbf{n}, \mathbf{s}, \mathbf{v}) = \rho \cos \alpha$$

Note that, since $\mathbf{s}$ is constant and ϕ is independent of $\mathbf{v}$, α depends only on $\mathbf{n}$. Let $\mathbf{n} = (p, q, 1)$ so that we represent the surface in gradient space, as before. Then reflectance is a function of (p, q), so we can write

$$R(p, q) = \phi(\mathbf{n}, \mathbf{s}, \mathbf{v})$$

for the reflectance. Now, if $\mathbf{s} = (p_s, q_s, 1)$, then

$$\begin{aligned}
\cos \alpha &= (1 + pp_s + qq_s)/\{\|\mathbf{s}\| . \|\mathbf{n}\|\} \\
&= (1 + pp_s + qq_s)/\{(1 + p^2 + q^2)^{1/2}(1 + p_s^2 + q_s^2)^{1/2}\} \\
&= R(p, q)/\rho
\end{aligned}$$

In photometric stereo, constant contours of R/ρ are drawn as functions of (p, q) for fixed (p_s, q_s). For example, if $(p_s, q_s) = (0, 0)$, then these contours are circles. The intensity information in the image will constrain the surface direction at any point of the image to a particular contour, say $R(p, q) = \rho c_1$ for some c_1. If another image of the scene is available with a different illumination, then the surface direction at the same point will be constrained to another contour, say $R(p, q) = \rho c_2$. These two contours will (generally) intersect in two points (p_1, q_1) and (p_2, q_2). A third image will identify one of these points, say (p_1, q_1) as the actual orientation of the surface. The main disadvantage with this method is the need for multiple images under different illumination conditions. However, using surface smoothness or some extra knowledge of the scene (for example, that it only contains polyhedra) it is possible to use a single image. For glossy surfaces the use of polarized light has also been demonstrated.

Shape of objects in a scene can also be estimated from known geometrical constraints and texture analysis. For example, if two lines are known to be parallel, the direction of a plane through the lines can be constrained. Moreover, if a surface carries a regular texture (for example, the pitted surface of a golf ball), then its shape can be inferred from the image by the change of shape of the texture elements. In the case of a golf ball, the small circular indentations will be circular at the centre of the ball image and become more ellipsoidal towards the edge.

Range data can be used to estimate the shape of objects in a scene. The light-stripe triangulation method has been used successfully in recognition of geometrical features. The image obtained can be segmented into straight lines by using a simple edge operator, giving rise to a line image of the form shown in Figure 13.31(a). These lines can be smoothed by a tracking algorithm, as in Figure 13.31(b), from which the regions are easily extracted (Figure 13.31(c)).

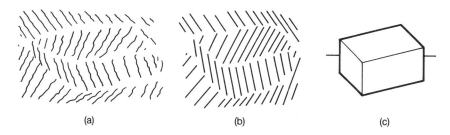

(a)   (b)   (c)

Figure 13.31   Using light-stripe data for shape analysis: (a) data from rectangular object; (b) after line enhancement; (c) after edge finding.

13.12 Stereo vision

Range data processing has been shown to be effective in obtaining the shape of three-dimensional objects in a scene. Another approach is to use two cameras to obtain slightly different images of the scene; the phase differences between the two images can then be used to reconstruct the scene, much as in human vision. Consider, first, a single camera geometry, as shown in Figure 13.32(a). It is convenient to redraw this diagram so that the image is between the lens and the scene, as in Figure 13.32(b). The image observed is identical to the first but is not inverted. A point (x, y, z) in the scene corresponds to $(\bar{x}, \bar{y})$ in the image given by

$$\bar{x} = fx/(f - z), \quad \bar{y} = fy/(f - z) \tag{13.12.1}$$

where f is the focal length of the lens.

Now consider two cameras with the same focal lengths and their optical axes at an angle 2θ to each other. The geometry is shown in Figure 13.33, with

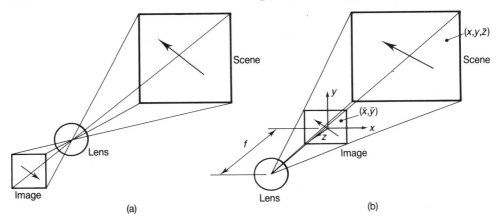

Figure 13.32 Camera geometry: (a) basic geometry; (b) equivalent geometry.

the y-axes perpendicular to the page. The image planes have coordinates (x_i, y_i, z_i), $i = 1, 2$, which are related to the central coordinates (x, y, z) by

$$
\begin{bmatrix} x_i \\ y_i \\ z \end{bmatrix} = \begin{bmatrix} \cos\theta & 0 & \pm\sin\theta \\ 0 & 1 & 0 \\ \mp\sin\theta & 0 & \cos\theta \end{bmatrix} \begin{bmatrix} x \pm d/2 \mp f\sin\theta \\ y \\ z \end{bmatrix} \tag{13.12.2}
$$

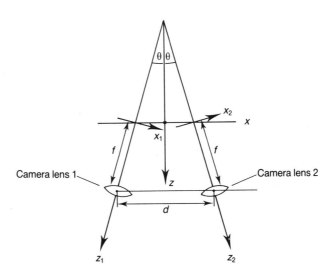

Figure 13.33 Stereo geometry.

for $i = 1, 2$, where the upper sign refers to $i = 1$ and the lower one to $i = 2$. Suppose the point (x, y, z) is observed by the two cameras to be at (x_i, y_i), $i = 1, 2$ in the two image planes. Then by (13.12.1),

$$\bar{x}_i = fx_i/(f - z_i), \quad \bar{y}_i = fy_i/(f - z_i) \qquad i = 1, 2 \qquad (13.12.3)$$

where (x_i, y_i, z_i) are the image coordinates of (x, y, z). If $(\bar{x}_1, \bar{y}_1)$ and $(\bar{x}_2, \bar{y}_2)$ are corresponding points in the two images, then we can solve (13.12.2,3) for the nine variables $(x, y, z, x_1, y_1, z_1, x_2, y_2, z_2)$. Note, however, that there are ten equations, which merely reflects the fact that $(\bar{x}_1, \bar{y}_1)$ and $(\bar{x}_2, \bar{y}_2)$ are not independent since they represent the same point of the scene.

Corresponding points $(\bar{x}_1, \bar{y}_1)$, $(\bar{x}_2, \bar{y}_2)$ in the images can be found in a variety of ways. The most common method is called *area-based stereo*, where one finds 'feature points' in one image and then uses some form of correlation analysis to find the corresponding points in the other image. Assuming the images are formed by a pair of cameras on the same horizontal line, feature points are found by one-dimensional differential operators used above to determine edges in an image. Corresponding points in the other image can be found by correlating the image pixels in windows, as shown in Figure 13.34. The correlation can be defined as being proportional to the covariance of the light intensities in windows w_1 and w_{2i}. Varying i (the pixel number) across the second image gives rise to a correlation function $C(i)$, the maximum of which determines the corresponding point.

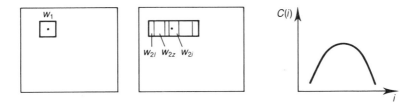

Figure 13.34 Correlation analysis to find corresponding image points.

13.13 Application of knowledge bases

Most of the techniques described above for image interpretation are effective only when some constraints are assumed to exist – general pictures are extremely difficult to interpret. These constraints take the form of *a priori* knowledge about the scene. Thus, for example, we may know that the image contains only polyhedra or circles and that certain areas have regular textures. It is believed that humans use very large knowledge data bases to help interpret scenes; some of the well-known optical illusions can be resolved if we know, for example, that a certain surface shown only in outline is in front of another surface. It is therefore natural that we should build into image processing systems large data bases of knowledge which can be used in parallel with the above algorithms in order to obtain a better and more efficient system. However, this implies some sophisticated data base management and we shall examine the basic ideas of this topic in this section.

Knowledge is usually classified into four types:

1. Knowledge about objects, e.g. cars usually have four wheels, cubes have six faces.
2. Knowledge about events, e.g. the ball is bouncing, the car is turning.
3. Knowledge about actions, e.g. how to drive a car, how to read.
4. Knowledge about knowledge (metaknowledge) – knowing what knowledge is applicable in a given situation.

Knowledge of types (1) and (4) is most often used in computer vision systems. Type (1) knowledge represents constraints on the images of some given scenes – we may know that a scene contains a ball and a cube near a wall. Type (4) knowledge is applied to control the processing of the data contained in the image; i.e. when to use a piece of knowledge, which knowledge to use and at what point in the processing.

The control of an image processing system by the knowledge subsystem can take a variety of forms. In the simplest form – that of *bottom–up processing* – the processing proceeds from the low-level processing and feature extraction (e.g. smoothing, removal of motion degradation, line enhancement, etc.) through feature description (line separation, texture analysis, etc.) to scene interpretation. Only in the last part is the knowledge system used to aid interpretation of the scene. In *top–down processing*, the knowledge is applied at all stages to improve the quality and efficiency of the processing. Such processing is often used to verify predictions about the nature of the scene; for example, if we suspect there are spheres in the scene we can use techniques specifically designed to find such objects, using the data base to simplify the processing.

In bottom–up and top–down processing the knowledge is applied in a simple sequential manner – first do the low-level processing, then the higher levels. In *feedback processing* we can feed information into the knowledge system from the low-level processing while it is proceeding, and feedback new knowledge to the low-level processors to speed up and improve the feature extraction, based on the results up to the present. The knowledge system will then decide on the best processing strategy at each step of the process. In the most general form of processing, namely *heterarchical control processing*, the general flow of processing from the lower levels to the higher levels is no longer maintained. After some low-level processing followed by high-level analysis the knowledge control system may return to low levels and then jump to much higher levels of processing. Thus, in heterarchical control the processing sequence from lower to higher levels may be reversed if it is decided that the preceding low-level processing is not sufficient for the interpretation of the scene.

Knowledge used in image processing is generally stored in one of two forms – procedural and declarative. Procedural knowledge is knowledge stored in the processing programs themselves, usually in the form of subroutines or *procedures*. The knowledge is accessed by running the appropriate procedure. Declarative knowledge, on the other hand, is simply knowledge stored in a static data base and retrieved by a data base search. Sophisticated imaging systems will contain a mixture of both types of knowledge in the form of *iconic models* (simply templates against which image features are compared), *graph models* (which store interrelations between objects and features in the form of a graph) and so-called *demons* (which activate the knowledge base only when the system reaches a certain state of processing). Further study of knowledge bases is beyond the scope of the present book and so we refer the reader to the bibliography.

Bibliographical notes

The technique of almost exact histogram matching for discrete histograms is due to Bidasaria (1986) and histogram hyperbolization is developed in Frei (1977). For a derivation of (13.2.7) see Zucker *et al*. (1977). The theory of image blur removal is given in Aboutalib and Silverman (1975) and generalized Wiener and Kalman filtering for two-dimensional images is discussed in Naki and Franco (1972), Pratt (1972) and Roberts (1963). For further analysis of the image restoration problem, see Helstrom (1967) and Mascarenhas and Pratt (1975). The Hough transform and various efficient algorithms are discussed in Ballard (1981), Deans (1981), Eichmann and Dong (1983), Hough (1962), Li *et al*. (1986), Merlin and Farber (1975) and Silberberg *et al*. (1984). Edge-finding techniques and edge linking are considered in Hueckel (1971), Shirai (1975, 1978) and Zucker *et al*. (1977) and region-splitting is covered in detail in Barrow and Popplestone (1971), and Horowitz (1974) and Tomita *et al*. (1973). For further results on interpretation of pictures and labelling methods see Clowes (1971), Huffman (1971), Roberts (1963), Rosenfeld *et al*. (1976) and Waltz (1975); gradient space was introduced in Mackworth (1973). Computational aspects of stereo vision are given in Marr and Poggio (1979) and photometric stereo is developed extensively in Horn (1975), Ikeuchi (1981) and Koshikawa (1979). For a more detailed description of range data processing, see Shirai (1972). Knowledge representations and their relative merits can be found, for example, in Cohen and Feigenbaum (1982), Fischler and Elschlager (1973), Hanson and Riseman (1978), Newell and Simon (1972), Stefik (1979) and Winograd (1975).

Exercises

1 Given the grey scale transformation

$$D_B = f(D_A) = D_A^2$$

show that the histogram

$$H_A(D_A) = e^{-D_A^2}$$

is mapped into the histogram

$$H_B(D_B) = \frac{e^{-D_B}}{2\sqrt{D_B}}$$

2 Show that the high-pass filter masks in (13.3.1) can be regarded as discrete differentiation operators.

3 Derive (13.6.1) and (13.6.2) in detail.

4 Interpret equation (13.6.4) explicitly.

5 If s and n are uncorrelated in Figure 13.17, show that

$$H_0(s) = \frac{P_s(s)}{P_s(s) + P_n(s)} \qquad s \neq 0$$

$$H_0(0) = 1/2$$

is the Wiener filter.

6 Discuss the two-dimensional generalization of Wiener filtering.

7 Prove (13.6.6).

8 Identify suitable vector spaces for the homomorphic system (13.7.1).

9 Put edge labels on the objects (i), (ii), (iv) in Figure 13.25(b) (as in Figure 13.26).

10 Show how to solve the system of equations (13.12.2,3).

References

Aboutalib, A. O. and L. M. Silverman (1975), 'Restoration of motion degraded images', *IEEE Trans. Circuits Sys.*, CAS-**22** (3), 278–86.

Ballard, D. H. (1981), 'Generalizing the Hough transform to detect arbitrary shapes', *Pattern Recognition*, **13**, 111–22.

Barrow, H. G. and R. J. Popplestone (1971), 'Relational description in picture processing', in *Machine Intelligence*, **6**, pp. 377–96 (B. Meltzer and D. Michie, eds.) Edinburgh: Edinburgh University Press.

Bidasaria, H. D. (1986), 'A method for almost exact histogram matching for two digitized images', *Computer Vision, Graphics and Image Processing*, **34**, 93–8.

Clowes, M. B. (1971), 'On seeing things', *Artificial Intelligence*, **2**(1), 79–116.

Cohen, P. R. and E. A. Feingenbaum (eds.) (1982), *The Handbook of Artificial Intelligence*, vol. 3, London: Pitman.

Deans, S. R. (1981), 'Hough transform from the radon transform', *IEEE Trans. Pattern Analysis and Machine Intelligence*, **3**, 185–8.

Eichmann, G. and B. Z. Dong (1983), 'Coherent optical production of the Hough transform', *Applied Optics*, **22** (6), 830–4.

Fischler, M. A. and R. A. Elschlager (1973), 'The representation and matching of pictorial structures', *IEEE Trans. Computers*, C-**22** (1), 67–92.

Frei, W. (1977), 'Image enhancement by histogram hyperbolization', *Computer Graphics and Image Processing*, **6**, 286–94.

Hanson, A. R. and E. M. Riseman (1978), 'Segmentation of natural scenes', in *Computer Vision Systems*, pp. 129–63 (A. R. Hanson and E. M. Riseman, eds.), NY: Academic Press.

Helstrom, C. W. (1967), 'Image restoration by the method of least squares', *J. Opt. Soc. Am.*, **57**, 297–303.

Horn, B. K. P. (1975), 'Obtaining shapes from shading information', in *The Psychology of Computer Vision* (P. H. Winston, ed.) NY: McGraw-Hill.

Hough, P. V. C. (1962), 'A Method and Means for Recognizing Complex Patterns', US Patent #3,039,654.

Hueckel, A. H. 'An operator which locates edges in digitized pictures'. *J. ACM*, **18** (1), 113–25.

Huffman, D. A. (1971), 'Impossible objects as nonsense sentences', in *Machine Intelligence*, **6**, pp. 295–323 (B. Meltzer and D. Michie, eds.), Edinburgh: Edinburgh University Press.

Ikeuchi, K. (1981), 'Determining surface orientations of specular surfaces by using the photometric stereo', *IEEE Trans. PAMI-2* (**6**), 661–9.

Koshikawa, K. (1979), 'A polarimetric approach to shape understanding of glossy objects', *Proc. 6th. IJCAI, Tokyo*, 493–5.

Ku, F-N. and J-M. Hu (1986), 'A new approach to the restoration of an image blurred by a linear uniform motion', *Computer Vision, Graphics and Image Processing*, **34**, 20–34.

Li, H., M. A. Lavin and R. J. LeMaster (1986), 'Fast Hough transform: a hierarchical approach', *Computer Vision, Graphics and Image Processing*, **36**, 139–61.

Mackworth, A. K. (1973), 'Interpreting pictures of polyhedral scenes', *Artificial Intelligence*, **4** (2), 121–37.

Marr, D. and T. Poggio (1979), 'A computational theory of human stereo vision', *Proc. Roy. Soc. (London)*, **B204**, 301–28.

Mascarenhas, N. D. A. and W. K. Pratt (1975), 'Digital image restoration under a regression model', *IEEE Trans. Circuits and Systems*, CAS-**22** (3), 252–66.

Merlin, P. M. and D. J. Farber (1975), 'A parallel mechanism for detecting curves in pictures', *IEEE Trans. Computers*, **24**, 96–8.

Nahi, N. E. and C. A. Franco (1972), 'Bayesian recursive image estimation', *IEEE Trans. Computers*, C-**21**, 734–8.

Newell, A. and H. A. Simon (1972), *Human Problem Solving*, Englewood Cliffs, NJ: Prentice Hall.

Pavlidis, T. and S. L. Horowitz (1974), 'Segmentation of plane curves', *IEEE Trans. Computers*, C-**23** (8), 860–70.

Pratt, W. K. (1972), 'Generalized Wiener filtering computation techniques', *IEEE Trans. Computers*, C-**21**, 636–41.

Roberts, L. G. (1963), 'Machine perception of three-dimensional solids', in *Optical and*

Electro-Optical Information Processing, pp. 157–97 (J. T. Tippet, ed.), Cambridge MA: MIT Press.

Rosenfeld, A., R. A. Hammel and S. W. Zucker (1976), 'Scene labeling by relaxation operations', *IEEE Trans.* SMC-**6** (6), 420–32.

Shirai, Y. (1972), 'Recognition of polyhedra with a range finder', *Pattern Recognition*, **4** (3), 243–50.

Shirai, Y. (1975), 'Edge finding, segmentation of edge and recognition of complex objects', *Proc. 4th. IJCAI*.

Shirai, Y. (1978), 'Recognition of real-world objects using edge cues', in *Computer Vision Systems*, pp. 353–62 (A. R. Hanson and E. M. Riseman, eds.), NY: Academic Press.

Silberberg, T. M., L. Davis and D. Harwood (1984), 'An iterative Hough procedure for 3D object recognition', *Pattern Recognition*, **17**, 621–9.

Stefik, M. (1979), 'An examination of a frame-structured representation system', *Proc. 6th. IJCAI*, Tokyo, 845–52.

Tomita, F., M. Yachida and S. Tsuji (1973), 'Detection of homogeneous regions by structural analysis', *Proc. 3rd. IJCAI, Stanford*, 572–7.

Waltz, D. L. (1975), 'Understanding line drawings of scenes with shadows', in *The Psychology of Computer Vision*, pp. 19–91 (P. H. Winston, ed.), NY: McGraw-Hill.

Winograd, T. A. (1975), 'Frame representation and the declarative/procedural controversy', in *Representation and Understanding: Studies in cognitive science*, pp. 185–210 (D. G. Bobrow and A. Collins, eds.) NY: Academic Press.

Woods, J. W. and C. H. Radewan (1977), 'Kalman filtering in two dimensions', *IEEE Trans. Inf. Theory*, IT-**23** (4), 473–82.

Wyszecki, G. and W. S. Stiles (1967), *Color Science*, NY: Wiley.

Zucker, S. W., R. A. Hummel and A. Rosenfeld (1977), 'An application of relaxation labeling to line and curve enhancement', *IEEE Trans. Computers*, C-**26** (4), 394–403.

14

Hardware and Software Implementation

14.1 Introduction
14.2 General Processor Types
14.3 Systolic Arrays
14.4 Transputer Systems
14.5 Parallel Languages
Bibliographical Notes
Exercises
References

14.1 Introduction

In Chapter 7 we discussed the hardware and software implementation of one-dimensional signal processing algorithms. These ideas can be generalized easily to the sequential processing of two-dimensional signals. In this chapter, therefore, we shall be specifically interested in *parallel* implementations of such algorithms, since it has been found in practice that standard sequential techniques are simply not fast enough for anything approaching real-time applications.

One important consideration in the use of several processing elements is the speed at which the memory can supply data to the processors; this is called the *memory bandwidth*. With many fast processing elements the memory bandwidth can be the main limiting factor in the system and so many designs take account of this aspect to the extent that the architecture itself may be influenced entirely by the memory cycle time.

In this chapter we shall discuss the main types of parallel architecture. In particular we shall consider in some detail pipelined computers, systolic arrays and the transputer. Software is, of course, at least as important as hardware and so we shall end the chapter with an introduction to some of the current parallel languages.

14.2 *General processor types*

The simplest type of stored-program computer is based on the von Neumann principle in which instructions and data are fetched from memory a byte or word at a time and processed one after the other. Since the earliest bit serial designs, where the arithmetic unit processed only a single bit at a time, it has been recognized that greater speeds (over and above that achieved by improvements in technology) can only be obtained by more and more parallelism. Thus, in the first place single-bit ALUs were replaced by processor units which operate on the whole data word in parallel. It was then recognized that when processing a single machine-level instruction not all parts of the processor are used each time and so useful processor capacity is lost. To overcome this problem several instructions are read into the processor at each time so that the next instruction can be decoded and partially executed before the last one is complete. The overlapping of instructions to maximize processor usage is called *pipelining* and is used by all modern computer systems.

The next level of parallelism came with the so-called *vector-processors* such as the CRAY-1 in which instead of operating on one or two words of data at any given time, the processor contains vectors which store several words which are operated on simultaneously. These were specially designed for efficient vector and matrix operations. Another approach to vectorization is the *orthogonal computer,* which can access the memory in two ways (Figure 14.1). Thus,

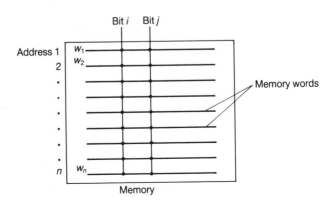

Figure 14.1 The principle of orthogonal computing.

words can be addressed in the normal way, so that we may fetch word w1 at address 1 and place it in the processor as in a conventional machine. However, an orthogonal computer can also access the memory bitwise across several words, enabling the system to process a particular bit of many words in parallel. This has led to the notion of *content-addressable memory* (or *associative memory*) in which a piece of data is referenced by the fact that part of its contents match a given mask, rather than by its address in memory. Content addressability takes on particular importance in neural networks and so we shall defer discussion of this topic until Chapter 21.

Since we are mainly interested here in specially designed hardware for image processing (and pattern recognition) the most important structure for us is the *processor array*. These usually have the form of one of the two general types shown in Figure 14.2(a), (b). In the first type, each processor has its own memory and information is transmitted between the processors by the switching network. In the second type the memory units are shared by the processors, the switching network determining which processor is connected to which memory unit at any given time; the first type is of course much easier to control, but is less flexible. The control logic of the system is usually contained in a central *control processor*, but some autonomous control is sometimes included in the processors themselves.

Processor complexity can vary between simple addition units to very powerful microprocessors. In the former case the arrays usually contain large numbers of processors, and are called *systolic arrays*. They are generally useful for tasks which involve large numbers of similar simple calculations such as

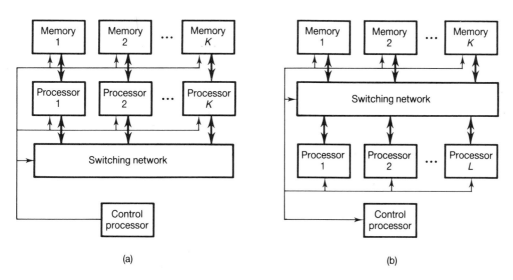

Figure 14.2 General processor arrays: (a) local memories; (b) shared memory.

matrix operations, FFT, etc. At the other end of the spectrum is the *transputer*, which is a very powerful processor with on-board floating point arithmetic and four serial connections to other transputers. Transputer systems are used for very general parallel processing and will be discussed later.

14.3 Systolic arrays

A *systolic array* is a collection of (usually) simple processor elements of the same type which are interconnected in a regular array. Each processor performs a simple operation on its inputs and produces one or more outputs which connect to other array elements. The elements can be connected in one-, two- or higher-dimensional arrays depending on their input–output connections and their intended use. Consider, for example, the implementation of a one-dimensional finite convolution given by

$$y_n = \sum_{i=0}^{k} x_{n-i}h_i = h_0x_n + h_1x_{n-1} + \ldots + x_{n-k}h_k$$

This operation is made up of a series of multiplications (h_i by x_{n-i}) and partial summations. A simple processor which can be used to implement the convolution is shown in Figure 14.3 (schematically). This element multiplies the input

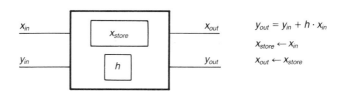

Figure 14.3   A simple processor element.

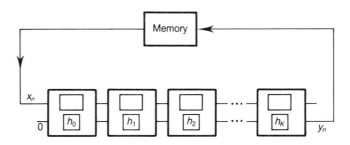

Figure 14.4   A systolic array for one-dimensional convolution.

x_{in} by h (stored permanently in the element) and adds y_{in} to produce y_{out}. A register in the element stores x_{in} for one cycle. A convolution array can be made by linking $k + 1$ of these elements, as in Figure 14.4. Note that the memory supplies the inputs $x_{-k}, \ldots, x_{-1}, x_0, x_1, x_2, \ldots$ and stores the results $y_0, y_1, \ldots$. The operation of the array is shown in Figure 14.5 for a number of cycles. (The number of clock cycles to generate the output from each element depends, of course, on the particular implementation of the element.) A two-dimensional convolution processor can be made from a set of one-dimensional ones, as in Figure 14.6, although if the memory bandwidth is not sufficient to supply the inputs at the correct rate, then the convolution can be rewritten in a one-dimensional form and the one-dimensional processor can then be used.

Another important application for systolic arrays in image processing and pattern recognition is in matrix operations. A given matrix operation, say multiplication, can be performed by one array and the result can be passed to another array to implement a further operation, perhaps inversion. Thus, although a sequence of operations can be performed by a distinct set of processor arrays, piping the inputs from the memory may be slow due to the limited memory bandwidth. In many cases the same processor array can be used

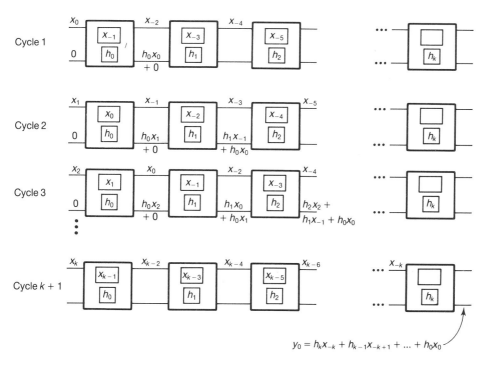

Figure 14.5 Progress of the partial sums of y_0 through the array.

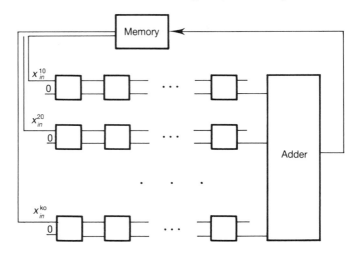

Figure 14.6   A two-dimensional convolution array processor.

to perform a sequence of operations by *reconfiguring* the array (i.e. changing the interconnections). Consider, for example, the problem of multiplying two matrices and inverting the result. If the matrix to be inverted is symmetric (as in the case of a covariance matrix, for example), then the inversion can be accomplished by performing an LU decomposition, as we shall see shortly. An array processor for matrix multiplication is shown in Figure 14.7(b), and consists of a square array of processors which store the elements of one matrix. The elements of the other matrix are piped in as shown, with a delay of one cycle between each column. The results $c_{ij} = \Sigma a_{ik} b_{kj}$ appear on the right and the operation of each processor is shown in Figure 14.7(a) where the outputs appear after a single processor cycle for the given inputs.

If we use Crout's algorithm to write C in the form LU, where L is upper triangular and U is lower triangular, then we have the recursive equations

$$t_{ij}^{(1)} = c_{ij}$$

$$t_{ij}^{(k+1)} = t_{ij}^{(k)} - l_{ik} u_{kj}$$

$$l_{ik} = \begin{cases} 0 & \text{if } i < k \\ 1 & \text{if } i = k \\ t_{ik}^{(k)} u_{kk}^{-1} & \text{if } i > k \end{cases}$$

and

$$u_{kj} = \begin{cases} 0 & \text{if } k > j \\ t_{kj}^{(k)} & \text{if } k \leq j \end{cases}$$

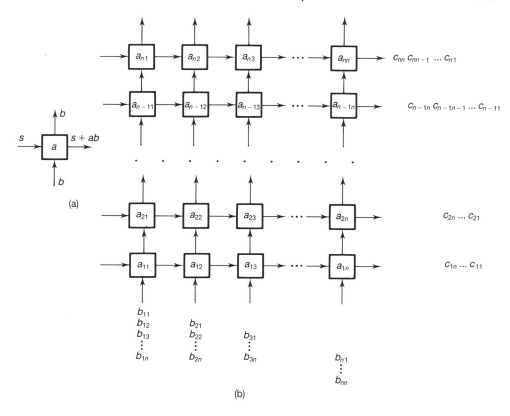

Figure 14.7 An array processor for matrix multiplication: (a) single processor; (b) matrix array.

It is not difficult to see that the system in Figure 14.7 can be reconfigured in the form of Figure 14.8 in order to implement this algorithm. (Only the upper triangular part is required to determine L and U.) A similar algorithm to determine L^{-1} and U^{-1} can be seen to require a further reconfiguration into a lower triangular form followed by a return to the original structure to evaluate $U^{-1}L^{-1}$.

Many other techniques related to systolic arrays have been implemented by various research groups. These include cellular arrays in which a simple processor is associated with each pixel of an image and which perform simple pixel-based operations. Three-dimensional wafer design is being actively investigated to minimize interconnection delays. An alternative to systolic arrays is to break a problem into noninteracting subproblems or hierarchies of subproblems and assign a (high-level) processor to each subproblem. The interconnections between processors can be represented in the form of a graph with computation

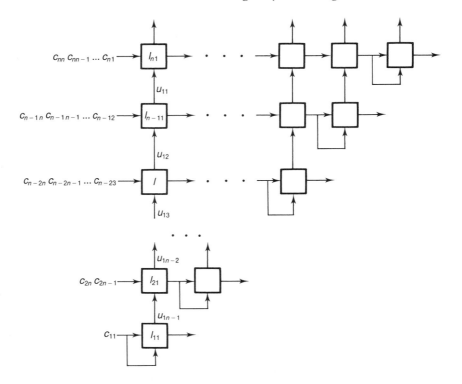

Figure 14.8   Reconfiguring Figure 14.7 to evaluate L and U.

times labelling the vertices (which represent the processors) and data transfer times labelling the edges. In some cases it is possible to choose the optimal network topology for the system to ensure minimum computation time. Such a system can be built using transputers, a topic which we shall discuss next.

14.4 Transputer systems

Conventional microprocessor systems use a uniformly accessible memory with addressing implemented by a global communication bus. As the system size increases, the speed of operation is reduced because of the capacitance of the bus and as a result of bus contention. As the ideas of parallelism developed, it became clear that local processors with their own memory could overcome the problems of standard bus architecture by including special communication lines within the processor. The *transputer* was developed for just this purpose and block diagrams of the internal structure of the INMOS T414 and T800

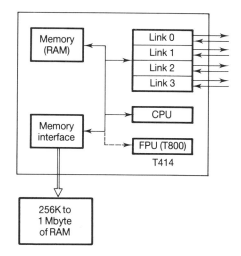

Figure 14.9   The   T414   and   T800
                        transputers.

processors are given in Figure 14.9. The basic structure is similar to a conventional microprocessor chip with local memory and data buses, CPU and, in the
case of the T800 chip, a floating point unit. The main difference between a
transputer and a conventional microprocessor is that a transputer is provided
with four serial bidirectional communication links to connect to other transputers. Since this is the only method of communication between transputers (the
local memory units are not shared in any way) the bus contention problem does
not arise.

The design of the transputer enables the development of large interconnected arrays of such devices. A standard architecture can be based on a simple
crossbar arrangement using four IMS C004 crossbar switches, as in Figure 14.10.
The IMS C004 chip has thirty-two input and output lines so that up to thirty-two
transputers can be connected in this way.

Another common arrangement for a network of transputers is the *hypercube*. In this case a transputer is placed at the corner of a hypercube and the
links form the edges of the hypercube. The hypercube designs of dimensions 0,
1, 2, 3 and 4 are shown in Figure 14.11 – of course, in dimensions 3 and 4 only a
two-dimensional projection of the 'real' geometrical figure can be drawn. In
dimension n, each transputer is connected to n others and the maximum
distance between two transputers is n interconnections, giving an upper bound
on the distance a signal must travel between transputers. Note that if $n > 4$,
then the links at each transputer must be multiplexed since the transputer has
only four bidirectional communication links.

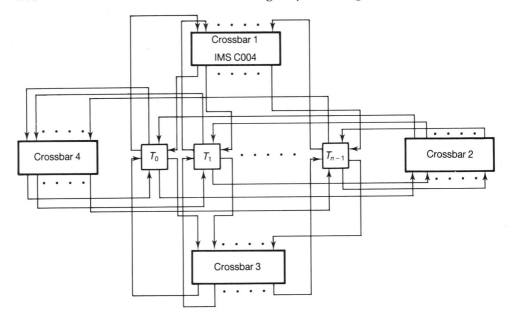

Figure 14.10   A simple crossbar connection for n transputers.

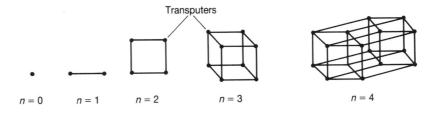

Figure 14.11   Hypercube transputer systems.

14.5 Parallel languages

Choosing parallel hardware is only part of the story, of course. Having decided on an appropriate hardware configuration, it is important to select a programming language with the flexibility to take full advantage of the hardware. Systolic arrays are no problem since each is a very simple processor containing its own microcode. High-level processors are a different matter and, basically, we can approach the parallel programming in one of two ways, depending on the hardware. For shared memory systems, which communicate along standard buses via the memory, we can use Modula-2 type concurrent languages, while for transputers, which communicate down serial lines and do not have shared memory, we must use a different approach based entirely on communicating processes. The language OCCAM has been specially designed for this purpose (although similar versions of parallel C, Pascal and FORTRAN are becoming available) and we shall discuss this briefly later.

In order to introduce parallel languages we shall first discuss Modula-2 since this has many of the constructs found in other parallel languages (although with a different syntax). (It is important to recognize, of course, that Modula-2 was developed as a language for writing operating systems on single processors, but the ideas are applicable to multiprocessor systems with shared memory.) Modula-2 is an outgrowth of Pascal and so much of the syntax is very similar to Pascal (the small syntactic differences need not concern us here). The main difference between Pascal and Modula-2 is that with the latter we can create *concurrent* processes. A *process* in Modula-2 is simply a PROCEDURE which has its own memory space and runs just like a normal PROCEDURE except that it can be interrupted by another process at any point. This is called *descheduling* of the process and when this happens the current state of the process is saved. When control is returned to the process the corresponding PROCEDURE will continue where it left off.

As an example, consider first two PROCEDUREs which are completely independent and can be run in parallel (with no shared variables). We can create two processes from these PROCEDUREs and run them concurrently with a special routine provided in Modula-2 which runs the time scheduler. Thus we have the outline program:

```
MODULE Ex1;
PROCEDURE proc1;
. . . . .
. . . . .
END proc1;
PROCEDURE proc2;
. . . . .
. . . . .
END proc2;
BEGIN
    StartProcess(proc1,space1,p1);
    StartProcess(proc2,space2,p2);
    StartScheduler;
END Ex1.
```

The PROCEDURE StartProcess has three parameters – the PROCEDURE from which we create the process, a space in memory of sufficient size to run the PROCEDURE and a priority level. Any process can interrupt another with lower priority. Note that we cannot pass any parameters through PROCED-UREs which are to be run as processes; thus proc1 and proc2 must be simple PROCEDURE types.

Now suppose that proc1 and proc2 are not completely independent, but share a common global variable. Then the processes created from proc1 and proc2 can 'communicate' via this global variable, but must do so in such a way that no bus contention arises over the access to this variable. This is done by using the Lock and Unlock procedures. If the Lock procedure is called in a process then the process cannot be descheduled until there is a corresponding call to Unlock. Thus we may extend the first module as in the following example:

```
MODULE Ex2;
VAR
    glob_var1;glob_var2:CARDINAL;
PROCEDURE proc1;
. . . .
    Lock;
    glob_var1:=glob_var1+1;
    glob_var2:=glob_var2*glob_var1;
    Unlock;
. . . .
END proc1;
PROCEDURE proc2;
. . . .
    Lock;
    If glob_var1>0 THEN glob_var1:=glob_var1−1;END;
    glob_var2:=glob_var2*2;
    Unlock;
. . . .
END proc2
BEGIN
. . . .
END Ex2.
```

There is another method of communicating in Modula-2, however, which is very similar to OCCAM in that it uses *signals*. The difference is that signals in Modula-2 are again stored in a common memory, whereas in OCCAM they are transmitted down serial communication lines. A *signal* in Modula-2 is basically a counter and a queue. The counter is used to determine whether any processes are waiting for the signal or whether there are signals waiting for processes to use them and the queue is used to determine the order in which any waiting processes are activated. Various predefined procedures are supplied in Modula-2 for the effective use of signals. These include the following:

PROCEDURE Init(VAR s:SIGNAL);	(This initializes s, i.e. sets the counter to zero and its queue to empty.)
PROCEDURE SEND(s:SIGNAL);	(This causes the first process waiting on s to become active. If no process is waiting the call is queued.)

PROCEDURE WAIT(s:SIGNAL);   (This causes the calling process to wait for a corresponding SEND unless the signal s has previously been queued.)

PROCEDURE Notify(s:SIGNAL);   (This causes a task waiting on s to be scheduled when possible, e.g. in the next time-slice.)

PROCEDURE
    Awaited(s:SIGNAL):BOOLEAN;   (This returns TRUE if any process is waiting on signal s.)

After this brief discussion of Modula-2 we shall end the chapter with a very short introduction to OCCAM. A full specification of the OCCAM language can be found in a complete OCCAM manual. In OCCAM the main functional units are processes, as in Modula-2, but in this case the processes *only* communicate via *channels*. (These correspond to the bidirectional serial links in transputer systems for processes running on different transputers. However, it should be noted that any OCCAM program can also be run on a single transputer. The 'channels' do not then correspond to physical communication lines.)

As a simple example of communicating processes, consider the three processes in Figure 14.12. In OCCAM we must name the channels and declare them before specifying the process. In the example there are five channels: in1,in2,out1,out2,out3. The three processes are run in parallel so we write the outline of the program in the following way:

```
CHAN in1,in2,out1,out2,out3:
PAR
     . . . . process1
     . . . . process2
     . . . . process3.
```

Process1 inputs a variable, multiplies it by 2 and outputs the result. The variable must be doubled *before* it is output, so these two operations must be performed sequentially. Then, process1 is written

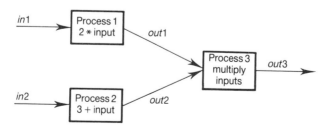

Figure 14.12   Three communicating processes.

```
VAR x:
SEQ
    in1 ? x
    out1 ! 2*x.
```

Various points should be noted here. First, we must define the (untyped) local variables for the process (there are no global variables, since processes do not have shared memory – they only communicate along the channels). Second, note the indentation; this is similar to Pascal, but here it is obligatory since the compiler determines precedence levels from the indentation. Finally, the symbols for channel input and output are ? and ! respectively. Process2 is given similarly by:

```
VAR x:
SEQ
    in2 ? x
    out2 ! 3+x
```

Process3 inputs two values and then multiplies them together before outputting the result. Inputting the two variables can be done in parallel since it does not matter which is received first. (Note, however, that we must input *both* before we can output the result.) Thus, process3 can be written

```
VAR x, y:
SEQ
    PAR
        out1 ? x
        out2 ? y
    out3 ! x*y
```

We can define processes as parameterized procedures, so that we can write

```
PROC proc1(CHAN in,out)=
    VAR x:
    SEQ
        in ? x
        out ! 2*x
PROC proc2(CHAN in,out)=
    VAR x:
    SEQ
        in ? x
        out ! 3+x
PROC proc3(CHAN in1,in2,out)=
    VAR x, y:
    SEQ
        PAR
            in1 ? x
            in2 ? y
        out ! x*y
```

The complete OCCAM program for the three processes is then

```
CHAN in1,in2,out1,out2,out3:
PAR
    proc1(in1,out1)
    proc2(in2,out2)
    proc3(out1,out2,out3)
```

We can make the processes above operate for a finite set of values (>1) by using the WHILE statement. Thus, for example, proc3 can be rewritten

```
PROC proc3(CHAN in1,in2,out)=
    VAR count:
      SEQ
        count:=0
        WHILE count<100
            VAR x:
              PAR
                count:=count+1
                SEQ
                    PAR
                        in1 ? x
                        in2 ? y
                    out ! x*y
```

By replacing 'count<100' by 'TRUE', the process will continue indefinitely.

OCCAM includes the IF and FOR statements, but it also has an ALT statement which allows any one of a number of processes to be selected arbitrarily if several conditions are true. Thus, consider the process

```
WHILE TRUE
    VAR x:
    ALT
        in1 ? x
            out ! x*x
        in2 ? x
            out ! x*x
```

If no input is available on channels in1 and in2, then the process will wait until such an input arrives. At this point the input is squared and the result is output to channel out. If inputs appear on both channel in1 and in2, then the process will choose arbitrarily between channel in1 and channel in2. The statements in1 ? x and in2 ? x can be regarded as tests which determine if an input is present and are called *guards*. We can also include Boolean expressions in guards, such as in:

```
ALT
    num<=1000 & in1 ? x
        PAR
            out ! x*x
            num:=num+1
```

```
num>=-1000 & in2 ? x
    PAR
        out ! x*x
        num:=num-1.
```

Bibliographical notes

Systolic arrays are treated in detail in Fu (1984) and many examples of their application to pattern recognition and image processing are included. Transputer hardware and software principles can be found in Hockney and Jesshope (1981) and INMOS (1989). For a general discussion of parallel processing, see Hockney and Jesshope (1981).

Exercises

1 Show how to reconfigure the two-dimensional convolution array processor into one-dimension. Explain the reason for doing this.
2 Draw the two-dimensional projection of a 5-cube.
3 Explain the equivalence

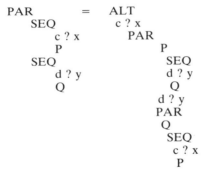

where P and Q are processes.

References

Fu, K-S. (ed.) (1984), *VLSI for Pattern Recognition and Image Processing*, Information Sciences, vol. 13, NY: Springer-Verlag.
Hockney, R. W. and C. R. Jesshope (1981), *Parallel Computers*. Bristol: Adam Hilger.
INMOS (1988), *Communicating Process Architecture*, Hemel Hempstead: Prentice Hall.
INMOS (1989), *Transputer Technical Notes*, Hemel Hempstead: Prentice Hall.

PART III

Pattern Recognition

15

Introduction to Pattern Recognition

15.1 Introduction

In Parts I and II of the book we have seen how to take pieces of one- or two-dimensional data, discretize them and process the resulting sequences to obtain transformed data which will represent 'more acceptable' forms of the input data. By 'more acceptable' we usually mean that unknown disturbances and distortions are removed from the given signal, in some optimum way. The signal processing described above is concerned with the handling of the data rather than its interpretation. Very often the purpose of this low-level data processing is to provide a digital signal which is suitable for the high-level processing involved in pattern recognition.

We are all constantly receiving data, processing it and then taking appropriate action based on our interpretation of the data. This interpretation depends on finding structure in the data or determining that the data is similar to some known structure. Similar structures can be grouped together to form a single class called a *pattern*. The notion of similarity is, however, relative and depends on what information we wish to extract from a set of data. Thus, for example, we may recognize that two animals are mammals and regard them as members

257

of the same pattern class. At a finer level we may be interested in their species; are they both human? Finer still, we can ask if they are known to us, so that we may have to recognize the 'pattern' which represents their facial features. Finally, we can consider the problem of whether two patterns represent the same human face, i.e. we require to recognize an individual face. Although we are extremely good at this apparently simple problem, it turns out to be an immensely complex problem to implement on conventional computer hardware. Thus, although most of the material in this part of the book will be oriented towards (von Neumann) sequential computer implementation, in the last chapter we shall introduce the parallel processing ideas implied by the use of 'neural nets'. The theory of neural nets seeks to model the action of biological neurons which are simple processing elements connected together in enormous numbers to form complex processing arrays. It now seems inevitable that such problems as the recognition of individual human faces by machine can only be solved (at least in any reasonable time) using many parallel processing elements.

Neural nets can solve many types of pattern recognition problems, but there are a substantial number which can also be solved by sequential computer systems and it is with these that the first chapters of this part of the book are concerned. Computer implementation of pattern recognition algorithms requires discrete digital representations of the patterns. These representations depend, of course, on the particular problem at hand and so we shall next describe some examples of pattern recognition problems which have been tackled by these methods.

15.2 Pattern recognition examples – obtaining measurement vectors

One of the earliest attempts at pattern recognition was the development of machine character readers. The standard method of discretizing a character is by covering it with a grid, as in Figure 15.1, and associating the character with a 'measurement' vector $z = (z_1, \ldots, z_N)$ where N is the number of small rectangles in the grid. Here $z_i = 1$ if part of the character intersects rectangle i, while $z_i = 0$ if it does not. (Some of the rectangles are numbered in Figure 15.1; in this case $N = 100$.)

For a given set of printed characters a, b, . . ., z, A, B, . . ., Z, 0, 1, . . ., 9 we can assume that a number of samples of each character is available; in the simplest case we can take a single sample S_i of each character ($1 \leq i \leq 62$). Discretizing each sample character as in Figure 15.1 gives a set of (distinct!) measurement vectors $z(i)$ ($1 \leq i \leq 62$), each belonging to the 100-dimensional Euclidean space $\mathbb{R}^{100}$. Of course, it is impossible to provide a visual impression of such a space and so we shall be content to draw a two-dimensional idealization of the real situation, as in Figure 15.2. (The axes are not labelled as

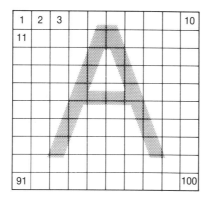

Figure 15.1   Discretizing a character.

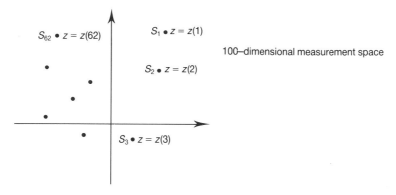

Figure 15.2   Representation of characters in measurement space.

they are not intended to coincide with any particular components of z.)

Now suppose a scanning device can read a printed character and produce a discretization of the form shown in Figure 15.1. Thus, for each character read by the device, we obtain a measurement vector, say z^*. The object is then to 'classify' z^*, i.e. to determine which of the sixty-two characters z^* represents. If we first imagine an ideal situation in which the printed characters are perfect (i.e. exactly match some 'ideal' characters) and the scanning device produces no errors, then z^* will exactly equal one of the samples $z(i)$, $1 \leqslant i \leqslant 62$. Thus, in order to classify z^* we can use the simple rule

$$z^* \text{ represents } S_i \text{ if } z^* = z(i)$$

Of course, in any practical system the scanning device will be subject to noise and disturbances and printed characters may vary in the quality of print, position alignment, etc., and so z^* is very unlikely to equal exactly $z(i)$ for any i. We can then seek to classify z^* by asking which $z(i)$ is z^* 'nearest' to. This depends on what we mean by 'near'. In the simplest case we may define distance in z-space by the standard Euclidean distance, so that the distance $d(z^*, z(i))$ from z^* to $z(i)$ is defined by

$$d(z^*, z(i)) = \|z^* - z(i)\| \triangleq \left(\sum_{k=1}^{100} (z_k^* - z_k(i))^2 \right)^{1/2}$$

The rule for classifying z^* now becomes

$$z^* \text{ represents } S_i \text{ if } d(z^*, z(i)) < d(z^*, z(j)) \qquad \text{(for all } j \neq i)$$

Of course, if $d(z^*, z(i)) = d(z^*, z(j))$ for some $j \neq i$ then we must assign z^* arbitrarily to any class S_j for which this holds. In this problem there are sixty-two classes and so we can define a class function $c(z)$ over measurement space by

$$c(z) = i \text{ if } z \text{ represents } S_i$$

Thus, our classification (or *decision rule*) can be written

$$c(z^*) = i \text{ if } d(z^*, z(i)) < d(z^*, z(j)) \qquad \text{(for all } j \neq i)$$

The decision rule therefore partitions measurement space into sixty-two disjoint regions, each of which represents a particular pattern class (i.e. character).

Another type of problem commonly arising in pattern recognition is that of recognizing a continuous waveform or at least one which is 'similar' to some known samples. For example, in voice processing, one can take the frequency spectrum of a given voice sample and compare it with a previously recorded sample to determine if they came from the same speaker. Consider, for example, the function $f(x)$ shown in Figure 15.3. This could be a sample of a voice pattern in the time or frequency domain (so that $x = $ time or $x = $ frequency, respectively) or it could be an EEG (electroencephalograph) or an ECG (electrocardiagraph) trace, etc. A simple way of obtaining a measure-

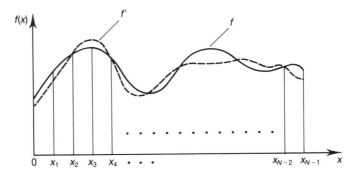

Figure 15.3 Typical function of one variable.

ment vector is to sample the signal at N points as shown, so that

$$z = (f(0), f(x_1), f(x_2), \ldots, f(x_{N-1}))$$

is the point in measurement space representing this particular waveform. Clearly, another 'similar' waveform f', shown in a dotted line, will have measurement vector z' such that $\|z - z'\|$ is 'small'.

Of course, in a similar way, a (monochrome) picture may be regarded as a two-dimensional function and sampled to give a measurement vector z specified by

$$z = (f(x_1, y_1), \ldots, f(x_1, y_n), f(x_2, y_1), \ldots, f(x_2, y_n),$$
$$\ldots, f(x_m, y_1), \ldots, f(x_m, y_n))$$

(Figure 15.4). Two-dimensional data may arise from seismic surveys, aerial reconnaissance, space photography and many other sources and the recognition of patterns is clearly of paramount importance.

Another method of obtaining a discrete measurement from a function such as that of Figure 15.3 (other than sampling) would be to express f in terms of a truncated Fourier series

$$f = \sum_{n=0}^{k} a_n \cos n\pi x + \sum_{n=1}^{k} b_n \sin n\pi x \qquad x \in [0, 1]$$

and taking z to be

$$z = (a_0, a_1, \ldots, a_k, b_1, \ldots, b_k)$$

Then patterns f_1 and f_2 are 'close' if they have similar Fourier coefficients up to order k. This method can be generalized by using functions other than cos and sin which are orthogonal on the interval of definition of f. The theory of orthogonal representations will be presented later.

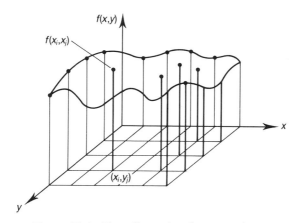

Figure 15.4 Two-dimensional pattern data.

15.3 *The general pattern recognition problem*

Given any particular pattern recognition problem the first task is to choose a discretization method, such as the ones discussed in the preceding section, in order to obtain a measurement vector for each sample pattern. A major difficulty often arises when using these discretization methods – namely, the dimension of the measurement space is usually very large. It is therefore common practice to try to reduce this dimension by mapping Z-space into X-space, where $\dim(X) \ll \dim(Z)$, while retaining as many properties or *features* of the original samples as possible. For this reason, this part of the pattern recognition problem is called *feature selection* (or preprocessing) and results in a set of samples which belong to *pattern space* or *feature space X* (Figure 15.5).

Suppose that a given pattern recognition problem has L patterns and denote the pattern classes by C_i, $1 \leq i \leq L$. In many types of problems we will have a number of sample patterns of known classification, say $x^{i,j}$, where

$$x^{i,j} \in C_i, 1 \leq i \leq L, 1 \leq j \leq M_i$$

i.e. we have M_i samples pattern class C_i. Note that each sample vector $x^{i,j}$ is an element of $\mathbb{R}^n$ (pattern space – we assume that feature selection has already been carried out). Thus, $x^{i,j}$ has n components, denoted by $x_k^{i,j}$, $1 \leq k \leq n$. We have used superscripts to denote pattern samples so as not to conflict with vector components.

A pattern recognition system is, then, a system which takes a new sample x^* of unknown classification and assigns it to some pattern class C_i ($1 \leq i \leq L$) on the basis of some *decision rule*. The decision rule is often obtained by partitioning pattern space into disjoint regions corresponding to the classes C_i (Figure 15.6). The hypersurfaces separating the pattern classes are called *decision boundaries* and will be $(n-1)$-dimensional. The unknown pattern x^* is then assigned to the class which corresponds to the region of pattern space to which x^* belongs; thus $x^* \in C_4$ in the example of Figure 15.6.

The selection of the decision boundaries can be made in a variety of ways. The simplest method is to use all the labelled samples simultaneously and find the 'best' partition of the pattern space which places the samples as far from the decision boundaries as possible. This type of decision boundary selection leads to the 'nearest neighbour' rule. One drawback with this kind of method is that once the decision boundaries are placed according to some finite set of samples

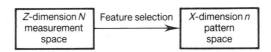

Figure 15.5   The feature selection map.

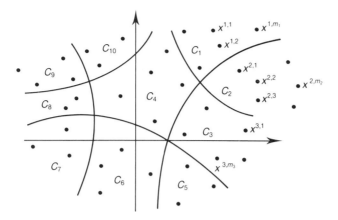

Figure 15.6 Pattern classes in pattern space (only a few samples are labelled).

they are fixed throughout the lifetime of the pattern recognition system. Alternatively, one can allow the decision boundaries to change on the basis of new information, giving rise to an adaptive system. This will lead to two distinct parts in the pattern recognition problem – learning (or training) and application. In the training phase, the labelled samples are presented to the system sequentially and the decision rule is altered by a 'teacher' which corrects any errors in the classification of the current sample on the basis of the previous decision rule. Once the system has been trained by the labelled samples, it can then be used in the application phase to classify new samples of unknown classification. A system which is trained on the basis of labelled samples is said to undergo *supervised learning*.

In some problems where one actually wishes to determine a classification scheme for a variety of types in a given problem (rather than assign new samples to an existing classification) there are no labelled samples, since the classes are not specified *a priori*. In this case we can use *unlabelled* samples to determine a 'natural' classification for the problem. A typical example of a classification problem is animal taxonomy in which one wishes to classify unknown species on the basis of comparative anatomical or genetic features. The basic method in the classification problem is called *clustering* and seeks to find subsets of the samples, called *clusters*, whose elements are mutually 'close' but far away from members of other clusters. An adaptive pattern classifier which is trained with unlabelled samples is said to have *unsupervised learning*. Such a system must remain adaptive even in the application phase since not all classes may have produced representative samples at any given stage. Thus, several new samples may not fit naturally into the existing clusters, but may be close enough to each other to indicate the existence of a new class. In the example in Figure 15.7

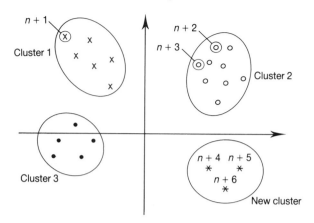

Figure 15.7   Cluster analysis.

three clusters have been determined up to sample n. The next three samples $n + 1$, $n + 2$, $n + 3$ fit into these clusters, but samples $n + 4$, $n + 5$, $n + 6$ seem to be forming a new cluster.

15.4 Pattern vector scaling

The above description of pattern recognition techniques is based on the use of a distance function in Euclidean space to measure similarity between samples in pattern space. The standard Euclidean distance

$$d(x, y) = ||x - y|| = \left\{ \sum_{i=1}^{n} (x_i - y_i)^2 \right\}^{1/2}$$

is often used, although other distances are sometimes more appropriate, as we shall see later. However, no matter which distance measure is chosen, each component of the pattern vector x represents a feature of the pattern, and as such may have physical units which are completely unconnected. For example, x_1 may represent a length while x_2 represents a time in some economic pattern recognition system. It follows that, in many pattern recognition problems, a careful scaling of the sample vectors must be performed. Thus, if x^{ij} are the samples, as above, two typical scaling methods are defined by

(i)   Set

$$D_k = \max_{i,j} \{x_k^{ij}\} - \min_{i,j} \{x_k^{ij}\} \qquad 1 \leqslant k \leqslant n$$

replace

$$x_k \text{ by } x_k/D_k \qquad (1 \leqslant k \leqslant n)$$

(ii) Set

$$\sigma_k^2 = \frac{1}{M} \sum_{i=1}^{L} \sum_{j=1}^{M_i} (x_k^{ij} - \bar{x}_k) \qquad 1 \leqslant k \leqslant n$$

where

$$M = \sum_{i=1}^{L} M_i, \; \bar{x}_k = \frac{1}{M} \sum_{i=1}^{L} \sum_{j=1}^{M_i} x_k^{ij}$$

replace

$$x_k \text{ by } x_k/\sigma_k \qquad (1 \leqslant k \leqslant n)$$

In the first case we find the greatest distance between the kth components of all samples and use this as a 'characteristic length', and in the second we use the variance of the kth components of all samples.

Bibliographical notes

There are many general texts, describing the deterministic and statistical methods of pattern recognition from a number of different viewpoints. A representative selection can be found in the following references: Andrews (1972), Duda and Hart (1973), Fu (1968, 1971, 1974), Kanal (1968), Meisel (1972), Nilsson (1965), Tou and Gonzalez (1974), Uhr (1969), Ullman (1973), van Trees (1968) and Watanabe (1969, 1971). We shall mention other more specific references in which the interested reader can find a wide variety of applications. These range from automatic character recognition (Kirsch 1964; Tou and Gonzalez, 1972a, b), picture analysis (Cofer, 1972; Cofer and Tou, 1971; and Guzman, 1968), automatic map reading (Cofer and Tou, 1972), fingerprint analysis (Hankley and Tou, 1968), biomedical applications (Gonzalez, 1972; Ledley, 1964; Rogers and Tanimoto, 1960; and Tou, 1972), to the surveillance of nuclear reactor components (Gonzalez *et al.*, 1974).

References

Andrews, H. C. (1972), *Introduction to Mathematical Techniques in Pattern Recognition*, NY: Wiley.

Cofer, R. H. (1972), 'Picture acquisition and graphical preprocessing system', *Proc. 9th Annual IEEE Region III Convention*, Charlottesville, Va.

Cofer, R. H. and J. T. Tou (1971), 'Preprocessing for pictorial pattern recognition', *Proc. of 21st NATO Technical Symposium on Artificial Intelligence*, Italy.

Cofer, R. H. and J. T. Tou (1972), 'Automated map reading and analysis by computer', *Proc. of Fall Joint Computer Conf.*

Duda, R. and P. Hart (1973), *Pattern Classification and Scene Analysis*, NY: Wiley.

Fu, K. S. (1968), *Sequential Methods in Pattern Recognition and Machine Learning*, NY: Academic Press.

Fu, K. S. ed. (1971), *Pattern Recognition and Machine Learning*, NY: Plenum Press.

Fu, K. S. (1974), *Syntactic Approaches to Pattern Recognition*, NY: Academic Press.

Fukunaga, K. (1972), *Introduction to Statistical Pattern Recognition*, NY: Academic Press.

Gonzalez, R. C., D. N. Fry and R. C. Kryter (1974), 'Results in the application of pattern recognition methods to nuclear reactor core component surveillance', *IEEE Trans. Nucl. Sci.*, **21**(1), 750–7.

Gonzalez, R. C., M. C. Lane, A. O. Bishop Jr. and W. P. Wilson (1972), 'Some results in automatic sleep-state classification', *Proc. 4th Southeastern Symp. on System Theory*.

Guzman, A. (1968), 'Decomposition of a visual scene into three dimensional bodies', *Proc. of Fall Joint Computer Conf.*

Hankley, W. J. and J. T. Tou (1968), 'Automatic fingerprint interpretation and classification via contextual analysis and topological coding', in *Pictorial Pattern Recognition* (G. C. Cheng, *et al.* eds.), Washington, DC: Thompson Book Company.

Kanal, L. ed. (1968), *Pattern Recognition*, Washington, DC: Thompson Book Company.

Kirsch, K. A. (1964), 'Computer interpretation of English text and picture patterns', *IEEE Trans. Electronic Computers*, EC-**13** (4), 363–76.

Ledley, R. S. (1964), 'High-speed automatic analysis of biomedical pictures', *Science*, **146** (3641), 216–23.

Meisel, S. M. (1972), *Computer Oriented Approaches to Pattern Recognition*, NY: Academic Press.

Nilsson, N. J. (1965), *Learning Machines*, NY: McGraw-Hill Book Company.

Patrick, E. A. (1972), *Fundamentals of Pattern Recognition*, Englewood Cliffs, NJ: Prentice Hall.

Rogers, D. and T. Tanimoto (1960), 'A computer program for classifying plants', *Science*, **132**, 1115–18.

Tou, J. T. (1972), 'Automatic analysis of blood smear micrographs', *Proc. 1972 Computer Image Processing and Pattern Recognition Symp., Univ. of Missouri, Columbia*.

Tou, J. T. and R. C. Gonzalez (1972a), 'Automatic recognition of handwritten characters via feature extraction and multilevel decision', *Int. J. Computer and Info. Sci.*, **1** (1), 43–65.

Tou, J. T. and R. C. Gonzalez (1972b), 'Recognition of handwritten characters by topological feature extraction and multilevel categorization', *IEEE Trans Computers*, C-**21**, (7), 776–85.

Tou, J. T. and R. C. Gonzalez (1974), *Pattern Recognition Principles*, NY: Addison-Wesley.

Uhr, L. ed. (1973), *Pattern Recognition*, NY: Wiley.

Ullman, J. R. (1973), *Pattern Recognition Techniques*, NY: Crane-Russak.

Van Trees, H. L. (1968), *Detection, Estimation and Modulation Theory* – Part I, NY: Wiley.

Watanabe, S. ed. (1969), *Methodologies of Pattern Recognition*, NY: Academic Press.

Watanabe, S. ed. (1971), *Frontiers of Pattern Recognition*, NY: Academic Press.

──────16──────

Decision Functions

16.1 Introduction
16.2 Decision Functions
16.3 Minimum Distance Algorithms
16.4 Weight Space
16.5 Training Pattern Classifiers
Bibliographical Notes
Exercises
References

16.1 Introduction

As we have discussed in the preceding chapter, one of the most basic techniques of pattern recognition is based on the partitioning of pattern (feature) space into disjoint regions, each of which corresponds to a pattern class. Thus, if we have a pattern recognition problem with L pattern classes and a number of labelled samples $\mathbf{x}^{i,j} \in \mathbb{R}^n$ ($1 \leq i \leq L, 1 \leq j \leq M_i$), then we try to find L subsets P_i, $1 \leq i \leq L$ of $\mathbb{R}^n$ such that

$$P_i \cap P_j = \varnothing \qquad \text{if } i \neq j$$

$$\bigcup_{1 \leq i \leq L} P_i = \mathbb{R}^n$$

$$\mathbf{x}^{i,j} \in P_i \qquad 1 \leq j \leq M_i$$

(In this case we have M_i samples of class i.) The sets P_i are usually determined by specifying their boundaries, which are always assumed to have a simple structure. In the most basic applications these boundaries are taken to be hyperplanes described by linear equations. In some situations, however, this is found to be too restrictive and we have to use piecewise-linear or general nonlinear boundaries.

This chapter is concerned with the methods of selecting the boundaries of the partitioning sets P_i and the decision rules to which they give rise. We shall see that this can be done in a relatively straightforward way using 'nearest neighbour'-type classification rules or by using training methods which are basically algorithms for moving the boundaries of the pattern sets P_i around until the labelled samples are correctly classified. It is also possible to use statistical estimation theory in the selection of classification boundaries, but this approach will be left until Chapter 17.

16.2 Decision functions

In order to illustrate the use of decision functions, consider the case of a three-class problem in two-dimensional pattern space (Figure 16.1). (As we have said before, the assumption of two-dimensionality is merely for convenience in visualizing the geometry of the situation. Real problems will have high dimensionality n in general and the decision boundaries will be $n - 1$ dimensional hypersurfaces.) A *decision function* $g_{ij}(\mathbf{x})$ is a function defined on pattern space with real values such that pattern classes i and j are on 'opposite sides' of the hypersurface

$$g_{ij}(\mathbf{x}) = 0$$

(This means that g_{ij} is a sufficiently 'well-behaved' function for $g_{ij} = 0$ to have

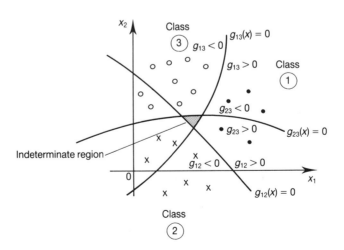

Figure 16.1   Decision functions for a three-class problem.

two sides.) We shall assume that g_{ij} is defined so that

(i) $\mathbf{x}^* \in \{\mathbf{x} : g_{ij}(\mathbf{x}) > 0)\}$ if $\mathbf{x}^*$ is in class i
(ii) $\mathbf{x}^* \in \{\mathbf{x} : g_{ij}(\mathbf{x}) < 0)\}$ if $\mathbf{x}^*$ is in class j

It is therefore convenient to define

$$g_{ji}(\mathbf{x}) = -g_{ij}(\mathbf{x})$$

A *choice function* $c(\mathbf{x})$ is a function $c : \mathbb{R}^n \to \{1, \ldots, L\}$ from pattern space to the set of the positive integers $1, \ldots, L$ (where L is the number of pattern classes) such that

$$c(\mathbf{x}) = i \qquad \text{if } \mathbf{x} \text{ is in class } i$$

Thus, in terms of the choice function, we have

$$c(\mathbf{x}) = i \text{ if } g_{ij}(\mathbf{x}) > 0 \qquad \text{for } j \neq i \tag{16.2.1}$$

(As usual, the boundaries themselves are indeterminate, so that if $g_{ij}(\mathbf{x}) = 0$, we must assign $\mathbf{x}$ arbitrarily to class i or j.) In the example of Figure 16.1 we have

$$c(\mathbf{x}) = \begin{cases} 1 & \text{if } g_{13} > 0,\ g_{12} > 0 \\ 2 & \text{if } g_{12} < 0 \text{ (or } g_{21} > 0),\ g_{23} > 0 \\ 3 & \text{if } g_{13} < 0 \text{ (or } g_{31} > 0),\ g_{23} < 0 \text{ (or } g_{32} > 0) \end{cases}$$

Note that, in general, if we choose decision functions of this form to separate the pattern classes then we require

$$L_{C_2} \triangleq L! / [(L - 2)! 2!] = L(L - 1)/2$$

(distinct) decision functions. (We are not considering g_{ij} and g_{ji} to be distinct functions.) Also note, from Figure 16.1, that there may be an *indeterminate region* where the decision function given by (16.2.1) cannot classify samples.

    The problems of requiring a large number of decision functions g_{ij} and the possible existence of indeterminate regions can be obviated by writing each g_{ij} in the form

$$g_{ij}(\mathbf{x}) = \theta_i(\mathbf{x}) - \theta_j(\mathbf{x}) \tag{16.2.2}$$

The L functions θ_i related to the decision functions g_{ij} by (16.2.2) are called *discriminant functions*. The choice function in (16.2.1) then becomes

$$c(\mathbf{x}) = i \text{ if } \theta_i(\mathbf{x}) > \theta_j(\mathbf{x}) \qquad \text{for } j \neq i \tag{16.2.3}$$

If we use discriminant functions then the example of Figure 16.1 will appear as in Figure 16.2. Note that there cannot be an indeterminate region since all the boundaries intersect at a common point.

    The most common type of decision function is given by a linear combination of the components of the pattern vector, i.e.

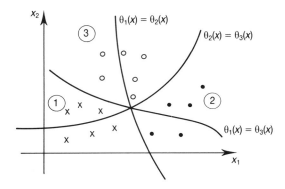

Figure 16.2   Discriminant functions.

$$g(\mathbf{x}) = w_1 x_1 + w_2 x_2 + \ldots + w_n x_n + w_{n+1} \qquad (16.2.4)$$
$$= \mathbf{w}^{\mathrm{T}}\mathbf{x} + w_{n+1}$$

where

$$\mathbf{w}^{\mathrm{T}} = (w_1, \ldots, w_n), \; \mathbf{x}^{\mathrm{T}} = (x_1, \ldots, x_n)$$

The equation $g(\mathbf{x}) = 0$ defines a hyperplane in n-dimensional pattern space (Figure 16.3). We can write (16.2.4) in the form

$$g(\mathbf{x}) = \mathbf{w}_a^{\mathrm{T}}\mathbf{x}_a$$

where

$$\mathbf{w}_a^{\mathrm{T}} = (w_1, \ldots, w_n, w_{n+1})$$
$$\mathbf{x}_a^{\mathrm{T}} = (x_1, \ldots, x_n, 1)$$

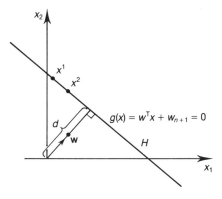

Figure 16.3   Decision hyperplane.

are called the *augmented parameter* (or *weight*) and *augmented pattern* vectors, respectively.

It is useful to have an expression for the distance d between the origin and a hyperplane H in n-dimensional space. Thus, referring to Figure 16.3, for any two distinct points $\mathbf{x}^1$ and $\mathbf{x}^2$ on H, we have

$$\mathbf{w}^\mathrm{T}\mathbf{w}^1 + w_{n+1} = 0$$
$$\mathbf{w}^\mathrm{T}\mathbf{x}^2 + w_{n+1} = 0$$

and so

$$\mathbf{w}^\mathrm{T}(\mathbf{x}^1 - \mathbf{x}^2) = 0$$

Since $\mathbf{x}^1 - \mathbf{x}^2$ is an arbitrary vector lying in H we see that the weight vector $\mathbf{w}^\mathrm{T}$ is perpendicular to H. Now to evaluate the distance d from the origin to H note that since $\mathbf{w}$ is perpendicular to H, d is given by $\|\mathbf{w}\alpha\|$ where α is chosen so that $\mathbf{w}\alpha \in H$. If $\mathbf{w}\alpha \in H$ we have

$$\mathbf{w}^\mathrm{T}\mathbf{w}\alpha + w_{n+1} = 0$$

and so

$$\|\mathbf{w}\|^2\alpha = -w_{n+1}$$

i.e.

$$\alpha = \frac{-w_{n+1}}{\|\mathbf{w}\|^2}$$

Hence,

$$d = \|\mathbf{w}\| \cdot |\alpha| = \frac{|w_{n+1}|}{\|\mathbf{w}\|}$$

We are not constrained to use linear discriminant (or decision) functions, however, even though they are easier to handle. In fact we could use a general polynomial function

$$d(\mathbf{x}) = \sum_{\substack{|i|=0 \\ i \geqslant 0}}^{k} \mathbf{w}_i \mathbf{x}^i \qquad (16.2.5)$$

where we have used the notations

$$\mathbf{i} = (i_1, \ldots, i_n)$$
$$|\mathbf{i}| = \sum_{j=1}^{n} i_j$$
$$\mathbf{i} \geqslant 0 \text{ if } i_j \geqslant 0 \qquad \text{for } 1 \leqslant j \leqslant n$$
$$\mathbf{x}^i = x_1^{i_1} x_2^{i_2} \ldots x_n^{i_n}$$

and

$$\mathbf{w}_i = w_{i_1 \dots i_n}$$

For example, of $n = 2$ and $k = 2$ then we have

$$d(\mathbf{x}) = w_{00} + w_{10}x_1 + w_{01}x_2 + w_{11}x_1x_2 + w_{20}x_1^2 + \dot{w}_{02}x_2^2$$

Although the decision function in (16.2.5) is a general nonlinear function we change it into a linear function in a higher dimensional space. Thus, if we write (16.2.5) in the form

$$d(\mathbf{x}) = \sum_{r=0}^{k} d^r(\mathbf{x})$$

where

$$d^0(\mathbf{x}) = w_0$$

$$d^r(\mathbf{x}) = \sum_{i_1=1}^{n} \sum_{i_2=i_1}^{n} \dots \sum_{i_r=i_{r-1}}^{n} w_{i_1 i_2 \dots j_r} x_{i_1} x_{i_2} \dots x_{i_r} \quad (r > 1)$$

then we can write

$$d(\mathbf{x}) = d(\mathbf{y}) = \sum_{r=0}^{k} \sum_{i_1=1}^{n} \sum_{i_2=i_1}^{n} \dots \sum_{i_r=i_{r-1}}^{n} w_{i_1 i_2 \dots i_r} y_{i_1 i_2 \dots i_r} \qquad (16.2.6)$$

where $\mathbf{y}$ is the vector containing the components $y_{i_1 i_2 \dots i_r}$ in some fixed order and we interpret $w_{i_1 \dots i_r}$ as w_0 and $y_{i_1 \dots i_r}$ as 1 if $r = 0$. The function $d(\mathbf{y})$ given by (16.2.6) is linear in $\mathbf{y}$ and depends on $^{n+r}C_r = (n + r)!/r!n!$ coefficients $w_{i_1 i_2 \dots i_r}$.

Of course, instead of using polynomials, we could define the decision function

$$d(\mathbf{x}) = \sum_{i=0}^{k} w_i \phi_i(\mathbf{x})$$

where $\phi_0(\mathbf{x}) = 1$ and $\phi_i(\mathbf{x})$ $(i > 0)$ is an arbitrary function of $\mathbf{x}$. Just as above, we can write

$$y_0 = 1, \, y_i = \phi_i(\mathbf{x}) \qquad (i > 0)$$

and then we obtain the linear function

$$d(\mathbf{y}) = \sum_{i=0}^{k} w_i y_i$$

This usually has the effect of increasing the dimension of pattern space.

16.3 Minimum distance algorithms

Having discussed the general principles of decision and discriminant functions we shall now give some examples of the simplest approach to the selection of the decision boundaries – namely that based on the minimum distance concept.

In this method a new unlabelled pattern sample is classified according to which pattern class contains a labelled sample to which the new pattern is closest. Thus, if we define

$$\theta_i(\mathbf{x}) = -\min_j d(\mathbf{x}, \mathbf{x}^{i,j}) \qquad\qquad (16.3.1)$$

where $\mathbf{x}^{i,j}$ are the samples of class i ($1 \le j \le M_i$) and d is the distance measure (which may not be the standard Euclidean distance), then we obtain the decision rule

$$c(\mathbf{x}) = i \text{ if } \theta_i(\mathbf{x}) > \theta_j(\mathbf{x}) \qquad \text{for all } j \ne i$$

The decision boundary for the nearest neighbour classification rule in a typical situation is shown in Figure 16.4, where we have taken d to be the standard Euclidean distance.

The nearest neighbour rule can be applied in the case where each pattern class has a single representative sample $\mathbf{x}^i$ ($1 \le i \le \mathrm{L}$), called a *prototype*. The general discriminant function (16.3.1) then becomes

$$\theta_i(\mathbf{x}) = -d(\mathbf{x}, \mathbf{x}^i) \qquad\qquad (16.3.2)$$

In the case of Euclidean distance d, we have the decision rule

$$c(\mathbf{x}) = i \text{ if } \sum_{k=1}^n (x_k - x_k^i)^2 < \sum_{k=1}^n (x_k - x_k^j)^2 \qquad \text{for all } j \ne i$$

This holds if and only if

$$-2 \sum_{k=1}^n x_k x_k^i + \sum_{k=1}^n (x_k^i)^2 < -2 \sum_{k=1}^n x_k x_k^j + \sum_{k=1}^n (x_k^j)^2$$

Hence we can use the linear discriminant function

$$\bar{\theta}_i(\mathbf{x}) = \sum_{k=1}^n x_k x_k^i - \frac{1}{2} \sum_{k=1}^n (x_k^i)^2$$

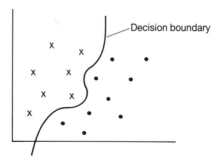

Figure 16.4 The nearest neighbour classification rule.

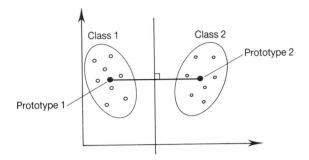

Figure 16.5   Single prototypes.

A simple way of obtaining a single prototype from a set of samples from a particular pattern class is to use their mean value. The decision boundary for single prototypes is shown in Figure 16.5.

We may choose to use more than one prototype for each class, however. Thus, suppose that $\mathbf{x}^{i,j}$, $1 \leq j \leq N_i$ are the prototypes for pattern class i. Then, instead of (16.3.2), we have the function

$$\theta_i(\mathbf{x}) = -\min_j d(\mathbf{x}, \mathbf{x}^{i,j})$$

This is similar to (16.3.1) except that N_i may be less than M_i (we may not use all the samples as prototypes). Again, in the case of Euclidean distance, we may use the discriminant functions

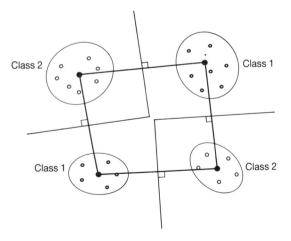

Figure 16.6   Decision boundaries for classes with
two prototypes.

$$\bar{\theta}_i(\mathbf{x}) = \max_{j} \{(\mathbf{x}^T\mathbf{x}^{i,j} - \tfrac{1}{2}(\mathbf{x}^{i,j})^T\mathbf{x}^{i,j}\} \qquad 1 \leq j \leq N_i$$

These functions are, however, only piecewise linear (Figure 16.6).

16.4 Weight space

We have seen that, in certain cases, we may use linear decision functions of the form

$$g(\mathbf{x}, \mathbf{w}_a) = \mathbf{w}^T\mathbf{x} + w_{n+1} \tag{16.4.1}$$

where we have explicitly denoted the dependence of g on the augmented weight vector $\mathbf{w}_a = (w_1, \ldots, w_n, w_{n+1})^T$. Consider a two-class problem with samples $\mathbf{x}^{1,j}$, $1 \leq j \leq M_1$ in class 1 and samples $\mathbf{x}^{2,j}$, $1 \leq j \leq M_2$ in class 2. Suppose we write the decision function in the form

$$c(\mathbf{x}) = 1 \text{ if } g(\mathbf{x}, \mathbf{w}_a) > 0$$

$$c(\mathbf{x}) = 2 \text{ if } g(\mathbf{x}, \mathbf{w}_a) < 0$$

Then, from (16.4.1), we have

$$\left.
\begin{aligned}
w_1 x_1^{1,1} + w_2 x_2^{1,1} + \ldots \quad + w_n x_n^{1,1} + w_{n+1} &> 0 \\
w_1 x_1^{1,2} + w_2 x_2^{1,2} + \quad\quad + w_n x_n^{1,2} + w_{n+1} &> 0 \\
\vdots \quad\quad\quad\quad\quad\quad\quad\quad & \\
w_1 x_1^{1,M_1} + w_2 x_2^{1,M_1} + \quad + w_n x_n^{1,M_1} + w_{n+1} &> 0 \\
w_1 x_1^{2,1} + w_2 x_2^{2,1} + \quad\quad + w_n x_n^{2,1} + w_{n+1} &> 0 \\
w_1 x_1^{2,2} + w_2 x_2^{2,2} + \quad\quad + w_n x_n^{2,2} + w_{n+1} &> 0 \\
\vdots \quad\quad\quad\quad\quad\quad\quad\quad & \\
w_1 x_1^{2,M_2} + w_2 x_2^{2,M_2} + \quad + w_n x_n^{2,M_2} + w_{n+1} &> 0
\end{aligned}
\right\} \tag{16.4.2}$$

The inequalities (16.4.2) must be satisfied if the decision boundary $g(\mathbf{x}, \mathbf{w}_a) = 0$ is to classify correctly the samples $\mathbf{x}^{i,j}$. For a fixed set of samples we can determine an appropriate weight vector $\mathbf{w}_a$ by finding a solution of (16.4.2). These inequalities are linear and the corresponding equations define hyperplanes in $(n + 1)$-dimensional *weight space* $\mathbf{w}_a$. Since each such hyperplane passes through the origin of $\mathbf{w}_a$-space the inequalities (16.4.2) define a closed convex cone in this space.

It is convenient to multiply the second set of inequalities in (16.4.2) by -1 so that all are of the same form; thus, we have

$$\left.\begin{array}{ll} w_1 x_1^{1,i} + w_2 x_2^{1,i} + \ldots + w_n x_n^{1,i} + w_{n+1} > 0 & 1 \leqslant i \leqslant M_1 \\ -w_1 x_1^{2,j} - w_2 x_2^{2,j} - \ldots - w_n x_n^{2,j} - w_{n+1} > 0 & 1 \leqslant j \leqslant M_2 \end{array}\right\} (16.4.3)$$

These inequalities will be useful in the next section where we consider various training algorithms.

16.5 Training pattern classifiers

As we have mentioned above, in a typical pattern recognition problem, we are presented with a set of labelled samples (i.e. samples of known classification) and we must find suitable decision boundaries which separate the samples into their correct classes. In this section we shall consider the determination of linear boundaries by the use of a variety of algorithms which recursively 'train' the weight vectors in (16.4.3) until these inequalities are satisfied. Typically, these algorithms consist of choosing a weight vector arbitrarily and then presenting each sample in turn to the system. If the sample is correctly classified by the decision function, then the weight vector is left unchanged. If, however, the decision function incorrectly classifies the sample, then the weight vector is corrected in some way.

The first method which we shall discuss is the celebrated *perceptron algorithm*. Here we shall merely describe the algorithm, leaving a detailed discussion of perceptrons until we consider general neural networks later. In the case of a system with just two pattern classes we can write the inequalities (16.4.3) in the form

$$\left.\begin{array}{ll} \mathbf{w}_a^{\mathrm{T}} \mathbf{x}_a^{1,i} > 0 & 1 \leqslant i \leqslant M_1 \\ -\mathbf{w}_a^{\mathrm{T}} \mathbf{x}_a^{2,j} > 0 & 1 \leqslant j \leqslant M_2 \end{array}\right\} \qquad (16.5.1)$$

where $\mathbf{w}_a = (w_1, \ldots, w_n, w_{n+1})^{\mathrm{T}}$, $\mathbf{x}_a = (x_1, \ldots, x_n, 1)^{\mathrm{T}}$ are the augmented weight and pattern vectors, respectively. For the given set of samples

$$\mathbf{x}^{1,i}, \; \mathbf{x}^{2,j}$$

we must find the weight vector $\mathbf{w}$ so that the inequalities (16.5.1) are satisfied. The algorithm may be written as follows:

STEP 1
Choose $\mathbf{w}$ arbitrarily.

STEP 2
For each sample pattern $\mathbf{x}_a^{1,i}$ in class 1 evaluate $p_i \triangleq \mathbf{w}_a^{\mathrm{T}} \mathbf{x}_a^{1,i}$. If $p_i \leqslant 0$ (i.e. $\mathbf{x}_a^{1,i}$ is misclassified), update $\mathbf{w}_a^{\mathrm{T}}$ by the rule

$$\mathbf{w}_a \leftarrow \mathbf{w}_a + c \mathbf{x}_a^{1,i}$$

where c is a correction parameter, which can be taken as 1. Otherwise leave $\mathbf{w}_a$ unchanged.

STEP 3

For each sample pattern $\mathbf{x}_a^{2,i}$ in class 2 evaluate $q_i \triangleq \mathbf{w}_a^T \mathbf{x}_a^{2,i}$. If $q_i \geq 0$ (i.e. $\mathbf{x}_a^{2,i}$ is misclassified), update $\mathbf{w}_a^T$ by the rule

$$\mathbf{w}_a \leftarrow \mathbf{w}_a - c\mathbf{x}_a^{2,i}$$

Otherwise leave $\mathbf{w}_a$ unchanged.

Repeat steps 2 and 3 until convergence.

We shall now prove that if the classes 1 and 2 are linearly separable then the perceptron algorithm converges. First recall from (16.5.1) that if we multiply class 2 pattern samples by -1, then the inequalities are the same way round and so we can write the perceptron algorithm in the form

$$\mathbf{w}_a \leftarrow \begin{cases} \mathbf{w}_a & \text{if } \mathbf{w}_a^T\mathbf{x}_a^* > 0 \\ \mathbf{w}_a + c\mathbf{x}_a^* & \text{if } \mathbf{w}_a^T\mathbf{x}_a \leq 0 \end{cases}$$

where $\mathbf{x}_a^*$ is any pattern sample (i.e. $\mathbf{x}_a^* = \mathbf{x}_a^{1,i}$ or $-\mathbf{x}_a^{2,i}$). Without loss of generality, we can assume that correction occurs at each step of the algorithm (by leaving out those steps where $\mathbf{w}_a$ remains unchanged). Thus, we can write the algorithm in the form

$$\mathbf{w}_a(k + 1) = \mathbf{w}_a(k) + \mathbf{x}_a^*(k) \tag{16.5.2}$$

where $\mathbf{x}_a^*(k)$ is the kth training sample (which will equal one of the given samples $\mathbf{x}_a^{1,i}$ or $-\mathbf{x}_a^{2,i}$ taken in order). From (16.5.2) we have

$$\mathbf{w}_a(k + 1) = \mathbf{w}_a(1) + \mathbf{x}_a^*(1) + \mathbf{x}_a^*(2) + \ldots + \mathbf{x}_a^*(k)$$

and so

$$\mathbf{w}_a^T(k + 1)\mathbf{\nabla}_a = \mathbf{w}_a^T(1)\mathbf{\nabla}_a + \sum_{i=1}^{k} \mathbf{x}_a^{*T}(i)\mathbf{\nabla}_a$$

where $\mathbf{\nabla}_a$ is any weight vector which correctly separates the classes. (It has been assumed that such a weight exists.) Thus,

$$\mathbf{w}_a^T(k + 1)\mathbf{\nabla}_a \geq \mathbf{w}_a^T(1)\mathbf{\nabla}_a + k\varepsilon \tag{16.5.3}$$

where

$$\varepsilon = \min_i \{\mathbf{x}_a^{*T}(i)\mathbf{\nabla}_a\}$$

Note that $\varepsilon > 0$ since $\mathbf{x}_a^{*T}(i)\mathbf{\nabla}_a > 0$ for each i. Hence,

$$\frac{(\mathbf{w}_a^T(1)\mathbf{\nabla}_a + k\varepsilon)^2}{\|\mathbf{\nabla}_a\|^2} \leq \|\mathbf{w}_a^T(k + 1)\|^2 \tag{16.5.4}$$

by applying the Cauchy–Schwartz inequality to (16.5.3). This provides a lower bound on $\mathbf{w}_a^T(k + 1)$. Conversely, we can obtain an upper bound from (16.5.2); i.e.

$$\|\mathbf{w}_a(i + 1)\|^2 \le \|\mathbf{w}_a(i)\|^2 + 2\mathbf{w}_a^T(i)\mathbf{x}_a^*(i) + \|\mathbf{x}_a^*(i)\|^2$$
$$\le \|\mathbf{w}_a(i)\|^2 + \delta$$

where $\delta = \max\|\mathbf{x}_a^*(i)\|^2$ (the maximum of the sample norm squares), since

$$\mathbf{w}_a^T(i)\mathbf{x}_a^*(i) \le 0$$

when a correction is made. Hence,

$$\|\mathbf{w}_a(k + 1)\|^2 \le \|\mathbf{w}_a(1)\|^2 + k\delta \qquad (16.5.5)$$

If we assume that correction steps are made for all k, then (16.5.4) and (16.5.5) are contradictory for large enough k. Hence the algorithm must converge. The number of steps in which a correction occurs must be less than or equal to the number k which solves the equation

$$\frac{(\mathbf{w}_a^T(1)\boldsymbol{\nabla}_a + k\varepsilon)^2}{\|\boldsymbol{\nabla}_a\|^2} = \|\mathbf{w}_a(1)\|^2 + k\delta$$

Consider next an L class problem with linear discriminant functions $\theta_i(\mathbf{x})$, $1 \le i \le L$, so that $\mathbf{x} \in$ class i if and only if

$$\theta_i(\mathbf{x}) > \theta_j(\mathbf{x}) \qquad \text{(for all } j \ne i)$$

If $\theta_i(\mathbf{x}) = \mathbf{w}_{ia}^T\mathbf{x}_a$, then we can formulate the following algorithm:

STEP 1
Choose $\mathbf{w}_{ia}(1)$ arbitrarily.

STEP 2
If

$$\theta_i(\mathbf{x}^*(k)) > \theta_j(\mathbf{x}^*(k)) \qquad (j = 1, \ldots, L, j \ne i)$$

for the kth training pattern $\mathbf{x}^*(k)$, such that $\mathbf{x}^*(k)$ is in class i, then set

$$\mathbf{w}_{ja}(k + 1) = \mathbf{w}_{ja}(k) \qquad (j = 1, \ldots, L)$$

STEP 3
If, for some l, we have

$$\theta_i(\mathbf{x}^*(k)) \le \theta_l(\mathbf{x}^*(k))$$

then set

$$\mathbf{w}_{ia}(k + 1) = \mathbf{w}_{ia}(k) + c\mathbf{x}_a^*(k)$$
$$\mathbf{w}_{la}(k + 1) = \mathbf{w}_{la}(k) - c\mathbf{x}_a^*(k)$$

$$\mathbf{w}_{ja}(k + 1) = \mathbf{w}_{ja}(k) \qquad (j = 1, \ldots, L; j \neq i, j \neq l)$$

where c is a positive constant.

Repeat steps 2, 3 until convergence.

It can be shown that if the pattern classes are linearly separable, then the algorithm converges in a finite number of steps.

The main disadvantage with the perceptron algorithm is that in the case when the classes are not linearly separable, it will give no indication of this and will continue forever trying to determine nonexistent linear boundaries. Another algorithm which does indicate when the classes are not linearly separable is the *least mean squared error algorithm* which we shall discuss next.

Consider again the two class problem and write the inequalities (16.5.1) in matrix form:

$$X\mathbf{w}_a > 0 \tag{16.5.6}$$

where

$$X = \begin{bmatrix} (\mathbf{x}_a^{1,1})^{\mathrm{T}} \\ \vdots \\ (\mathbf{x}_a^{1,M_1})^T \\ (\mathbf{x}_a^{2,1})^{\mathrm{T}} \\ \vdots \\ (\mathbf{x}_a^{2,M_2})^T \end{bmatrix}$$

Then we must find an $(n + 1)$-dimensional vector $\mathbf{w}_a$ such that (16.5.6) is satisfied. Instead of trying to solve this inequality it is clearly equivalent to solving the equality

$$X\mathbf{w}_a = \mathbf{b} \tag{16.5.7}$$

where $\mathbf{b} = (b_1, \ldots, b_M)^{\mathrm{T}}$, $M = M_1 + M_2$ and $b_i > 0$ for each i. This, in turn is equivalent to minimizing the cost function

$$J(\mathbf{w}_a, \mathbf{b}) = \tfrac{1}{2}\|X\mathbf{w}_a - \mathbf{b}\|^2$$
$$= \frac{1}{2} \sum_{j=1}^{M_1} (\mathbf{w}_a^{\mathrm{T}}\mathbf{x}_a^{1,j} - b_j) + \frac{1}{2} \sum_{j=1}^{M_2} (\mathbf{w}_a^{\mathrm{T}}\mathbf{x}_a^{2,j} - b_{j+M_1})$$

Now,

$$\frac{\partial J}{\partial \mathbf{w}_a} = X^{\mathrm{T}}(X\mathbf{w}_a - \mathbf{b}) \tag{16.5.8}$$

and

$$\frac{\partial J}{\partial \mathbf{b}} = -(X\mathbf{w}_a - \mathbf{b}) \tag{16.5.9}$$

Since $\mathbf{w}_a$ is unconstrained we have

$$X^T X \mathbf{w}_a = X^T \mathbf{b}$$

and so

$$\mathbf{w}_a = (X^T X)^{-1} X^T \mathbf{b} = X^\dagger \mathbf{b}$$

where

$$X^\dagger \triangleq (X^T X)^{-1} X^T$$

is called the *generalized inverse* of X and exists if $n + 1$ of the samples are in 'general position'.

We cannot set $\partial J/\partial \mathbf{b} = 0$, however, since $\mathbf{b}$ is constrained to be positive. In order to keep $\mathbf{b}$ positive we must find a correction $\Delta \mathbf{b}(k)$ which is positive and define

$$\mathbf{b}(k + 1) = \mathbf{b}(k) + \Delta \mathbf{b}(k).$$

Since we are trying to make $X\mathbf{w}_a(k)$ equal to $\mathbf{b}$ it is reasonable to define

$$\Delta \mathbf{b}(k) = \begin{cases} 2c[X\mathbf{w}_a(k) - \mathbf{b}(k)]_i & \text{if } [X\mathbf{w}_a(k) - \mathbf{b}(k)]_i > 0 \\ 0 & \text{if } [X\mathbf{w}_a(k) - \mathbf{b}(k)]_i \leq 0 \end{cases}$$

for some positive correction constant c. Clearly,

$$\Delta \mathbf{b}(k) = c\{X\mathbf{w}_a(k) - \mathbf{b}(k) + |X\mathbf{w}_a(k) - \mathbf{b}(k)|\}$$

where

$$|\mathbf{x}| = (|x_1|, \ldots, |x_n|)^T$$

for any $\mathbf{x} \in \mathbb{R}^n$. Put

$$\mathbf{e}(k) = X\mathbf{w}_a(k) - \mathbf{b}(k)$$

Then, since

$$\mathbf{w}_a(k + 1) = X^\dagger \mathbf{b}(k + 1) = X^\dagger (\mathbf{b}(k) + \Delta \mathbf{b}(k)) = \mathbf{w}_a(k) + X^\dagger \Delta \mathbf{b}(k)$$

we have the algorithm

$$\mathbf{w}_a(1) \quad = X^\dagger \mathbf{b}(1), \text{ arbitrary } b_i(1) > 0 \quad (1 \leq i \leq L)$$
$$\mathbf{w}_a(k + 1) = \mathbf{w}_a(k) + cX^\dagger(\mathbf{e}(k) + |\mathbf{e}(k)|) = X^\dagger \mathbf{b}(k + 1)$$
$$\mathbf{b}(k + 1) \quad = \mathbf{b}(k) + c(\mathbf{e}(k) + |\mathbf{e}(k)|)$$

We shall now show that this algorithm converges in a finite number of steps if $0 < c \leq 1$ and, of course, if a solution exists. By convergence we mean that $\mathbf{e}(k) = 0$ for some k; for then we have

$$X\mathbf{w}_a = \mathbf{b}$$

for some positive **b**. In the course of the proof we shall see that if $\mathbf{e}(k) \leq 0$ with at least one component $e_i(k) < 0$, then this will indicate that a solution does not exist. Since

$$\mathbf{e}(k) = X\mathbf{w}_a(k) - \mathbf{b}(k)$$
$$= (XX^\dagger - I)\mathbf{b}(k)$$

we have

$$\mathbf{e}(k + 1) = (XX^\dagger - I)\mathbf{b}(k + 1)$$
$$= (XX^\dagger - I)\{\mathbf{b}(k) + c[\mathbf{e}(k) + |\mathbf{e}(k)|]\}$$
$$= \mathbf{e}(k) + c(XX^\dagger - I)[\mathbf{e}(k) + |\mathbf{e}(k)|]$$

Hence,

$$\|\mathbf{e}(k + 1)\|^2 = \|\mathbf{e}(k)\|^2 + 2c\mathbf{e}^T(k)(XX^\dagger - I)(\mathbf{e}(k) + |\mathbf{e}(k)|)$$
$$+ \|c(XX^\dagger - I)(\mathbf{e}(k) + |\mathbf{e}(k)|)\|^2$$
$$= \|\mathbf{e}(k)\|^2 + 2c\mathbf{e}^T(k)(XX^\dagger - I)\mathbf{e}'(k) + \|c(XX^\dagger - I)\mathbf{e}'(k)\|^2$$

where

$$\mathbf{e}'(k) = \mathbf{e}(k) + |\mathbf{e}(k)|$$

Now,

$$XX^\dagger\mathbf{e}(k) = XX^\dagger[X\mathbf{w}_a(k) - \mathbf{b}(k)]$$
$$= XX^\dagger(XX^\dagger\mathbf{b}(k) - \mathbf{b}(k))$$
$$= 0$$

Moreover, $XX^\dagger$ is symmetric, so $\mathbf{e}^T(k)XX^\dagger = 0$. Thus we have

$$\|\mathbf{e}(k + 1)\|^2 = \|\mathbf{e}(k)\|^2 - 2c\mathbf{e}^T(k)\mathbf{e}'(k) + \|c(XX^\dagger - I)\mathbf{e}'(k)\|^2$$
$$= \|\mathbf{e}(k)\|^2 - c\|\mathbf{e}'(k)\|^2 + \|c(XX^\dagger - I)\mathbf{e}'(k)\|^2$$

since $\mathbf{e}^T(k)\mathbf{e}'(k) = \frac{1}{2}\|\mathbf{e}'(k)\|^2$. Also, we have

$$\|c(XX^\dagger - I)\mathbf{e}'(k)\|^2 = c^2\mathbf{e}'^T(k)(XX^\dagger - I)^T(XX^\dagger - I)\mathbf{e}'(k)$$
$$= c^2\|\mathbf{e}'(k)\|^2 - c^2\mathbf{e}'^T(k)XX^\dagger\mathbf{e}'(k)$$

and so

$$\|\mathbf{e}(k)\|^2 - \|\mathbf{e}(k + 1)\|^2 = c(1 - c)\|\mathbf{e}'(k)\|^2 + c^2\mathbf{e}'^T(k)XX^\dagger\mathbf{e}'(k)$$
$$\geq 0$$

if $0 < c \leq 1$, since $c^2\mathbf{e}'^T(k)XX^\dagger\mathbf{e}'(k) \geq 0$ because $XX^\dagger \geq 0$. Hence,

$$\|\mathbf{e}(k)\|^2 \geq \|\mathbf{e}(k + 1)\|^2$$

Since $\mathbf{e}'(k) = \mathbf{e}(k) + |\mathbf{e}(k)|$, it follows that if

$$\|\mathbf{e}(k)\|^2 = \|\mathbf{e}(k+1)\|^2$$

for all $k \geqslant$ some K, then $\mathbf{e}(k) \leqslant 0$ (i.e. $e_i(k) \leqslant 0$ for each i). If, for some k, $\mathbf{e}(k) = 0$ then we have found a solution and the algorithm terminates. We must show that, in the separable case, not all components of $\mathbf{e}(k)$ become negative. Suppose, on the contrary that $e_i(k) < 0$ for all i. Since the problem is assumed to be separable, we can find $\hat{\mathbf{w}}_a$ and $\hat{\mathbf{b}} > 0$ such that $X\hat{\mathbf{w}}_a = \hat{\mathbf{b}}$. Since $\hat{\mathbf{b}} > 0$ we have

$$\mathbf{e}^{\mathrm{T}}(k)\hat{\mathbf{b}} < 0 \tag{16.5.10}$$

and so

$$\begin{aligned}
X^{\mathrm{T}}\mathbf{e}(k) &= X^{\mathrm{T}}[X\mathbf{w}_a(k) - \mathbf{b}(k)] \\
&= X^{\mathrm{T}}(XX^{\dagger} - I)\mathbf{b}(k) \\
&= (X^{\mathrm{T}} - X^{\mathrm{T}})\mathbf{b}(k) \\
&= 0
\end{aligned}$$

Hence, $(X\hat{\mathbf{w}})^{\mathrm{T}}\mathbf{e}(k) = \hat{\mathbf{w}}^{\mathrm{T}}X^{\mathrm{T}}\mathbf{e}(k) = 0$ and since $X\hat{\mathbf{w}} = \hat{\mathbf{b}}$ it follows that $\hat{\mathbf{b}}^{\mathrm{T}}\mathbf{e}(k) = 0$, which contradicts (16.5.10), and so, in the separable case, not all components of $\mathbf{e}(k)$ can become negative. This, of course, implies that if $\mathbf{e}(k) < 0$ for some k, then the problem is nonseparable.

All that remains is to prove that $\|\mathbf{e}(k)\| \to 0$. Since $V = \|\mathbf{e}(k)\|^2$ is a Lyapunov function for the error equation, it follows that $\|\mathbf{e}(k)\| \to 0$ as $k \to \infty$. To show that $\|\mathbf{e}(k)\| \to 0$ for finite k note that $X\mathbf{w}_a(k) = \mathbf{b}(k) + \mathbf{e}(k)$. Since $\|\mathbf{e}(k)\| \to 0$ we must have

$$\|\mathbf{e}(k')\| \leqslant \min(b_1(1), \ldots, b_m(1))$$

for some finite k', and since $\mathbf{b}(k)$ increases we have

$$X\mathbf{w}_a(k') > 0$$

and this completes the proof.

We shall complete this section by noting an algorithm which is similar to the perceptron algorithm but is expressed in the form of *potential functions*. The algorithm determines the decision function $d_k(\mathbf{x})$ in a two-class problem directly according to the rule

$$d_{k+1}(\mathbf{x}) = d_k(\mathbf{x}) + r_{k+1}K(\mathbf{x}, \mathbf{x}_{k+1})$$

where

$$r_{k+1} = \begin{cases} 0 & \text{if } \mathbf{x}_{k+1} \in \text{class 1 and } d_k(\mathbf{x}_{k+1}) > 0 \\ 0 & \text{if } \mathbf{x}_{k+1} \in \text{class 2 and } d_k(\mathbf{x}_{k+1}) < 0 \\ 1 & \text{if } \mathbf{x}_{k+1} \in \text{class 1 and } d_k(\mathbf{x}_{k+1}) \leqslant 0 \\ -1 & \text{if } \mathbf{x}_{k+1} \in \text{class 2 and } d_k(\mathbf{x}_{k+1}) \geqslant 0 \end{cases}$$

($\mathbf{x}_{k+1}$ is the $(k + 1)$th training pattern) and

$$K(\mathbf{x}, \mathbf{y}) = \sum_{i=1}^{\infty} \phi_i(\mathbf{x})\phi_j(\mathbf{y})$$

where $\{\phi_i\}$ is a set of orthonormal *potential* functions for which the series converges. Typical potential functions are

$$K_1(\mathbf{x}, \mathbf{y}) = \exp\{-\alpha\|\mathbf{x} - \mathbf{y}\|^2\}$$

$$K_2(\mathbf{x}, \mathbf{y}) = \frac{1}{1 + \alpha\|\mathbf{x} - \mathbf{y}\|^2}$$

$$K_3(\mathbf{x}, \mathbf{y}) = \left| \frac{\sin \alpha\|\mathbf{x} - \mathbf{y}\|^2}{\alpha|\mathbf{x} - \mathbf{y}|^2} \right|$$

The algorithm can be written in perceptron form by defining

$$z_i = \phi_i(\mathbf{x}), \; v_i = \phi_i(\mathbf{y})$$

Then, taking a finite number R of functions ϕ_i we have

$$d_k(\mathbf{x}) = \sum_{i=1}^{R} w_i(k)z_i$$

for some weights w_i.

Bibliographical notes

The theory of perceptrons and learning machines was introduced in Rosenblatt (1961). Once a system has been trained, its *extension properties* must be checked, i.e. its ability to classify correctly new samples. The number of training samples required to give good extension capability is considered in Cover (1965). Further training algorithms are discussed in detail in Meisel (1972), Tou and Gonzalez (1974), and Warmack and Gonzalez (1973).

Exercises

1 Find a condition for two hyperplanes in $\mathbb{R}^n$

$$H_1 : \boldsymbol{\omega}_1 \cdot \mathbf{x} = c_1$$

$$H_2 : \boldsymbol{\omega}_2 \cdot \mathbf{x} = c_2$$

to intersect in a proper $(n - 2)$-dimensional plane. Find the distance of that plane to the origin.

2 Prove that there are $^{n+r}C_r$ coefficients in (16.2.6).
3 Prove the convergence of the L-class perceptron algorithm.
4 Derive a multiclass version of the potential function algorithm.

References

Cover, T. M. (1965), 'Geometrical and statistical properties of systems of linear inequalities with applications to pattern recognition', *IEEE Trans. Electronic Computers*, EC-**14** (3), 326–34.

Meisel, W. S., *Computer Oriented Approaches to Pattern Recognition*, NY: Academic Press.

Rosenblatt, F. (1961), *Principles of Neurodynamics: Perceptrons and the theory of brain machines*, Washington DC: Spartan Books.

Tou, J. T. and R. C. Gonzalez (1974), *Pattern Recognition Principles*, NY: Addison Wesley.

Warmack, R. E. and R. C. Gonzalez (1973), 'An algorithm for the optimal solution of linear inequalities and its application to pattern recognition', *IEEE Trans. Computers*, C-**22** (12), 1065–75.

17

Statistical Decision Theory

17.1 Introduction

Up to now we have treated pattern recognition problems in a deterministic sense, assuming that no noise is present in the samples. In practice, of course, we may introduce significant amounts of noise in the process of measurement or feature extraction from the real data. We shall see in this chapter that it is possible to interpret discriminant functions in a statistical sense and choose decision boundaries to minimize the expected number of misclassifications. Since our samples are noisy it is impossible to know whether a particular sample is classified correctly; only its probability of correct classification can be determined.

We shall begin by introducing the notion of *risk*, which is the expectation of the 'cost' of assigning a pattern sample to class c when its correct class is i. Decision rules can then be determined by minimizing the risk. This will depend, of course, on how we define the 'cost' of making an incorrect decision. In the last part of the chapter we shall show how to extend the training algorithms developed in the last chapter to the case of noisy samples.

17.2 Probability densities and decision functions

We have seen that it is useful to write a decision function $g_{ij}(\mathbf{x})$ which separates classes i and j in the form

$$g_{ij}(\mathbf{x}) = \theta_i(\mathbf{x}) - \theta_j(\mathbf{x})$$

where $\theta_i(\mathbf{x})$ is called a discriminant function. Moreover, we have considered the case of linear functions $\theta_i(\mathbf{x})$ in some detail. In this chapter we shall give the discriminant function $\theta_i(\mathbf{x})$ a different interpretation in terms of the probability of occurrence of a sample of class i. In other words $\theta_i(\mathbf{x})$, when appropriately normalized, can be chosen to be the probability density function of the ith class. The choice function

$$c(\mathbf{x}) = i \qquad \text{if } \theta_i(\mathbf{x}) > \theta_j(\mathbf{x}) \qquad \text{for all } j \neq i$$

as defined above is now interpreted as follows: assign sample $\mathbf{x}$ to class i if the probability of the occurrence of $\mathbf{x}$, given that it is in class i, is greater than the corresponding probability for all other classes. Figure 17.1 shows the situation for a two-class problem in one-dimension.

By being normalized we mean, of course, that

$$\int_{\mathbb{R}^n} \theta_i(\mathbf{x})d\mathbf{x} = 1$$

for each i, so that θ_i *is* a probability density function. Note that, since $\theta_i(\mathbf{x})$ is the probability of the occurrence of $\mathbf{x}$ given that $\mathbf{x}$ is in class i, we can write

$$\theta_i(\mathbf{x}) = p(\mathbf{x}|i)$$

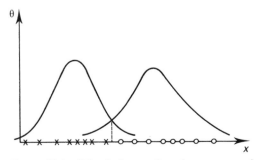

Figure 17.1 Discriminant functions as probability densities.

where $p(.|i)$ denotes the conditional probability. We shall write

$$p_i(\mathbf{x}) = p(\mathbf{x}|i) = \theta_i(\mathbf{x})$$

One of the major problems with statistical decision theory is the estimation or approximation of the probability densities $\theta_i(\mathbf{x})$ – more will be said about this later. We shall also require the *a priori* probability ρ_i of the occurrence of class i. In cases where there exist a large number of samples, a reasonable estimate for ρ_i is given by

$$\rho_i = \frac{M_i}{\sum_{j=1}^{L} M_j} \tag{17.2.1}$$

i.e. the number of samples in class i divided by the total number of samples.

17.3 Bayesian estimation

When we give a statistical interpretation to the discriminant functions which represent the pattern classes, it is impossible to determine the 'correct' class for a particular sample; only the 'most likely' class is a well-defined concept. Hence when determining decision rules we may seek to assign a sample to the best class or to the class which gives the least probability of error. In order to define precisely what 'best' should mean we must have some quantitative measure or cost associated with incorrect decisions. This is done in terms of a *loss function* $L(c, i)$ which is the loss or cost associated with assigning a sample to class c when its correct class is i. Of course, the function L is a design parameter and must be chosen in some way which is related to the intended use of the desired pattern recognition system. Various examples of typical loss functions will be given later.

As stated above, we cannot know which is the correct class for any particular sample since they are effectively random variables and so we cannot use the loss function directly. Instead, we use as our cost function the *risk* or expected loss defined by

$$R = E_i E_{\mathbf{x}}\{L[c(\mathbf{x}), i]\}$$

where E_i denotes the expectation over the classes and $E_{\mathbf{x}}$ denotes the expectation within a class. Thus,

$$R = \sum_{i=1}^{L} \int_{\mathbb{R}^n} L[c(\mathbf{x}), i] \rho_i p_i(\mathbf{x}) \mathrm{d}\mathbf{x} \tag{17.3.1}$$

Note that $\rho_i p_i(\mathbf{x})$ is the joint probability density of sample $\mathbf{x}$ occurring and being in class i.

Having defined the 'cost function' for our problem we can now state the required minimization in the following form: determine the choice function $c(\mathbf{x})$

which minimizes the risk R given by (17.3.1). As stated above we can go no further until we have specified the loss function L. As an example, consider the typical loss function defined by

$$L(c, i) = \begin{cases} -h_i & \text{for } c = i \\ 0 & \text{for } c \neq i \end{cases}$$

where $h_i > 0$. Thus, we assign a negative loss (i.e. a positive gain) to a correct decision and a zero loss to an incorrect decision. From (17.3.1) we have

$$R = \int_{\mathbb{R}^n} \sum_{i=1}^{L} L[c(\mathbf{x}), i] \rho_i p_i(\mathbf{x}) d\mathbf{x}$$

and R is clearly minimized if the integrand

$$F(c) = \sum_{i=1}^{L} L[c(\mathbf{x}), i] \rho_i p_i(\mathbf{x})$$

is minimized. However,

$$F(1) = -h_1 \rho_1 p_1(\mathbf{x})$$
$$F(2) = -h_2 \rho_2 p_2(\mathbf{x})$$
$$\vdots$$
$$F(L) = -h_L \rho_L p_L(\mathbf{x})$$

and so the minimum of R over c is attained by $c = i$ if

$$h_i \rho_i p_i(\mathbf{x}) \geq h_j \rho_j p_j(\mathbf{x}) \qquad j \neq i$$

This leads to the choice function

$$c(\mathbf{x}) = i \text{ if } h_i \rho_i p_i(\mathbf{x}) \geq h_j \rho_j p_j(\mathbf{x}) \qquad j \neq i \qquad (17.3.2)$$

For a more practical example consider the problem where we have radar images of aircraft of two types – friendly and enemy. We wish to classify incoming aircraft optimally so that we define

$$L(c, i) = \begin{cases} K_2 \ (>0) & \text{if } c = 1, i = 2 \\ K_1 \ (>0) & \text{if } c = 2, i = 1 \\ 0 \end{cases}$$

where class 1 is the class of enemy aircraft and class 2 is that of friendly aircraft. Thus, K_2 is the loss in classifying a friendly aircraft as an enemy and K_1 is the loss in classifying an enemy as a friend. For obvious reasons we would therefore choose $K_1 > K_2$! As above, we can determine the following choice function:

$$c(\mathbf{x}) = \begin{cases} 1 & \text{if } K_1 \rho_1 p_1(\mathbf{x}) \geq K_2 \rho_2 p_2(\mathbf{x}) \\ 2 & \text{otherwise} \end{cases}$$

17.4 Selection of linear discriminant functions

In the last chapter we considered deterministic methods of choosing appropriate linear discriminant functions. Here we shall show how the risk may be used to develop an algorithm for the positioning of discriminant functions which best separate the classes. Thus, suppose we have L classes, each with an associated linear discriminant function

$$l_i(\mathbf{x}) = \boldsymbol{\omega}_i \mathbf{x} - c_i \qquad 1 \leqslant i \leqslant L$$

where $\boldsymbol{\omega}_i$ and c_i are unknown parameters to be determined. Recall that we have defined the choice function by

$$c(\mathbf{x}) = i \text{ if } \boldsymbol{\omega}_i \mathbf{x} - c_i \geqslant \boldsymbol{\omega}_j \mathbf{x} - c_j \qquad \text{for all } j \neq i$$

Also the risk has been defined as

$$R = \sum_{i=1}^{L} \rho_i \int_{\mathbb{R}^n} L[c(\mathbf{x}), i] p_i(\mathbf{x}) d\mathbf{x}$$

The integral term is the expectation of L for fixed i and so if $\mathbf{x}^{i,j}$ are the given samples we may approximate R by

$$R \cong \sum_{i=1}^{L} \frac{\rho_i}{M_i} \sum_{j=1}^{M_i} L[c(\mathbf{x}^{i,j}), i]$$

where there are M_i samples in class i. If we assume reasonably large samples we may also use the approximation (17.2.1) and thus write R in the form

$$R \cong \frac{1}{M} \sum_{i=1}^{L} \sum_{j=1}^{M_i} L[c(\mathbf{x}^{i,j}), i] \qquad (17.4.1)$$

where

$$M = \sum_{j=1}^{L} M_i$$

As before, we must now specify the loss function L. In this case, since we are trying to place the hyperplanes defined by $l_i = 0$ so that all the samples will be correctly classified, it is reasonable to take L to be 1 for each misclassification and 0 otherwise, so that R will be proportional to the number of misclassifications. Thus we define

$$L[c(\mathbf{x}), i] = \begin{cases} 0 & \text{if } \boldsymbol{\omega}_i \mathbf{x} - c_i \geqslant \boldsymbol{\omega}_j \mathbf{x} - c_j \qquad \text{for all } j \neq i \\ 1 & \text{otherwise} \end{cases} \qquad (17.4.2)$$

The problem now consists of minimizing the risk given by (17.4.1) over the parameters $\boldsymbol{\omega}_i$, c_i when L is defined by (17.4.2). This is a nonlinear, discontinuous optimization problem and must be solved numerically. The main problem with the loss function (17.4.2) is its discontinuity which considerably complicates the numerical procedure. In order to modify L to make it continuous but still retain the desirable properties which make R proportional to the number of misclassifications, consider first a two-class problem and note that L can be written in the form

$$L[c(\mathbf{x}), 1] = \begin{cases} 0 & \text{if } \boldsymbol{\omega}.\mathbf{x} - c \geqslant 0 \\ 1 & \text{otherwise} \end{cases}$$

$$L[c(\mathbf{x}), 2] = \begin{cases} 0 & \text{if } \boldsymbol{\omega}.\mathbf{x} - c \leqslant 0 \\ 1 & \text{otherwise} \end{cases}$$

where $\boldsymbol{\omega} = \boldsymbol{\omega}_1 - \boldsymbol{\omega}_2$, $c = c_1 - c_2$. In order to make L continuous we introduce a 'dead zone' of width $2d/\|\boldsymbol{\omega}\|$ around the hyperplane $\boldsymbol{\omega}\cdot\mathbf{x} = c$ (Figure 17.2). We then define a modified loss function by

$$L[c(\mathbf{x}), 1] = \begin{cases} 0 & \text{if } \boldsymbol{\omega}\cdot\mathbf{x} - c \geqslant d \\ \dfrac{d - \boldsymbol{\omega}\cdot\mathbf{x} + c}{\|\boldsymbol{\omega}\|} & \text{if } \boldsymbol{\omega}\cdot\mathbf{x} - c < d \end{cases}$$

$$L[c(\mathbf{x}), 2] = \begin{cases} 0 & \text{if } \boldsymbol{\omega}\cdot\mathbf{x} - c \leqslant -d \\ \dfrac{\boldsymbol{\omega}\cdot\mathbf{x} - c + d}{\|\boldsymbol{\omega}\|} & \text{if } \boldsymbol{\omega}\cdot\mathbf{x} - c > -d \end{cases}$$

With this choice of loss function we are assigning zero loss to a decision only if the sample is on the correct side of the decision boundary *and* is outside the deadzone. Samples within the deadzone have a nonzero loss, even when they are on the correct side of the boundary. Again, this problem can be solved by using an appropriate numerical technique. We shall return to the positioning of linear discriminant boundaries later when we consider stochastic versions of the learning algorithms presented in the last chapter.

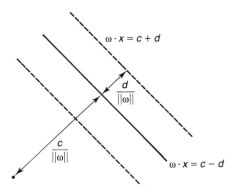

Figure 17.2 Introducing a dead zone (it is assumed that $c > 0$).

17.5 Determination of probability densities

In the preceding discussion on Bayesian estimation we have assumed that the probability distribution $p_i(\mathbf{x})$ of samples in the ith class is known, since the choice functions which we obtained depend on this function. In this section we shall indicate a number of ways in which one may obtain approximations to $p_i(\mathbf{x})$. The first method seeks to express $p_i(\mathbf{x})$ in terms of a finite number of orthonormal functions $\phi_1(\mathbf{x}) \ldots \phi_R(\mathbf{x})$. Thus we write

$$p_i(\mathbf{x}) = \sum_{j=1}^{R} c_{ij}\phi_j(\mathbf{x})$$

and find the coefficients c_{ij} which minimize the cost function

$$J = \int_{\mathbb{R}^n} \left[p_i(\mathbf{x}) - \sum_{j=1}^{R} c_{ij}\phi_j(\mathbf{x}) \right]^2 \mathrm{d}\mathbf{x} \tag{17.5.1}$$

We therefore require $\partial J/\partial c_{ik} = 0$, so that

$$\sum_{j=1}^{R} c_{ij} \int_{\mathbb{R}^n} \phi_j(\mathbf{x})\phi_k(\mathbf{x})\mathrm{d}\mathbf{x} = \int_{\mathbb{R}^n} \phi_k(\mathbf{x})p_i(\mathbf{x})\mathrm{d}\mathbf{x}$$

i.e.

$$c_{ij} = \int_{\mathbb{R}^n} \phi_j(\mathbf{x})p_i(\mathbf{x})\mathrm{d}\mathbf{x} \tag{17.5.2}$$

(which, of course, are just the usual Fourier coefficients of $p_i(\mathbf{x})$ with respect to the orthonormal functions $\phi_j(\mathbf{x})$). However, the expression on the right of (17.5.2) is the expectation of $\phi_j(\mathbf{x})$ and so we may approximate c_{ij} (for large samples) by

$$c_{ij} = \frac{1}{M_i} \sum_{l=1}^{M_i} \phi_j(\mathbf{x}^{il})$$

(where we recall that $\mathbf{x}^{il}$ are the samples of class i). Hence we have

$$p_i(\mathbf{x}) \cong \frac{1}{M_i} \sum_{j=1}^{R} \sum_{l=1}^{M_i} \phi_j(\mathbf{x}^{il})\phi_j(\mathbf{x})$$

for any number R. Note that it is possible to use a positive weighting function g in (17.5.1) which then becomes

$$J_g = \int_{\mathbb{R}^n} \left[p_i(\mathbf{x}) - \sum_{j=1}^{R} c_{ij}\phi_j(\mathbf{x}) \right]^2 g(\mathbf{x})\mathrm{d}\mathbf{x}$$

A second method of approximation of probability densities is to construct $p_i(\mathbf{x})$ directly in terms of *potential functions* $\gamma(\mathbf{x}, \mathbf{y})$. Thus, we write

$$p_i(\mathbf{x}) = \frac{1}{M_i} \sum_{j=1}^{M_i} \gamma(\mathbf{x}, \mathbf{x}^{ij}) \tag{17.5.3}$$

where $\mathbf{x}^{ij}$ is again the jth sample of the ith class. Here, γ should be normalized, i.e.

$$\int_{\mathbb{R}^n} \gamma(\mathbf{x}, \mathbf{y})d\mathbf{x} = 1 \qquad \text{for all } \mathbf{y} \in \mathbb{R}^n$$

so that, from (17.5.3), we have

$$\int_{\mathbb{R}^n} p_i(\mathbf{x})d\mathbf{x} = \frac{1}{M_i} \sum_{j=1}^{M_i} \int_{\mathbb{R}^n} \gamma(\mathbf{x}, \mathbf{x}^{ij})d\mathbf{x}$$

$$= \frac{1}{M_i} \sum_{j=1}^{M_i} 1$$

$$= 1$$

so that $p_i(\mathbf{x})$ *is* a probability density function. A typical function $\gamma(\mathbf{x}, \mathbf{y})$ is a Gaussian distribution with mean $\mathbf{y}$, i.e.

$$\gamma(\mathbf{x}, \mathbf{y}) = \frac{1}{(2\pi)^{n/2}\sigma^n} \exp\left(\frac{-\|\mathbf{x} - \mathbf{y}\|^2}{2\sigma^2}\right) \qquad (17.5.4)$$

If we recall the decision function

$$c(\mathbf{x}) = i \text{ if } h_i\rho_i p_i(\mathbf{x}) \geq h_j\rho_j p_j(\mathbf{x}) \qquad \text{for all } j \neq i \qquad (17.5.5)$$

then the following result shows that a potential function can always be chosen so that the decision rule (17.5.5) correctly classifies samples provided the samples are distinct. (We shall prove the result with the simplifying assumptions that $h_i\rho_i = h_j\rho_j$ for each i, j and for the case of a two-class problem. The general case can be proved similarly.)

THEOREM
Let $Y = \{\mathbf{y}_1, \ldots, \mathbf{y}_M\}$, $Z = \{\mathbf{z}_1, \ldots, \mathbf{z}_N\}$ be samples of two classes for which $\mathbf{y}_i \neq \mathbf{z}_j$ for all i, j. Then there exists a function $\gamma(\mathbf{x}, \mathbf{y})$ such that the discriminant functions $p_1(\mathbf{x})$, $p_2(\mathbf{x})$ defined by

$$p_1(\mathbf{x}) = \frac{1}{M} \sum_{j=1}^{M} \gamma(\mathbf{x}, \mathbf{y}_j), \ p_2(\mathbf{x}) = \frac{1}{N} \sum_{j=1}^{N} \gamma(\mathbf{x}, \mathbf{z}_j)$$

classify all points of Y and Z correctly using the decision rule (17.5.5), with $h_1\rho_1 = h_2\rho_2$.

Proof   We must prove that

$$p_2(\mathbf{y}_k) \leq p_1(\mathbf{y}_k)$$

for all k and that

$$p_1(\mathbf{z}_l) \leq p_2(\mathbf{z}_l)$$

for all l. We shall prove the former since the latter follows similarly. Thus let

$$D = \min_{1 \leqslant i \leqslant M} \min_{1 \leqslant j \leqslant N} \|\mathbf{y}_i - \mathbf{z}_j\|$$

and define

$$\gamma(\mathbf{x}, \mathbf{y}) = \exp\left[-(1/\alpha)\|\mathbf{x} - \mathbf{y}\|^2\right]$$

where

$$\alpha < D^2/\ln\left[\max(M, N)\right]$$

Now, if $\mathbf{y}_k \in Y$, then

$$
\begin{aligned}
p_2(\mathbf{y}_k) &= \frac{1}{N} \sum_{i=1}^{N} \exp\left[-(1/\alpha)\|\mathbf{y}_k - \mathbf{z}_i\|^2\right] \\
&\leqslant \max_{1 \leqslant i \leqslant N} \exp\left[-(1/\alpha)\|\mathbf{y}_k - \mathbf{z}_i\|^2\right] \\
&\leqslant \exp\left[-(1/\alpha) \min_{1 \leqslant i \leqslant N} \|\mathbf{y}_k - \mathbf{z}_i\|^2\right] \\
&\leqslant \exp\left[-D^2/\alpha\right] \\
&< \exp\left(-\ln M\right) \\
&= 1/M \\
&\leqslant \frac{1}{M} \exp\left[-(1/\alpha)\|\mathbf{y}_k - \mathbf{z}_k\|^2\right] \\
&\leqslant \frac{1}{M} \sum_{i=1}^{M} \exp\left[-(1/\alpha)\|\mathbf{y}_k - \mathbf{y}_i\|^2\right] \\
&= p_1(\mathbf{y}_k)
\end{aligned}
$$

This proves the result.

Finally, we shall mention another direct method of probability distribution construction called the *parametric method*. Here we assume that $p_i(\mathbf{x})$ is Gaussian and choose the mean and variance as discussed below. Thus, dropping the subscript i for simplicity, we write

$$p(\mathbf{x}) = \frac{1}{(2\pi)^{n/2}|C|^{1/2}} \exp\left[-\tfrac{1}{2}(\mathbf{x} - \mathbf{m})C^{-1}(\mathbf{x} - \mathbf{m})^{\mathrm{T}}\right]$$

where $C = (c_{ij})$ is positive definite. Then,

$$\mathbf{m} = \int_{\mathbb{R}^n} \mathbf{x}p(\mathbf{x})\mathrm{d}\mathbf{x} = E\{\mathbf{x}\}$$

$$
\begin{aligned}
c_{ij} = \sigma_{ij} &= \int_{\mathbb{R}^n} (x_i - m_i)(x_j - \mathbf{m}_j)p(\mathbf{x})\mathrm{d}\mathbf{x} \\
&= E\{(x_i - m_i)(x_j - m_j)\}
\end{aligned}
$$

Hence, again assuming a reasonably large sample set,

$$\mathbf{m} \cong \frac{1}{M} \sum_{j=1}^{M} \mathbf{x}^j \qquad\qquad (17.5.6)$$

$$\sigma_{ij} \cong \frac{1}{M} \sum_{l=1}^{M} (x_i^l - m_i)(x_j^l - m_j)$$

where $\mathbf{x}^j$, $1 \le j \le M$ are the samples in the given class. These expressions provide estimates of the parameters in terms of the samples. Often, these expressions are rewritten in an iterative form so that they can be used for training by presenting the samples to the system sequentially. Thus, we can write

$$\sigma_{ij}(k) = \frac{1}{k} \sum_{l=1}^{k} x_i^k x_j^k - m_i(k)m_j(k)$$
$$= s_{ij}(k) - m_i(k)m_j(k)$$

where

$$s_{ij}(k) = \frac{1}{k} \sum_{l=1}^{k} x_i^k x_j^k$$

and

$$m_i(k) = \frac{1}{k} \sum_{j=1}^{k} x_i^k$$

By (17.5.6) we have

$$m_i(k+1) = \frac{1}{k+1}(km_i(k) + x_i^{k+1})$$
$$s_{ij}(k+1) = \frac{1}{k+1}(ks_{ij}(k) + x_i^{k+1}x_j^{k+1})$$

and

$$\sigma_{ij}(k+1) = s_{ij}(k+1) - m_i(k+1)m_j(k+1)$$

These specify recursive relationships between $m_i(k)$ and $\sigma_{ij}(k)$.

17.6 Training pattern classifiers

In this section we shall generalize the deterministic algorithms discussed in Chapter 16 to the stochastic case. We have seen that a decision function based on Bayesian estimation is given by

$$d_i(\mathbf{x}) = p(\mathbf{x}|i)\rho_i \qquad 1 \le i \le L$$

and we have described methods of approximating ρ_i and $p(\mathbf{x}|i)$. Note, however, that in determining $p(\mathbf{x}|i)$ no training is involved since the class i is fixed and so the probability density $p(\mathbf{x}|i)$ is independent of the other classes. However, we can write

$$p(\mathbf{x}|i) = p(i|\mathbf{x})p(\mathbf{x})/\rho_i$$

by Bayes' rule and so d_i becomes

$$d_i(\mathbf{x}) = p(i|\mathbf{x})p(\mathbf{x})$$

However, $p(\mathbf{x})$ is independent of i and so can be omitted from d_i, giving finally

$$d_i(\mathbf{x}) = p(i|\mathbf{x})$$

When the discriminant functions are written in this form we can obtain useful training algorithms. Note that in the two-class case we have

$$d_1(\mathbf{x}) > d_2(\mathbf{x})$$

if

$$p(1|\mathbf{x}) > p(2|\mathbf{x})$$
$$= 1 - p(1|\mathbf{x})$$

so that we obtain the decision rule

$$c(\mathbf{x}) = \begin{cases} 1 & \text{if } p(1|\mathbf{x}) > \tfrac{1}{2} \\ 2 & \text{if } p(1|\mathbf{x}) < \tfrac{1}{2} \end{cases}$$

The algorithms we seek are based on the well-known Robbins–Monro regression algorithm which is designed to determine a solution of an equation of the form $g(w) = 0$ from noisy observations $h(w)$ of g. It is assumed that

$$h(w) = g(w) + r(w),$$

where r is some random process, and that r satisfies the assumptions:

(i) $E\{h(w)\} = g(w)$
(ii) $\sigma^2(r) = E\{[g(w) - h(w)]^2\}$ is bounded.

Under these conditions (and some mild conditions on the function g) it can be shown that the algorithm

$$w(k + 1) = w(k) - \alpha_k h[w(k)] \qquad (17.6.1)$$

converges to a root $\bar{w}$ of g in the mean square sense:

$$\lim_{k \to \infty} \{E[(w(k) - \bar{w})^2]\} = 0$$

and even with probability 1, i.e.

$$\text{Prob}\,\{\lim_{k \to \infty} w(k) = \bar{w}\} = 1$$

In (17.6.1) the coefficients α_k must satisfy the conditions

$$\sum_{k=1}^{\infty} \alpha_k, \quad \sum_{k=1}^{\infty} \alpha_k^2 < \infty \tag{17.6.2}$$

for example, $\alpha_k = 1/k$ will be acceptable coefficients. Note that (17.6.1) can be directly generalized to the case of a scalar valued function $g(\mathbf{w})$ of a vector variable. Thus, we have

$$\mathbf{w}(k + 1) = \mathbf{w}(k) - \alpha_k h[\mathbf{w}(k)] \tag{17.6.3}$$

where α_k satisfies (17.6.2).

We now wish to develop an algorithm which will determine $p(i|\mathbf{x})$ from the training patterns. To express $p(i|\mathbf{x})$ in a form similar to that used for training deterministic decision functions we write

$$p(i|\mathbf{x}) = \sum_{j=1}^{k+1} w_{ij}\phi_j(\mathbf{x}) = \mathbf{w}_i^T\phi(\mathbf{x})$$

where $\mathbf{w}_i = (w_{i1}, \ldots, w_{ik}, w_{ik+1})^T$ is a weight vector and $\phi(\mathbf{x}) = (\phi_1(\mathbf{x}), \ldots, \phi_k(\mathbf{x}), 1)^T$ is a vector of basis functions. However, as in the case of generalized non-linear discriminant functions, by regarding $\phi(\mathbf{x})$ as a new coordinate vector we may write

$$p'(i|\mathbf{x}') = p(i|\mathbf{x}) = \mathbf{w}_i^T\mathbf{x}'_a$$

where

$$\mathbf{x}'_a = (\phi_1(\mathbf{x}), \ldots, \phi_k(\mathbf{x}), 1)^T$$

Hence, dropping the ' notation we may assume that p is a linear form

$$p(i|\mathbf{x}) = \mathbf{w}_i^T\mathbf{x} \tag{17.6.4}$$

However, unlike the deterministic case we have no knowledge of $\mathbf{w}_i^T\mathbf{x}_a$ (since this is what we are trying to determine) so we introduce the function

$$r_i(\mathbf{x}) = \begin{cases} 1 & \text{if } \mathbf{x} \in \text{class } i \\ 0 & \text{otherwise} \end{cases}$$

This function is, of course, known during the training phase and we can write

$$r_i(\mathbf{x}) = p(i|\mathbf{x}) + \theta \tag{17.6.5}$$

where θ is a zero mean random process, for we have

$$p[r_i(\mathbf{x}) = 1|\mathbf{x}] = p(i|\mathbf{x})$$

Thus $r_i(\mathbf{x})$ represents a noisy measurement of $p(i|\mathbf{x})$. Now we wish to determine $\mathbf{w}_i$ so that (17.6.4) holds and so we consider the cost functional

$$J = E\{|p(i|\mathbf{x}) - \mathbf{w}_i^T\mathbf{x}_a|\}$$

J is a minimum when (17.6.4) is satisfied and so we require

$$\frac{\partial J}{\partial \mathbf{w}_i} = E\{-\mathbf{x}_a \operatorname{sgn}[p(i|\mathbf{x}) - \mathbf{w}_i^T \mathbf{x}_a]\} = 0$$

However, by (17.6.5), r_i is a noisy measurement of $p(i|\mathbf{x})$, so if we consider the function

$$h(\mathbf{w}_i) = -\mathbf{x}_a \operatorname{sgn}[r_i(\mathbf{x}) - \mathbf{w}_i^T \mathbf{x}_a]$$

the Robbins–Monro algorithm becomes

$$\mathbf{w}_i(k + 1) = \mathbf{w}_i(k) + \alpha_k \mathbf{x}_a(k) \operatorname{sgn}\{r_i[\mathbf{x}(k)] - \mathbf{w}_i^T(k)\mathbf{x}_a(k)\}$$

where $\mathbf{w}_i(1)$ is chosen arbitrarily. This gives the algorithm

$$\mathbf{w}_i(k + 1) = \begin{cases} \mathbf{w}_i(k) + \alpha_k \mathbf{x}_a(k) & \text{if } \mathbf{w}_i^T(k)\mathbf{x}_a(k) < r_i[\mathbf{x}(k)] \\ \mathbf{w}_i(k) - \alpha_k \mathbf{x}_a(k) & \text{otherwise} \end{cases}$$

which should be compared with the deterministic perceptron algorithm. The main difference here is that this algorithm converges even when the pattern classes are not linearly separable.

As in the deterministic case we can derive a least-mean-square-error algorithm by using the cost function

$$J(\mathbf{w}_i, \mathbf{x}_a) = \tfrac{1}{2} E\{[r_i(\mathbf{x}) - \mathbf{w}_i^T \mathbf{x}_a]^2\}$$

Thus,

$$\frac{\partial J}{\partial \mathbf{w}_j} = E\{-\mathbf{x}[r_i(\mathbf{x}) - \mathbf{w}_i^T \mathbf{x}_a]\}$$

and if we put $h(\mathbf{w}_i) = -\mathbf{x}[r_i(\mathbf{x}) - \mathbf{w}_i^T \mathbf{x}_a]$ in the general Robbins–Monro algorithm, we obtain

$$\mathbf{w}_i(k + 1) = \mathbf{w}_i(k) + \alpha_k \mathbf{x}_a(k)[r_i(\mathbf{x}(k)) - \mathbf{w}_i^T(k)\mathbf{x}_a(k)] \qquad (17.6.6)$$

where $\mathbf{w}_i(1)$ is arbitrary and $r_i(\mathbf{x}(k)) = 1$ if $\mathbf{x}(k)$ belongs to class i and is zero otherwise. It can be shown that this algorithm converges if α_k satisfies (17.6.2) and if

1. $E\{\mathbf{x}\mathbf{x}^T\}$ and $E\{(\mathbf{x}\mathbf{x}^T)^2\}$ exist and are positive definite.
2. $E\{\mathbf{x}p(i|\mathbf{x})\}$ and $E\{\mathbf{x}\mathbf{x}^T p(i|\mathbf{x})\}$ exist.

We note finally that the deterministic potential function algorithm can be generalized in the form:

1. Set $f_0(\mathbf{x}) = 0$.
2. if $\mathbf{x}_k \in$ class i and $f_k(\mathbf{x}_k) > 0$, or $\mathbf{x}_k \notin$ class i and $f_k(\mathbf{x}_k) < 0$, then set

$$f_{k+1}(\mathbf{x}) = f_k(\mathbf{x}).$$

3. if $\mathbf{x}_k \in$ class i and $f_k(\mathbf{x}_k) < 0$, then set

$$f_{k+1}(\mathbf{x}) = f_k(\mathbf{x}) + \alpha_k K(\mathbf{x}, \mathbf{x}_k)$$

4. if $\mathbf{x}_k \notin$ class i and $f_k(\mathbf{x}_k) > 0$, then set

$$f_{k+1}(\mathbf{x}) = f_k(\mathbf{x}) - \alpha_k K(\mathbf{x}, \mathbf{x}_k)$$

where $\{\alpha_k\}$ satisfies (17.6.2). The potential function K can be chosen as in Chapter 16. However, the functions $f_k(\mathbf{x}_k)$ defined by this recursive procedure are not probability densities and so we define

$$\bar{f}_k(\mathbf{x}) = \begin{cases} f_k(\mathbf{x}) & \text{if } 0 \leqslant f_k(\mathbf{x}) \leqslant 1 \\ 0 & \text{otherwise} \end{cases}$$

It can then be shown that $\bar{f}_k(\mathbf{x})$ converges in the mean to the recognition function $p(i|\mathbf{x})$, i.e.

$$\lim_{k \to \infty} E\{\bar{f}_k(\mathbf{x}) - p(i|\mathbf{x})\}^2 = 0$$

We can express the algorithm in a different form by writing

$$\bar{f}_k(\mathbf{x}) = \sum_{j=1}^{R} c_j(k)\phi_j(\mathbf{x}) \tag{17.6.7}$$

for some orthonormal functions ϕ_j and some fixed R. Then if

$$K(\mathbf{x}, \mathbf{x}_k) = \sum_{j=1}^{R} \lambda_j^2 \phi_j(\mathbf{x})\phi_j(\mathbf{x}_k)$$

we have

$$f_{k+1}(\mathbf{x}) = f_k(\mathbf{x}) \pm \alpha_k \sum_{j=1}^{R} \lambda_j^2 \phi_j(\mathbf{x})\phi_j(\mathbf{x}_k)$$

and so by (17.6.7) we have

$$\sum_{j=1}^{R} c_j(k+1)\phi_j(\mathbf{x}) = \sum_{j=1}^{R} [c_j(k) \pm \alpha_k \lambda_j^2 \phi_j(\mathbf{x}_k)]\phi_j(\mathbf{x})$$

This leads to the algorithm

1. Choose $c_j(0)$, $1 \leqslant j \leqslant R$ arbitrarily.
2. for a correct classification set

$$c_j(k+1) = c_j(k)$$

3. if $\mathbf{x}_k \in$ class i and $\mathbf{x}_k$ is misclassified, set

$$c_j(k+1) = c_j(k) + \alpha_k \lambda_j^2 \phi_j(\mathbf{x}_k)$$

4. if $\mathbf{x}_k \notin$ class i and $\mathbf{x}_k$ is misclassified, set

$$c_j(k+1) = c_j(k) - \alpha_k \lambda_j^2 \phi_j(\mathbf{x}_k)$$

Bibliographical notes

A detailed analysis of the statistical approach to pattern recognition can be found in Meisel (1972) and Patrick (1972). The Robbins–Monro algorithm was given in Robbins and Monro (1951) and generalized to the multidimensional case in Blum (1954); see also Dvoretzky (1956) and Wilde (1964). The method of stochastic approximation by potential functions is taken from Aizerman *et al.* (1964a, b, 1965).

Exercises

1 Determine the choice function as in (17.3.2) when the loss function is given by

$$L(i, c) = \begin{cases} -h_i & \text{for } c = i \\ k & \text{for } c \neq i \end{cases}$$

$(h_i, k > 0)$.

2 Generalize the expressions given in Section 17.4 for L in the case when a deadzone is introduced around each hyperplane.

3 Derive an expression for c_{ij} as in (17.5.2) when J_g is used instead of J.

4 Generalize the theorem in Section 17.5 to the multiclass case.

5 Write a Pascal program to implement the training algorithms given in the last part of the chapter.

References

Aizerman, M. A., E. M. Braverman and L. I. Rozonoer (1964a), 'The method of potential functions in the problem of determining the characteristics of a function generator from randomly observed points', *Automation and Remote Control,* **25** (12), 1546–56.

Aizerman, M. A., E. M. Braverman and L. I. Rozonoer (1964b), 'Theoretical foundations of the potential function method in pattern recognition', *Automation and Remote Control,* **25** (6), 821–37.

Aizerman, M. A., E. M. Braverman and L. I. Rozonoer (1965), 'The Robbins–Monro process and the method potential functions', *Automation and Remote Control,* **26** (11), 1882–5.

Blum, J. R. (1954), 'Multidimensional stochastic approximation methods', *Ann. Math. Stat.,* **25**, 737–44.

Dvoretzky, A. (1956), 'On stochastic approximation', in *Proc. 3rd. Berkeley Symp. on Math. Statistics and Probability* (J. Neyman, ed.), Berkeley: University of California Press, 39–55.

Meisel, S. M. (1972), *Computer-Oriented Approaches to Pattern Recognition,* NY: Academic Press.

Patrick, E. A. (1972), *Fundamentals of Pattern Recognition,* Englewood Cliffs, NJ: Prentice Hall.

Robbins, H. and S. Monro (1951), 'A stochastic approximation method', *Ann. Math. Stat.*, **22**, 400–7.

Wilde, D. J. (1964), *Optimum Seeking Methods,* Englewood Cliffs, NJ: Prentice Hall.

18

Cluster Analysis and Unsupervised Learning

18.1 Introduction

Up to now we have considered pattern recognition in the case where a set of samples of known classification are used to train a system (i.e. to select a decision function which correctly classifies the samples). New samples are then classified on the basis of the decision rule which was derived in the training phase. In some problems, however, the samples presented to the system are not preclassified, since natural pattern classes are not known, *a priori*. Thus, for example, in animal taxonomy or code breaking, we must find the 'natural' pattern classes before we can begin classifying new samples. When the classes are not known in advance we must seek 'clusters' of samples in pattern space which will then represent the classes inherent in the problem. In this chapter we develop training algorithms for finding such clusters, and systems which use these algorithms are said to undergo *unsupervised learning* (or learning without a teacher) since no *a priori* knowledge of the classes is presented to the system.

It should be observed, however, that, unlike the methods developed in

301

preceding chapters, unsupervised learning is an interactive procedure between the computer system implementing the algorithms and the designers of the system, since the computer can never 'know' when suitable clusters have been found. The clusters determined by computer algorithm must be examined to ensure that they are 'sensible' with respect to the particular problem in hand. Only the designers of the system for that problem can know if the resulting clusters are reasonable. It is thus seen that cluster analysis is somewhere between a science and an art.

18.2 Basic principles of cluster analysis

Decision-theoretic pattern recognition (as opposed to syntactic pattern recognition, to be discussed later) is based on the concept that points in pattern space which are 'close' together are assumed to represent the same pattern class. Thus, even if the classes are not known, *a priori*, we can seek natural pattern classes by finding groups of pattern samples which are close to each other but far away from samples of other classes. Typical situations which can occur are shown in Figure 18.1. In the first case (a) the clusters form roughly spherical regions, whereas in (b) they can be seen to be arranged in sheets. Note that in case (a) there are two obvious clusters, whereas it is not clear whether the third region is a single cluster or represents two distinct clusters. It will be seen that the algorithms developed in the next section can predict either case, depending on the thresholds, initial conditions, etc. This is the point at which the designer of the system must decide whether two distinct clusters or a single one is more appropriate for the given system.

Stated formally, cluster analysis seeks to divide pattern space $\mathbb{R}^n$ into K disjoint regions X_i, $1 \leq i \leq K$ such that

$$X_1 \cup X_2 \cup \ldots \cup X_K = \mathbb{R}^n \qquad (18.2.1)$$

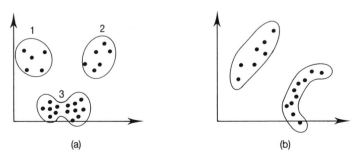

(a)   (b)

Figure 18.1 Typical cluster formations: (a) well-separated clusters; (b) linear clusters.

$$X_i \cap X_j = \phi \qquad \text{if } i \neq j \tag{18.2.2}$$

i.e. $\{X_i : 1 \leqslant i \leqslant K\}$ is a *partition* of $\mathbb{R}^n$. (Some definitions of cluster analysis omit condition (18.2.2), thus allowing clusters to overlap in cases where it can be argued that some samples naturally belong to several classes.) The subset X_i defines a cluster of sample $\mathcal{C}_i$ by the rule

$$\mathbf{x} \in \mathcal{C}_i \text{ if } \mathbf{x} \in X_i$$

The derivation of the subsets X_i will be based on a distance measure, which does not have to be the standard Euclidean distance $d(\mathbf{x}, \mathbf{y}) = \|\mathbf{x} - \mathbf{y}\|$. In fact the following *measures of similarity* have been used in practice:

(i) $d(\mathbf{x}, \mathbf{y}) = (\mathbf{x} - \mathbf{y})^{\mathrm{T}} C^{-1} (\mathbf{x} - \mathbf{y})$

(ii) $s(\mathbf{x}, \mathbf{y}) = \dfrac{\mathbf{x}^{\mathrm{T}}\mathbf{y}}{\|\mathbf{x}\| \cdot \|\mathbf{y}\|}$

(iii) $s(\mathbf{x}, \mathbf{y}) = \dfrac{\mathbf{x}^{\mathrm{T}}\mathbf{y}}{\|\mathbf{x}\|^2 + \|\mathbf{y}\|^2 - \mathbf{x}^{\mathrm{T}}\mathbf{y}}$

Note that s given by (ii) or (iii) is *not* a metric since $s(\mathbf{x}, \mathbf{y}) = 0 \not\Rightarrow \mathbf{x} = \mathbf{y}$. Since $\mathbf{xy} = \|\mathbf{x}\|^{\mathrm{T}}\|\mathbf{y}\| \cos \theta$, where θ is the angle between $\mathbf{x}$ and $\mathbf{y}$, s is a maximum when $\mathbf{x}$ and $\mathbf{y}$ are colinear. The similarity measures s in (ii) and (iii) are therefore useful when clusters tend to develop in a linear form; (iii) is called the *Tanimoto measure* and is used in disease classification, taxonomy, etc.

18.3 Algorithms for cluster seeking

The simplest approach to cluster analysis is to choose a threshold θ which represents the radius of the proposed clusters. (This must be chosen in accordance with some intuitive understanding of the particular problem at hand.) Then, if we have a set $\{\mathbf{x}_1, \ldots, \mathbf{x}_N\}$ of (unlabelled) samples we choose one sample arbitrarily, say $\mathbf{x}_1$ and put

$$\mathbf{c}_1 \triangleq \mathbf{x}_1$$

so that $\mathbf{x}_1$ becomes the first cluster centre. Then we find the first index k such that

$$d(\mathbf{x}_k, \mathbf{c}_1) > \theta$$

If no such k exists, then there is one cluster with all samples assigned to this cluster, i.e.

$$C_1 = \{\mathbf{x}_1, \ldots, \mathbf{x}_N\}$$

Otherwise, we set

$$C_1 = \{\mathbf{x}_1, \ldots, \mathbf{x}_{k-1}\}$$

$$\mathbf{c}_2 \stackrel{\triangle}{=} \mathbf{x}_k$$

If $k < N$ we then let

$$\left.\begin{array}{ll}\mathbf{x}_{k+1} \in C_1 & \text{if } d(\mathbf{x}_{k+1}, \mathbf{c}_1) \leqslant \theta \\[2mm] \mathbf{x}_{k+1} \in C_2 & \text{if } d(\mathbf{x}_{k+1}, \mathbf{c}_2) \leqslant \theta \\[4mm] \mathbf{c}_3 = \mathbf{x}_{k+1} & \text{if } d(\mathbf{x}_{k+1}, \mathbf{c}_i) > \theta \quad i = 1, 2 \end{array}\right\} \quad (18.3.1)$$

and

We then proceed in this way until all the samples have been assigned to clusters. The conditions in (18.3.1) simply state that a new sample is assigned to an existing cluster if it is within a distance θ of that cluster centre, or that the sample forms a new cluster centre otherwise. It is clear that this simple algorithm depends not only on the threshold θ but also on the order in which the samples are considered. The algorithm does, however, give a quick insight into the rough nature of the clusters in the given problem.

If we know the number of clusters which occur in a given problem, then we can use the celebrated *K-means algorithm* for cluster seeking. Given a set of unlabelled samples $\{\mathbf{x}_1, \ldots, \mathbf{x}_N\}$ we can specify the algorithm in the following way:

STEP 1   Choose K initial cluster centres $\mathbf{c}_1(1), \ldots, \mathbf{c}_K(1)$. These could be arbitrary, but are usually defined by

$$\mathbf{c}_i(1) = \mathbf{x}_i \quad 1 \leqslant i \leqslant K$$

(i.e. we choose the first K samples).

STEP 2   At the kth step, assign the sample $\mathbf{x}_l$, $1 \leqslant l \leqslant N$ to cluster j if

$$\|\mathbf{x}_l - \mathbf{c}_j(k)\| < \|\mathbf{x}_l - \mathbf{c}_i(k)\|$$

for all $i \neq j$. (In the case of equality we assign $\mathbf{x}_l$ arbitrarily to i or j.)

STEP 3   Let $C_j(k)$ denote the jth cluster after Step 2. Determine new cluster centres by

$$\mathbf{c}_j(k + 1) = \frac{1}{N_j} \sum_{\mathbf{x} \in C_j(k)} \mathbf{x}$$

where N_j = number of samples in $C_j(k)$. Thus, the new cluster centre is the mean of the samples in the old cluster.

STEP 4   Repeat until convergence is achieved.

Although it is possible to find pathological cases where convergence never occurs, the algorithm does converge in most examples. Note that it depends on the number, K, of cluster centres chosen, the choice of initial cluster centres and the order in which the samples are used.

A variation of the K-means algorithm which includes a number of heuristic parameters is the *isodata algorithm* (*Iterative Self-Organizing Data Analysis Technique Algorithm*). We shall simply state the steps of the algorithm and leave the reader to interpret the steps in obvious ways:

Let the samples be $\{x_1, \ldots, x_N\}$ and let K be the desired number of cluster centres. Set $n = 1$.

STEP 1   Select initial cluster centres $\{c_1, \ldots, c_L\}$ (from the samples). Note that L may be different from K.

STEP 2   Choose the following parameters:

m = minimum number of samples per cluster;

σ_d = a desired standard deviation for clusters;

θ = lumping parameter;

M = maximum number of pairs of cluster centres which can be lumped;

I = maximum number of iterations.

STEP 3   If C_i denotes the ith cluster, distribute the samples by the rule

$$x \in C_i \text{ if } \|x - c_i\| < \|x - c_j\| \qquad 1 \leq i \leq L, j \neq i$$

STEP 4   If C_i has less than m samples, then discard C_i and replace L by $L - 1$.

STEP 5   Define new cluster centres by

$$c_j = \frac{1}{N_j} \sum_{x \in C_j} x \qquad 1 \leq j \leq L$$

as in the K-means algorithm.

STEP 6   Determine the average distances

$$D_j = \frac{1}{N_j} \sum_{x \in C_j} \|x - x_j\| \qquad 1 \leq j \leq L$$

STEP 7   Find the overall average distance D of the samples from their respective cluster centres by

$$D = \frac{1}{N} \sum_{j=1}^{L} N_j D_j$$

STEP 8   If this is iteration number I, or if it is an even-numbered iteration or if $L \geq 2K$, then **goto** step 12; otherwise continue.

STEP 9   Evaluate the standard deviation vector $\sigma_j = (\sigma_{j1}, \sigma_{j2}, \ldots, \sigma_{jn})^{\mathrm{T}}$ for each cluster:

$$\sigma_{ij} = \left\{ \frac{1}{N_j} \sum_{x^k \in C_j} (x_i^k - c_{ji})^2 \right\}^{1/2} \quad 1 \leq i \leq n, 1 \leq j \leq L$$

where x_i^k is the ith component of the kth sample of C_j, and c_{ji} is the ith component of c_j.

STEP 10   Set

$$\sigma_{j\max}^l = \max_{1 \leq i \leq n} \{\sigma_{ji}\} \quad 1 \leq j \leq L$$

where l is the value which satisfies $\sigma_{j\max}^l = \sigma_{jl}$.

STEP 11   If $\sigma_{j\max} > \sigma_d$ and $((D_j > D$ and $N_j > 2(m + 1))$ or $(L \leq K/2))$, then split c_j into two cluster centres c_j^+, c_j^- where

$$c_{ji}^+ = c_{ji} + k\sigma_{j\max}^l \delta_i$$
$$c_{ji}^- = c_{ji} - k\sigma_{j\max}^l \delta_i$$

for some $k \in (0, 1)$, where l is as in Step 10, and **goto** Step 3. Otherwise continue.

STEP 12   Evaluate

$$D_{ij} = \|\mathbf{c}_i - \mathbf{c}_j\| \quad i = 1, \ldots, L, j = i + 1, \ldots, L$$

STEP 13   Compare each D_{ij} with θ, and arrange the M smallest such distances which are less than θ in ascending order:

$$D_{i_1 j_1} < D_{i_2 j_2} < \ldots < D_{i_M j_M}.$$

STEP 14   For $l = 1, \ldots, M$ let $\mathbf{c}_{i_l}$, $\mathbf{c}_{j_l}$ be the centres associated with the distance $D_{i_l j_l}$. If neither $\mathbf{c}_{i_l}$ nor $\mathbf{c}_{j_l}$ has been used in lumping in this iteration, replace $\mathbf{c}_{i_l}$, $\mathbf{c}_{j_l}$ by a single centre given by

$$\mathbf{c}_{i_l}^* = \frac{1}{N_{i_l} + N_{j_l}} (N_{i_l} \cdot c_{i_l} + N_{j_l} \cdot c_{j_l})$$

and replace L by $L - 1$.

STEP 15   If $n = L$ then stop. Otherwise set $n = n + 1$ and return to Step 2 (or Step 1 if any of the parameters m, σ_d, θ, M or I is to be changed – this makes the algorithm interactive).

As a final algorithm of this type we mention the following recursive technique which is usually applied with a single pass through the data. The algorithm may be stated in the form:
Define

$$d_\sigma^2(\mathbf{x}, \mathbf{y}) = \sum_{i=1}^n \left(\frac{\mathbf{x}_i - \mathbf{y}_i}{\sigma_j} \right)^2$$

1. Put $\mathbf{m}_1 = \mathbf{x}_1$ (the first sample) and $\boldsymbol{\sigma}_1 = 0$.
2. At the kth step suppose there are L_k clusters, and let $\mathbf{x}_{k+1}$ be the next sample.
   (a) If

   $$d_{\sigma_i}^2(\mathbf{x}_{k+1}, \mathbf{m}_i) \leq \theta\tau \qquad \text{for some } i \in \{1, \ldots, L_k\}$$

   assign $\mathbf{x}_{k+1}$ to cluster i and update m_i, σ_i by

   $$\mathbf{m}_i \leftarrow \frac{1}{N_i + 1} [N_i\mathbf{m}_i] + \mathbf{x}_{k+1}]$$

   $$\sigma_{ij}^2 \rightarrow \frac{1}{N_i + 1} [N_i\sigma_{ij}^2 + (x_{k+1j} - \mathbf{m}_{ij})^2] \qquad 1 \leq j \leq n$$

   where cluster i has N_i samples.
   (b) If

   $$\theta\tau < d_{\sigma_i}^2(\mathbf{x}_{k+1}, \mathbf{m}_i) \leq \tau \qquad \text{for some } i \in \{1, \ldots, L_k\}$$

   do not assign $\mathbf{x}_{k+1}$ to any cluster; instead hold $\mathbf{x}_{k+1}$ in a buffer.
   (c) If

   $$d_{\sigma_i}^2(\mathbf{x}_{k+1}, \mathbf{m}_i) > \tau \qquad \text{for all } i \in \{1, \ldots, L_k\}$$

   then $\mathbf{x}_{k+1}$ forms a new cluster. Put $\mathbf{m}_{L_k+1} = \mathbf{x}_{k+1}$, $\boldsymbol{\sigma}_{L_k+1} = 0$.
3. If the buffer formed in 2(b) reaches a certain length, then assign each sample in the buffer to the nearest cluster, and change the corresponding cluster parameters $\mathbf{m}_i$ and $\boldsymbol{\sigma}_i$ as in (2)(a).
4. **Goto** (2) if some samples remain.

The parameters θ and τ are often chosen in some *ad hoc* way. To understand the significance of the algorithm consider Figure 18.2, where a typical cluster is shown. The parameters $\mathbf{m}_i$ and $\boldsymbol{\sigma}_i$ represent the mean and standard deviations of the clusters, respectively, and the algorithm proceeds by assigning a new sample x to an existing cluster if the 'distance' $d_{\sigma_i}^2(\mathbf{x}, \mathbf{m}_i)$ of the sample to $\mathbf{m}_i$ is less than or equal to $\theta\tau$. If the sample lies at a distance $d_\sigma^2 > \tau$ for all existing clusters, then it is assigned to a new cluster. The remaining regions of pattern space form the 'guard zones' around the existing clusters. Any new sample falling in these regions is regarded as 'doubtful' and is held in a buffer until the buffer is full, at which time these samples are assigned to their nearest clusters. The guard zones effectively postpone the classification of

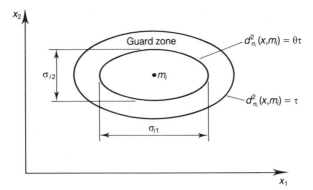

Figure 18.2   Defining clusters with guard zones.

doubtful samples and thus reduce the effect of initial parameter choices and of the order in which samples are taken.

18.4 Graph theoretic clustering

A simple and easily implemented clustering technique which uses elementary graph theoretic ideas will be discussed in this section. First we shall briefly describe those parts of graph theory which are necessary for an understanding of this method. A *graph* $G = (V, E)$ consists of a set $V = \{v_1, v_2, \ldots\}$ of *vertices* and a set E of *edges*, with elements of the form $\{v_i, v_j\}$. Informally, V can be thought of as a set of points in $\mathbb{R}^n$ and E as a set of lines joining certain pairs of elements of V. (Strictly speaking, we have defined an *unordered* graph. An *ordered* graph consists of vertices and ordered pairs of vertices $E \subseteq V \times V$.)

A *path* in a graph is a sequence of edges of the form $\{v_{i_1}, v_{i_2}\}$, $\{v_{i_2}, v_{i_3}\}$, $\{v_{i_3}, v_{i_4}\}$, ... and a *circuit* is a closed path, i.e. a sequence of the form $\{v_{i_1}, v_{i_2}\}$, $\{v_{i_2}, v_{i_3}\}$, ..., $\{v_{i_k}, v_{i_1}\}$. A *tree* is a graph without any circuits. A graph is *connected* if there exists a path joining any two vertices. A *spanning tree* in a graph is a connected tree which contains all the vertices of the graph.

After these preliminary definitions we now associate a graph with a set of pattern samples in the following way. First choose a threshold parameter θ which will measure how close samples have to be so that they are regarded as being in the same cluster. Here, again, this parameter must be chosen with reference to the particular problem. Then we define the graph $G = (V, E)$ by

(i) $\mathbf{x} \in V$ if $\mathbf{x}$ is a pattern sample,
(ii) $\{\mathbf{x}, \mathbf{y}\} \in E$ if $d(\mathbf{x}, \mathbf{y}) \le \theta$,

where d is any desired distance measure. A simple example is shown in Figure

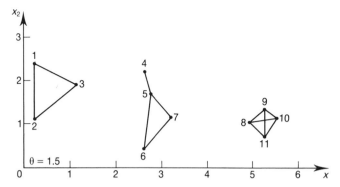

Figure 18.3 Graph associated with pattern samples.

18.3. We can also express the graph in the form of a similarity matrix $S = (s_{ij})$ by defining

$$s_{ij} = \left\{ \begin{array}{ll} 1 & \text{if } d_{ij} \leq \theta \\ 0 & \text{if } d_{ij} > \theta \end{array} \right.$$

where $d_{ij} = d(\mathbf{x}_i, \mathbf{y}_j)$, and $\mathbf{x}_i$, $\mathbf{y}_i$ are the ith and jth samples. Thus, for the example in Figure 18.3 we obtain the similarity matrix S given by

$$S = \begin{bmatrix} 1 & 1 & 1 & & & & & & & & \\ 1 & 1 & 1 & & & & & & & & \\ 1 & 1 & 1 & & & & & & & & \\ & & & 1 & 1 & & & & & & \\ & & & 1 & 1 & 1 & 1 & & & & \\ & & & & 1 & 1 & 1 & & & & \\ & & & & 1 & 1 & 1 & & & & \\ & & & & & & & 1 & 1 & 1 & 1 \\ & & & & & & & 1 & 1 & 1 & 1 \\ & & & & & & & 1 & 1 & 1 & 1 \\ & & & & & & & 1 & 1 & 1 & 1 \end{bmatrix}$$

The clusters can be seen clearly from the similarity matrix since they correspond to the submatrix blocks along the diagonal of S.

We can study the effect of changing θ by considering a spanning tree of the graph for various values of θ. If we associate a *weight* with each edge of the graph which equals the distance d_{ij} between samples i and j, where $E = \{\mathbf{x}_i, \mathbf{x}_j\}$ then we define a *minimal* spanning tree to be a spanning tree with minimal total weight. A minimal spanning tree for the example in Figure 18.3 is shown in Figure 18.4. Starting with θ large enough for all the edges of a minimal spanning

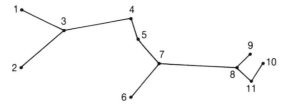

Figure 18.4 A minimal spanning tree for Figure 18.3.

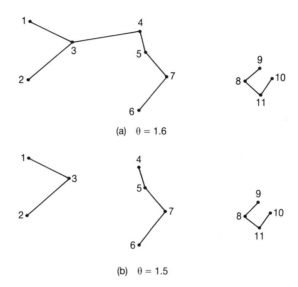

Figure 18.5 Splitting the spanning tree.

tree to have weight less than θ we reduce θ gradually and observe the way in which this spanning tree splits into connected subtrees. Each connected subtree then represents a cluster with threshold given by the particular value of θ which is reached at that point. The minimal spanning tree of Figure 18.4 splits, as shown in Figure 18.5, for the values (a) $\theta = 1.6$ and (b) $\theta = 1.5$. The clusters given by the connected subtrees in (b) are the same as those shown in Figure 18.3.

18.5 Indirect methods

We can also approach the problem of cluster analysis indirectly by optimizing some performance index which measures the relative merits of a given clustering of the samples. Of course, the methods depend on the performance index we choose, which must again be based on the particular properties of the problem at hand. We shall mention two approaches here: a deterministic distance algorithm and a stochastic method based on probability densities.

In a typical distance measuring algorithm we specify the clusters according to the rule

$$C_i = \{x : d_i(\mathbf{x}, \mathbf{c}_i) \leq d_j(\mathbf{x}, \mathbf{c}_j) \qquad \text{for } j \neq i\} \qquad (18.5.1)$$

where $\mathbf{c}_i$ is the 'centre' of cluster i (to be determined by the algorithm). The distance d_i can be defined by

$$d_i^2(\mathbf{x}, \mathbf{c}_i) = \sum_{j=1}^{n} \left(\frac{\mathbf{x}_j - c_{ij}}{\sigma_{ij}} \right)^2 \qquad (18.5.2)$$

where σ_{ij}^2 is the variance of the ith cluster along axis j. If the number of clusters K is known we can define the performance measure

$$Q = \sum_{j=1}^{K} \sum_{\mathbf{x} \in C_j} d_j^2(\mathbf{x}, \mathbf{c}_j) \qquad (18.5.3)$$

Minimizing Q with respect to $c_1, \ldots, c_K$ and $\boldsymbol{\sigma}_1, \ldots, \boldsymbol{\sigma}_K$ (where $\boldsymbol{\sigma}_i = (\sigma_{i1}, \ldots, \sigma_{in})$) will then find the optimal clusters for this particular performance index. If K is unknown, then other performance measurements must be sought, perhaps by adding a term which penalizes small clusters.

A statistical approach to cluster analysis, very much in the spirit of pattern classification by the minimization of the risk discussed earlier, can be derived. Thus we define a *mixture*

$$p(\mathbf{x}) = \sum_{i=1}^{K} \rho_i p_i(\mathbf{x})$$

where $p_i(\mathbf{x})$ is the probability density of cluster i and ρ_i is the probability of the occurrence of cluster i. Note that $p(\mathbf{x})$ is a probability density function. Let C_i (cluster i) be defined by some conditions similar to (18.5.1) and (18.5.2) so that we can write $C_i(\boldsymbol{\alpha})$ to indicate that the ith cluster depends on some parameters ($\mathbf{c}_i$ and $\boldsymbol{\sigma}_i$ in the above instance). A suitable performance index can be written in terms of the overlap of the component density functions, i.e.

$$Q(\boldsymbol{\alpha}) = E\left\{ \sum_{i=1}^{K} \sum_{\substack{j=1 \\ i \neq j}}^{K} \rho_i \rho_j p_i(\mathbf{x}) p_j(\mathbf{x}) \right\} \qquad (18.5.4)$$

with the constraint

$$\sum_{i=1}^{K} \rho_i = 1$$

The densities ρ_i and $p_i(\mathbf{x})$ can be estimated by any of the methods of Section 17.5. Thus, for example, we could write

$$\rho_i \simeq \frac{M_i}{\Sigma_{j=1}^{K} M_j}$$

where there are M_i samples in cluster i, and

$$p_i(\mathbf{x}) \simeq \frac{1}{M_i} \sum_{j=1}^{R} \sum_{l=1}^{M_i} \phi_j(\mathbf{x}^{il}) \phi_j(\mathbf{x})$$

where $\mathbf{x}^{il}$, $1 \leqslant l \leqslant M_i$ are the samples in cluster i. (Note that M_i depends on $\boldsymbol{\alpha}$.) The function $Q(\boldsymbol{\alpha})$ given by (18.5.4) can then be minimized by a suitable numerical technique.

Bibliographical notes

The K-means algorithm is discussed in detail in MacQueen (1967) and the ISODATA algorithm was developed in Ball and Hall (1966); an interesting example of its application can be found in Gonzalez (1974). Graph theoretical techniques have been used with success in Zahn (1981). The choice of the parameters θ and τ in the algorithm represented in Figure 18.2 is discussed in Macciadi and Gose (1970). For general results on unsupervised learning, see [1, 3, 4].

Exercises

1 Explain the significance of the measures of similarity (ii), (iii) given in Section 18.2.
2 Write a Pascal program to implement the K-means algorithm.
3 Repeat exercise 2 for the ISODATA algorithm.
4 Find relations for $\mathbf{c}_i$ and $\boldsymbol{\sigma}_i$ when (18.5.3) is minimized.

References

Agrawala, A. K. (1970), 'Learning with a probabilistic teacher', *IEEE Trans. Inf. Theory*, **16**, 373–9.
Ball, G. H. and D. J. Hall (1966), 'ISODATA: An iterative method of multivariate data analysis and pattern classification', *Proc. IEEE Int. Commun. Conf.*, 116–17.
Braverman, E. M. (1966), 'The method of potential functions in the problem of training machines to recognize patterns without a trainer', *Automat. Remote Contr.*, **27**, 1748–71.
Dorofeyuk, A. A. (1966), 'Teaching algorithm for a pattern recognition machine without

a teacher, based on the method of potential functions', *Automat. Remote Contr.*, **27**, 1728–37.

Gonzalez, R. C., D. N. Fry and R. C. Kryter (1974), 'Results in the application of pattern recognition methods to nuclear reactor core component surveillance', *IEEE Trans. Nucl. Sci.*, **21**, (1), 750–7.

Macciadi, A. N. and E. L. Gose (1970), 'An algorithm for automatic clustering in *N*-dimensional spaces using hyperellipsoidal cells', *Proc. IEEE Sys. Sci. Cybernetics Conf., Pittsburgh*.

MacQueen, J. (1967), 'Some methods for classification and analysis of multivariate data', *Proceedings of 5th Berkeley Symp. on Probability and Statistics*, Berkeley: University of California Press.

Zahn, C. T. (1971), 'Graph-theoretical methods for detecing and describing Gestalt clusters', *IEEE Trans. Computers*, **20**, 68–86.

19

Feature Selection

19.1 Introduction

One of the main problems in pattern recognition is the choice of the 'best' features in a given problem, while ignoring inessential data. In this context 'best' means the features which separate the clusters representing pattern classes in some optimal way. There are two approaches to this problem – direct and indirect. The former technique tends to be applied to specific problems and has strong connections with syntactic methods and layered networks. Since these will be discussed in detail later, we shall concentrate on the indirect methods in this chapter.

Most of the indirect methods can be formulated as follows. First recall that we began this part of the book by showing how to determine a measurement space Z for a particular pattern recognition problem. A *feature map* is a function

$$\mathbf{x} = F(\mathbf{z})$$

from Z-space into X-space, where $\dim X < \dim Z$. The feature selection problem can be regarded as the selection of an appropriate feature map from a collection of such maps, parameterized by a set of symbols $\lambda = (\lambda_1, \lambda_2, \ldots)$ belonging to some set L. Thus, let

$$\mathcal{F} = \{F(\mathbf{z}, \lambda) : \lambda \in L\}$$

be the set of these feature maps. The effectiveness of any given feature map $F(\mathbf{z}, \lambda)$ in separating the samples is measured by a *quality index* $Q(\lambda)$ which is designed to be small when the samples are tightly clustered and well separated and larger otherwise. The 'best' feature map $F(.,\lambda)$ is then given by the solution of the optimization problem:

$$\min_{\lambda \in L} Q(\lambda)$$

In the next section we shall discuss various quality indices and then, in the following section, the construction of feature maps will be considered.

19.2 Measures of quality

Measures of quality are often chosen on the basis of how any given feature map separates clusters and keeps the samples of individual clusters close together. This can be achieved by using interset and intraset distances. Consider first the intraset distance (i.e. a measure of the average distance between samples of the same cluster). If $\{\mathbf{x}^i\}$ are the samples in a given cluster, then the mean square distance $D(\mathbf{x})$ of any point $\mathbf{x}$ to the samples is given by

$$D(\mathbf{x}) = \frac{1}{M} \sum_{i=1}^{M} d^2(\mathbf{x}, \mathbf{x}^i) \tag{19.2.1}$$

where M is the number of samples in the cluster and d is any distance measure. In particular, the mean square distance from sample i to the other samples of the cluster is

$$D(\mathbf{x}^i) = \frac{1}{M-1} \sum_{j=1}^{M} d^2(\mathbf{x}^i, \mathbf{x}^j) \tag{19.2.2}$$

We then define the *intraset distance* D_{intra} by

$$D_{intra} = \frac{1}{M(M-1)} \sum_{i=1}^{M} \sum_{j=1}^{M} d^2(\mathbf{x}^i, \mathbf{x}^j) \tag{19.2.3}$$

i.e. the mean of (19.2.2) over all samples.

The *interset distance* D_{inter} is defined similarly. This time the samples of one cluster are (generally) distinct from those of another and so we put

$$D_{inter} = \frac{1}{M_1 M_2} \sum_{i=1}^{M_1} \sum_{j=1}^{M_2} d^2(\mathbf{x}^i, \mathbf{y}^j) \qquad (19.2.4)$$

where $\{\mathbf{x}^i\}$ $(1 \le i \le M_1)$ are the samples of one cluster and $\{\mathbf{y}^j\}$ $(1 \le j \le M_2)$ are the samples of the other.

A measure of quality $Q(\lambda)$ can now be defined in terms of the interset and intraset distances as follows. Let $F(\mathbf{z}, \lambda)$ be a given feature map and let $C_i(\lambda)$ be the sets

$$C_i(\lambda) = \{\mathbf{x} \in X : \mathbf{x} = F(\mathbf{z}, \lambda), \qquad \mathbf{z} \in C_i\}$$

where C_i are the classes in measurement (Z-) space. Denote by D^i_{intra} and D^{ij}_{inter} the intraset and interset distances, respectively, of the mapped clusters $C_i(\lambda)$, $C_j(\lambda)$. Then we can define a measure of quality by

$$Q(\lambda) = \frac{\sum_{i=1}^{K} D^i_{intra}}{\sum_{\substack{i=1 \\ i \ne j}}^{K} \sum_{j=1}^{K} D^{ij}_{inter}} \qquad (19.2.5)$$

Note that in (19.2.1), the distance d^2 is often taken to be the standard Euclidean norm. However, this is not appropriate for multimodal distributions or clusters which tend to form sheets. One suggested approach is to use a 'localized distance' defined by

$$\bar{d}(\mathbf{x}, \mathbf{y}) = \begin{cases} d(\mathbf{x}, \mathbf{y}) & \text{for } d(\mathbf{x}, \mathbf{y}) \le D \\ D & \text{for } d(\mathbf{x}, \mathbf{y}) > D \end{cases} \qquad (19.2.6)$$

Alternatively, we could set

$$\bar{d}(\mathbf{x}, \mathbf{y}) = 1 - \exp\left[-\frac{1}{2D^2} d^2(\mathbf{x}, \mathbf{y})\right] \qquad (19.2.7)$$

These measures have the effect of not significantly weighting distant samples of the same cluster. In many cases, the samples lie on lower-dimensional manifolds and so it is better to use a measure of quality which merely reduces the dimension of the space, while preserving the distances between the samples. Such a measure is given by

$$Q(\lambda) = \frac{2}{M(M-1)} \sum_{i<j} \{d_n[F(\mathbf{z}_i, \lambda), F(\mathbf{z}_j, \lambda)] - d_N(\mathbf{z}_i, \mathbf{z}_j)\}^2 \quad (19.2.8)$$

where M is now the total number of samples in the sample set $\{\mathbf{z}_1, \ldots, \mathbf{z}_N\}$ and d_n, d_N are distances in pattern and measurement spaces respectively. This measure can be localized as in (19.2.7) to obtain the measure

$$Q(\lambda) = \frac{2}{M(M-1)} \sum_{i<j} \{d_n[F(\mathbf{z}_i, \lambda), F(\mathbf{z}_j, \lambda)] - d_N(\mathbf{z}_i, \mathbf{z}_j)\}^2$$

$$\times \exp\left(-\frac{1}{2D^2} d_n[F(\mathbf{z}_i, \lambda) F(\mathbf{z}_j, \lambda)]\right) \qquad (19.2.9)$$

This measure can be used when the samples lie on curved manifolds of lower dimension (surfaces of spheres, etc.).

19.3 Clustering transformations and feature ranking

Feature selection can be approached by separating the problems of optimal clustering and dimension reduction. The latter problem is solved by some form of *feature ranking* which places the features in an order of significance. The dimension of the space can then be reduced merely by choosing the n most significant features. The former problem can be solved by minimizing a measure of quality such as one of those defined above with an appropriate feature map $F(z, \lambda)$. The simplest type of transformation F is given by a linear function

$$z' \triangleq F(\mathbf{z} \ \lambda) = \Lambda \mathbf{z} \tag{19.3.1}$$

where

$$\Lambda = (\lambda_{ij}) \qquad 1 \leqslant i, j \leqslant N$$

is a matrix of parameters. Note that Λ is a square matrix since we are first trying to cluster the samples without reducing the dimension of the measurement space. A simple numerical procedure can then be used to minimize any of the measures of quality derived in Section 19.2. The dimension of the feature space can be reduced by a second transformation

$$\mathbf{x} = \Lambda' \mathbf{z}'$$

where Λ' is chosen to diagonalize the covariance matrix of the samples. The features are then ordered according to the increasing size of the covariance eigenvalues. Larger eigenvalues of the covariance matrix imply more spread in the samples in that direction, which in turn implies less confidence in that feature. The directions corresponding to the n smallest covariances are then chosen as the features. It is important in such 'feature ranking' procedures to ensure that the retained features are reasonably uncorrelated; otherwise the data will contain a large amount of redundancy.

Linear transformations are somewhat restrictive, however, and it is sometimes useful to try a piecewise-linear map of the form

$$\mathbf{x} = F(\mathbf{z}) = \begin{cases} \Lambda_1 \mathbf{z} + \mathbf{c}_1 & \mathbf{z} \in Z_1 \\ \vdots & \\ \Lambda_R \mathbf{z} + \mathbf{c}_R & \mathbf{z} \in Z_R \end{cases} \tag{19.3.2}$$

where $\{Z_1, \ldots, Z_R\}$ is a partition of $Z = \mathbb{R}^N$ (or a partition of a subset of $\mathbb{R}^N$ containing all the pattern samples). As an example, consider the three-class example in Figure 19.1(a). Note that two of the classes are multimodal in two-dimensional feature space. Consider the piecewise-linear map

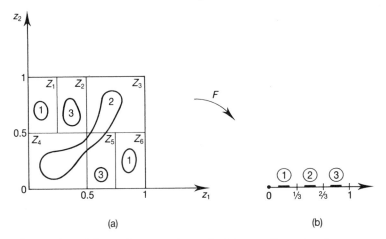

Figure 19.1   Three-class sample set in (a) two-dimensional measurement space, and (b) one-dimensional pattern space.

$$F(z_1, z_2) = \begin{cases} (z_2 - 1/2) \cdot 2/3 & \mathbf{z} \in Z_1 \\ 2/3 + (z_2 - 1/2) \cdot 2/3 & \mathbf{z} \in Z_2 \\ 1/3 + (z_2 - 1/2) \cdot 2/3 & \mathbf{z} \in Z_3 \\ 1/3 + z_1 \cdot 2/3 & \mathbf{z} \in Z_4 \\ 1/3 + 4/3 \cdot (1/2 - z_2) & \mathbf{z} \in Z_5 \\ z_2 \cdot 2/3 & \mathbf{z} \in Z_6 \end{cases}$$

The map F keeps the clusters separate and even changes the classes 1 and 3 to unimodal distributions. Also, F reduces the dimension and so clustering and feature extraction are performed with the same map. The use of piecewise-linear transformation is therefore much more powerful than with linear ones.

19.4 Entropy methods

When we perform a pattern recognition operation we are trying to determine how 'close' a given sample is to some ideal pattern. As we have seen in the last chapter, it is important for the samples of a given class to be tightly clustered. The more dispersed the samples are along a given direction in measurement (or pattern) space, the more uncertainty there is in the data. We would therefore like to minimize the uncertainty in each direction and choose the features corresponding to the n smallest uncertainties. Entropy is a measure of uncertainty and so we must first define this concept.

To define entropy we shall begin by outlining the basic ideas of information theory. Information content is, of course, related to uncertainty; in fact, we could regard information content in a signal to be the amount of unpredictable change. If a signal is completely predictable (for example, an electronic signal of a constant voltage), then it contains no information. To quantify the amount of information in a signal, consider a discrete signal over a time interval $[0, T]$ such that the signal is constant over sampling periods of length τ and takes values in a discrete set $\{v_0, \ldots, v_{n-1}\}$ (i.e. there are n possible levels for each signal value in a sampling interval – see Figure 19.2). The number of possible signals (or messages) which can be generated in $[0, T]$ is therefore $n^{T/\tau}$. This could reasonably be used as a measure of the information content in a set of message samples. However, it is natural to expect that if we double the signal time interval to $[0, 2T]$, then we should double the information content. For this reason we define the information in T seconds to be

$$H = \frac{T}{\tau} \ln n$$

(We can take the log to any base. Here we shall use the natural logarithm as being the most appropriate. In computer communications, base 2 is used and then information is measured in *bits*.) If each level $v_0, \ldots, v_{n-1}$ is equally likely, then the probability of any one level is $p = 1/n$. Hence,

$$H = \frac{T}{\tau} \ln n = -\frac{T}{\tau} \ln p$$

In many cases, the levels are not equally likely and so we must modify the definition of H. Thus, if v_i occurs $R_i(N)$ times in a long series of N trials, then the information content in N intervals is

$$H = -\sum_{i=0}^{n-1} R_i(N) \ln p_i$$

where p_i is the probability of v_i. However,

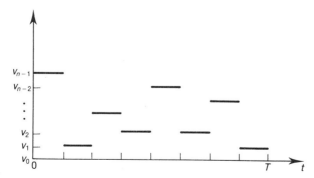

Figure 19.2   A discrete signal.

$$\lim_{N \to \infty} \frac{R_i(N)}{N} = p_i$$

and so in T/τ intervals (assuming T/τ is large) we have

$$H = -\frac{T}{\tau} \sum_{i=0}^{n-1} p_i \ln p_i$$

Returning to the case of pattern populations with probability densities $p(\mathbf{x}|i) = p_i(\mathbf{x})$ we define the *entropy* of the ith class to be

$$H = -\int_x p(\mathbf{x}|i) \ln p(\mathbf{x}|i) \mathrm{d}x = -E\{\ln p(\mathbf{x}|i)\} \tag{19.4.1}$$

which we recognize as a continuous version of the information in a discrete signal. Of course, if $p(\mathbf{x}|i) = 1$, then $H = 0$ and there is no uncertainty.

Returning now to the problem of feature selection, let

$$\mathbf{x} = A\mathbf{z} \tag{19.4.2}$$

be a linear feature map where the elements of A are the parameters which are to be found (A is an $n \times N$ matrix, where $n < N$). We shall suppose for simplicity that the probability densities of the clusters in Z-space $p(\mathbf{z}|i)$ are given by

$$p(\mathbf{z}|i) = \frac{1}{(2\pi)^{N/2}|C|^{1/2}} \exp\left[-\tfrac{1}{2}(\mathbf{z} - \mathbf{m}_i)^{\mathrm{T}} C^{-1}(\mathbf{z} - \mathbf{m}_i)\right] \tag{19.4.3}$$

where the covariance is independent of i. By (19.4.2), we have

$$\mathbf{m}_i' = A\mathbf{m}_i$$

and

$$C' = E\{(\mathbf{x} - \mathbf{m}_i')(\mathbf{x} - \mathbf{m}_i')^{\mathrm{T}}\}$$

for the transformed mean and covariances. Thus,

$$C' = AE\{(\mathbf{z} - \mathbf{m}_i')(\mathbf{z} - \mathbf{m}_i')^{\mathrm{T}}\}A^{\mathrm{T}} = ACA^{\mathrm{T}}$$

Hence, the probability density functions for the transformed clusters are

$$p(\mathbf{x}|i) = \frac{1}{(2\pi)^{n/2}|ACA^{\mathrm{T}}|^{1/2}} \exp\left[-\tfrac{1}{2}(\mathbf{x} - \mathbf{m}_i')^{\mathrm{T}}(ACA^{\mathrm{T}})^{-1}(\mathbf{x} - \mathbf{m}_i')\right] \tag{19.4.4}$$

Substituting (19.4.4) into the definition of entropy (19.4.1) and minimizing with respect to the elements of A shows that $A = (a_{ij})$ is given by

$$C\mathbf{a}_i = \lambda_i \mathbf{a}_i \qquad 1 \leqslant i \leqslant n \tag{19.4.5}$$

where $\mathbf{a}_i = (a_{i1}, \ldots, a_{iN})$ is the ith row of A and $\lambda_1, \ldots, \lambda_n$ are the n smallest eigenvalues of C.

19.5 *Functional methods*

In Chapter 12 we have discussed the ideas of data compression by functional expansion. For example, if $f(x, y)$ is an image representation (in terms of grey levels) over some rectangle $[0, 1] \times [0, 1]$, say, then it is possible to write

$$f(x, y) = \sum_{i=1}^{\infty} \langle f, \phi_i \rangle \phi_i(x, y) \tag{19.5.1}$$

where

$$\langle f, \phi_i \rangle = \int_0^1 \int_0^1 f(x, y) \phi_i(x, y) \mathrm{d}x \mathrm{d}y$$

and $\{\phi_i\}$ is a set of orthonormal functions; i.e.

$$\langle \phi_i, \phi_j \rangle = \begin{cases} 0 & \text{if } i \neq j \\ 1 & \text{if } i = j \end{cases}$$

The first n Fourier coefficients $a_i \triangleq \langle f, \phi_i \rangle$, $1 \leqslant i \leqslant n$, of f are then selected as the features representing the 'pattern' f. Although examples of orthonormal sequences of functions were given, only a brief mention was made about the 'best' choice of the functions ϕ_i. To clarify what is meant by best, consider the error $E(x, y)$ between f and the truncated expansion of f in terms of $\phi_1, \ldots, \phi_n$, i.e.

$$E(x, y; f, \{\phi_i\}) = f(x, y) - \sum_{i=1}^{n} \langle f, \phi_i \rangle \phi_i(x, y)$$

We have explicitly indicated the fact that E depends on the orthonormal sequence $\{\phi_i\}$ and f. The best o.n. sequence then, will be the one which minimizes $\|E(x, y; f, \{\phi_i\})\|^2$ for a given picture $f(x, y)$. In fact, we can determine the best o.n. sequence $\{\phi_i\}$ for a finite set of sample pictures or patterns $f_1(x, y), \ldots, f_n(x, y)$ by minimizing

$$Q \triangleq \sum_{i=1}^{m} \left\| f_i - \sum_{j=1}^{n} \langle f_i, \phi_j \rangle \phi_j \right\|^2 \tag{19.5.2}$$

with respect to ϕ_j, $1 \leqslant j \leqslant n$. Q is a function defined on the infinite-dimensional space of functions $\phi(x, y)$, $(x, y) \in [0, 1] \times [0, 1]$ and so we cannot optimize Q merely by 'differentiating with respect to the variables'. However, we can define a derivative on such a space which is equivalent to partial differentiation in finite-dimensional vector spaces. Thus, let C^2 denote the space of functions $\phi(x, y)$ defined on $[0, 1] \times [0, 1]$ which are twice continuously differentiable. Clearly, C^2 is a vector space of infinite dimension. Let $F : C^2 \to \mathbb{R}$ be a real-valued function defined on C^2 and write

$$\delta F(\phi_0; \psi) = \frac{\mathrm{d}}{\mathrm{d}\varepsilon} F(\phi_0 + \varepsilon\psi) \bigg|_{\varepsilon=0}, \ \psi \in C^2$$

Then $\delta F(\phi_0; \psi)$ is called the *directional* (or *Gateaux*) *derivative* of F (with respect to ϕ) at ϕ_0 in the direction ψ. For example, if $F(\phi) = \langle \phi, \xi \rangle$ for some fixed ξ, then

$$\delta F(\phi; \psi) = \frac{d}{d\varepsilon} \langle \phi + \varepsilon\psi, \xi \rangle \bigg|_{\varepsilon=0}$$

$$= \langle \psi, \xi \rangle \tag{19.5.3}$$

Similarly, if $F(\phi) = \|\phi\|^2$, then

$$\delta F(\phi; \psi) = \frac{d}{d\varepsilon} \langle \phi + \varepsilon\psi, \phi + \varepsilon\psi \rangle \bigg|_{\varepsilon=0}$$

$$= 2\langle \phi, \psi \rangle \tag{19.5.3}$$

It can be shown that a necessary condition for a minimum of $F(\phi)$ at ϕ_0 is that

$$\delta F(\phi_0; \psi) = 0$$

for all $\psi \in C^2$.

Returning to (19.5.2), a necessary condition for a minimum of Q is that

$$\delta Q(\phi; \psi) = 0$$

for all ψ. Now,

$$Q = \sum_{i=1}^{m} \left\langle f_i - \sum_{j=1}^{n} \langle f_i, \phi_j \rangle \phi_j, f_i - \sum_{k=1}^{n} \langle f_i, \phi_k \rangle \phi_k \right\rangle$$

$$= \sum_{i=1}^{m} \langle f_i, f_i \rangle - \sum_{i=1}^{m} \sum_{j=1}^{n} \langle f_i, \phi_j \rangle^2 \tag{19.5.5}$$

since the ϕs are orthonormal. We want to minimize Q with respect to the ϕ_js subject to the constraint

$$\langle \phi_i, \phi_i \rangle = \|\phi_i\|^2 = 1 \qquad 1 \le i, j \le n$$

As in the case of finite-dimensional optimization, it can be shown that this is equivalent to minimizing

$$Q_\lambda \triangleq Q + \sum_{j=1}^{n} \lambda_j (\langle \phi_j, \phi_j \rangle - 1)$$

where λ_j are Lagrange multipliers. Since the first term in Q given by (19.5.5) is constant we can simply minimize

$$Q'_\lambda \triangleq -\sum_{i=1}^{m} \sum_{j=1}^{n} \langle f_i, \phi_j \rangle^2 + \sum_{j=1}^{n} \lambda_j (\langle \phi_j, \phi_j \rangle - 1)$$

By (19.5.3) and (19.5.4), we have

$$\delta Q'_\lambda(\phi_k; \psi) = -2 \sum_{i=1}^{m} \langle f_i, \phi_k \rangle \langle f_i, \psi \rangle - 2\lambda_k \langle \phi_k, \psi \rangle$$

This is zero for all ψ if and only if

$$\sum_{i=1}^{m} \langle f_i, \phi_k \rangle f_i - \lambda_k \phi_k = 0$$

i.e.

$$\sum_{i=1}^{m} \int_0^1 \int_0^1 f_i(x, y) f_i(x', y') \phi_k(x', y') dx' dy' = \lambda_k \phi_k(x, y)$$

Let $K : C^2 \rightarrow C^2$ be the map defined by

$$(K\phi)(x, y) = \sum_{i=1}^{m} \int_0^1 \int_0^1 f_i(x, y) f_i(x', y') \phi(x', y') dx' dy'$$

Then we have

$$K\phi_k = \lambda_k \phi_k \qquad (19.5.6)$$

and so the optimal choice of the o.n. sequence $\{\phi_k\}$ is given by the orthonormal eigenfunctions of the operator K. The expression (19.5.1) for f in terms of such functions ϕ_k is called the *Karhunen–Loève* expansion. Note that a similar derivation can be given in the discrete case, giving rise to a matrix equation of the form (19.5.6).

19.6 *Stochastic methods and divergence maximization*

We have seen in Chapter 17 the application of Bayes' rule to the determination of statistical decision boundaries. In particular, we derived the decision rule

$$c(\mathbf{x}) = i \qquad \text{if } \rho_i p_i(\mathbf{x}) \geq \rho_j p_j(\mathbf{x}) \qquad \text{for all } j \neq i \qquad (19.6.1)$$

We can use the probability densities ρ_i, $p_i(\mathbf{x})$ to measure the separability of clusters when a feature transformation $\mathbf{x} = F(\mathbf{z}, \boldsymbol{\lambda})$ is applied to measurement space. Many such measures of quality have been suggested – we shall mention only the most obvious, namely that of *divergence*. Thus we define

$$\begin{aligned}
Q_{ij}(\boldsymbol{\lambda}) &= \int_X \{\rho_i p_i(\mathbf{x}) - \rho_j p_j(\mathbf{x})\} \log\left[\frac{\rho_i p_i(\mathbf{x})}{\rho_j p_j(\mathbf{x})}\right] d\mathbf{x} \\
&= \int_Z \{\rho_i p_i(F(\mathbf{z}, \boldsymbol{\lambda})) - \rho_j p_j(F(\mathbf{z}, \boldsymbol{\lambda}))\} \log\left[\frac{\rho_i p_i(F(\mathbf{z}, \boldsymbol{\lambda}))}{\rho_j p_j(F(\mathbf{z}, \boldsymbol{\lambda}))}\right] \frac{\partial F}{\partial \mathbf{z}} d\mathbf{z}
\end{aligned}$$

It is easily seen that $Q_{ij}(\boldsymbol{\lambda})$ increases as the probability densities $\rho_i p_i(\mathbf{x})$, $\rho_j p_j(\mathbf{x})$ become more separated (Figure 19.3). Here, Q_{12} in Figure 19.3(a) is smaller than Q_{12} in Figure 19.3(b). (Note that $Q_{ij}(\boldsymbol{\lambda}) \geq 0$.)

In the case of normal populations, with

$$p_i(\mathbf{x}) = \frac{1}{(2\pi)^{n/2} |C_i|^{1/2}} \exp\left[-\tfrac{1}{2}(\mathbf{x} - \mathbf{m}_i)^{\mathrm{T}} C_i^{-1} (\mathbf{x} - \mathbf{m}_i)\right]$$

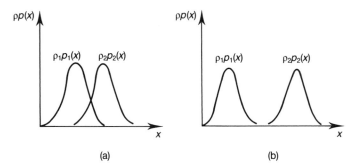

Figure 19.3 Typical probability densities in a two-class problem: (a) intersecting; (b) distinct densities.

and $\rho_i = 1$ then the divergence is given by

$$Q_{ij} = \tfrac{1}{2}\mathrm{tr}\,[(C_i - C_j)(C_j^{-1} - C_i^{-1})] + \tfrac{1}{2}\mathrm{tr}\,[(C_i^{-1} + C_j^{-1})(\mathbf{m}_i - \mathbf{m}_j)(\mathbf{m}_i - \mathbf{m}_j)^{\mathrm{T}}]$$

$$(19.6.2)$$

If $C_i = C_j = C$, then

$$Q_{ij} = (\mathbf{m}_i - \mathbf{m}_j)^{\mathrm{T}} C^{-1} (\mathbf{m}_i - \mathbf{m}_j)$$

which is just the *Mahalanobis distance*. Hence the divergence can be regarded as a generalized distance.

For a problem with K clusters, we can minimize (numerically) the measure of quality

$$Q = \sum_{\substack{i,j \\ i \neq j}} Q_{ij}(\lambda)$$

over the set $\mathcal{F}$ of all feature maps in the given class. In the case of a two-cluster problem with normal populations as above (with $C_1 = C_2$), and linear transformations of the form

$$x = \lambda \mathbf{z}$$

where x is a scalar and λ is a vector of parameters, the necessary condition for Q_{12} to be a maximum is that

$$(C^{-1}(\mathbf{m}_1 - \mathbf{m}_2)(\mathbf{m}_1 - \mathbf{m}_2)^{\mathrm{T}})\lambda = \left(\frac{\lambda^{\mathrm{T}}(\mathbf{m}_1 - \mathbf{m}_2)(\mathbf{m}_1 - \mathbf{m}_2)^{\mathrm{T}}\lambda}{\lambda^{\mathrm{T}} C \lambda} \right) \lambda \quad (19.6.3)$$

so that λ is an eigenvector of $C^{-1}(\mathbf{m}_1 - \mathbf{m}_2)(\mathbf{m}_1 - \mathbf{m}_2)^{\mathrm{T}}$. If the probability densities are not known, *a priori*, then they can be estimated by any of the methods discussed earlier.

19.7 Binary feature selection

The feature selection methods described above are all used mainly for continuous patterns. In Chapter 15 we discussed several methods for discretizing patterns; in particular, for the character recognition problem the discretized samples consisted of a binary array, the elements of which are 1 or 0 depending on whether part of the character intersects the corresponding grid element. Feature selection for such binary patterns requires special techniques, one of which will be described in this section.

In order to specify the method, consider the binary patterns shown in Figure 19.4, where a black square indicates a '1' and a white square a '0'. We introduce the Boolean operations '.' and '+' on such patterns by setting

$$\left.\begin{array}{c} (P \cdot Q)_{ij} = p_{ij} \cdot q_{ij} \\ (P + Q)_{ij} = p_{ij} + q_{ij} \end{array}\right\} \qquad (19.7.1)$$

where p_{ij} ($= 0$ or 1) is the (i, j)th element of the binary matrix P and the symbols '.' and '+' on the right-hand sides of (19.7.1) have their usual (Boolean) meanings. (Note that $(P)_{ij}$ also denotes the (i, j)th element of P.) With this definition of Boolean operations we have the Boolean *identity pattern*

$$(I)_{ij} = 1 \qquad \text{for all } i, j$$

Then we have

$$P \cdot I = P \qquad P + I = I$$

For any binary pattern $P = (p_{ij})$ let

$$|P| = \sum_i \sum_j p_{ij}$$

Thus, in the case of 4×4 patterns, $|I| = 16$.

Now let $P_1, \ldots, P_N$ be a given set of patterns, then we wish to find the minimum number of features $F_1, \ldots, F_n$ (which are themselves patterns of the same size as the Ps) such that each P_i can be written (nonuniquely!) as a sum of Fs, i.e.

$$P_i = F_{i_1} + \ldots + F_{i_l}$$

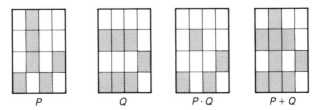

Figure 19.4   Binary patterns and Boolean operations.

for some l, where $i_1, \ldots, i_l \in \{1, \ldots, n\}$. Two algorithms are commonly used to determine the Fs – a sequential or a parallel algorithm. In the sequential algorithm, the features are determined sequentially, each one being obtained by a single pass through the given patterns $P_1, \ldots, P_N$. Thus, for example, F_1 is first set equal to I and an arbitrary threshold θ is chosen. Then we replace F_1 by $F_1 \cdot P_1$ if $|F_1 \cdot P_1| \geq \theta$ and otherwise leave F_1 unchanged. Similarly, if $|F_1 \cdot P_2| \geq \theta$, then we replace F_1 by $F_1 \cdot P_2$ and otherwise leave F_1 unchanged. This is repeated for all $P_1, \ldots, P_N$. Next we set $F_2 = I$ and follow a similar procedure to that in which F_1 was obtained. However, this time the threshold is changed at each step. Thus we define the threshold $\theta' = \theta + |F_1 \cdot (F_2 \cdot P_1)|$ to start the second iteration, and if $|F_2 \cdot P_1| \geq \theta'$ we replace F_2 by $F_2 \cdot P_1$ and otherwise leave F_2 unchanged. (In the definition of θ', F_1 is the final value of

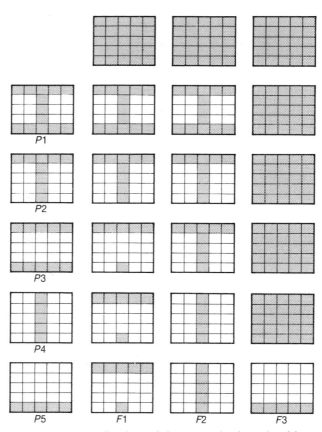

Figure 19.5 Application of feature selection algorithm for binary patterns P1, . . ., P5, ($\theta = 3$).

the first feature obtained at the end of the first iteration.) In general, at the ith stage of the second iteration we replace F_2 by $F_2 \cdot P_i$ if $\theta' = \theta + |F_1 \cdot (F_2 \cdot P_i)| \leq |F_2 \cdot P_i|$ and otherwise leave F_2 unchanged. At the end of the second iteration we check to see if each P_i is equal to F_1, F_2 or $F_1 + F_2$. If not then we continue to the third iteration, and so on until each P_i can be written in terms of the features found up to that iteration.

Stated formally, the sequential algorithm may be written:

(i)   Choose θ; set i = 1.
(ii)   repeat
        (a) $F_i = I$
        (b) for $j = 1$ to N:
                if $i > 1$ then set $\theta' = \theta + |F_{i-1} \cdot (F_i \cdot P_j)|$
                if $i = 1$ then set $\theta' = \theta$
                if $|F_i \cdot P_j| \geq \theta'$ then replace F_i by $F_i \cdot P_j$
                otherwise leave F_i unchanged.
        (c) $i := i + 1$.
until each P_k can be written as a sum of Fs.

An example of this procedure is shown in Figure 19.5, where the features for five simple patterns are found. Note that the algorithm depends strongly on the initial value of θ and different values of this parameter must be tried to obtain the best results.

It is possible to determine a parallel algorithm where the patterns are again presented in sequence, but each new pattern becomes a new feature if it cannot be expressed in terms of existing features. Thus, new features appear in the algorithm before existing features are completely fixed.

Bibliographical notes

The ideas of inter- and intraset distances are discussed in detail in Babu (1973) and Sebestyen (1962) and further consideration of feature ranking is given in Henrichon and Fu (1969) and Nelson and Levy (1968). The minimum entropy technique is taken from Tou and Heydorn (1967) and functional expansions were developed successively in Karhunen (1960), Watanabe (1965) and Chien and Fu (1967). Divergence and other statistical measures are discussed in Kullback (1958), Reza (1961), Tou and Heydorn (1967), Kailath (1967), Meisel (1971), Patrick Fischer (1969). Finall the binary feature selection algorithm is taken from Block *et al.* (1964), where details of the parallel algorithm can be found.

Exercises

1 Discuss the effect of using a localized distance such as (19.2.6) in a measure of quality.

2 Prove that the example in Figure 19.1 can be generalized to any dimension; i.e. that there exists a piecewise-linear map from $Z \subseteq \mathbb{R}^N$ to $\mathbb{R}^1$ which separates clusters and changes multimodal distributions to unimodal ones, provided the clusters in Z-space are contained in nonintersecting compact sets.

3 Prove (19.4.5).

4 Derive the discrete version of the Karhunen-Loève equation (19.5.6).

5 Discuss the effect of varying the initial value of θ in the sequential binary feature selection algorithm.

References

Babu, C. (1973), 'On the application of probabilistic distance measures for the extraction of features from imperfectly labelled patterns', *Int. J. Computer and Inf. Sci.*, **2**, 103–14.

Block, H. D., N. J. Nilsson and R. O. Duda (1964), 'Determination and detection of features in patterns', in *Computer and Inf. Sciences* – I (J. T. Tou and R. H. Wilcox, eds.) Washington DC: Spartan Books.

Chien, Y. T. and K. S. Fu. (1967), 'On the generalized Karhunen–Loève expansion', *IEEE Trans. Inf. Theory*, **IT-13** (3), 518–20.

Henrichon, E. G. Jr. and K. S. Fu (1969), 'A nonparametric partitioning procedure for pattern classification', *IEEE Trans. Computers.*, **18**, 614–24.

Kailath, T. (1967), 'The divergence and Bhattacharyya distance measure in signal selection', *IEEE Trans. Comm. Technol.*, **15**, 52–60.

Karhunen, K. (1947), 'Uber Lineare Methoden in der Wahrscheinlichkeitsrechnung', *Ann. Acad. Sci. Fennicae, Ser. A137* (translated by I. Selin in 'On linear methods in probability theory', T-131, 1960, California: the RAND Corp., Santa Monica).

Kullback, S. (1958), *Information Theory and Statistics*, NY: Wiley.

Meisel, W. S. (1971), 'On nonparametric feature selection', *IEEE Trans. Inf. Theory*, **17**, 105–6.

Nelson, G. D. and D. M. Levy (1968), 'A dynamic programming approach to the selection of pattern features', *IEEE Trans. Sys. Science and Cybernetics*, **4**, 145–51.

Patrick, E. A. and F. P. Fischer II (1969), 'Nonparametric feature selection', *IEEE Trans. Inf. Theory*, **15**, 577–84.

Reza, F. M. (1961), *An Introduction to Information Theory*, NY: McGraw-Hill.

Sebestyen, G. S. (1962), *Decision Making Processes in Pattern Recognition* NY: Macmillan.

Tou, J. T. and R. P. Heydorn (1967), 'Some approaches to optimum feature extraction', in *Computer and Inf. Sciences* – II (J. T. Tou, ed.), NY: Academic Press.

Watanabe, S. (1965), 'Karhunen–Loève expansion and factor analysis – theoretical remarks and applications', *Proc. of 4th Conf. on Inf. Theory, Prague*.

20

Syntactic Methods

20.1 Introduction

In the preceding chapters on pattern recognition we have described techniques which use only the lowest level of information in the patterns to be recognized. Thus, discretization schemes use a simple regular sampling approach or a general functional expansion method, neither of which takes account of the pattern interpretation, or its structure. For example, we began by discussing the character recognition problem and introduced the obvious discretization consisting of regular sampling on a rectangular grid. Each element of the grid is coded with a '1' or a '0' depending on whether or not the character intersects the grid. This leads to a large number of features, however, and it is better to seek methods which take into account the shape of the characters directly. Thus, an 'A' has three straight lines meeting in a certain way and so can be recognized from three features and a rule for their combination.

The idea of the syntactic approach to pattern recognition is therefore to decompose a complex pattern into a hierarchy of simpler subpatterns and to develop a rule by which the subpatterns are to be combined to form a high-level pattern. The act of decomposing a pattern is called *parsing* and the rules of combination of subpatterns are based on formal language theory. The latter uses techniques similar to those used in ordinary languages which have syntactic rules for the combination of words – indeed, sentences in ordinary language can be regarded as complex patterns which we comprehend by syntactic rules learned in childhood.

The lowest-level pattern features which are to be the component forms of all the given high-level patterns are often called *pattern primitives* and correspond to the basic symbols in formal language theory. One of the most difficult aspects of syntactic pattern recognition is the selection of pattern primitives (which is essentially a feature selection problem). These primitives are then combined to form the given patterns. The method of combination is defined by the *pattern grammar* so that given primitives may or may not 'fit together'. The overall pattern recognition process proceeds in a similar way to the decision-theoretic approaches discussed earlier. Thus, a given set of sample patterns is analysed to find the pattern primitives and the associated pattern grammar, i.e. the rules for combining the pattern primitives. This is the training phase, as before. Then new patterns are presented to the machine, which separates each pattern into its primitives and then decides whether it is an acceptable pattern by *parsing* the string consisting of the pattern primitives making up the sample pattern. The parsing can be done in one of two ways – bottom–up or top–down. In bottom–up processing the primitive string is reduced to a starting symbol, if possible, by applying the grammatical rules 'in reverse'. In top–down parsing the initial symbol and other 'nonterminal' symbols are replaced using the rules of the grammar by other symbol strings until only 'terminal' symbols (which in this case are pattern primitives) remain. The pattern is accepted if it can be obtained from the initial symbol in this way. A simple syntactic recognition system is shown in Figure 20.1.

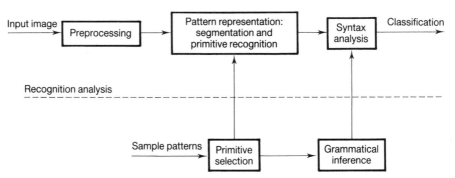

Figure 20.1 Syntactic pattern recognition system.

20.2 *Formal language theory*

We begin by abstracting the basic elements of an ordinary (written) language. An *alphabet* is a finite nonempty set V whose elements are called *letters*. A *word w* (over V) is a finite string of zero or more letters of V, its length $|w|$ being the number of letters in the string. The (unique) word of length 0 is denoted by Λ. The set of all words over V is denoted by $W(V)$ or just W if no confusion over the set of letters is likely.

If $P, Q \in W$ then PQ denotes their *concatenation*. Note that concatenation is associative and $P\Lambda = \Lambda P = P$ for all $P \in W$. P is a *subword* of Q if $Q = P_1 P P_2$ for some $P_1, P_2 \in W$. Subsets of W are called *languages* (over V).

A *generative grammar* (or *phrase structure grammar*) is a quadruple $G = (V_N, V_T, S, F)$ where V_N and V_T are disjoint alphabets, $S \in V_N$ and F is a finite set of ordered pairs (P, Q) such that $P, Q \in W(V)$, where $V = V_N \cup V_T$ and P contains at least one letter of V_N. The elements of V_N are called *nonterminals* and those of V_T *terminals*, while S is called the *initial letter*. If $(P, Q) \in F$ we write

$$P \to Q$$

Such an element (P, Q) is called a *rewriting rule* or *production*. We say that P *generates Q directly* and write $P \Rightarrow Q$ if there exist words R, T and a production $P_1 \to Q_1 \in F$ such that $P = RP_1T$ and $Q = RQ_1T$. Similarly, we say that P *generates Q* and write $P \Rightarrow^* Q$ if there exists a finite sequence of words $P_0, \ldots, P_k$ such that $P_0 = P$, $P_k = Q$ and $P_i \Rightarrow P_{i+1}$ for $0 \leqslant i \leqslant k - 1$. Thus,

$$P \Rightarrow^* Q = P = P_0 \Rightarrow P_1 \Rightarrow \ldots \Rightarrow P_k = Q$$

The *language $L(G)$ generated by G* is then defined by

$$L(G) = \{P : P \in W(V_T), S \Rightarrow^* P\}$$

A generative grammar is useful in top–down parsing; for bottom–up parsing we can use the dual concept of *analytic* grammar. This is an ordered quadruple $G = (V_N, V_T, S, F)$ where V_N, V_T, S are as before and F is a finite set of ordered pairs (P, Q) of words such that $P, Q \in W(V)$ and Q contains at least one letter from V_N. The relations $\Rightarrow$ and $\Rightarrow^*$ are then defined as before and we define the language $L(G)$ *recognized* (or *accepted*) by G by

$$L(G) = \{P : P \in W(V_T), P \Rightarrow^* S\}$$

Two grammars G_1 and G_2 (either both generative or both analytic) are said to be *equivalent*, written $G_1 = G_2$, if $L(G_1) = L(G_2)$.

The rules of production (i.e. elements of F) defined above are very general and without some restrictions lead to significant problems in formal language theory. A hierarchy of types of grammars is therefore introduced, each being more general than the following grammar. The four main types may be defined as follows:

Type 0, or *unrestricted grammar* allows all productions as defined above.

Type 1, or *context-sensitive grammar* allows only productions of the form $R_1 A R_2 \to R_1 P R_2$ where R_1, $R_2 \in W(V) = W(V_N \cup V_T)$, $P \in W(V) \backslash \Lambda$ and $A \in V_N$, and possibly the production $S \to \Lambda$.

Type 2, or *context-free grammar* allows productions of the form $A \to P$, where $A \in V_N$ and $P \in W(V)$.

Type 3, or *finite-state* or *regular grammar* allows productions of the forms $A \to BP$ or $A \to P$ where A, $B \in V_N$, $P \in W(V_T)$.

Note that, for type 1 grammars, if the production $S \to \Lambda$ is included in the grammar, then S cannot occur on the right of any production of F. Another type of grammar is often defined, namely a *length-increasing grammar*, where each production $P \to Q$ must satisfy $|P| \le |Q|$. However, it can be shown that G is of type 1 if and only if there is an equivalent length-increasing grammar.

Examples of grammars

(1) *Type 0*, the unrestricted grammar

$$G = (V_N, V_T, S, F)$$

defined by

$$V_N = \{S, A, B\}, V_T = \{a, b, c\}$$

$$F = \{S \to aAbc, Ab \to bA, Ac \to Bbcc, bB \to Bb, aB \to aaA, aB \to \Lambda\}$$

generates sentences of the form

$$w = a^n b^{n+2} c^{n+2} \tag{20.2.1}$$

for $n \ge 0$, where $a^n = aa \ldots a$ (n terms).

(2) *Type 1*, the context-sensitive (or length-increasing) grammar

$$G = (V_N, V_T, S, F)$$

defined by

$$V_N = \{S, A, B\}, V_T = \{a, b, c\}$$

$$F = \{S \to abc, S \to aAbc, Ab \to bA, Ac \to Bbcc, bB \to Bb,$$

$$aB \to aaA, aB \to aa\}$$

generates sentences of the form

$$w = a^n b^n c^n \tag{20.2.2}$$

for $n \ge 1$.

(3) *Type 2*, the context-free grammar

$$G = (V_N, V_T, S, F)$$

with

$$V_N = \{S\}, \; V_T = \{a, b\}$$
$$F = \{S \to ab, \; S \to aSb\}$$

generates sentences of the form

$$w = a^n b^n \tag{20.2.3}$$

$n \geqslant 1$.

(4) *Type 3*, the finite-state grammar

$$G = (V_N, V_T, S, F)$$

with

$$V_N = \{S, A\}, \; V_T = \{a, b\}$$
$$F = \{S \to Aa, \; A \to Aa, \; A \to b\}$$

generates sentences of the form

$$w = ba^n \qquad (n \geqslant 1) \tag{20.2.4}$$

Each type of language can be generated by a particular type of automaton, which we shall now describe briefly. To begin with the simplest type (i.e. Type 3) we define a *finite automaton A* over an alphabet $V = \{v_1, \ldots, v_n\}$ to be a finite directed graph in which every vertex has n arrows leading from it with each arrow labelled by a distinct v_i. One vertex is labelled '$-$' and is called the *initial vertex* and there is a set of vertices (possibly empty) labelled '$+$' *final vertices*. The vertices are also called *states*. A word $w \in W(V)$ is associated with a path in A from vertex i to vertex j if the letters on the arrows along this path when concatenated form the word w. We call such a path the *w-path*. A word $w \in W(V)$ is *accepted* by A if there exists a w-path from the initial vertex to a final vertex. (Note that the empty word Λ is accepted by A if and only if the initial vertex is also a final vertex.) For example, the finite automaton in Figure 20.2 accepts any word with an even number of *a*s and an even number of *b*s.

It is also possible to define a *nondeterministic finite automaton* in which each arrow is labelled by more than one letter of the alphabet (and otherwise is the same as a finite automaton). In this case the operation of the automaton is not completely specified since there is a choice at some vertices as to which letter to take ·in a word generated by following a path. However, it can be shown that for any nondeterministic finite automaton there is a finite automaton which accepts the same set of words and so we need not consider nondeterministic finite automata further.

The main importance of finite automata for syntactic pattern recognition is that the language generated by a Type 3 grammar is accepted by a finite automaton and conversely. Thus a Type 3 language can be generated by determining all the words accepted by a finite automaton.

An alternative representation for a finite automaton is a finite machine. For simplicity we shall define such a machine for the alphabet $V = \{a, b\}$. A *finite machine M* over $V = \{a, b\}$ is a flow diagram with one variable x (which can take on as a value any word over $\{a, b\}$) in which each statement has one of the following three forms:

1. START statement (of which there is exactly one)

2. HALT statements

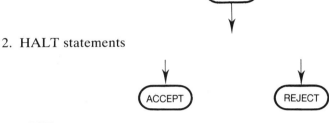

3. TEST statement

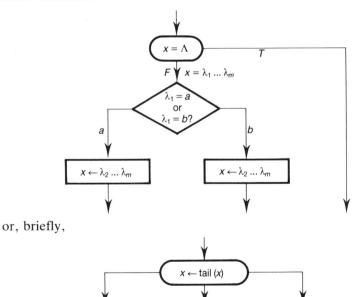

or, briefly,

where tail $(x) = \lambda_2 \ldots \lambda_m$ if $x \neq \Lambda$ and $x = \lambda_1 \ldots \lambda_m$ (where λ_i is a or b, $1 \leq i \leq m$). A word $w \in W(V)$ is *accepted* (*rejected*) by a finite machine M if the computation of M starting with input $x = w$ (at START) eventually reaches an ACCEPT (respectively REJECT) halt.

It can be shown that finite automata and finite machines have the same power in the sense that both can be designed to accept the same set of words. For example, the finite machine corresponding to the finite automaton in Figure 20.2 is shown in Figure 20.3.

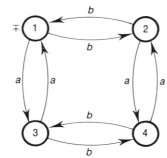

Figure 20.2 A simple finite automaton.

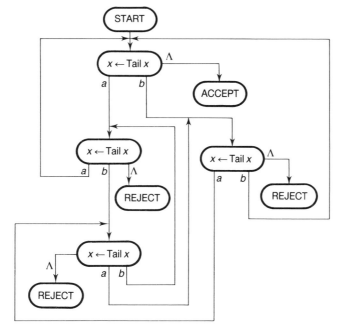

Figure 20.3 A finite machine equivalent of Figure 20.2.

In order to determine the machines which accept Type 2 languages we need to extend the notion of finite machine by adding a 'stack'. A *finite machine with one pushdown store* (over $\{a, b\}$) is a finite machine (with variable x) with a distinct variable y such that all operations on y appear in the forms:

1. TEST y

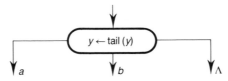

(as in the TEST statement for x).

2. ASSIGN TO y

Thus we can add a letter to the start of y. For example, the machine in Figure 20.4 accepts the set of words $\{a^n b^n : n \geqslant 0\}$. It can then be shown that finite machines with one pushdown store are precisely the acceptors of Type 2 languages.

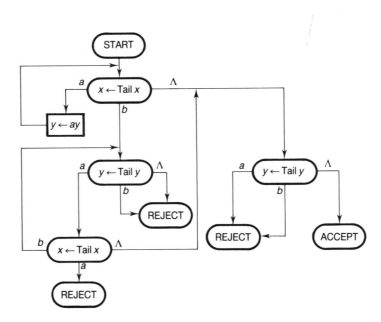

Figure 20.4   A finite machine with one pushdown store.

We shall consider next the Type 0 (unrestricted) languages. These are accepted by (according to Church's thesis) the most general form of computing device, namely the Turing machine, which we shall now describe. A *Turing machine M* over an alphabet *V* consists of four things:

1. A *tape* divided into cells. The tape has a leftmost cell (although in some descriptions it is infinite to the left) and is infinite to the right. Each cell of the tape holds one symbol which is either an element of *V* or a blank symbol Δ.

2. A *tape head* which scans one cell of the tape in each computation step. The head can erase and write characters to a cell and move left or right one cell. For example, the tape and tape head may appear in the form:

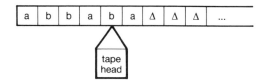

3. A *program* which is a finite directed graph (the vertices of which are called states). There is a unique START state and a (possibly empty) set of HALT states. Each arrow of the graph is of the form

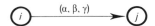

where $\alpha, \beta \in V \cup \{\Delta\}$ and $\gamma \in \{L, R\}$. This is interpreted by the machine as follows: if during the computation the machine is in state *i* and scans the symbol α, then the tape head replaces α by β, moves one cell to the left if $\gamma = L$ and one cell to the right if $\gamma = R$ and finally changes to state *j*.

4. A set of initial states $\Sigma \subseteq V$.

Note that all arrows leading from the same vertex must have distinct αs. If we remove this restriction we obtain nondeterministic Turing machines.

Let *w* be a word over Σ, and suppose that *w* is placed on the left-hand side of the tape in a Turing machine, while all the remaining cells hold the blank symbol Δ. Beginning with the START state we follow the program specified by the Turing machine. If we reach a HALT state (of course in a finite number of steps) then we say that *w* is *accepted* by the Turing machine. It can be shown that the class of sets of words accepted by the class of Turing machines is precisely the class of Type 0 languages. Type 1 languages are accepted by a special class of nondeterministic Turing machines, for which Σ contains two special symbols placed on the tape to prevent the machine leaving the portion of the tape on which the input is placed.

There are a variety of other grammars which have been introduced because context-free languages are not powerful enough to describe programming languages whereas context-sensitive languages are very complex to analyse. We shall mention two such modifications. In *programmed grammars* the structure is similar to those introduced above. However, the application of the productions is restricted in the following way. Each production is numbered $1, \ldots, m$ for some finite m, so that production 1 is always applied first. Suppose we try to apply production i at any given stage of a derivation. The next production will then be restricted to one of two sets, depending on i, called the ith success *field* $\mathcal{S}_i$ and the ith *failure field* $\mathcal{F}_i$. Each of these fields is a subset of the set $\{1, \ldots, m\}$. If we were successful in applying production i at the present stage, then the next production must be chosen from $\mathcal{S}_i$. If we were not successful in applying production i (i.e. if the production is of the form $\alpha \rightarrow \beta$ and the word α is not a subword of the derived word up to the present production) then the next production must be chosen from $\mathcal{F}_i$. Note that $\mathcal{S}_i$ or $\mathcal{F}_i$ may be empty, in which case the derivation halts if a production must be chosen from such a set. A programmed grammar is of Type i ($0 \le i \le 4$) if each production is from a grammar of Type i. Thus a *context-sensitive programmed grammar* is a programmed grammar with productions from a context-sensitive grammar.

Another modified grammar is the *indexed grammar*. This is a grammar (V_N, V_T, S, F, P) where V_N, V_T, S are as before, elements of P are finite sets of special productions (sometimes called *flags*) of the form $A \rightarrow \alpha$ where $A \in V_N$, $\alpha \in (V_N \cup V_T)^* = V^*$ and the normal productions F are of the form $A \rightarrow R_1 P_1 R_2 P_2 \ldots R_m P_m$, where $R_1, \ldots, R_m \in V_N$ or V_T and $P_1, \ldots, P_m \in P^*$ with the condition that $P_i = \Lambda$ if $R_i \in V_T$. It can be shown that the class of indexed languages includes the class of context-free languages (properly) and is a proper subclass of the context-sensitive languages.

An an example of an indexed grammar, let

$$G = (\{S, T, A, B\}, \{0, 1\}, S, F, \{P_1, P_2\})$$

where

$$F = \{S \rightarrow TP_2, T \rightarrow TP_1, T \rightarrow ABA\}$$

and

$$P_1 = \{A \rightarrow 0A, B \rightarrow 1B\}, P_2 = \{A \rightarrow 0, B \rightarrow 1\}$$

Then applying $S \rightarrow TP_2$ once, $T \rightarrow TP_1$ $(n - 1)$ times and then $T \rightarrow ABA$, we have

$$S \Rightarrow TP_2 \Rightarrow TP_1 P_2 \Rightarrow \ldots \Rightarrow TP_1^{n-1} P_2 \Rightarrow AP_1^{n-1} P_2 BP_1^{n-1} P_2 AP_1^{n-1} P_2$$

Finally, using the productions in P_1, P_2 gives

$$AP_1^{n-1} P_2 BP_1^{n-1} P_2 AP_1^{n-1} P_2 \Rightarrow 0AP_1^{n-2} P_2 1 BP_1^{n-2} P_2 0 AP_1^{n-2} P_2 \Rightarrow \ldots \Rightarrow$$
$$0^{n-1} AP_2 1^{n-1} BP_2 0^{n-1} AP_2 \Rightarrow 0^n 1^n 0^n$$

Thus, G generates the context-sensitive language $\{0^n 1^n 0^n : n = 1, 2, \ldots\}$.

20.3 Special languages – string language and pattern grammars

In this section we shall describe some of the more widely used pattern languages and their primitives. The first was developed to deal with two-dimensional picture type objects which do not link together naturally at single points. This means that simple concatenation of symbols cannot be applied without some simplification of the picture primitives. In order to reduce the problem to a concatenation language the *picture description language* (PDL) is defined in terms of primitives, each of which has only two points (*head* and *tail*) which can be joined to other primitives. Each pattern primitive can then be represented by a vector with a head and a tail (Figure 20.5). The primitives can be connected in one of four ways, as shown in Figure 20.6. If b is a primitive, we denote by $\sim b$ the *reverse* of b, represented by an arrow in the opposite direction from b. Also the *null primitive* Λ is an arrow of zero length with identical head and tail. A grammar which generates PDL sentences is the context-free grammar

$$G = (V_N, V_T, S, F)$$

where V_N will contain objects which are required to be formed from the pattern primitives and V_T will contain the primitives (which will depend on the

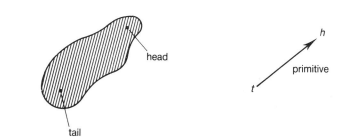

Figure 20.5 Primitive of the PDL.

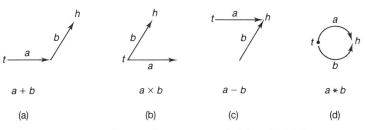

Figure 20.6 Connecting pattern primitives in PDL.

particular problem) and the symbols (,), $+$, $\times$, $-$, $*$, $\sim$. For example, suppose we wish to recognize the letter 'A' and the 'envelope' object shown in Figure 20.7. A suitable grammar is given by

$$G = (V_N,\ V_T,\ S,\ F)$$

where

$$V_N = \{S,\ A,\ \text{Envelope},\ \text{Triangle}\},\ V_T = \{\underset{\rightarrow}{a},\ b\nearrow,\ \searrow c,\ \downarrow d,\ (,),\ +,\ \times,\ -,\ *,\ \sim\}$$

and F consists of the productions

$$S \rightarrow A,\ S \rightarrow \text{Envelope}$$

$$A \rightarrow (b + (\text{Triangle} + c))$$

$$\text{Envelope} \rightarrow ((((c + c) + (\sim d))*(d + (a \times (b + b))))*\text{Triangle})$$

$$\text{Triangle} \rightarrow ((b + c)*a)$$

Then,

$$L(G) = \{(b + ((b + c)*a) + c)),\ ((((c + c) + (\sim d))*$$
$$\times (d + (a \times (b + b)))))*((b + c)*a))\}$$

Parsing trees are shown in Figure 20.8 for the simple structures in Figure 20.7.

  Another interesting grammar has been developed for the recognition of chromosomes which are usually of two types, as shown in Figure 20.9. A context-free grammar which will generate submedian and telocentric chromosome types is given by

$$G = (V_N,\ V_T,\ S_1,\ S_2,\ F)$$

where

$$S_1 = \text{Submedian},\ S_2 = \text{Telocentric}$$

$$V_N = \{S_1,\ S_2,\ \text{Bottom},\ \text{Side},\ \text{Armpair},\ \text{Rightpart},\ \text{Leftpart},\ \text{Arm}\}$$

Figure 20.7 Simple PDL structural descriptions.

$F = \{S_1 \rightarrow$ Armpair. Armpair, $S_2 \rightarrow$ Bottom. Armpair,

    Armpair $\rightarrow$ Side.Armpair, Armpair $\rightarrow$ Armpair.Side,

    Armpair $\rightarrow$ Arm.Righpart, Armpair $\rightarrow$ Leftpart.Arm,

    Leftpart $\rightarrow$ Arm.c, Rightpart $\rightarrow$ c.Arm, Bottom $\rightarrow$ b.Bottom,

    Bottom $\rightarrow$ Bottom.b, Bottom $\rightarrow$ e, Side $\rightarrow$ b.Side, Side $\rightarrow$ Side.b,

    Side $\rightarrow$ b, Side $\rightarrow$ d, Arm $\rightarrow$ b.Arm, Arm $\rightarrow$ Arm.b, Arm $\rightarrow$ $a\}$.

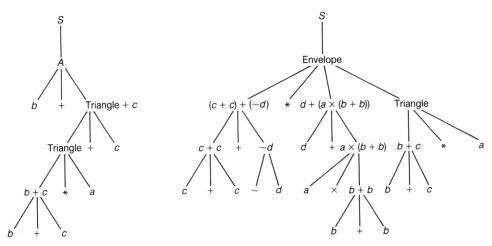

Figure 20.8 Parsing trees for 'A' and 'Envelope'.

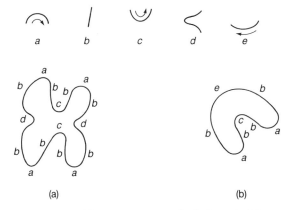

Figure 20.9 Chromosomes and their primitives:
(a) submedian type; (b) telocentric type.

Note that this grammar has two initial symbols S_1, S_2. We could equally well have considered two similar grammars each with a single initial symbol S_1 or S_2. A submedian chromosome is described (in the clockwise direction) by the word

$$w = abcbabdbabcbabdb$$

A generating sequence for w is as follows:

$S_1 \rightarrow$ Armpair.Armpair

$\rightarrow$ (Armpair.Side).(Armpair.Side)

$\rightarrow$ ((Arm.Rightpart).Side).((Armpair.Side).b)

$\rightarrow$ (((Arm.b).(c.Arm)).d).(((Arm.Rightpart).d).b)

$\rightarrow$ (((a.b).(c.(Arm.b))).d).((((Arm.b).(c.Arm)).d).b)

$\rightarrow$ (((a.b).(c.((b.Arm).b))).d).(((((b.Arm).b).(c.(Arm.b))).d).b)

$\rightarrow$ (((a.b).(c.((b.a).b))).d).(((((b.a).b).(c.((b.Arm).b))).d).b)

$\rightarrow$ (((a.b).(c.((b.a).b))).d).(((((b.a).b).(c.((b.a).b))).d).b)

Note that the parentheses are not part of the language and are introduced merely for convenience in reading.

The grammars introduced so far are essentially one-dimensional, i.e. the primitives are connected at single points giving linear sentences. Higher-dimensional patterns are difficult to analyse in this way and so a variety of different grammars have been developed to deal with more complex two- and three-dimensional pictures. Objects which can be defined by a hierarchical structure naturally fit into the theory of tree grammars. A *tree* in this sense is the same as an unoriented tree in graph theory with a distinguished node (the *root* of the tree). Two examples are given in Figure 20.10. A *tree grammar* is a quintuple $G = (V_N, V_T, S, F, R)$ where V_N, V_T, S, F are as before (S can be a tree) and R is a ranking function which determines how many nodes are connected directly below a given node in the tree. For example, for the first picture in Figure 20.10 we could use the grammar

$$V_N = \{A_1, A_2, S\}, \; V_T = \{r, h, c, w_1, w_2, d, w_3, w_4\}$$

The ranking function R is given by

$$R(r) = 2, \; R(h) = 3, \; R(c) = 2, \; R(w_1) = R(w_2) = R(w_3) = R(w_4) = R(d) = 0.$$

Two other grammars related to trees are webb and graph grammars. These will not be discussed here.

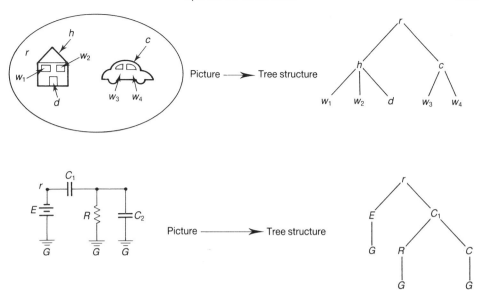

Figure 20.10 Two images and their associated tree structures.

20.4 Theory of parsing

Having introduced the basic ingredients of abstract language theory we shall now indicate how these ideas are applied to syntactic pattern recognition. Suppose we require a system to recognize patterns in m given classes $\omega_1, \ldots, \omega_m$. Then we must first reduce the patterns to their basic features or *primitives* in terms of which all pattern samples are constructed. The primitives are then taken as the terminals for m pattern grammars $G_1, \ldots, G_m$ where

$$G_i = \{V_{N,i}, V_{T,i}, S_i, F_i\} \qquad 1 \leqslant i \leqslant m$$

and $V_{T,i} =$ the set of pattern primitives of the ith class. (It is often possible to take $V_{N,i}$, $V_{T,i}$, S_i to be independent of i, so that only the production rules depend on the pattern class.) Each sample pattern P can be regarded as a set of primitives connected in the form of a string, say $P = A_1 A_2 \ldots A_m$ where A_j is a pattern primitive for $1 \leqslant j \leqslant m$. Let $W_i = W_i(V_{N,i} \cup V_{T,i})$ denote the language generated by G_i. Then we assign P to class i if

$$P \in W_i \qquad\qquad (20.4.1)$$

(Of course, if P belongs to more than one language, say W_i and W_j, then we must assign P arbitrarily to class i or class j, while if P does not belong to any W_i we must reject P as being an abnormal or noisy sample.)

The two main problems with syntactic pattern recognition are (i) determining the grammars G_i, $1 \leq i \leq m$, for the pattern classes, and (ii) deciding whether or not (20.4.1) is valid. We shall discuss the generation of the grammars later and assume for now that these are available. In this section we shall consider the problem of determining the value of i for which (20.4.1) is true (assuming that it is true for some i). Deciding whether or not a given word belongs to the language generated by a grammar is solved by *parsing* the word in accordance with the production rules of the grammar.

Parsing, as stated earlier, may proceed in either a top–down or a bottom–up manner. In top–down parsing of a word $w = v_1 \dots v_m$ we start with the symbol S and essentially try all possible productions at each node of the parse tree until the terminal word $v_1 \dots v_m$ is obtained or a production is applied which cannot derive (a part of) w. If such a point is reached we 'backtrack' up the tree and try the next possible production. (This is very similar to computer game theory in which a game tree consisting of all possible next moves is searched.) It may be possible, of course, to eliminate redundant branches of the parse tree before we reach the terminal symbols. As an example, consider the grammar $G = (V_N, V_T, S, F)$ given by

$$V_N = \{S, A, B\}, \ V_T = \{a, b, c, d\}$$

$$F = \{S \to A, \ S \to AdS, \ A \to BcA, \ A \to B, \ B \to a, \ B \to b, \ B \to c\}$$

Then $W(V_N \cup V_T)$ contains the word $w = acbda$ which can be obtained by the following sequence of productions

$$S \Rightarrow AdS \Rightarrow BcAdS \Rightarrow BcBdS \Rightarrow acBdS \Rightarrow acbdS$$

$$\Rightarrow acbdA \Rightarrow acbdB \Rightarrow acbda.$$

A naive computer algorithm may parse the word w by trying all possible productions as shown in Figure 20.11. In this diagram each edge of the tree corresponds to a production and at each node we have shown the word obtained up to that point. Only a small portion of the complete tree has been shown. In particular, one terminal leaf appears with the word '*aca*'. This is not w of course and so we must backtrack to the previous node and try the next possible production. In principle, the parse tree is of infinite extent; however, since the sought for word w has only five characters we can 'prune' the tree at any branch which will generate words of length greater than five. Note that we may also use other syntactic information to prune the tree. Thus, for example, the whole left-hand branch shown in Figure 20.11 may be removed since the first production $S \to A$ cannot lead to a word containing '*d*', and so only the branch beginning with the production $S \to AdS$ needs to be searched.

The principles of bottom–up parsing are similar. This time we start at the bottom of the parse tree with the word w and apply the productions in reverse order, attempting to achieve the 'goal' S. The main drawback with these

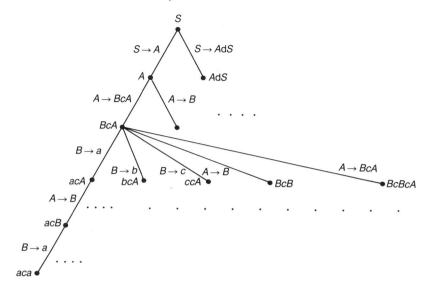

Figure 20.11 A partial parse tree.

methods is the amount of redundant computation required and so various efficient parsing algorithms have been derived. We shall proceed to outline just two of the more widely used versions.

The *Cocke–Younger–Kasami parsing algorithm* can be described as follows. It is assumed that we are given a context-free grammar $G = (V_N, V_T, S, F)$ with no Λ-production in *Chomsky normal form*, i.e. all productions are of the types $A \rightarrow BC$ or $A \rightarrow a$, with $A, B, C \in V_N, a \in V_T$. (It can be shown that any context-free grammar can be put in this form.) Let $w = w_1 w_2, \ldots, w_n$ be an input word. Then the algorithm generates a parse table T with cells t_{ij} such that t_{ij} contains $A \in V_N$ if and only if $A \Rightarrow^* w_i w_{i+1} \ldots w_{i+j-1}$. The table is built up from the bottom line (with $j = 1$) by the iterative steps:

STEP 1 Let $t_{i1} = \{A : A \rightarrow w_i \text{ is in } F\}$ for each $i \in \{1, \ldots, n\}$.

STEP 2 If t_{ik} has been found for all i and $1 \leqslant k < j$, then set

$$t_{ij} = \{A : \text{for some } k, 1 \leqslant k < j, A \rightarrow BC \text{ is in } F,$$

$$B \text{ is in } t_{ik} \text{ and } C \text{ is in } t_{i+k,j-k}\}.$$

STEP 3 Repeat Step 2 for $1 \leqslant i \leqslant n, 1 \leqslant j \leqslant n - i + 1$

STEP 4 If $S \in t_{1n}$, then $w \in L(G)$.

Example

$$\text{Let } G = (V_N, V_T, S, F), \ V_N = \{S, A\}, \ V_T = \{a, b\}$$

$$F = \{S \to AA, \ S \to AS, \ S \to b, \ A \to SA, \ A \to AS, \ A \to a\}$$

and consider the word $w = abaab$. We obtain the parse table shown below:

$j \uparrow$					
5	A, S				
4	A, S	A, S			
3	A, S	S	A, S		
2	A, S	A	S	A, S	
1	A	S	A	A	S
	1	2	3	4	5 $\to i$

Another efficient parsing algorithm for context-free grammars is due to Earley. Again let $G = (V_N, V_T, S, F)$ be a context-free grammar and let $w = w_1 \ldots w_n$ be an input word. Then *Earley's parsing algorithm* may be stated in the following form:

A parse list $L_0, L_1, \ldots, L_n$ for w is determined where each L_i contains expressions of the form $[A \to \alpha, k]$ where $A \in V_N$, $\alpha \in W(V_N \cup V_T \cup \{.\})$ and k is a positive integer. The lists are found by applying the following steps:

Find I_0:

Step 1_0 If $S \to \alpha$ is in F add $[S \to .\alpha, 0]$ to I_0.

REPEAT

Step 2_0 If $[B \to \gamma., 0]$ is in list I_0, add $[A \to \alpha B. \beta, 0]$ for all.

$\quad [A \to \alpha.B\beta, 0]$ in I_0.

Step 3_0 If $[A \to \alpha. B\beta, 0]$ is in I_0, add $[B \to .\gamma, 0]$ to I_0 for all productions $B \to \gamma$ in F.

UNTIL no new items are added to I_0.

Find I_j from $I_0, \ldots, I_{j-1}$ for $j = 1, \ldots, n$:

Step 1_j For each $[B \to \alpha.x\beta, i]$ in I_{j-1} such that $x = w_j$ add $[B \to \alpha x.\beta, i]$ to I_j.

REPEAT

Step 2_j Suppose $[A \to \alpha., i]$ is in I_j. If $[B \to \alpha.A\beta, k]$ is in I_i, add $[B \to \alpha A.\beta, k]$ to I_j.

Step 3ⱼ Suppose $[A \to \alpha . B\beta, i]$ is in I_j. If $B \to \gamma$ is in F, add $[B \to \gamma, j]$ to I_j.

UNTIL no new items are added to I_j.

It can be shown that $w \in L(G)$ if and only if a term of the form $[S \to \alpha., 0]$ is in I_n.

20.5 Stochastic languages and error correction

As in the decision-theoretic approach to pattern recognition, the patterns and primitives used in syntactic recognition may be noisy and may not therefore be modelled by a fixed grammar. Stochastic languages have been developed to cope with this situation and we shall briefly outline some of the basic ideas involved in this section. Thus, a *stochastic grammar* is a five-tuple $G = (V_N, V_T, S, F, \mathcal{P})$ where V_N, V_T, S, F are as before and $\mathcal{P}$ is a set of probability assignments over the productions of F. One can define context-free, context-sensitive and regular grammars much as before. Let $P_1, \ldots, P_m$ be a set of productions in F and consider the following derivation of the word w:

$$S \overset{P_1}{\Rightarrow} \alpha_1 \overset{P_2}{\Rightarrow} \alpha_2 \overset{P_3}{\Rightarrow} \ldots \overset{P_m}{\Rightarrow} \alpha_m = w$$

where α_i is an intermediate word. Each production of P_i, $1 \le i \le m$, is assigned a probability from $\mathcal{P}$ written $p(P_i)$. Thus, the probability of generating the word w is

$$p(w) = p(P_1)p(P_2|P_1)p(P_3|P_1, P_2) \ldots p(P_m|P_1, \ldots, P_{m-1})$$

where $p(P_j|P_1, \ldots, P_{j-1})$ is the probability of P_j given that the productions $P_1, \ldots, P_{j-1}$ have already been applied. If $p(P_j|P_1, \ldots, P_{j-1}) = p(P_j)$, then the probability of assignment associated with P_j is *unrestricted*. If this is true for all assignments, $\mathcal{P}$ is said to be *unrestricted*. A *stochastic* language $L(G) = \{[w, p(w)]: S \Rightarrow^* w, w \in V_T^+\}$ is the language generated by a stochastic grammar G. We say that $\mathcal{P}$ is *consistent* if

$$\sum_{w \in L(G)} p(w) = 1$$

where there are k distinct generations of w (k depending on w) with probabilities $p_i(w)$, $1 \le i \le k$ and

$$p(w) = \sum_{i=1}^{k} p_i(w)$$

An example of a stochastic context-free grammar is given by

$$G = (V_N, V_T, S, F, \mathcal{P})$$

where

$$V_N = \{S\}, \; V_T = \{a, b\}$$

$$F = \{S \xrightarrow{p} aSb, \; S \xrightarrow{1-p} ab\}$$

$$\mathcal{P} = \{p, 1 - p\}$$

Note that the probability assignments of each production are usually shown above the production arrow. Consider the word $w = aaabbb$. Then we can generate w in the unique way:

$$S \Rightarrow aSb \Rightarrow aaSSbb \Rightarrow aaabbb = w$$

Clearly, $p(w) = p^2(1 - p)$, and so

$$L(G) = \{[a^n b^n, \; p^{n-1}(1 - p)] : n \geq 1\}$$

Parsing theory for stochastic languages is similar to that for deterministic languages. However, the parse tree can be effectively minimized by choosing, at each node, the most probable production followed by the next most probable, etc. Stochastic generalizations of the parsing algorithms mentioned above are also possible.

One of the most difficult problems associated with stochastic syntactic recognition theory is that of determining the production probabilities. A simple method for estimating these probabilities during the training phase will now be described. Suppose we have an M class problem defined by M stochastic grammars $G_k = (V_{Nk}, V_{Tk}, S_k, F_k, \mathcal{P}_k)$, $1 \leq k \leq M$, where only the production probabilities $\mathcal{P}_k$ are unknown. Assume that we have a set of sample words $W' = \{w_1, \ldots, w_K\}$ where each word belongs to one (or more) of the languages $L(G_k)$. Let $n(w_i)$, $1 \leq i \leq K$, be the number of times w_i occurs in W'. For simplicity we shall assume that each G_k is regular or context-free, so that each production is of the form $A \rightarrow \beta$ where $A \in V_N$.

We proceed by taking each sample word w_i and parsing it with respect to each grammar. For any production $A_l \rightarrow \beta_j$ of grammar G_k, let $N_{klj}(w_i)$ denote the number of times this production is used in parsing w_i. Finally, let $p(w_i | G_k)$ be the probability that w_i is generated by G_k. Clearly, if w_i is in class k only, then $p(w_i | G_k) = 1$, while if w_i is not in class k then $p(w_i | G_k) = 0$. If w_i belongs to $L(G_k)$ for several values of k, then we can estimate $p(w_i | G_k)$ by the relative frequency with which w_i occurs in the classes. We must impose the restriction

$$\sum_{k=1}^{m} p(w_i | G_k) = 1$$

however.

Now, the expected number of times n_{klj} that the production $A_l \rightarrow \beta_j$ from F_k is used in parsing a sample string is thus

$$n_{klj} = \sum_{i=1}^{K} n(w_i)p(w_i|G_k)N_{klj}(w_i)$$

and so the probability p_{klj} associated with the production $A_l \rightarrow \beta_j$ of F_k can be estimated by

$$p_{klj} \cong \frac{n_{klj}}{\sum_j n_{klj}}$$

where the sum is taken over all productions in F_k of the form $A_l \rightarrow \beta_j$. It can be shown, under some mild conditions, that p_{klj} converges to the true value as $K \rightarrow \infty$ (provided the sample set is sufficiently general).

Another way of handling noisy patterns is by the use of similarity measures as in decision theoretic pattern recognition. We can think of poorly defined patterns as introducing errors into their string representations in terms of primitives. Such errors can be one of three types:

(i)   substitution error: $\alpha_1 a \alpha_2 \vdash \alpha_1 b \alpha_2, \, a, \, b \in V_T$ $(a \neq b)$
(ii)   deletion error: $\alpha_1 a \alpha_2 \vdash \alpha_1 \alpha_2, \, a \in V_T$
(iii)   insertion error: $\alpha_1 \alpha_2 \vdash \alpha_1 a \alpha_2, \, a \in V_T$

where $\alpha_1, \, \alpha_2 \in W(V_T)$.

The basic idea of *minimum-distance error correction* is to minimize the number of such errors in a given parse. Thus we must first define a suitable distance function. A simple distance $d(w_1, w_2)$ between two words w_1 and w_2 can be defined in terms of the minimum number of error transformations of the above three types which are required to obtain w_2 from w_1. For example, if $w_1 = abd$, $w_2 = accd$, then we can obtain w_2 from w_1 by substituting c for b and inserting another c, so that $d(w_1, w_2) = 2$. (The three types of errors could be weighted differently leading to a slightly different measure.) Now let $L(G)$ be a given language and w a given word (which may not belong to $L(G)$). In *minimum-distance error correcting parsing* we find a word $\bar{w}$ in $L(G)$ such that

$$d(w, \bar{w}) = \min_{w' \in L(G)} d(w, w') \tag{20.5.1}$$

This is achieved by adding the extra symbols in w to G, giving G', and extending $L(G)$ to $L(G')$. The productions of G are augmented with the three error transformations defined above and a parse Π for w in $L(G')$ which uses the minimum number of error productions is found. Finally, $\bar{w}$ is obtained by running the same parse Π with the error productions omitted. Earley's parsing algorithm can be extended to determine a parse Π which minimizes the number of error productions. The above ideas can also be extended to stochastic grammars. Note finally that the introduction of a distance function such as (20.5.1) into abstract languages allows us to use all the ideas of decision-theoretic pattern recognition. In particular, the clustering algorithms described earlier apply to syntactic pattern recognition via the metric (20.5.1).

20.6 Grammatical inference

In our discussion of syntactic pattern recognition we have assumed above that the grammars describing the pattern classes in a given problem are already known and the object is to parse sample words (built up from the primitives) to determine if they are in any of the given languages. In most cases, however, the grammars are not known *a priori* and they must therefore be inferred from a given set of sample strings. Obtaining a grammar G which will generate a given set of sample words is called *grammatical inference* and we shall briefly describe a simple algorithm which solves a simple form of this problem.

The basic idea behind grammatical inference is to find a set of productions which will generate a given sample word (and only that word). This is done for each sample word, giving rise to a nonrecursive grammar which generates all the sample words. Redundant productions are removed and the grammar is made recursive in order that it will generate an infinite number of words. (This is required so that the system will recognize patterns which are close to, but not identical with, the sample words.)

As an example of the simple algorithm described below, consider the sample set $W' = \{abbbc, ccbbc, abbc, ccbc, abc, ccc, ac\}$. We must find a grammar $G = (V_N, V_T, S, F)$ for which $W' \subseteq W(V_N \cup V_T)$. Let $V_T = \{a, b, c\}$. We process the words in W' in order of decreasing length. Thus start with $abbbc$ (or $ccbbc$). A set of productions which generates abbbc (and only this word) is

$$F_1 = \{S \to aA_1, A_1 \to bA_2, A_2 \to bA_3, A_3 \to bc\}$$

The last production, namely $A_3 \to bc$, is called a *residue production*. We require at least two symbols from V_T on the right of this production in order to obtain a recursive grammar later in the procedure, as we shall see below. The second word $ccbbc$ can be generated by the productions

$$F_2 = \{S \to cA_4, A_4 \to cA_5, A_5 \to bA_6, A_6 \to bc\}$$

Similarly, we obtain the following productions for the remaining words:

$$abbc: F_3 = F_1 \cup \{A_3 \to c\}$$
$$ccbc: F_4 = F_2 \cup \{A_6 \to c\}$$
$$abc: F_5 = F_1 \cup \{A_2 \to c\}$$
$$ccc: F_6 = F_2 \cup \{A_5 \to c\}$$
$$ac: F_7 = F_1 \cup \{A_1 \to c\}$$

This leads to the intermediate set of productions

$$\bar{F} = \bigcup_{i=1}^{7} F_i = \{S \to aA_1, S \to cA_4, A_1 \to c, A_1 \to bA_2, A_2 \to c, A_2 \to bA_3,$$
$$A_3 \to c, A_3 \to bc, A_4 \to cA_5, A_5 \to c, A_5 \to bA_6, A_6 \to c, A_6 \to bc\}$$

The language generated by $\bar{F}$ is clearly nonrecursive and so the next task is to extend the language to a recursive one. To do this we take a residue production (with two terminal characters), say $A_3 \rightarrow bc$, find a production of the form $A' \rightarrow c$ for which there exists a production $A'' \rightarrow bA'$, replace A_3 by A'' and delete the production $A_3 \rightarrow bc$. (These productions are assumed to exist; this indicates the main limitation of the method.) In the present example we may take the productions $A_3 \rightarrow c$ and $A_2 \rightarrow bA_3$, and replace A_3 by A_2. Similarly, using the residue production $A_6 \rightarrow bc$ we find the productions $A_6 \rightarrow c$, $A_5 \rightarrow bA_6$ so that A_6 may be replaced by A_5. This method thus leads to the recursive productions $A_2 \rightarrow bA_2$, $A_5 \rightarrow bA_5$ and the new set of productions is

$$\bar{\bar{F}} = \{S \rightarrow aA_1, \; S \rightarrow cA_4, \; A_1 \rightarrow c, \; A_1 \rightarrow bA_2, \; A_2 \rightarrow c, \; A_2 \rightarrow bA_2,$$

$$A_4 \rightarrow cA_5, \; A_5 \rightarrow c, \; A_5 \rightarrow bA_5\}$$

The grammar developed so far may have equivalent productions. Two productions $A \rightarrow \alpha$, $B \rightarrow \beta$ are *equivalent* if they generate the same set of words. In this case we can equate A and B and thus obtain the productions $A \rightarrow \alpha$, $A \rightarrow \beta$. In the above example given by $\bar{\bar{F}}$, it is clear that we may equate A_1 with A_2 and A_1 with A_5. This gives the required finite-state grammar:

$$G = (V_N, V_T, S, F), \; V_N = \{S, A_1, A_2\}, \; V_T = \{a, b, c\}$$

$$F = \{S \rightarrow aA_1, \; S \rightarrow cA_2, \; A_1 \rightarrow bA_1, \; A_2 \rightarrow cA_1, \; A_1 \rightarrow c\}$$

20.7 Texture analysis

In the last section of this chapter we shall describe an interesting application of syntactic pattern recognition to texture analysis. Texture, as discussed briefly in Part 2 of the book, is a quality or feature of a surface which is determined by a repetitive, or almost repetitive, pattern. Texture analysis is useful in scene segmentation, which is an important precursor to image interpretation. The *primitive* for syntactic texture analysis is a small region of the image in which the grey level is nearly uniform. It could be a single pixel or it could consist of a number of pixels. In the former case, if the image has n grey levels, then we would have n pattern primitives.

Having chosen the primitive, the image is divided into *windows* consisting of a square array of primitives, say $k \times k$. The image is assumed to be a semiregular repetition of the windows (see Figure 20.12). By semiregular we mean that the pattern in one window may be a shifted version of that in another. Because of the high dimensionality imposed by considering reasonable sized windows (say 10×10 primitives) it is usually best to use a tree grammar to describe texture patterns. Thus we take a window and represent it in the form of a tree, each node of which is labelled by the pattern primitive at the corresponding pixel point. For example, the window in Figure 20.12 is 7 × 7 and the image is binary (black and white), so we can label the nodes with 0 or 1 depending on whether the pixel is white or black respectively (Figure 20.13). Note that many different tree structures are possible for any window – the choice of a particular one such as in Figure 20.13(a) will affect the efficiency of the processing.

When a tree structure has been chosen, the next task is to determine a

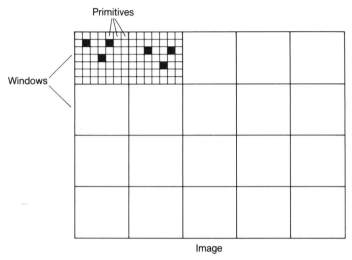

Figure 20.12 Primitives and window selection for texture analysis.

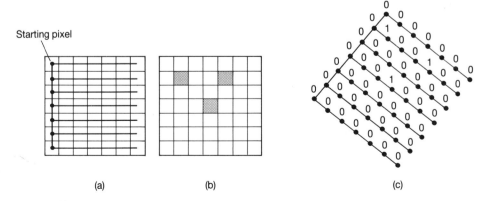

Figure 20.13 Generating the tree structure for a window: (a) chosen tree stucture; (b) sample window; (c) corresponding tree.

grammar which will generate the tree for the given texture window (such as the tree in Figure 20.13(c)). The following tree grammar $G = (V_N, V_T, S, F, R)$ will generate the tree in Figure 20.13(c):

$$V_N = \{S, A_1, A_2, A_3, A_4, A_5, K\}, V_T = \{0, 1\}, R = \{0, 1, 2\}$$

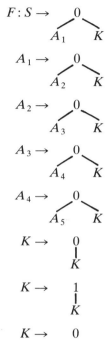

To apply these ideas to texture analysis we divide the image into windows and parse the sample tree corresponding to that window to determine if it is part of the texture defined by the grammar. The union of all such windows determines the part of the image which contains the given texture. All the other techniques described above, such as clustering, error correction, etc., are of course available in the texture analysis problem.

Bibliographical notes

The theory of formal languages and automata is discussed in detail in McNaughton (1982) and Saloman (1973). PDL was developed by Shaw (1969) and a grammar suitable for speech recognition can be found in De Mori (1972). Chromosome grammars are studied more extensively in Lee and Fu (1972) and high-dimensional tree, webb and graph grammars appear in Brainerd (1969), Brayer and Fu (1976), Gips (1974), Narasimhan (1969), Pavlidis (1972), Rounds (1970) and Shaw (1972). The Cocke–Younger–Kasami parsing algorithm is discussed in detail in Aho and Ullman (1972) and the Earley parsing algorithm is developed in Earley (1970). For a more general discussion of stochastic languages and error-correction the reader may consult Fu (1973), Fu and Huang (1972), Huang and Fu (1971), Lu and Fu (1978), Nasu and Honda (1971), Swain and Fu (1972) and Tanaka and Fu (1978). Cluster analysis for syntactic pattern recognition is described in Fu and Lu (1977) and Lu (1979), and a more detailed discussion of grammatical inference can be found in Feldman (1972), Fu and Booth (1975) and Sauvain and Uhr (1969). Finally, further ideas on the application of syntactic pattern recognition to texture analysis are presented in Haralick *et al.* (1973), Lu and Fu (1978), Sutton and Hall (1972), Weszka and Rosenfeld (1970) and Zucker (1976).

Exercises

1 Prove that Type 1 grammars and length-increasing grammars are equivalent.

2 Prove that the automaton in Figure 20.2 accepts words with an even number of as and bs.

3 Demonstrate that the machine in Figure 20.4 accepts the set of words

$$\{a^n b^n : n \geq 0\}$$

4 Derive a PDL for the following shapes:

5 Discuss the Cocke–Younger–Kasami algorithm in detail.

6 Apply the Earley parsing algorithm to the word $w = a*a$ formed by the grammar

$$G = (V_N, V_T, S, F), \quad V_N = \{S, T, P\}, \quad V_T = \{a, +, *, (,)\}$$

$$F = \{S \to S + T, S \to T, T \to T*P, T \to P, P \to (S), P \to a\}$$

7 Apply the inference algorithm in Section 20.6 to the samples set

$$W' = \{aabdc, acbcc, abd, cad, bd\}.$$

8 Demonstrate a parse for the tree in Figure 20.13(c) using the tree grammar given in the text.

References

Aho, A. V. and J. D. Ullman (1972), *The Theory of Parsing, Translation and Compiling* vol. I, *Parsing*, Englewood Cliffs NJ: Prentice Hall.

Brainerd, W. S. (1969) 'Tree generating regular systems', *Inf. Control*, **14**, 207–31.

Brayer, J. M. and K. S. Fu (1976), 'Application of a Webb grammar model to an earth resources satellite picture', *Proc. 3rd. Int. Joint Conf. Pattern Recognition, Coronado, Calif, Nov. 8–11.*

De Mori, R. (1972), 'A descriptive technique for automatic speech recognition', *IEEE Trans Audio Electroacoust.*, AU-**21**, 89–100.

Earley, J. (1970) 'An efficient context-free parsing algorithm', *Commun. ACM*, **13**, 94–102.

Feldman, J. A. (1972), 'Some decidability results on grammatical inference and complexity', *Inf. Control*, **20**, 244–62.

Fu, K. S. (1973), 'Stochastic languages for picture analysis', *Comput. Graphics, Image Process.*, **2**, 433–53.

Fu, K. S. and T. Huang (1972), 'Stochastic grammars and languages', *Int. J. Comput. Inf. Sci.*, **1**, 135–70.

Fu, K. S. and T. L. Booth, (1975), 'Grammatical inference: introduction and survey', parts I and II, *IEEE Trans. Sys., Man, Cybern.*, SMC-**5**, 59–72, 409–23.

Fu, K. S. and S. Y. Lu (1977), 'A cluster procedure for syntactic patterns', *IEEE Trans. Sys., Man, Cybern.*, SMC-**7**, 734–42.

Gips, J. (1974), 'A syntax-directed program that performs a three-dimensional perceptual task', *Pattern Recognition*, **6**, 189–200.

Haralick, R. M., K. Shanmugam and I. Dinstein (1973), 'Texture features for image classification', *IEEE Trans. Sys., Man, Cybern.*, SMC-**3**, 610–21.

Huang, T. and K. S. Fu (1971), 'On stochastic context-free languages', *Inf. Sci.*, **3**, 201–24.

Lee, H. C. and K. S. Fu (1972), 'A stochastic syntax analysis procedure and its application to pattern classification', *IEEE Trans. Computers*, C-**21**, 660–6.

Lu, S. Y. (1979), 'A tree-to-tree distance and its application to cluster analysis', *IEEE Trans. Pattern Anal. Mach. Intell.*, PAMI-**1**, 219–24.

Lu, S. Y. and K. S. Fu (1978a), 'Error-correcting tree automata for syntactic pattern recognition', *IEEE Trans. Computers*, C-**27**, 1040–53.

Lu, S. Y and K. S. Fu (1978b), 'A syntactic approach to texture analysis', *Comput. Graphics, Image Process.*, **7**, 303–30.

McNaughton, R. (1982), *Elementary Computability, Formal Languages and Automata*, Englewood Cliffs NJ: Prentice Hall.

Narasimhan, R. (1969), 'On the description, generation and recognition of classes of pictures', in *Automatic Interpretation and Classification of Images* (A. Grasselli, ed.) NY: Academic Press.

Nasu, M. and N. Honda (1971), 'A context-free language which is not acceptable by a probabilistic automaton', *Inf. Control*, **18**, 233–6.

Pavlidis T. (1972), 'Linear and context-free graph grammars', *J. Assoc. Comput. Mach.*, **19**, 11–22.

Rounds, W. C. (1970), 'Mappings and grammars on trees', *J. Math. Sys. Theory,* **4** (3), 257–87.

Saloman, A. (1973), *Formal Languages*, NY: Academic Press.

Sauvain, R. and L. Uhr (1969), 'A teachable pattern describing and recognizing program', *Pattern Recognition*, **1**, 219–32.

Shaw, A. C. (1969), 'The formal picture description scheme as a basis for picture processing', *Inf. Control*, **14**, 9–52.

Shaw, A. C. (1972), 'Picture graphs, grammars and parsing', in *Frontiers of Pattern Recognition* (S. Watanabe, ed.), NY: Academic Press.

Sutton, R. N. and E. L. Hall (1972), 'Texture measures for automatic classification of pulmonary disease', *IEEE Trans. Computers*, C-**21**, 667–76.

Swain, P. H. and K. S. Fu (1972), 'Stochastic programmed grammars for syntactic pattern recognition', *Pattern Recognition*, **4**, Special Issue on Syntactic Pattern Recognition.

Tanaka, E. and K. S. Fu (1978), 'Error-correcting parsers for formal languages', *IEEE Trans. Computers*, C-**27**, 605–16.

Weszka, J. S. and A. Rosenfeld (1970), 'An application of texture analysis to material inspection', *Pattern Recognition*, **8** (4), 195–200.

Zucker, S. W. (1976), 'Toward a model of texture', *Comput. Graphics Image Process.*, **5**, 190–202.

21

Neural Networks

21.1 Introduction

All the ideas and algorithms described in this book up to now have been based on conventional computer hardware (including the latest parallel machines discussed in Chapter 14). Such hardware consists of processing units and a separate memory (or memories) in which the data is stored. One major disadvantage of using computers designed on these conventional lines is that if part of the system fails then the whole system fails (although some parallel architectures can overcome this problem to some extent). Moreover, in conventional memory units, pieces of data are stored in one or more individual memory locations with definite addresses. If these memory units fail then that data is lost, and again the whole system may fail.

In an attempt to overcome the above problems much work is currently in progress into the use of *neural networks* which seek to model the processing capability of the human brain. The latter, of course, consists of a large number $\sim 10^9$) of neurons interconnected in highly complex ways. Thus the human brain is a large-scale parallel computer, among other things. Since we are so good at

357

pattern recognition it is argued that such neural computers should perform better than conventional hardware, at least in the area of pattern recognition. A *neuron* is a simple computing device which can be connected to a large number of other such devices. In a neural computer there is no specific unit identified as the 'central processor' and no separate memory. The whole system consisting of the interconnected neurons *is* the processor *and* the memory. Thus, not only is the processing distributed over the system, so also is the data in such a way that no single piece of data or *pattern* is associated with a single neuron. Only part of a pattern 'exists' at any given neuron – the complete pattern only exists on the whole system. A major advantage of this design is that if one neuron fails then 'most' of the pattern (and the processing capability) is still functional and the system will be almost as good as it was before the failure. Another important advantage is that such systems can be very good at *generalization*, i.e. if a system is designed to recognize certain patterns and a sample is 'similar' to the training samples then the system will correctly classify the new sample.

Neural computers are ideally suited to the pattern recognition problem since they can be 'taught' new patterns simply by presenting the sample at the input of the system. Knowledge (i.e. data) is stored in the system in the form of the interconnection strengths between the neurons. A neuron can either *excite* or *inhibit* other neurons to which it is connected. When a new pattern is presented to the system the connection strengths will change with time until a new stable configuration is reached. At this point we can say that the new pattern has been 'learned'. Of course, the system must learn the new pattern without destroying other knowledge stored in the neurons. That this is possible is due to a basic property of large-scale neural networks, i.e. if the new pattern only changes the connection strengths at each node by a small amount the previous data will not be lost. It is these small changes summed over the large number of neurons which account for the storage of the new pattern. Of course, any given system must have a limit to the number of 'distinct' patterns it can store, a point which will be discussed later.

Some neural computers have yet another important property – that of self-organization. Since the data is stored in the connection strengths of the neurons which stabilize according to well-defined dynamical equations, the network effectively organizes itself into a particular set of connection strengths – this is ideal for unsupervised learning.

21.2 *General networks*

In this section we shall discuss general networks of neurons and various learning modes. A single *neuron* is a computing device which has a number of inputs i_j $(1 \leq j \leq n)$ and a single output o (Figure 21.1). The neuron computes the output from the inputs in the following way. First the inputs are combined (usually linearly) to form the *weighted input I*, given by

$$I = \sum_{j=1}^{n} w_j i_j \qquad (21.2.1)$$

where w_j is the weight which the neuron assigns to the jth input. (It is these values which store the data in the neurons.) The neuron has an internal state dynamic given by the equation

$$a(t + 1) = F(a(t), I(t)) \qquad (21.2.2)$$

(or by a corresponding continuous-time equation) where a is the 'state of activation' of the neuron. Finally, the output is computed as some given function of the state a:

$$o = f(a).$$

The output function f is often a threshold device, as in Figure 21.2. The

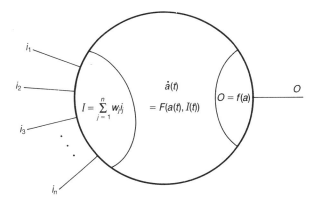

Figure 21.1   A single neuron.

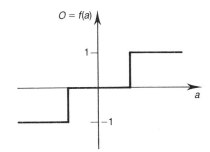

Figure 21.2   A   threshold   output
function.

dynamic state activation is often replaced by a static rule of the form

$$a = F(I)$$

where F is a sigmoid function of the type shown in Figure 21.3.

Following Hinton, we may define a neural network as a 'collection of interconnected processors in which long-term memory is stored in the connection strengths[1] (Figure 21.4(a)). These can be represented in a more orderly form, as in Figure 21.4(b). Note that we have shown the output of a neuron feeding back into its own input. Clearly, this is the most general topology possible – other topologies, where such connections do not exist, can be represented in this form with a zero input weighting. In a general network of this form we shall denote the ith neuron by N_i, its input, activation and output

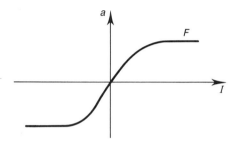

Figure 21.3 A sigmoid static activation rule.

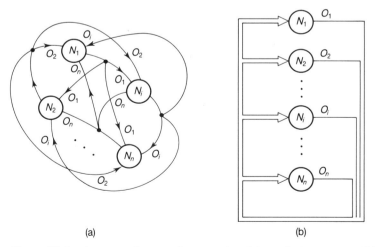

(a)   (b)

Figure 21.4 A general neural network: (a) typical system; (b) 'canonical' representation.

by I_i, a_i and o_i, respectively, and its jth weight by w_{ij}. Thus, the weighted input to the ith neuron is

$$I_i = \sum_{j=1}^{n} w_{ij}o_j \qquad (21.2.4)$$

This is often called the *propagation rule*. It defines a family of hyperplanes in $(o_1, \ldots, o_n)$ space, the positions of which are determined by the weights. The weights determine the strengths of interconnections (as stated above, if $w_{ij} = 0$ then the jth neuron has no direct effect on N_i). If $w_{ij} < 0$ we say that N_j *inhibits* N_i, while if $w_{ij} > 0$ we say that N_j *excites* N_i. Again as we have already remarked, whether or not $w_{ij} \neq 0$ determines the topology of the network, which affects what the system can learn.

The main purpose of a neural network is to learn patterns of information and store them in the weights w_{ij}. The training phase of a neural network consists of a dynamic relationship for the evolution of the weights; this dynamic propagation equation for w_{ij} is called the *learning rule* and is usually a generalization of the perceptron algorithm described earlier. A basic idea, which leads to *Hebb's rule*, is that if the ith neuron receives an input from the jth neuron and both are highly active, then the connection between N_i and N_j should be strengthened. This learning rule can be expressed in the form

$$w_{ij}(t + 1) = w_{ij}(t) + \eta a_i o_j \qquad (21.2.5)$$

(for a discrete system), where η is a constant which determines the learning rate. This simple rule is not particularly effective, however, and more general ones will be introduced later. Most learning rules are of the form

$$w_{ij}(t + 1) = w_{ij}(t) + g(a_i(t), T_i(t))h(o_j(t), w_{ij}) \qquad (21.2.6)$$

where T is a 'teaching input' used in training the system. For example, a generalized Hebb's rule, including a teaching input is given by

$$w_{ij}(t + 1) = w_{ij}(t) + \eta(T_i(t) - a_i(t))o_j(t). \qquad (21.2.7)$$

From (21.2.1), (21.2.2) and (21.2.6) we see that a neural network can be described by the dynamic equations

$$a_i(t + 1) = F(a_i(t), \sum_{j=1}^{n} w_{ij}f_j(a_j))$$

$$w_{ij}(t + 1) = w_{ij}(t) + g(a_i(t), T_i(t))h(f_j(a_j(t)), w_{ij}(t))$$

or

$$\phi(t + 1) = \mathcal{F}(\phi(t), T(t)) \qquad (21.2.8)$$

where

$$\phi = (a_1, \ldots, a_n, w_{11}, \ldots, w_{nn})^{\mathrm{T}}$$

and $\mathcal{F}$ is an obvious function. Thus a neural network is represented by a very general nonlinear dynamical system with a teaching (or control) input.

For pattern recognition we are interested in two basic types of learning for a neural network. The first is called *associative learning*, where the system learns to produce a particular pattern of activation on one set of units whenever another pattern occurs on another set of units. This is used, in particular, in *associative memories* for storing patterns. If the input and output patterns are the same we have *auto-association*; a system of this kind can be trained to 'fill in' missing pieces of incomplete or noisy patterns. The other type of learning of importance in pattern recognition is *regularity discovery*, in which one trains the system to respond to 'interesting' patterns, i.e. to recognize structure in input data. Such systems are clearly of use in feature and primitive detection.

We end this section by mentioning some specific models – others will be discussed later. The simplest learning device is the *linear associator* given by the equations

$$a_i(t + 1) = \sum_{j=1}^{n} w_{ij}(t)a_j(t)$$

or

$$\mathbf{a}(t + 1) = W\mathbf{a}(t)$$

where $\mathbf{a} = (a_1, \ldots, a_n)^\mathrm{T}$, $W = (w_{ij})$. The learning rule is

$$w_{ij}(t + 1) = w_{ij}(t) + \eta a_j T_i(t) \tag{21.2.9}$$

Note that

$$\mathbf{a}(t + k) = W^k \mathbf{a}(k)$$

and so what can be learned in k steps can also be learned in one step by the system with weights W^k. This severely restricts the amount which the linear associator can learn.

A *linear threshold system* is one in which the output function f_i of each neuron is the identity function, so that $o_i = a_i$ and where the activation is two-valued, e.g.

$$a_i(t + 1) = \begin{cases} 0 & \text{if } I_i(t) \leq \theta_i \\ 1 & \text{if } I_i(t) > \theta_i \end{cases}$$

for some thresholds θ_i, $1 \leq i \leq n$, where

$$I_i = \sum_{j=1}^{n} w_{ij} a_j$$

The learning rule is of the form

$$w_{ij}(t + 1) = w_{ij}(t) + \eta(T_i - a_i)a_j \tag{21.2.10}$$

The perceptron is an example of a linear threshold system, as can be seen from the perceptron algorithm described earlier.

Another example of a neural network is the so-called 'brain state in a box'. Here the activation is of the form

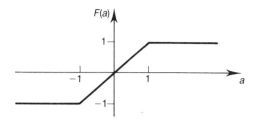

Figure 21.5 Activation function for the brain state in a box.

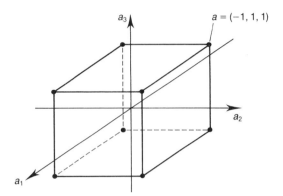

Figure 21.6 Eventual states for the brain state in a box.

$$a_i(t + 1) = F(a_i(t) + \sum_{j=1}^{n} w_{ij}a_j(t))$$

where F is a simple limiter as shown in Figure 21.5.

The learning rule is either (21.2.9) or (21.2.10). Note that each state a_i, is forced to either $+1$ or -1 as t increases, and so $a = (a_1, \ldots, a_n)$ eventually lies at the corner of a hypercube in n-dimensional space, as in Figure 21.6 (for $n = 3$), hence the name 'brain state in a box'.

21.3 Neural networks as parallel memories and content addressability

In a conventional computer memory, a word of data is accessed by placing its address on the address bus and instructing the memory to supply the byte at that address. The contents of the byte are irrelevant as far as the processing is concerned since the processor operates on bytes (or words) in parallel irrespective of what their contents may be. The interpretation of the final results is a matter for the programmer. Humans, on the other hand, are extremely good at retrieving contextually useful information from the memory. Such information is not stored at a particular address but is distributed over a large number of neurons in the form of appropriate weights. Addressing by content, then, means activating the neurons according to the attributes of a particular piece of information we wish to retrieve.

As an example of the use of neural nets as content-addressable memories, consider the simplified problem of animal classification shown in Figure 21.7. Each attribute is modelled by a single neuron which excites other neurons (the exact connection strengths are not particularly important in this qualitative example). An exciting terminal is shown by an arrowhead, so that neurons connected by a line with an arrowhead at each end are mutually exciting.

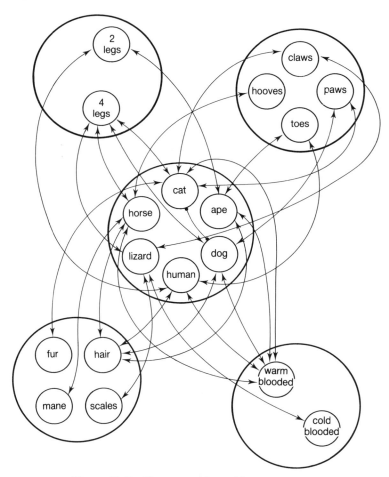

Figure 21.7 Content addressable memory.

Suppose we wish to recall the attributes of a horse (only a small number of attributes are shown here, of course). If we activate the 'horse' neuron in the central set, then the 'mane', 'hair', '4 legs', 'hooves' and 'warm blooded' neurons will then be activated since the 'horse' neuron is exciting for the latter neurons. Note that if one connection fails, say the 'horse' to '4 legs' exciting connection, then we will still retrieve the remaining attributes 'mane', 'hair', 'hooves' and 'warm blooded' and the system will certainly not fail totally. Another important property of this type of memory is that we can 'interrogate' it at any particular feature or attribute. Thus if we activate the 'hooves' neuron, then the 'horse' neuron will be activated, and then all the other horse attributes, as before. Note, however, that when the 'warm blooded' neuron is activated this will active the other mammalian neurons. It is thus important to choose the weights representing the interconnection strengths carefully so that activating 'hooves' does not activate 'cat' too strongly (via the connection hooves → horses → warm blooded → cat). One way to improve this situation is to include inhibitory neurons such as the one connecting dog to cat (with the dots at the ends of the line), since an animal cannot be a dog and a cat simultaneously.

One advantage of 'hooves' activating 'cat' (even if only slightly) and the other mammals via the 'warm blooded' neuron is that of *generalization*. Although a cat does not have hooves it shares many other attributes with related mammals and so activating a particular attribute activates closely related ones (to a greater or lesser extent).

An important neural memory for pattern recognition is the *pattern asso-ciator* or *linear associator* described earlier. Suppose we wish to design a system which associates an output pattern, say $(1, 1, -1, 1, -1, -1)$ with a given input pattern, say $(1, -1, -1, -1, 1, 1)$ (pattern variables are taken to be ± 1 for simplicity). A neural network which will achieve this is given in Figure 21.8. We have seen that the activations in a linear associator are given by

$$a_i = \Sigma w_{ij} a_j$$

(in the static case) so that we simply choose the correct weight for which the output activation has the appropriate value. Thus,

$$\bar{a}_1 = \tfrac{1}{6}a_1 - \tfrac{1}{6}a_2 - \tfrac{1}{6}a_3 - \tfrac{1}{6}a_4 + \tfrac{1}{6}a_5 + \tfrac{1}{6}a_6$$

giving $\bar{a}_1 = 1$ if $(a_1, \ldots, a_6) = (1, 1, -1, 1, -1, -1)$ is the input pattern. (The pattern of weights for a_1 is just the input vector multiplied by $1/6$. We could omit the factor $1/6$ and threshold the result.) In matrix form we can write

$$\bar{\mathbf{a}} = W\mathbf{a}$$

where

$$\mathbf{a} = (a_1, \ldots, a_6)^{\mathrm{T}}, \bar{\mathbf{a}} = (\bar{a}_1, \ldots, \bar{a}_6)^{\mathrm{T}}, W = (w_{ij}).$$

Since the weights w_{ij}, $1 \leq j \leq 6$, in the ith row of W are simply the normalized

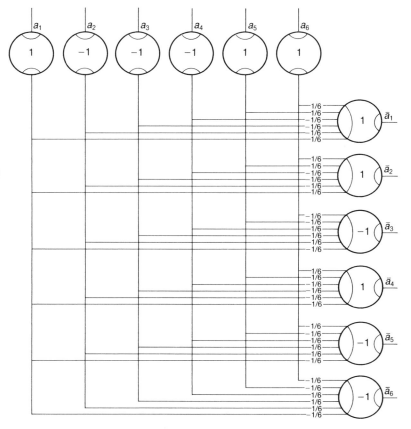

Figure 21.8   A pattern associator.

vector components of the input, we have

$$W = \begin{bmatrix} \mathbf{a}^T/6 \\ \mathbf{a}^T/6 \\ -\mathbf{a}^T/6 \\ \mathbf{a}^T/6 \\ -\mathbf{a}^T/6 \\ -\mathbf{a}^T/6 \end{bmatrix}$$

where a^T is regarded as a row vecor, for then we have

$$W\mathbf{a} = (\mathbf{a}^T\mathbf{a}/6, \mathbf{a}^T\mathbf{a}/6, -\mathbf{a}^T\mathbf{a}/6, \mathbf{a}^T\mathbf{a}/6, -\mathbf{a}^T\mathbf{a}/6, -\mathbf{a}^T\mathbf{a}/6)$$

$$= (1, 1, -1, 1, -1, -1) = \bar{\mathbf{a}}.$$

Now suppose we wish to store a second pattern pair $(\mathbf{b}, \bar{\mathbf{b}})$ in the system (i.e. to associate $\mathbf{b}$ with $\bar{\mathbf{b}}$). Assume that a and b are orthogonal, so that

$$\mathbf{a}^T\mathbf{b} = 0$$

Moreover, suppose that $\bar{\mathbf{b}} = (-1, -1, -1, 1, -1, 1)$. Define the weight matrix by

$$W = \begin{bmatrix} \mathbf{a}^T/6 - \mathbf{b}^T/6 \\ \mathbf{a}^T/6 - \mathbf{b}^T/6 \\ -\mathbf{a}^T/6 - \mathbf{b}^T/6 \\ \mathbf{a}^T/6 + \mathbf{b}^T/6 \\ -\mathbf{a}^T/6 - \mathbf{b}^T/6 \\ -\mathbf{a}^T/6 + \mathbf{b}^T/6 \end{bmatrix}$$

Then

$$W\mathbf{a} = (\mathbf{a}^T\mathbf{a}/6 - \mathbf{b}^T\mathbf{a}/6, \mathbf{a}^T\mathbf{a}/6 - \mathbf{b}^T\mathbf{a}/6, -\mathbf{a}^T\mathbf{a}/6 - \mathbf{b}^T\mathbf{a}/6, \mathbf{a}^T\mathbf{a}/6 + \mathbf{b}^T\mathbf{a}/6,$$
$$-\mathbf{a}^T\mathbf{a}/6 - \mathbf{b}^T\mathbf{a}/6, -\mathbf{a}^T\mathbf{a}/6 + \mathbf{b}^T\mathbf{a}/6)$$
$$= \bar{a},$$

since $\mathbf{a}^T\mathbf{b} = \mathbf{b}^T\mathbf{a} = 0$. Similarly,

$$W\mathbf{b} = \bar{\mathbf{b}}$$

and so the pattern pairs $(\mathbf{a}, \bar{\mathbf{a}})$, $(\mathbf{b}, \bar{\mathbf{b}})$ are correctly stored in the system. Note, however, that if $\mathbf{a}$ and $\mathbf{b}$ are not orthogonal then the patterns will 'interfere' and the association will not be perfect. Hence an $n \times n$ linear pattern associator can store, at most n (orthogonal) patterns.

A linear pattern associator of the above type can be used for *autoassociation* in which we associate a pattern with itself (i.e. the system learns pattern pairs of the form $(\mathbf{a}, \mathbf{a})$). This is useful in pattern recognition for recognizing imperfect patterns. Thus, in Figure 21.8, suppose we associate $\mathbf{a} = (1, -1, -1, -1, 1, 1)$ with itself, so that $\bar{\mathbf{a}} = \mathbf{a}$. Then the weight matrix is

$$W = \begin{bmatrix} \mathbf{a}^T/6 \\ -\mathbf{a}^T/6 \\ -\mathbf{a}^T/6 \\ -\mathbf{a}^T/6 \\ \mathbf{a}^T/6 \\ \mathbf{a}^T/6 \end{bmatrix}$$

Suppose that part of the input pattern is missing, so that we actually input $\hat{\mathbf{a}} = (1, -1, 0, -1, 1, 1)$ into the system. Then the output will be

$$W\hat{\mathbf{a}} = (5/6, -5/6, -5/6, -5/6, 5/6, 5/6)^T$$
$$= 5/6\mathbf{a}$$

and so thresholding the output gives the correct pattern **a**. Hence the pattern associator can recreate the correct pattern from an imperfect copy.

In the above discussion we have assumed that the activation levels are fixed at the correct levels. Now consider the dynamic situation where the input vector is presented to the system (with fixed weights) and the activation levels are allowed to find the correct values in accordance with the discrete equation

$$\mathbf{a}(k + 1) = W\mathbf{a}(k) \qquad (21.3.1)$$

for some initial value **a**(0). Then

$$\mathbf{a}(k) = W^k\mathbf{a}(0)$$

and it is important to study the stability of this system.

In the autoassociative case, W is symmetric and has zero diagonal. To apply Lyapunov stability theory to the system, consider the energy function

$$E(\mathbf{a}) = -\mathbf{a}W\mathbf{a}^{\mathrm{T}}$$

Then

$$\frac{\Delta E}{\Delta a_k} = -\mathbf{a}\mathbf{w}_k^{\mathrm{T}} - \mathbf{a}\mathbf{w}^k$$

where $\mathbf{w}_k(\mathbf{w}^k)$ is the kth row (column) of W. Since W is symmetric we have

$$\frac{\Delta E}{\Delta a_k} = -2\mathbf{a}\mathbf{w}^k$$

Now if $\mathbf{a}\mathbf{w}^k > 0$ (< 0) then a_k is thresholded to 1 (-1) and so

$$\Delta E = -2\mathbf{a}\mathbf{w}^k \cdot \Delta a_k < 0$$

and E is decreasing along the motion of the system. Thus, since E is bounded below, **a** tends to a finite limit and so the system is stable.

If W is not symmetric then the above result does not hold and so stability in the non-autoassociative case may not occur. To overcome this difficulty the *bidirectional associative memory* (BAM) has been proposed in which we associate pairs of data $(\mathbf{a}_i, \mathbf{b}_i)$. Instead of using the dynamics (21.3.1), in which **a**(k) is input to the associator and the new value **a**$(k + 1)$ at the output is again fedback to the input, we use the dynamics

$$\mathbf{b}(k + 1) = W\mathbf{a}(k)$$

$$\mathbf{a}(k + 1) = W^{\mathrm{T}}\mathbf{b}(k).$$

This means that we feed **a** *forwards* to obtain **b** and then **b** *backwards* to obtain the next **a**, hence the name BAM. These equations determine a second-order system

$$\begin{bmatrix} \mathbf{b} \\ \mathbf{a} \end{bmatrix}(k + 1) = \begin{bmatrix} 0 & W \\ W^{\mathrm{T}} & 0 \end{bmatrix}\begin{bmatrix} \mathbf{b} \\ \mathbf{a} \end{bmatrix}(k)$$

which is effectively an autoassociative system with patterns

$$\begin{bmatrix} \mathbf{b}_i \\ \mathbf{a}_i \end{bmatrix}$$

Since

$$\begin{bmatrix} 0 & W \\ W^{\mathrm{T}} & 0 \end{bmatrix}$$

is symmetric, stability follows as before. The encoding matrix W is given by

$$W = \sum_i \mathbf{a}_i^{\mathrm{T}} \mathbf{b}_i$$

where $\mathbf{a}_i^{\mathrm{T}}$ is a column vector and $\mathbf{b}_i$ is a row vector, assuming bipolar patterns $\mathbf{a}_i$, $\mathbf{b}_i$ (i.e. each element of $\mathbf{a}_i$ and $\mathbf{b}_i$ is ± 1). Note, finally, that stability of the system can also be proved in the continuous-time case and for *adaptive* networks in which the weight matrix changes in accordance with a simple Hebbian learning rule

$$\dot{w}_{ij} = -w_{ij} + S(a_i)S(b_j)$$

where S is a monotone increasing sigmoid function as in Figure 21.3.

21.4 Neural network types

One of the main problems in neural network theory is to obtain a topological structure and learning rule which guarantee the stability of the network, i.e. so that the weights and activations settle down to some equilibrium values. Many simple dynamical systems have a small number of equilibria and so the search for a stable one is usually quite easy. In general networks, however, there are many equilibria representing the local minima of an energy function. Convergence of the dynamical system to some equilibrium does not guarantee that a global minimum of the energy has been found – there may be many local minima in some region with the global minimum being far away. In this section we shall briefly review some of the existing types of neural networks and their properties.

Systems containing a single layer of perceptrons have been studied extensively in the past and it was found that there were many problems which could not be solved by such systems. This led to a pessimism about the effectiveness of neural networks until Hopfield and others considered multilayered networks. The basic *Hopfield net* is simply an autoassociative memory, with fixed weights, of the type considered in the last section. If the pattern samples from m classes are $\mathbf{x}^k = (x_n^k, \ldots, x_n^k)$, $1 \leq k \leq m$, where $x_j^k = \pm 1$ then the weights are chosen to be

$$w_{ij} = \sum_{k=1}^{m} x_i^k x_j^k \qquad i \neq j$$

$$w_{ii} = 0 \qquad\qquad 1 \leqslant i \leqslant n$$

Given any unknown input pattern $(\bar{x}_i)$ the activation levels a_i of the nodes are chosen to satisfy the dynamics

$$a_j(t + 1) = f\left(\sum_{i=0}^{n} w_{ij} a_i(t)\right) \qquad 1 \leqslant j \leqslant n$$

$$a_j(0) = \bar{x}_j \qquad\qquad 1 \leqslant j \leqslant n$$

Here, f is the hard limiter function defined by

$$f(\zeta) = \begin{cases} 1 & \text{if } \zeta \geqslant 0 \\ -1 & \text{if } \zeta < 0 \end{cases}$$

A refinement of the basic Hopfield net is the *Hamming net* which is a minimum error classifier. Again we suppose that m binary pattern samples are given as above. For any given unknown input pattern $(\bar{x}_i)$ we measure the *Hamming distance* between $\bar{x}$ and the sample $\mathbf{x}^k$ by

$$H(\mathbf{x}^k, \bar{\mathbf{x}}) = \sum_{j=1}^{n} v_j$$

where

$$v_j = 1 \quad \text{if } x_j^k \neq \bar{x}_j$$

$$ = 0 \quad \text{if } x_j^k = \bar{x}_j$$

i.e. $H(\mathbf{x}^k, \bar{\mathbf{x}})$ measures the number of bits of $\bar{x}$ which do not match the corresponding bits of $\mathbf{x}^k$. A Hamming net is a multilayer network consisting of a feedforward system, the outputs of which (after convergence) are n minus the Hamming distances to the pattern samples, and a Hopfield-like system which chooses the maximum of these values. The output of the feedforward network will be a maximum at the node corresponding to the sample pattern which is closest to the (unknown) input sample (Figure 21.9). The weights in the top net are inhibitory (with value $-\varepsilon$) and work on a 'winner takes all' basis, i.e. the activation levels converge to values of which only one is positive, corresponding to the maximum of the outputs of the nodes in the middle layer. The equations for the Hamming net may be written in the form

WEIGHTS

$$\text{Lower net: } w_{ij} = \frac{x_i^j}{2}, \; \theta_j = n/2 \quad 1 \leqslant i \leqslant n, \, 1 \leqslant j \leqslant m$$

(x^j is the jth sample pattern, θ_j is a threshold)

Output

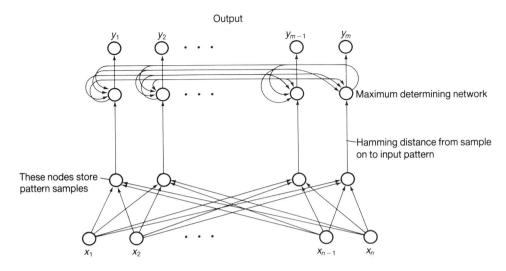

Figure 21.9 Hamming net.

$$\text{Upper net: } w_{ij} = \left\{ \begin{array}{ll} 1 & i = j \\ -\varepsilon & i \neq j, \ \varepsilon < 1/m \quad 0 \leqslant i, j \leqslant m \end{array} \right.$$

DYNAMICS

$$\text{(Upper net): } a_j(t + 1) = f\left(a_j(t) - \varepsilon \sum_{i \neq j} a_i(t)\right), \quad 0 \leqslant i, j \leqslant m$$

with initial value

$$a_j(0) = f\left(\sum_{i=1}^{n} w_{ij}x_i - \theta_j\right), \quad 0 \leqslant j \leqslant m$$

where f is a threshold logic nonlinearity as in Figure 21.10. The Hamming net can be shown to be stable for $\varepsilon < 1/m$.

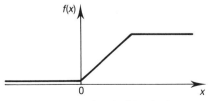

Figure 21.10 Threshold logic non-linearity for Hamming net.

Another generalization of the Hopfield net is the multilayered feedforward network. In these systems only the first layer is in direct contact with the 'external world' – the other layers are free to settle into any consistent internal representation. There are no connections within each layer and each layer is fully connected to the next layer (Figure 21.11). Let a_i^l be the activation of the ith neuron in layer l, $(1 \leq i \leq N, 1 \leq l \leq L)$ where there are N neurons in each layer. If w_{ij}^l is the coupling weight on the connection between the jth neuron in layer l and the ith neuron in layer $l + 1$, then we define

$$a_i^{l+1} = \text{sgn}\left\{ \sum_{j=1}^{N} w_{ij}^l a_j^l \right\}$$

As in an associative memory, the initial weights are chosen to be

$$w_{ij}^l = \frac{1}{N} \sum_{\gamma=1}^{p} x_{i,\gamma}^{l+1} x_{j,\gamma}^l \tag{21.4.1}$$

where $x_{i\gamma}^l$, $1 \leq \gamma \leq p$ are the stored patterns (i.e. $x_{j,\gamma}^1$ are p input samples and the patterns $x_{j,\gamma}^l$ for $l > 1$ are arbitrarily assigned initially). In the learning stage we begin by initializing $x_{i,\gamma}^2(0) = \pm 1$ randomly and update the stored patterns according to the dynamics

$$w_{ij}^1(t) = \frac{1}{N} \sum_{\gamma=1}^{p} x_{i,\gamma}^2(t) x_{j,\gamma}^1$$

$$x_{i,\gamma}^2(t + 1) = \text{sgn}\left\{ \sum_{j=1}^{N} w_{ij}^1(t) x_{j,\gamma}^1 \right\} \tag{21.4.2}$$

where $x_{j,\gamma}^1$, $1 \leq \gamma \leq p$ are the input samples. These equations can be shown to be stable and after convergence of $x_{i,\gamma}^2(t)$ we train the third layer from the second in the same way, and so on for each pair of layers. It can be shown that if $\alpha \triangleq p/N < 0.18$, then the system learns the input samples perfectly and also has good noise characteristics in the sense that it will recall exactly a learned sample pattern from a noisy version of the pattern if the noise is not too large. It should be noted, however, that if L is large, then the stored patterns in the last layer can become completely correlated (i.e. all input samples are mapped onto the same output).

Instead of allowing the 'internal representations' of the sample patterns to be updated dynamically (according to (21.4.2)) another popular training method for feedforward networks is via back error propagation which alters the weights directly. In this case we do not allow the last layer to be self-organizing – instead we choose a set of desired outputs and train the system on the basis of the errors between the actual outputs obtained by passing the input data through the feedforward network and the desired outputs. These errors are then propagated through the network in the reverse direction. Consider the system in Figure 21.12. Note that we allow different numbers of neurons in each layer. Forward propagation is similar to that of the feedforward network considered earlier. This time a bias is added to the activation to shift the output of the

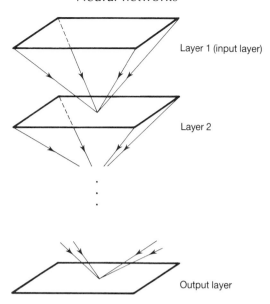

Figure 21.11 A general feedforward network.

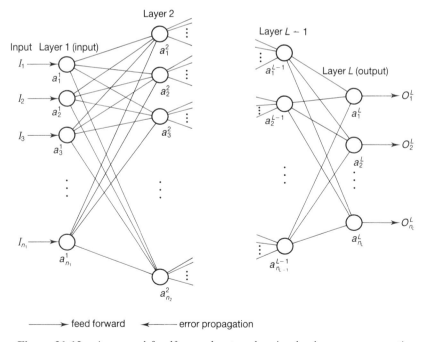

feed forward ⟵ error propagation

Figure 21.12 A general feedforward network using back error propagation.

neuron (via the sigmoid nonlinearity F). The equations for feedforward propagation are as follows:

$$o_i^1 = I_i$$

(the output of the first layer neurons is just the corresponding input)

$$\left. \begin{array}{l} a_i^k = \left(\sum_j w_{ji}^{k-1} o_j^{k-1} \right) + B_i^k \\[2em] o_i^k = F(a_i^k) \end{array} \right\} \quad 2 \leqslant k \leqslant L,\ 1 \leqslant i \leqslant n_i$$

where B_i^k is the bias in the kth layer.

Once the inputs I_i have propagated to the outputs o_j^L of layer L, we
determine the errors

$$\varepsilon_j^L = F'(a_j^L)(d_j - o_j^L) \quad 1 \leqslant j \leqslant n_L$$

between the actual outputs o_j^L and some desired outputs d_j. (Here F' is the
derivative of F.) These errors are then propagated backwards through the
network towards the input layer according to the rules:

$$\left. \begin{array}{l} \varepsilon_j^L = F'(a_j^L)(d_j - o_j^L) \\[1em] \Delta w_{ij}^{L-1} = \beta o_i^{L-1} \varepsilon_j^L \\[1em] \Delta B_i^L = \beta \varepsilon_i^L \end{array} \right\} \qquad \text{layer } L$$

$$\left. \begin{array}{l} \varepsilon_j^k = F'(a_j^k) \left(\sum_i w_{ji}^k \varepsilon_i^k \right) \\[1em] \Delta w_{ij}^{k-1} = \beta o_i^{k-1} \varepsilon_j^k \\[1em] \Delta B_i^k = \beta \varepsilon_i^k \end{array} \right\} \qquad \text{layer } k, \quad 2 \leqslant k \leqslant L - 1$$

where $0 < \beta \ll 1$ is a 'small' parameter. This parameter must be small so that
stability of the system is achieved; this implies slow learning, requiring a large
number of iterations of the type described above, until the error ε converges to
zero.

The systems described above are designed to approach an equilibrium point
of a certain dynamical system. Such equilibrium points can be regarded as
(local) minima of energy (or Lyapunov) functions of the systems. In many cases
there are a large number of local minima, some close to the global minimum
and some significantly higher. The latter do not represent good solutions to the
learning problem, but techniques such as steepest descent minimization (which is
the basis of many learning algorithms) may 'hang' on such a local minimum.
One can obviate this difficulty by allowing some randomness in the search for a
minimum in the hope that after a large number of random starting values the
global minimum will be found eventually. The *Boltzmann machine* is a neural
network which seeks the global minimum of its 'energy' in this way and we shall
describe this type of network briefly in the remainder of this section.

A Boltzmann machine is a neural network consisting of units with activation values $a_i = 0$ or 1 (off or on) and with symmetric weights, i.e. $w_{ij} = w_{ji}$. The *energy* of the system is defined by

$$E(w_{ij}, a_i) = -\sum_{i=1}^{n}\sum_{j=1}^{n} w_{ij}a_i a_j$$

The energy is minimized during training over the values of a_i which correspond to *hidden units* (i.e. ones which are not fixed by input or output patterns which are to be learned). This minimization is done for fixed weights w_{ij}. When this minimum has been found the weights are altered by minimizing another function (to be specified below) over w_{ij} with the activation values a_i fixed at the ones found in the previous minimization of E. This cycle is then repeated until learning is complete.

Consider, first, the minimization of E. As stated above, some of the activation values a_i correspond to input or output units which are clamped during training to some desired patterns. By renumbering, we can assume these are $a_1, \ldots, a_k$. We then require to minimize E over $a_{k+1}, \ldots, a_n$ (the activation values of the hidden or internal units). It should be noted that it is the values $a_{k+1}, \ldots, a_n$ which generate the internal model of the external environment. We minimize E by using the random search method discussed above. However, rather than let new values of $a_{k+1}, \ldots, a_n$ be totally random we adopt the following strategy. With completely deterministic minimization algorithms we accept only new values of $a_{k+1}, \ldots, a_n$ which make E smaller. This often has the effect of finding only a single local minimum. In the random search method new values of the activations which actually increase E are also accepted, but only with probability $\exp(-E/T)$, where T is some parameter. This will lead to a Boltzmann distribution of the neural states. By analogy with many physical processes we think of the network as being in 'thermal equilibrium' and regard T as the 'temperature'. For large temperature T, $\exp(-E/T)$ is much larger than the corresponding value for small T, and so at high temperatures the probability of accepting uphill moves is quite large and equilibrium is achieved quickly. For low temperatures, equilibrium takes longer to find, but lower energy states are favoured. Thus a good strategy for minimizing E is to start at a high temperature and reduce T slowly. For this reason this method is called *optimization by simulated annealing*, by analogy with the annealing of metals.

Next we must consider the training of the weights w_{ij}. Since we have assigned k states as visible units there are 2^k possible patterns which can be imposed on the system and so, at most, 2^k patterns can be learned. However, for large k this requires many internal nodes and so most networks will have fewer such nodes than are necessary to learn all possible input patterns. We therefore need a measure of how well such a real system is performing relative to a perfect system which can learn all possible input patterns. Such a measure is provided by the information metric

$$G = \sum_{\alpha} p_{\alpha} \ln [p_{\alpha}/\bar{p}_{\alpha}] \tag{21.4.3}$$

where α is a state of the visible units (for example, $\alpha = (a_1, \ldots, a_k)$ may be $(1, 1, 0, 0, \ldots, 0)$), p_{α} is the probability of the visible units being in state α when the state is determined by the input pattern and $\bar{p}_{\alpha}$ is the probability of the visible units being in state α when the system is free running, i.e. when no patterns are imposed on the visible units. Note that p_{α} is the 'environmental distribution' and does not depend on w_{ij}. The probability distributions p_{α} and $\bar{p}_{\alpha}$ will be equal (so that $G = 0$) only when the system is perfect, i.e. can learn all possible input patterns – otherwise G is positive. To minimize G we use a steepest descent algorithm which requires the derivative of G with respect to w_{ij}. It is not difficult to show that

$$\partial G/\partial w_{ij} = -(1/T)(p_{ij} - \bar{p}_{ij}) \tag{21.4.4}$$

where

$$p_{ij} = \sum_{\alpha} \sum_{\beta} p_{\alpha\beta} s_i^{\alpha\beta} s_j^{\alpha\beta}$$

$$\bar{p}_{ij} = \sum_{\alpha} \sum_{\beta} \bar{p}_{\alpha\beta} s_i^{\alpha\beta} s_j^{\alpha\beta}$$

and α is summed over visible unit states and β over hidden unit states. ($s_i^{\alpha\beta}$ is the state of unit i when the visible units are in state α and the hidden units are in state β; $p_{\alpha\beta}$, $\bar{p}_{\alpha\beta}$ are the obvious joint probabilities.) The probability distributions p_{ij} and $\bar{p}_{ij}$ can be approximated by averaging during the training stage.

21.5 Application of neural networks to pattern recognition

In this section we shall consider briefly the application of general neural networks to a specific problem in pattern recognition – that of recognizing image patterns which are translated or rotated versions of the trained patterns. Before doing this we shall first show the connections between neural networks and decision-theoretic pattern recognition, as discussed earlier. We recall that the basic idea of decision-oriented pattern recognition is to represent patterns by a feature vector in some n-dimensional space and then try to separate the sample patterns in different classes by decision boundaries. In the case of linear boundaries, this led to the perceptron and LMS algorithms for moving the boundary hyperplane until all patterns samples were correctly classified. This process can be modelled by the *perceptron* or *adaptive linear neuron* (ADALINE) shown in Figure 21.13. The input vector is simply a pattern and the

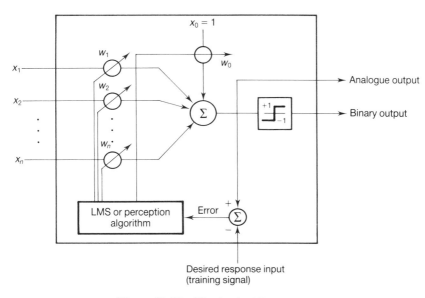

Figure 21.13 The basic ADALINE.

weights $w_1, \ldots, w_n$ correspond to the coefficients of the hyperplane. These coefficients are changed adaptively by the perceptron or LMS algorithms which place the hyperplane in such a way as to classify the input pattern correctly (in accordance with the training signal). The weight w_0 and the fixed value $x_0 = 1$ correspond to the augmented vectors introduced earlier.

As we saw before, not all pattern samples in a given pattern recognition problem are linearly separable and so there are many problems which single layer perceptrons cannot solve. For example, suppose the binary patterns $(+1, +1), (+1, -1), (-1, -1), (-1, +1)$ are classified as follows:

$$\text{Class 1: } \{(+1, +1), (-1, -1)\}$$

$$\text{Class 2: } \{(+1, -1), (-1, +1)\}$$

Then no straight line in two-dimensional space will separate class 1 from class 2. We can solve this problem with a two-layer network, however. In fact, if we first design an AND gate using a single (nonadaptive) ADALINE, as in Figure 21.14, then we can solve the problem using the two-layer network shown in Figure 21.15.

This demonstrates the importance of multilayered neural networks in pattern recognition, and in principle shows how to solve almost any given problem (at the expense of a very large network). A typical problem in adaptive image pattern analysis is to recognize new patterns which are simply rotated or translated (possibly noisy) versions of known image patterns. To solve this

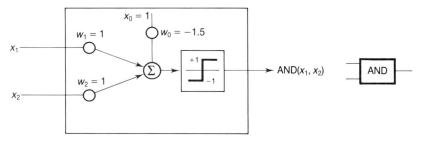

Figure 21.14 Implementing an AND gate using a single ADALINE.

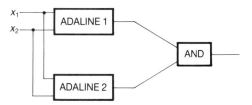

Figure 21.15 Solving a nonlinear separation
problem.

problem consider an input image made up of $N \times N$ pixels and map this onto a
slab of neurons which is translation invariant in the sense that the (single)
output of this slab is the same no matter how the input pattern is translated
(Figure 21.16). (Note that the majority voting output neuron can be made using
a single ADALINE.)

The weights in the slab of neurons can be chosen to make it translation-
invariant in the following way. First note that every pixel in the image feeds into
every neuron in the slab (the number of neurons in the slab is the same as the
number of pixels). Let the weights on the inputs to neuron $(1, 1)$ be given by
the matrix

$$W^{(1,1)} = (w_{ij}^{(1,1)}) \quad 1 \leq i, j \leq N.$$

Then the weights on the inputs to the other neurons are the same except that
they are permuted by rows or columns across the slab. Thus,

$$W^{(1,2)} = CW^{(1,1)}$$

$$W^{(2,1)} = RW^{(1,1)}$$

where C is the elementary operation of moving the columns of a matrix to the
right and replacing the first column by the last, and R is the similar operation
performed on the rows. In general,

$$W^{(i,j)} = R^{i-1}C^{j-1}W^{(1,1)}$$

Input image pattern (5 × 5)

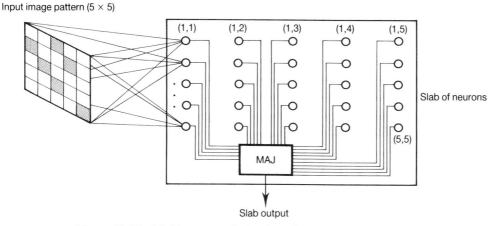

Figure 21.16 Making a translation-invariant slab of neurons ($N = 5$).

It is easily seen that the slab of neurons and their corresponding weights so generated are translation-invariant.

Now suppose we have a neural network $\mathcal{S}$ (of one of the types discussed in the preceding section) which is designed to recognize the given patterns (in fixed position), and suppose that $\mathcal{S}$ has M inputs. Then we make M identical slabs of the type discussed above and use the outputs of the slabs as inputs to $\mathcal{S}$ (Figure 21.17).

Rotation-invariance can be dealt with similarly and will be left as an interesting exercise for the reader.

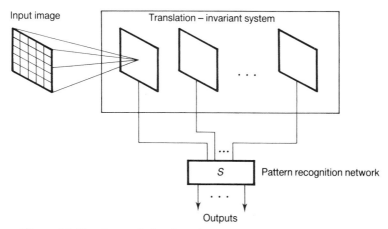

Figure 21.17 A translation-invariant pattern recognition system.

21.6 Application of neural networks to image processing

In the last section of this chapter we shall mention very briefly two typical applications of neural networks to image processing. In the first example we consider the removal of a known shift-invariant blur and noise by a neural network. The system will require a network with $L^2 \times M$ mutually interconnected neurons for an image with $L \times L$ pixels and M grey levels. The activation level of neuron (i, k) will be denoted by $a_{i,k}$ $(1 \leq i \leq L^2, 1 \leq k \leq M)$ and the connection weight between neurons (i, k) and (j, l) by $w_{i,k;j,l}$. The weights are required to be symmetric, so that

$$w_{i,k;j,l} = w_{j,l;i,k} \quad 1 \leq i, j \leq L^2, 1 \leq l, k \leq M.$$

Then we let the activation be defined by

$$a_{i,k} = \sum_{j=1}^{L^2} \sum_{l=1}^{M} w_{i,k;j,l} o_{j,l} + I_{i,k} \tag{21.6.1}$$

where $I_{i,k}$ is an input bias. The (binary) output of neuron (i, k) is given by

$$o_{i,k} = g(a_{i,k}) \tag{21.6.2}$$

where

$$g(x) = \begin{cases} 1 & \text{if } x \geq 0 \\ 0 & \text{if } x < 0 \end{cases}$$

Let x be an $L \times L$ image with grey level $x(i, j)$ at the (i, j)th pixel $(1 \leq i, j \leq L)$. Then we shall design the network so that

$$x(i, j) = \sum_{k=1}^{M} o_{m,k} \tag{21.6.3}$$

where $m = (i - 1)xL + j$.

The network will operate in a nonadaptive way by first determing the parameters w and I and then letting the outputs evolve according to (21.6.1) and (21.6.2). The reconstructed image is found from the stablized outputs using (21.6.3). The parameters will be found by equating the energy of the neural network to the energy function obtained when the restoration problem is rewritten in a minimum error formulation. Thus, first note that the blurred and noise degraded image y can be written in the matrix form

$$Y = HX + N \tag{21.6.4}$$

where x is the original image and H is an L^2 by L^2 matrix. The optimal estimate $\hat{X}$ of X is given by minimizing the error

$$E = \tfrac{1}{2}||Y - H\hat{X}||^2 + \tfrac{1}{2}\lambda||D\hat{X}||^2 \tag{21.6.5}$$

where the second term is a constraint on the smoothness of $\hat{X}$. Thus, D could be a block Toeplitz matrix with blocks of the form

$$\frac{1}{6}\begin{bmatrix} 1 & 4 & 1 \\ 4 & -20 & 4 \\ 1 & 4 & 1 \end{bmatrix}$$

which is a 3×3 windowed approximation to the Laplacian. The energy function of the neural network can be written in the form

$$E_N = \frac{-1}{2} \sum_{i=1}^{L^2} \sum_{j=1}^{L^2} \sum_{k=1}^{M} \sum_{l=1}^{M} w_{i,k;j,l} o_{i,k} o_{j,l} - \sum_{i=1}^{L^2} \sum_{k=1}^{M} I_{i,k} o_{i,k}. \qquad (21.6.6)$$

Expanding (21.6.5) and equating it with (21.6.6) it is easy to show that

$$w_{i,k;j,l} = -\sum_{p=1}^{L^2} h_{pi} h_{pj} - \lambda \sum_{p=1}^{L^2} d_{pi} d_{pj} \qquad (21.6.7)$$

$$I_{i,k} = \sum_{p=1}^{L^2} y_p h_{pi}$$

where

$$H = (h_{ij}), \ D = (d_{ij}).$$

Thus, given the blurred image Y and the blurring function H we can find the neural network parameters and the problem is solved, in principle. Note, however, that $w_{i,k;i,k} \neq 0$ and so the neurons have self-feedback which means that the change in energy

$$\Delta E = -\left(\sum_{j=1}^{L^2} \sum_{l=1}^{M} w_{i,k;j,l} o_{j,l} + I_{ik} \right) \Delta o_{ik} - \tfrac{1}{2} w_{i,k;i,k} (\Delta o_{i,k})^2$$

is not always negative during reconstruction. Hence we must be careful in allowing the network to evolve according to (21.6.1) and (21.6.2). We can either allow only those changes in $o_{i,k}$ which lead to ΔE being negative, or operate the system by a method similar to simulated annealing, as described above. Note, finally, that it is also possible to generalize the system to evaluate the parameters w and I adaptively.

The second example which we shall discuss is related to data compression of images. In particular we shall design a neural network for evaluating the coefficients of an image when expanded in terms of some (generally non-orthogonal) basis functions. (As we have seen in Part 2 of the book, this is important in many areas, notably data compression, feature extraction, etc.) Let $I(k, l)$, $1 \leq k$, $l \leq n$ be a discrete image and let $G_i(k, l)$, $1 \leq k$, $l \leq n$, $1 \leq i \leq N$ be a set of discrete functions (not necessarily orthogonal) in terms of which we wish to expand I. Thus, we write

$$I(k, l) = \sum_{i=1}^{N} a_i G_i(k, l) \quad 1 \leq k, l \leq n, \qquad (21.6.8)$$

and we wish to determine the coefficients a_i. (We *do* assume that the functions G_i are complete in the sense that any function I can be expanded in this way.) Of course, if the G_is are orthonormal with respect to the inner product

$$\langle G_i, G_j \rangle = \sum_{k,l} G_i(k, l)G_j(k, l)$$

then we have

$$a_i = \langle G_i, I \rangle$$

In general, when the G_is are not orthonormal we can find the a_is by minimizing the error

$$E = \left\| I - \sum_{i=1}^{N} a_i G_i \right\|^2$$

$$= \sum_{k,l} (I(k, l) - \sum_{i=1}^{N} a_i G_i(k, l))^2$$

Now,

$$\frac{\partial E}{\partial a_i} = -2\langle I, G_i \rangle + 2\left\langle \sum_{k=1}^{n} a_k G_k, G_i \right\rangle \tag{21.6.9}$$

and the minimum is given by $\partial E / \partial a_i = 0$.

Consider the neural network in Figure 21.18. In the first layer the neurons each have the n^2 inputs $I(1, 1), \ldots, I(n, n)$ and the (fixed) weights are $G_i(1, 1), \ldots, G_i(n, n)$ for the ith neuron. The output of the ith neuron is

$$\sum_{k,l} G_i(k, l)I(k, l)$$

The second layer has adjustable states a_i and identity output functions so that the outputs are also a_i, $1 \leq i \leq N$. (Each second layer neuron has n^2 outputs.) The third layer neurons are single-input single-output units with fixed weights $G_i(k, l)$, and the last layer neurons again have fixed weights $G_i(k, l)$ and outputs

$$\sum_{k,l} G_i(k, l)\sum_j a_j G_j(k, l) \quad 1 \leq i \leq N$$

The first and fourth layer feed into the second layer with respective weights $+1$, -1. It can be seen by comparison with the 'energy' change (21.6.9) that if the state of the second layer is changed iteratively according to the rule

$$a_i(t + 1) = a_i(t) + \Delta_i(t) \quad 1 \leq i \leq N$$

where

$$\Delta_i = \langle I, G_i \rangle - \left\langle \sum_{k=1}^{n} a_k G_k, G_i \right\rangle$$

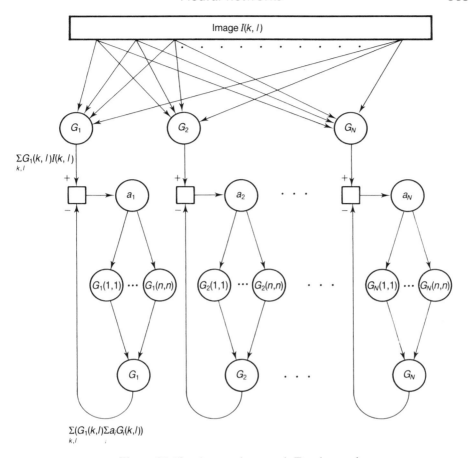

Figure 21.18 A neural network Fourier analyser.

then the network will stabilize to the minimum of E, i.e. the a_i will solve the equation $\partial E/\partial a_i = 0$.

Bibliographical notes

A general discussion of the psychological properties of neural networks is given in Rumelhart and McClelland (1986) and a summary of the main types can be found in Lippmann (1987). Hopfield nets were introduced in Hopfield (1982) and Boltzmann machines are considered in more detail in Rumelhart and McClelland (1986), Ackley *et al.* (1985) and Hinton and Sejnowsky (1983). A complete discussion of bidirectional associative memories is given in Kosko (1988) and stability and learning capacity are considered in Guez *et al.* (1988) and Cohen and Grossberg (1983), while in Meir and Domany (1988) feedforward networks are analysed in detail. Forgetting as a way of improving neural network performance is discussed in Sasiela (1986), where it is argued that the human brain uses such behaviour during REM (rapid eye movement) sleep.

Neural networks for pattern recognition and image processing are given in Daugman (1988), Fukushima (1988), Widrow *et al.* (1988) and Zhou *et al.* (1988). In particular, the application of the Fourier analyser discussed above to Gabor transforms is considered in Daugman (1988).

Exercises

1 Complete Figure 21.7 by adding more inhibitory neurons.
2 Write a Pascal program to implement a Hopfield net.
3 Repeat exercise 2 for a Hamming net.
4 Prove (21.4.4).
5 Design a majority voting neuron for use in Figure 21.16.
6 Design a slab of neurons, similar to that in Figure 21.16, which is invariant under a clockwise 90° rotation.
7 Prove (21.6.7).
8 Write a Pascal program to simulate the Fourier analyser in Figure 21.18.

References

Ackley, D. H., G. E. Hinton and T. J. Sejnowski (1985), 'A learning algorithm for Boltzmann machines', *Cognitive Science*, **9**, 147–68.

Cohen, M. A. and S. Grossberg (1983), 'Absolute stability of global pattern formation and parallel memory storage by competitive neural networks', *IEEE Trans. Sys., Man, Cybern.*, SMC-**13** (no. 5), 815–26.

Daugman, J. G. (1988), 'Complete discrete 2-D Gabor transforms by neural networks for image analysis and compression', *IEEE Trans. Acoust., Speech, Signal Process.*, ASSP **36** (7), 1169–79.

Fukushima, K. (1988), 'A neural network for visual pattern recognition', *Proc. IEEE Computer Soc.*, 65–75.

Guez, A., V. Protopopsecu, and J. Barhen (1988), 'On the stability, storage capacity and design of nonlinear continuous neural networks', *IEEE Trans. Sys., Man, Cybern.*, SMC-**18** (1), 80–7.

Hinton, G. E. and T. J. Sejnowski (1983), 'Optimal perceptive inference', *Proc. IEEE Computer Soc. on Computer Vision and Pattern Recognition*, Washington DC, 448–53.

Hopfield, J. J. (1982), 'Neural networks and physical systems with emergent collective computational abilities', *Proc. Nat. Acad. Sci., USA*, **79**, 2554–8.

Kosko, B. (1988), 'Bidirectional associative memories', *IEEE Trans. Sys. Man, Cybern.* SMC-**18** (1), 49–60.

Lippmann, R. P. (1987), 'An introduction to computing with neural nets', *IEEE Trans. Acoust. Speech, Signal Process., ASSP Magazine*, **34**, 4–22.

Meir, R. and E. Domany (1988), 'Iterated learning in a layered feed-forward neural network', *Phys. Rev. A.*, **20** 2660–8.

Rumelhart, D. E. and J. L. McClelland (1986), *Parallel and Distributed Processing,* vol. 1, Massachusetts: Mass. Inst. of Tech. Press.

Sasiela, R. J. (1986), 'Forgetting as a way to improve neural-net behaviour', *Amer. Inst. Phys.,* **94**, 386–91.

Widrow, B., R. G. Winter and R. A. Baxter (1988), 'Layered neural nets for pattern recognition', *IEEE Trans. Acoust., Speech, Signal Process.,* ASSP **36** (7), 1109–18.

Zhou, Y-T., R. Chellappa, A. Vaid and B. K. Jenkins (1988), 'Image restoration using a neural network', *IEEE Trans. Acoust., Speech, Signal Process.,* ASSP, **36** (7), 1141–51.

Appendices

Mathematical Background

A1.1 Sets and functions

We shall use the standard theory of sets. In particular, a set will be specified by listing its elements or in terms of a defining property $P(x)$ in the form

$$\{x : P(x) \text{ is true}\}$$

We write $x \in X$ if x belongs to the set X. Unions and intersections of sets are defined in the normal way:

$$X \cup Y = \{x : x \in X \text{ or } x \in Y\}$$

$$X \cap Y = \{x : x \in X \text{ and } x \in Y\}.$$

Special sets will have their usual notations; thus,

$$\mathbb{Z} = \text{set of integers} = \{\ldots, -2, -1, 0, 1, 2, \ldots\}$$

$$\mathbb{N} = \text{set of natural numbers} = \{0, 1, 2, \ldots\}$$

$\mathbb{N}^+$ = set of positive natural numbers = $\{1, 2, \ldots\}$

$\mathbb{R}$ = set of real numbers

$\mathbb{R}^+$ = set of nonnegative real numbers

$\mathbb{C}$ = set of complex numbers.

The *Cartesian product* of sets X, Y is defined by

$$X \times Y = \{(x, y) : x \in X, y \in Y\}$$

i.e. the set of all ordered pairs with first element in X and second element in Y.

A *function* from a set X into a set Y (written $f : X \to Y$) is a subset of $X \times Y$ such that

$$(x, y_1), (x, y_2) \in f \Rightarrow y_1 = y_2$$

Thus, to each element $x \in X$, f associates a *unique* element y of Y; then we write

$$y = f(x)$$

Sometimes, however, it is convenient to write $y = f_x$. In particular, if $X = \mathbb{Z}$, a function $s : \mathbb{Z} \to Y$ is called a *sequence* and we write $s(n) = s_n$ for all $n \in \mathbb{Z}$. The set of all functions from X into Y is often denoted by X^Y and, in particular, the set of all sequences with values in Y is denoted by $Y^{\mathbb{Z}}$. Thus, $\mathbb{C}^{\mathbb{Z}}$ denotes the set of all complex sequences, i.e. sequences of the form

$$\ldots, c_{-2}, c_{-1}, c_0, c_1, c_2, \ldots$$

where $c_n \in \mathbb{C}$ for each $n \in \mathbb{Z}$.

A1.2 Complex functions

Let $f : \mathbb{C} \to \mathbb{C}$ be a function and recall that f is *analytic at z* if it is differentiable at every point in some neighbourhood of z_0, and f is *analytic* if it is analytic at each point $z \in \mathbb{C}$. A *singular point* z_0 of f is a point such that f is analytic at some point of every neighbourhood of z_0 except at z_0. Let R be the 'annulus'

$$R = \{z : r_1 < |z - z_0| < r_2\}$$

and suppose that f is analytic in R. Then we can write f in the form of the *Laurent series*:

$$f(z) = \sum_{n=-\infty}^{\infty} a_n (z - z_0)^n \tag{A1.2.1}$$

where, for $n \geqslant 0$,

$$a_n = \frac{1}{2\pi j} \int_\Gamma \frac{f(\xi)d\xi}{(\xi - z_0)^{n+1}}, \quad a_{-n} = \frac{1}{2\pi j} \int_\Gamma \frac{f(\xi)d\xi}{(\xi - z_0)^{-n+1}} \qquad \text{(A1.2.2)}$$

and Γ is any positively oriented circle centered at z_0 and lying in R.

If f is analytic and C is a closed contour with z_0 in its interior, then

$$f(z_0) = \frac{1}{2\pi j} \int_C \frac{f(z)}{z - z_0} \, dz$$

(Cauchy's integral formula). More generally, if $f^{(n)}$ denotes the nth derivative of f, then

$$f^{(n)}(z_0) = \frac{n!}{2\pi j} \int_C \frac{f(z)dz}{(z - z_0)^{n+1}} \qquad \text{(A1.2.3)}$$

Thus, if f is analytic, (A1.2.1), (A1.2.2) and (A1.2.3) give *Taylor's theorem*:

$$f(z) = \sum_{n=0}^{\infty} a_n(z - z_0)^n$$

where

$$a_n = \frac{f^{(n)}(z_0)}{n!}$$

An isolated singular point of a function $f : \mathbb{C} \to \mathbb{C}$ is called a *pole of order n* if

$$\lim_{z \to z_0} (z - z_0)^n f(z)$$

exists. If z_0 is such a point, then

$$R = \frac{1}{2\pi j} \int_\Gamma f(z)dz \qquad \text{(A1.2.4)}$$

is called the *residue* of f at z_0, where Γ is a simple closed contour around z_0 (and containing no other singularity). Now if C is a simple closed, positively oriented contour such that f is analytic on C and inside C, except for isolated singular points $z_1, \ldots, z_n$, inside C, then

$$\int_C f(z) = 2\pi j \sum_{k=1}^n R_k$$

(*residue theorem*), where R_k is the residue of f at z_k. By (A1.2.2) and (A1.2.4) we have

$$R_k = a_{-1}(z_k)$$

where $a_{-1}(z_k)$ is the coefficient of $(z - z_k)^{-1}$ in the Laurent expansion of f about z_k.

A function $f : \mathbb{C} \to \mathbb{C}$ is called *meromorphic* if its only singularities are poles and if the function $g(z) = f(1/z)$ has only a pole (or is analytic) at $z = 0$.

A particularly simple type of meromorphic function is a *rational function* of the form

$$f(z) = \frac{a_m z^m + a_{m-1} z^{m-1} + \ldots + a_0}{b_n z^n + b_{n-1} z^{n-1} + \ldots + b_0}$$

The poles of f are the zeros of the polynomial $b_n z^n + b_{n-1} z^{n-1} + \ldots + b_0$ while the zeros of f are simply the zeros of the polynomial $a_m z^m + \ldots + a_0$. If $p_1, \ldots, p_n$ are the poles of f and $z_1, \ldots, z_m$ are the zeros of f, then

$$f(z) = \prod_{i=1}^{m}(z - z_i) \Big/ \prod_{j=1}^{n}(z - p_j).$$

If the poles p_j are distinct we can write f in the form

$$f(z) = \sum_{j=1}^{n} \frac{A_j}{(z - p_j)} \tag{A1.2.5}$$

where

$$A_j = f(z)(z - p_j)|_{z=p_j}. \tag{A1.2.6}$$

This is called the *partial fraction expansion* of f. The reader may like to obtain a similar form when the poles are not distinct.

We shall require two particularly important special functions – the exponential and logarithmic functions. The *exponential function* is defined by the series

$$\exp(z) \text{ (or } e^z) = \sum_{n=0}^{\infty} \frac{z^n}{n!}$$

and this defines an (entire) analytic function; exp is not 1–1 everywhere, however, and its 'inverse' w defined by

$$z = \exp w$$

is called the *logarithm*. It is a multivalued function and is written

$$w = \log z.$$

It can be shown that w is given by

$$w = \text{Log}|z| + j(\arg z + 2k\pi) \qquad k = 0, \pm 1, \pm 2, \ldots$$

where $\text{Log}|z|$ is the ordinary real logarithm of the real-valued function $|z|$. The function

$$w = \text{Log}|z| + i\text{Arg}\, z$$

where $\text{Arg}\, z$ is the standard argument $\angle z$ of z such that $-\pi < \angle z \leqslant \pi$, is called the *principal value* of $\log z$.

Finally, when transforming filters from the s- to the z-plane we shall need the concept of conformal mapping. A *conformal mapping* $f: D \to \mathbb{C}$ from a region $D \subseteq \mathbb{C}$ into $\mathbb{C}$ is an analytic function such that $f'(z_0) \neq 0$ for all $z_0 \in D$.

Then f is invertible on D and preserves angles between any pair of smooth curves in D.

A1.3 Vector spaces, norms and Hilbert space

Only the most elementary parts of linear mathematics is required in this book. In fact, all we need is the definition of vector spaces, norms and some simple Hilbert space theory. A *vector space* over a field F is a set V together with two maps $+ : V \times V \to V$ (*addition*) and $\cdot : F \times V \to V$ (*scalar multiplication*) which satisfy the axioms:

(i) $x + y = y + x$ for all $x, y \in V$
(ii) $(x + y) + z = x + (y + z)$ for all $x, y, z \in V$
(iii)   there exists $0 \in V$ such that $x + 0 = x$ for all $x \in V$
(iv)   for each $x \in V$, there exists $-x \in V$ such that $x + (-x) = 0$
(v) $\lambda(x + y) = \lambda x + \lambda y$ for all $\lambda \in F, x, y \in V$
(vi) $(\lambda + \mu)x = \lambda x + \mu x$ for all $\lambda, \mu \in F, x \in V$
(vii) $(\lambda\mu)x = \lambda(\mu x)$ for all $\lambda, \mu \in F, x \in V$
(viii) $1x = x$ for all $x \in V$

In this book, F will either be $\mathbb{R}$ or $\mathbb{C}$. Standard examples of vector spaces are $\mathbb{R}^n$ and $\mathbb{C}^n$ defined respectively by

$$\mathbb{R}^n = \{(x_1, \ldots, x_n) : x_i \in \mathbb{R} \quad 1 \le i \le n\}$$

$$\mathbb{C}^n = \{(z_1, \ldots, z_n) : z_i \in \mathbb{C} \quad 1 \le i \le n\}$$

Addition and scalar multiplication are defined in the obvious way. A *basis* of a vector space V (over F) is a set $\{v_1, \ldots, v_n\} \in V$ such that each $v \in V$ has a unique representation in the form

$$v = \sum_{i=1}^{n} \alpha_i v_i$$

where $\alpha_i \in F$; in this case n is called the *dimension* of v.

A *norm* on a vector space V is a map $\|.\| : V \to \mathbb{R}^+$ such that

$$\|x\| = 0 \qquad \text{if and only if } x = 0$$

$$\|\alpha x\| = |\alpha|\,\|x\| \qquad \text{for all } \alpha \in F, x \in V$$

$$\|x + y\| \le \|x\| + \|y\| \qquad \text{for all } x, y \in V$$

A vector space with a norm defined on it is called a *normed (vector) space*. For example, if $V = \mathbb{R}^n$, the standard (Euclidean) norm is defined by

$$\|\mathbf{x}\| = \left(\sum_{i=1}^{n} x_i^2 \right)^{1/2} \qquad \mathbf{x} \in \mathbb{R}^n$$

while, if $V = \mathbb{C}^n$, then

$$|\mathbf{z}| = \left(\sum_{i=1}^{n} |z_i|^2 \right)^{1/2} \qquad \mathbf{z} \in \mathbb{C}^n$$

A vector space V over F ($=\mathbb{R}$ or $\mathbb{C}$) is called an *inner product space* if there is defined a map $\langle .,. \rangle : V \times V \to F$ such that

$$\langle x, x \rangle \geq 0 \qquad \qquad \text{for all } x \in V$$

$$\langle x, x \rangle = 0 \qquad \qquad \text{if and only if } x = 0$$

$$\langle x, y \rangle = \overline{\langle y, x \rangle} \qquad \text{for all } x, y \in V$$

$$\langle \lambda x + \mu y, z \rangle = \lambda \langle x, z \rangle + \mu \langle y, z \rangle \text{ for all } \lambda, \mu \in F, x, y, z \in V.$$

Note that $\|x\| \triangleq \langle x, x \rangle^{1/2}$ defines a norm on the inner product space V.

A sequence $\{x_n\}$ in a normed space V *converges* (to $x \in V$) if

$$\lim_{n \to \infty} \|x_n - \mathbf{x}\| = 0$$

A convergent sequence $\{x_n\}$ is a *Cauchy sequence*; i.e.

$$\|x_n - x_m\| \leq \varepsilon$$

for any $\varepsilon > 0$ and for all $n, m \geq$ some $M \geq 0$. If, conversely, every Cauchy sequence in a normed vector space V converges (to an element of the space) then we say that V is *complete* and that V is a *Banach space*. A *Hilbert space H* is a Banach space whose norm comes from an inner product, i.e.

$$\|x\| = \langle x, x \rangle^{1/2}$$

The most important example of a Hilbert space in signal processing is the space $L^2(\Omega)$ of square integrable functions $f : \Omega \to \mathbb{C}$ defined on some region $\Omega \subseteq \mathbb{R}^n$. The inner product is defined by

$$\langle f, g \rangle_{L^2} = \int_{\Omega} f(x) g^*(x) \mathrm{d}x \qquad (* \text{ denotes complex conjugation})$$

Clearly, $L^2(\Omega)$ is not finite-dimensional. Similarly, if $\xi = \{\xi_n\}$ is a sequence of complex numbers, then we define

$$\|\xi\|_{l^2} = \left(\sum_{i=1}^{\infty} |\xi_n|^2 \right)^{1/2}$$

and we denote by l^2 the Hilbert space of all sequences ξ such that $\|\xi\|_{l^2} < \infty$. More generally, for $p \geq 1$ we define l^p to be the Banach space of sequences $\xi = \{\xi_n\}$ such that

$$\|\xi\|_{l^p} \triangleq \left(\sum_{i=1}^{\infty} |\xi_n|^p \right)^{1/p} < \infty$$

An *orthonormal basis* of a Hilbert space H is an indexed set $\{e_i\}_{i \in I} \subseteq H$ such that

$$\langle e_i, e_j \rangle = \delta_{ij} \qquad i, j \in I$$

and such that for any $h \in H$ and any $\varepsilon > 0$ we can find a finite subset $J \subseteq I$ such that

$$\left\| h - \sum_{i \in J'} \langle h, e_i \rangle e_i \right\| \leq \varepsilon$$

for all finite subsets $J' \subseteq J$ of I. If I is countable then H is called *separable*. $L^2(\Omega)$ and l^2 are separable Hilbert spaces (when Ω is open in $\mathbb{R}^n$).

A1.4 Matrices and eigenvalues

We shall use the standard theory of matrices and eigenvalues. In particular A^{-1} will denote the inverse of an invertible matrix A. If A is not invertible (or if it is not square) we can define other types of inverse in the following way. First, if A is of order $m \times n$ and $m > n$, then we can define the *generalized inverse* $A^\dagger$ of A by

$$A^\dagger = (A^\mathrm{T} A)^{-1} A^\mathrm{T}$$

provided A is of rank n. If $m < n$ and A is of rank m, then we define $A^\dagger$ by

$$A^\dagger = A^\mathrm{T} (A A^\mathrm{T})^{-1}$$

Note that, in either case, $A^\dagger$ satisfies the relations

$$A A^\dagger = (A A^\dagger)^\mathrm{T}$$
$$A^\dagger A = (A^\dagger A)^\mathrm{T}$$
$$A A^\dagger A = A$$
$$A^\dagger A A^\dagger = A^\dagger$$

Consider a set of equations of the form

$$A x = b$$

If A is square and invertible then, clearly, $x = A^{-1} b$ is the unique solution to these equations. If A is not square, but a solution to the equations exists, then any solution can be written in the form

$$x = A^\# b + (I - A^\# A) c$$

where c is arbitrary $n \times 1$ vector and $A^\#$ is a (nonunique!) *conditional inverse* of A which satisfies

$$AA^{\#}A = A$$

Note that a solution x of the system exists if and only if

$$AA^{\#}b = b$$

If no solutions of the system exist then a vector of the form

$$x = A^{ls}b$$

where A^{ls} is a (nonunique) least squares inverse of A defined by

$$AA^{ls}A = A$$

$$AA^{ls} = (AA^{ls})^{\mathrm{T}}$$

minimizes the error $||Ax - b||^2$ over all x. Thus, the least squares inverse of A gives the 'best' approximate solution to the system in the least squares sense.

An important decomposition of an $m \times n$ matrix A (other than the standard Jordan form) which finds many applications in signal processing is the *singular value decomposition* (SVD). This is given by

$$A = U^{\mathrm{T}}\Lambda^{1/2}V$$

where U and V are unitary $m \times m$ and $n \times n$ matrices, respectively (i.e. $UU^{\mathrm{T}} = I_m$, $VV^{\mathrm{T}} = I_n$) and

$$\Lambda^{1/2} = \begin{bmatrix} \Lambda_1 & 0 \\ 0 & 0 \end{bmatrix}$$

where

$$\Lambda_1 = \mathrm{diag}(\lambda_1^{1/2}, \ldots, \lambda_r^{1/2})$$

and 0 represents a zero matrix of appropriate dimension. Here, r is the rank of A and $\lambda_1, \ldots, \lambda_r$ are the nonzero (real) eigenvalues of AA^{T}. We can also write

$$A = \sum_{j=1}^{r} \lambda_j^{1/2}\mathbf{u}_j\mathbf{v}_j^{\mathrm{T}}$$

where $\mathbf{u}_1, \ldots, \mathbf{u}_m$ are the columns of U and $\mathbf{v}_1, \ldots, \mathbf{v}_n$ are the columns of V. Note that $\mathbf{u}_1, \ldots, \mathbf{u}_m$ are also the eigenvectors of AA^{T} while $\mathbf{v}_1, \ldots, \mathbf{v}_n$ are the eigenvectors of $A^{\mathrm{T}}A$.

A1.5 Optimization

Since optimization theory plays an important role in digital filter design we shall briefly recall the Lagrange multiplier method for constrained optimization. First note that the optima (i.e. maxima and minima) of a function $f(\mathbf{x})$, $\mathbf{x} \in \mathbb{R}^n$ in the unconstrained case are given by the solutions of the equations

$$\partial f(\mathbf{x}^*)/\partial x_i = 0 \qquad 1 \le i \le n \tag{A1.5.1}$$

for which the matrix $(\partial^2 f(\mathbf{x}^*)/\partial x_i \partial x_j)$ is positive or negative definite.

Consider, next, the constrained optimization problem

$$\text{optimize } f(\mathbf{x}) \tag{A1.5.2}$$

subject to

$$g_i(\mathbf{x}) = b_i \qquad 1 \le i \le m$$

where $m < n$. Then it can be shown that a necessary condition for $\mathbf{x}^*$ to be a solution to this problem, provided

$$\text{rank}\left(\frac{\partial g_i(\mathbf{x}^*)}{\partial x_j}\right) = m$$

is that the function

$$F(\mathbf{x}, \lambda) \triangleq f(\mathbf{x}) + \sum_{i=1}^{m} \lambda_i(g_i(\mathbf{x}) - b_i) \tag{A1.5.3}$$

has an optimum at $(\mathbf{x}^*, \lambda^*)$ for some λ^*. Thus, we can solve the unconstrained optimization problem

$$\text{optimize } F(\mathbf{x}, \lambda)$$

over $\mathbf{x}, \lambda$ instead of (A1.5.2). From (A1.5.1) and (A1.5.3) the solutions x^* are given by solutions of the equations

$$\frac{\partial F}{\partial \mathbf{x}}(\mathbf{x}^*, \lambda^*) = 0$$

$$\frac{\partial F}{\partial \lambda}(\mathbf{x}^*, \lambda^*) = 0$$

i.e.

$$\frac{\partial f}{\partial \mathbf{x}}(\mathbf{x}^*) + \sum_{i=1}^{m} \lambda_i \frac{\partial g_i}{\partial \mathbf{x}}(x^*) = 0$$

and

$$g_i(\mathbf{x}^*) = b_i \qquad 1 \le i \le m$$

The vector λ is called a *Lagrange multiplier* vector.

A1.6 The Huygens–Fresnel principle

In chapter 11 we have used a simple scattering equation in order to obtain the point spread function for a simple lens. We shall now give a brief derivation of this equation using elementary electromagnetic theory and an integral theorem. Readers unfamiliar with these topics may omit this section and accept the Huygens–Fresnel equation at face value.

We begin with the well-known Maxwell's equations describing an electromagnetic field in free space:

(i) $\text{div } \mathbf{E} = 0$

(ii) $\text{div } \mathbf{B} = 0$

(iii) $\text{curl } \mathbf{E} + \dfrac{1}{c}\dfrac{\partial \mathbf{B}}{\partial t} = 0$

(iv) $\text{curl } \mathbf{B} - \dfrac{1}{c}\dfrac{\partial \mathbf{E}}{\partial t} = 0$

From (iii) we have

$$\text{curl curl } \mathbf{E} + \frac{1}{c}\frac{\partial}{\partial t}\text{curl } \mathbf{B} = 0$$

and since

$$\text{curl curl} = \text{grad div} - \nabla^2$$

it follows from (i) and (iv) that

$$\nabla^2 \mathbf{E} - \frac{1}{c^2}\frac{\partial^2 \mathbf{E}}{\partial t^2} = 0$$

Similarly,

$$\nabla^2 \mathbf{B} - \frac{1}{c^2}\frac{\partial^2 \mathbf{B}}{\partial t^2} = 0$$

Hence the components of the electric and magnetic vectors satisfy wave equations. The development of a vector scattering theory is very difficult and so it is usual to solve the problem for the scalar amplitude of a light wave Ψ which satisfies the same equation. Thus,

$$\nabla^2 \Psi - \frac{1}{c^2}\frac{\partial^2 \Psi}{\partial t^2} = 0$$

For a monochromatic wave,

$$\Psi(r, t) = \psi(r)e^{-j\omega t}$$

and so

$$\nabla^2 \psi + k^2 \psi = 0$$

where

$$k = \omega/c$$

Let $\chi(r)$ be any function which satisfies Helmholtz' equation:

$$\nabla^2\chi + k^2\chi = 0$$

By Green's theorem, we have

$$-\int_S (\psi\,\mathrm{grad}\,\chi - \chi\,\mathrm{grad}\,\psi)\mathrm{d}s = \int_V (\psi\nabla^2\chi - \chi\nabla^2\psi)\mathrm{d}v \qquad \text{(A1.6.1)}$$

for any volume V bounded by the closed surface S. Here, $\mathrm{d}s$ is a vector element of surface pointing *inwards*. Since χ, ψ both satisfy Helmholtz' equation, the right-hand side of (A1.6.1) is zero. Now choose, in particular,

$$\chi(r) = \frac{e^{jkr}}{r}$$

Then $\nabla^2\chi + k^2\chi = 0$, as required. However, there is a singularity at $r = 0$ and so we surround this point by a small sphere of radius ρ and surface element $\mathrm{d}a$. Then, by (A1.6.1),

$$\int_S \left(\psi\,\mathrm{grad}\frac{e^{jkr}}{r} - \frac{e^{jkr}}{r}\,\mathrm{grad}\,\psi\right)\mathrm{d}s + \int_{\text{sphere}}\left(\psi\,\mathrm{grad}\frac{e^{jk\rho}}{\rho} - \frac{e^{jk\rho}}{\rho}\,\mathrm{grad}\,\psi\right)\mathrm{d}a = 0$$

$$\text{(A1.6.2)}$$

Now,

$$\mathrm{d}a = \mathbf{n}\rho^2\sin\theta\mathrm{d}\theta\mathrm{d}\phi = \mathbf{n}\rho^2\mathrm{d}\Omega,$$

where $\mathrm{d}\Omega$ is an element of solid angle. Hence the second term in (A1.6.2) equals

$$\int_{\text{sphere}}\left\{\psi\left(\frac{jk}{\rho} - \frac{1}{\rho^2}\right)e^{jk\rho}\mathbf{n} - \frac{1}{\rho}e^{jk\rho}\,\mathrm{grad}\,\psi\right\}\mathbf{n}\rho^2\mathrm{d}\Omega \to -\int_{\text{sphere}}\psi\mathrm{d}\Omega \text{ as } \rho \to 0$$

$$\text{(A1.6.3)}$$

But $\psi \to \psi(\rho = 0)$ and $\int \mathrm{d}\Omega = 4\pi$ as $\rho \to 0$, so the right-hand side of (A1.6.3) equals $-4\pi\psi(r = 0)$. Hence, by (A1.6.2),

$$\psi(r = 0) = \frac{1}{4\pi}\int_S\left(\psi\,\mathrm{grad}\frac{e^{jkr}}{r} - \frac{e^{jkr}}{r}\,\mathrm{grad}\,\psi\right)\mathrm{d}s$$

This is the *Helmholtz–Kirchhoff equation*. Now consider the case of a flat screen with a circular aperture as in Figure A1. If ψ_{inc} is the incident wave, then

$$\psi(r = 0) = \frac{1}{4\pi}\int_\sigma\left(\psi_{inc}\,\mathrm{grad}\frac{e^{jkr}}{r} - \frac{e^{jkr}}{r}\,\mathrm{grad}\,\psi_{inc}\right)\mathrm{d}s$$

since ψ, $\partial\psi/\partial n = 0$ on σ' and σ'' as $R \to \infty$ (where n is the unit normal). For a spherical wave

$$\psi_{inc} = A\frac{e^{jkr_0}}{r_0}$$

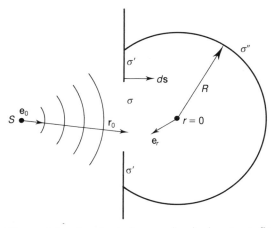

Figure A.1   A spherical wave impinging on a flat
screen.

and so

$$\psi(r = 0) = \frac{1}{4\pi} \int_\sigma \left\{ \left(A \, \frac{e^{jkr_0}}{r_0} \right) \left(\frac{jk}{r} - \frac{1}{r^2} \right) e^{jkr} \mathbf{e}_r - \left(\frac{e^{jkr}}{r} \right) \left(\frac{jk}{r_0} - \frac{1}{r_0^2} \right) A \, e^{jkr_0} \mathbf{e}_0 \right\} \mathrm{d}s$$

For large r, r_0 we can neglect terms in $1/r^2$, $1/r_0^2$ and finally obtain

$$\psi(r = 0) = j \, \frac{Ak}{4\pi} \int_\sigma \frac{e^{jk(r+r_0)}}{rr_0} \, (\mathbf{e}_r - \mathbf{e}_0).\mathrm{d}s$$

which is the desired Huygens–Fresnel equation.

References

Set theory: A. Abian (1965), *The Theory of Sets*, NY: Saunders.
Complex function theory: Knopp (1945), *Theory of Functions*, NY: Dover.

    Titchmarsh (1978), *The Theory of Functions*, Oxford: Oxford University Press.

Vector Spaces and Hilbert spaces: N. Dunford and J. T. Schwartz (1957), *Linear Operators*, vol. I, NY: Interscience.
Matrices and eigenvalues: G. Hadley (1979), *Linear Algebra*, Reading, Mass.: Addison Wesley.
Optimization: K. V. Mital (1976), *Optimization Methods*, New Delhi: Wiley.

    S. P. Banks (1968), *Control Systems Engineering*, London: Prentice Hall.

    D. G. Luenberger (1969), *Optimization by Vector Space Methods*, NY: Wiley.

EM theory: J. D. Kraus and K. R. Carver (1973), *Electromagnetics*, NY: McGraw-Hill.

Statistical Background

A2.1 Probability theory

We shall require only the simplest aspects of the probability theory of real random variables. In order to define a random variable we must introduce the notion of Borel subset of $\mathbb{R}$. Consider the set $\mathcal{B}$ of subsets of $\mathbb{R}$ which is the smallest such set having the properties

(i)   The intervals (a, b), $(a, b]$, $[a, b)$, $[a, b]$, where a, b are real numbers or $\pm\infty$, belong to $\mathcal{B}$.

(ii)   If $A \in \mathcal{B}$ then $\mathbb{R}\backslash A \in \mathcal{B}$.

(iii) If $A_1, A_2, \ldots$ is an infinite sequence of sets in $\mathcal{B}$ then

$$\bigcup_{n=1}^{\infty} A_n \in \mathcal{B}$$

Any set in $\mathcal{B}$ is called a *Borel* set.

Next let X be any set and let S be a subset of the set of subsets of X which is closed under complements and finite unions and such that ϕ, $X \in S$. Then we define a *probability* P on S to be a function $P : S \rightarrow R$ such that

(i)　　　$P(E) \geqslant 0$ for all $E \in S$.
(ii)　　$P(X) = 1$.
(iii)　　$P(E \cup F) = P(E) + P(F)$ if $E \cap F = \phi$.

We call (X, S, P) or simply X a *probability space*. Elements of S are called *events*. A *random variable* $v : X \to \mathbb{R}$ is then a function defined on a probability space (X, S, P) such that $v^{-1}(B) \in S$ for each Borel set B in $\mathbb{R}$.

The *conditional probability* $P[E|F]$ of a set $E \in S$ given the event $F \in S$ is defined by

$$P[E|F] = \frac{P[E \cap F]}{P[F]}$$

if $P[F] > 0$.

We say that E is *independent* of F if

$$P[E|F] = P[E]$$

Thus,

$$P[E \cap F] = P[E]P[F]$$

In general, we have

$$P[E|F] = \frac{P[E \cap F]}{P[F]}$$

$$= \frac{P[E \cap F]}{P[E]} \cdot \frac{P[E]}{P[F]}$$

$$= \frac{P[F|E]P[E]}{P[F]}$$

This is called *Bayes' theorem*.

A2.2 Density functions

Let $P : S \to \mathbb{R}$ be a probability defined on the probability space (X, S, P). A (probability) *density function* for P is a function $f : X \to \mathbb{R}$ such that $f(x) \geqslant 0$ for all $x \in X$ and

$$P(E) = \int_E f(x)\mathrm{d}x$$

for all $E \in S$. Then,

$$P(X) = 1 = \int_X f(x)\mathrm{d}x$$

and so the integral of a density function over the whole probability space must be equal to 1.

Suppose that $(\mathbb{R}, S, P)$ is a probability space; i.e. S is a set of subsets of $\mathbb{R}$ with the properties stated above. Also, let f be a density function for P. Then we call the function F defined by

$$F(x) = \int_{-\infty}^{x} f(x')\mathrm{d}x'$$

the (cumulative) *distribution function associated with f*. Clearly,

$$f(x) = F'(x)$$

(assuming that f is sufficiently 'nice' – we shall not require the theory of Lebesgue integration here, as we shall assume all distribution functions are smooth).

A2.3 Moments

When performing experiments involving random phenomena, we cannot predict the outcome of any particular experiment in advance. We can only predict certain 'average values' of random variables. These average values are defined most conveniently in terms of a probability density function. Thus, let (X, S, P) be a probability space with density function f. We define the *expectation* of a function $g : X \to \mathbb{R}$ (if it exists) by

$$E(g) = \int_{X} g(x)f(x)\mathrm{d}x$$

(Of course, we are assuming that X is a measure space with measure $\mathrm{d}x$.) In particular, if $g(x) = x$ for all $x \in X$, we call

$$m = E(x) \overset{\triangle}{=} \int_{X} xf(x)\mathrm{d}x$$

the *mean* of the probability function P. Also, $E((x - E(x))^n)$ is called the *n*th *central moment of P*. For $n = 2$ we obtain the *variance* σ^2 of P given by

$$\sigma^2 = E((x - m)^2)$$

The square root σ of the variance is called the *standard deviation*.

A2.4 The normal distribution

A particularly important probability distribution is defined by the *Gaussian density* on $\mathbb{R}^n$ by

$$p(\mathbf{x}) = \frac{1}{(2\pi)^{n/2}|C|^{1/2}} \exp\left[-\tfrac{1}{2}(\mathbf{x} - \mathbf{m})C^{-1}(\mathbf{x} - \mathbf{m})^{\mathrm{T}}\right], \qquad (\text{A}2.4.1)$$

where

$$\mathbf{m} = \int_X \mathbf{x}p(\mathbf{x})\mathrm{d}\mathbf{x} = E\{\mathbf{x}\} \qquad (\text{A}2.4.2)$$

and $C = (c_{ij})$ is a positive definite matrix defined by

$$c_{ij} = \int_X (x_i - m_i)(x_j - m_j)p(\mathbf{x})\mathrm{d}\mathbf{x}$$
$$= E\{(x_i - m_i)(x_j - m_j)\} \qquad (\text{A}2.4.3)$$

Here, $|C|$ denotes the determinant of C. A simple way of demonstrating the relations (A2.4.2) and (A2.4.3) is by diagonalizing C in the form

$$C = \begin{bmatrix} \sigma_1^2 & 0\ldots & & 0 \\ 0 & \sigma_2^2 & 0 & 0 \\ \vdots & & & \\ 0 & & & \sigma_n^2 \end{bmatrix}$$

so that (A2.4.1) becomes

$$p(\mathbf{x}) = \frac{1}{(2\pi)^{n/2}\sigma_1 \ldots \sigma_n} \exp\left[-\frac{1}{2}\sum_{i=1}^{n} \frac{(x_i - m_i)^2}{\sigma_i^2}\right]$$

A2.5 Correlation

An important measure of 'similarity' between two distributions is provided by correlation. Thus, if $y(i)$, $z(i)$ are discrete sequences, then the *correlation function* of y and z is defined as the sequence

$$r_{yz}(k) = E(y(i)z(i + k))$$

In particular, if $y = z$, we write $r_y(k) = r_{yy}(k)$ and call this the *autocorrelation* of y. The *power spectral density* S_y of a (real) sequence $y(k)$ is defined as the Z-transform of $r_y(k)$, i.e.

$$S_y(z) = Z(r_y(k))(z)$$

or, in terms of real frequencies,

$$S_y(\omega) = Z(r_y(k))(z)|_{z=e^{j\omega T}}$$

For continuous time (complex) signals f(t) we define the *autocorrelation* of f by

$$E\{f(t)f^*(\tau)\} = R_f(t, \tau)$$

Frequently, R_f is a function of $t - \tau$ and so we write

$$R_f(\tau) = E\{f(t)f^*(t + \tau)\}$$

Finally, we define the *power spectral density* $\mathcal{P}_f$ of f as the Fourier transform of R_f. Thus,

$$\mathcal{P}_f(\omega) = \mathcal{F}R_f(\omega)$$

A *white noise process* is a stochastic signal with unity power spectral density over the whole frequency band $(-\infty, \infty)$. (This is, of course, a mathematical idealization.)

References

Probability theory: E. Parzen (1960), *Modern Probability Theory and its Applications*, NY: Wiley.

C. W. Burrill (1972), *Measure, Integration and Probability*, NY: McGraw-Hill.

Correlation and stochastic processes: A. Papoulis (1965), *Probability, Random Variables and Stochastic Processes*, NY: McGraw-Hill.

Index